LEYTE GULF

OSPREY
PUBLISHING

LEYTE GULF

A New History of the World's
Largest Sea Battle

MARK E. STILLE

OSPREY PUBLISHING
Bloomsbury Publishing Plc
Kemp House, Chawley Park, Cumnor Hill, Oxford OX2 9PH, UK
29 Earlsfort Terrace, Dublin 2, Ireland
1385 Broadway, 5th Floor, New York, NY 10018, USA
E-mail: info@ospreypublishing.com
www.ospreypublishing.com

OSPREY is a trademark of Osprey Publishing Ltd

First published in Great Britain in 2023

A catalog record for this book is available from the British Library.

ISBN: HB 9781472851758; PB 9781472851765; eBook 9781472851772;
ePDF 9781472851727; XML 9781472851734

23 24 25 26 27   10 9 8 7 6 5 4 3 2 1

Plate section images are from Naval History and Heritage Command.
Maps by www.bounford.com
Index by Angela Hall

Typeset by Deanta Global Publishing Services, Chennai, India
Printed and bound in Great Britain by CPI (Group) UK Ltd, Croydon CR0 4YY

To find out more about our authors and books visit www.ospreypublishing.com.
Here you will find extracts, author interviews, details of forthcoming events and the option
to sign up for our newsletter.

Contents

Introduction

The Battle of Leyte Gulf has no counterpart. It simply remains the largest and most complex naval battle in history. Up until the present day, it is the last battle between fleets.

In sheer size, it has no rival. Of the two American fleets involved in the battle, one was comprised of 738 ships and carried an invasion force of approximately 165,000 men in addition to the 50,000 sailors aboard the ships.[1] The other American fleet was the most powerful in the world, with a total of 16 aircraft carriers and six of the world's most powerful battleships. In total, the two fleets brought 235 surface combatants and 1,500 aircraft to the battle. Opposed to this collection of naval might was the Imperial Japanese Navy. Once the most powerful navy in the Pacific, the Imperial Fleet was forced into a desperate fight with all its remaining strength. In total, the Japanese committed 69 ships and some 375 aircraft, most of which were land based.[2]

Both sides committed so much because the stakes were so high. The Americans planned to invade Leyte Island in the Philippines as a potential first step to occupying the entire archipelago. The Leyte invasion force was larger than the initial American contribution to the assault force at Normandy. If the Philippines could be occupied, Japanese sea lines of communications between the Home Islands and the resource areas in Southeast Asia would be severed, fatally compromising Japan's ability to continue the war. This demanded that the Japanese respond to the invasion with all of their remaining strength.

The ensuing battle was the most complex naval battle of the entire Second World War. Its complexity makes it compelling. Instead of being a single battle as the name implies, it was actually comprised of four major engagements and several lesser actions fought over the span of three days.

The characteristics of the battle continue to astound – it contained the largest air-sea battle in history; it included the last carrier and battleship clashes in history; it was the only time that a surface force engaged a carrier force while under air attack; and it featured the first pre-planned use of suicide attacks during the Pacific War.

Adding to the drama of this momentous event was the role personalities played in the battle. On the American side were the flamboyant General Douglas MacArthur, the steady Admiral Chester Nimitz, and the impulsive Admiral William Halsey. Overlooked but still key commanders included Vice Admiral Thomas Kinkaid and the brilliant Clifton Sprague, commander of the escort carrier group known as Taffy 3.

For the Japanese, the taciturn Vice Admiral Kurita Takeo was placed in command of their most important force. He was charged to execute a plan devised by Admiral Toyoda Soemu, who cared more about presenting the Imperial Navy's Combined Fleet with an opportunity to die fighting than to produce a plan in the best interests of the nation. The most competent Japanese admiral, Ozawa Jisaburo, was placed in charge of a force ordered to decoy Halsey's powerful Third Fleet. Ozawa expected to lose his entire fleet in the process, but he ended up being the only Japanese commander to complete his mission. Vice Admiral Nishimura Shoji led the Japanese force at the Battle of Surigao Strait. His force was virtually annihilated, making him the only Japanese commander to exhibit such determination.

It was a battle decided by mistakes on both sides. The overarching American mistake was their divided command structure. Incredibly, the two fleets in the battle did not have a direct and secure means of communicating with each other. The bifurcated command structure and a general lack of awareness of what each fleet was doing led to Halsey's controversial decision and prevented the Americans from bringing their full power to bear. While Halsey's errors are the focus of most accounts, those committed by Kinkaid were also important and deserve additional scrutiny.

The biggest mistake of all was the fatuous Japanese plan named *Sho-Go* (Victory Plan), devised by Toyoda. He admitted after the war that his plan was against accepted wisdom, but he felt he had to commit the Combined Fleet's remaining strength before it became irrelevant. In fact, with so little chance that his plan would achieve a strategic result and so high a probability that the Combined Fleet would be destroyed in the process, Toyoda should not have accepted battle under the conditions prevailing in October 1944. The Imperial Navy admitted to the Imperial Army that the plan was an "all-or-nothing" operation. The planning basis for *Sho-Go* was complete and utter desperation – not the best ingredient for success.

Predictably, the plan resulted in an utter debacle. The Japanese neither stopped the invasion of Leyte, slowed the pace of the American advance in the Pacific, nor inflicted severe losses on the American fleet. Toyoda intended the battle to be decisive and to turn the tide of war in favor of the Japanese. Instead, it resulted in a decisive defeat for the Imperial Navy. Over the span of four days, the Japanese lost 28 ships comprising over 300,000 tons. The scale of such losses is unparalleled in naval history. In the sense that it resulted in the end of the Imperial Navy as an effective force, the battle was decisive. For the remainder of the war, the Americans had no real concerns about the ability of the Imperial Navy's surface fleet to shape events. If any naval battle in the Pacific War can be defined as decisive, it was the Battle of Leyte Gulf. But Toyoda achieved his aim of providing the Combined Fleet with a fitting opportunity to die fighting.

Even though *Sho-Go* had no prospects of success, and the battle resulted in an undisputed victory for the Americans, there is still controversy attached to it. Almost 80 years after the event, the myths created around the battle continue to gain strength. Providing cover for the enduring mythology are the two key decisions of the battle. The first was Halsey's decision to take his entire Third Fleet to the north to attack Ozawa's decoy force. This clever diversionary aspect of *Sho-Go* has been treated like it provided the Japanese with victory or at least the foundation of victory. It did neither, but it did provide Kurita with the opportunity to exploit the divided American command structure and enter the Philippine Sea unchecked, where he fell upon a group of American escort carriers known as Taffy 3. In the resulting Battle off Samar, the Americans sustained heavy losses but denied the Japanese an immediate victory. This led directly to the second key controversy of the battle, when Kurita failed to press his attack to destroy Taffy 3 and then steam into Leyte Gulf in accordance with Toyoda's plan.

Since the most alluring aspects of the battle are bound up in its mythology, this book focuses on the myths of Leyte Gulf. The first myth surrounds the Japanese plan for the battle. Even in October 1944, the Japanese thought they could fight and win a decisive battle. In fact, the Japanese had no chance to reverse the tide of war. *Sho-Go* was not a serious plan for victory, but a vehicle to allow the Combined Fleet a fitting and honorable death. As framed, the variant of *Sho-Go* used to defend the Philippines (*Sho-1*) had no strategic purpose, since it was literally impossible for the Combined Fleet to defeat the invasion before it was firmly established on Leyte. Even if the large force under Kurita had successfully attacked into the gulf as planned on October 25, it had no chance to generate any strategic impact.

The second myth seems to be the one held most firmly. Any discussion of how American naval commanders performed at Leyte Gulf begins with Halsey. Most accounts of the battle make Halsey the scapegoat for a lost American victory or even an American defeat. This is curious, since Leyte Gulf was the greatest American naval victory of the war. Halsey's controversial decisions often overshadow that fact. In trying to assess Halsey's performance, two key decisions are held up for examination – his decision to go north after Ozawa late on October 24, and his decision to bring his battleships and a carrier task force back south late in the morning of October 25. These certainly were key decisions that shaped the entire battle, but focusing solely on them leaves out the bigger issue of Halsey's handling of the Third Fleet for the entire period of the battle. Even more damning than any shortcomings in the two decisions mentioned above is the fact that during the entire period of the battle the full power of the Third Fleet was never brought to bear at any time.

Accepted wisdom is that Halsey acted stupidly on the night of October 24 when he decided to take the Third Fleet north to attack the Japanese carrier force. The author believes Halsey acted correctly with the information he had available at the time. In fact, his decision was virtually pre-ordained. Given Halsey's mindset, his orders, existing US Navy doctrine, and the manner in which the battle developed, there was no chance of Halsey acting differently. Criticism of Halsey's action is extremely easy with the benefit of hindsight, but this criticism is built on knowledge that Halsey could not have possessed in the moment.

This is not to say that Halsey should be forgiven for his shortcomings during the battle. Everything he did was magnified, since he commanded the most powerful naval force in the world during history's largest naval battle. Even if he is excused for taking the bait so cleverly presented by the Japanese, his other actions before and after this decision were poor. As is detailed in this account, Halsey failed to bring his full power against either of the two main Japanese forces in the battle. This denied him the battle of annihilation he so earnestly desired.

The hardest myth to dispel is the notion that Kurita's force should have utterly annihilated Taffy 3 at the Battle off Samar. In the accepted version of the battle, the underdog American force prevailed against overwhelming odds. Unparalleled American bravery provided the edge while the Japanese blundered their way to defeat. There is no doubt that the bravery of American sailors played a prominent role in the battle, but the battle was not just a David and Goliath contest with American destroyers attacking Japanese battleships. The battle was unlike anything else ever fought in naval history. A force of heavy ships surprised and attacked a carrier force during daylight and fought a prolonged surface battle while under persistent air attack. The Battle off Samar was not just a surface battle; it was an air-sea battle of immense proportions. In addition to the brave and much-heralded attacks by the escorting destroyers, the Americans brought over 200 aircraft into play. The primary American weapon was aircraft, not the heroic escorting destroyers and destroyer escorts. The fact that a large force of aircraft defeated a surface force should be no surprise. That was the established norm from the very first day of the Pacific War.

Even if the aircraft had not been present, it is unreasonable to assume that one force of surface ships could quickly cripple another by long-range gunnery. During the Pacific War, earlier battles of this type demonstrated the innate difficulty of hitting targets at long range. During the Battle off Samar, the Japanese were facing the worst possible conditions for conducting long-range gunnery. Without the benefit of radar, they were firing against targets hidden by weather and smoke. In addition, the Japanese ships were under consistent air attack, making it even more difficult to develop accurate fire control solutions. Under these conditions, the Japanese should be given credit for what they did manage to achieve (sinking four ships by gunfire and damaging another four), not what they failed to achieve. This was a creditable performance; expecting the quick destruction of the well-handled and well-fought Taffy 3 is not realistic.

The next myth is one that is hardly even examined. It is generally assumed that Kurita acted stupidly by not pressing into the gulf when he had the chance. By declining to do so, he threw away victory. On the contrary, Kurita did not act stupidly. He carefully considered his options and acted out of conscience by deciding not to throw away the lives of his men. He realized the utter futility of *Sho-1*. Because it offered no prospect of success, Kurita was totally justified in declining its suicidal design. As is detailed in this account, Kurita correctly discerned there was no possible gain to following his orders to a dramatic but futile finish. Even Imperial Navy officers had a limit to their willingness to sacrifice thousands of men for no purpose.

The last myth is directly tied to Kurita's refusal to commit his force on a suicidal path. As prevailing wisdom goes, had he only pressed his attack, Kurita would have found nothing in his way (in fact, entirely false) and once inside the gulf, there were targets of such importance that their destruction would have changed the course of the American campaign to retake the Philippines or even of the war itself. Few myths are easier to refute. Kurita would have faced a force larger than his own, supported by hundreds of aircraft, even before he could have entered the gulf. If by chance he had successfully forced his way into the gulf to attack the shipping present, there was relatively little of value to attack (with the exception of the three command ships and the cruiser that MacArthur was embarked on). The invasion force was long gone, but there were 28 Liberty ships and 23 landing ship tanks (LSTs) remaining. Even in the extremely unlikely event that all had been sunk, their loss would have made no difference to the Philippines campaign or the pace of the American advance in the final months of the war. A nation that could build over 2,700 Liberty ships and over 1,000 LSTs would shrug off such losses.

Each of the engagements that make up the Battle of Leyte Gulf are fascinating in their own right. Though largely unknown, the battle actually began a week before the invasion of Leyte when Halsey's carriers attacked Japanese airfields and installations on Formosa (present-day Taiwan). What resulted was the largest air-sea battle in history up to that point between Third Fleet and the vast number of aircraft Toyoda had massed to destroy the American carrier fleet. The great air-sea battle off Formosa resulted in a massive Japanese defeat that had immense implications for the Battle of Leyte Gulf. The key to the upcoming battle was air power, and the failure of Japanese air power to inflict any serious losses on the Americans was a portent of things to come. After the air-sea battle off Formosa, it would not be an exaggeration to state that the outcome of the Battle of Leyte Gulf was a foregone conclusion.

In the opening engagement of the Battle of Leyte Gulf, the Battle of the Sibuyan Sea, most accounts focus on the sinking of superbattleship

Musashi and how she was pounded under the waves by an unprecedented barrage of torpedo and bomb hits. This was an undeniable American success, but the battle had turned out much better than Kurita had a right to expect. A full day of strikes from Halsey's carriers had accounted for a single ship sunk – *Musashi* – and damage to a heavy cruiser that forced her to return to base. This overconcentration on *Musashi* left Kurita's force still extremely formidable. The failure of the Third Fleet to stop the advance of Kurita's force, the centerpiece of *Sho-1*, made the battle a tactical victory for the Japanese. It also led directly to Halsey's controversial decision to focus on the Japanese carrier force to the north and ignore Kurita's force.

The second major engagement of the battle was nothing more than a maritime execution. The Battle of Surigao Strait was the least important of the four actions making up the Battle of Leyte Gulf, since it was fought by a Japanese decoy force against insurmountable odds. It did contain the second and last battleship action of the Pacific War, and the last battleship clash ever fought. Given enough warning, the Americans prepared an elaborate ambush for Nishimura's small force. Never before had the Americans planned a night battle so carefully with such overwhelming force. Of the seven attacking Japanese ships, all but one was sunk, three by a single torpedo salvo from an American destroyer. Both Japanese battleships present were also sunk by torpedoes. The gunnery phase of the battle was anticlimactic, but witnessed the last big-gun salvo aimed at another battleship in naval history.

The most important action in the battle of Leyte Gulf is the Battle off Samar. As already mentioned, the action is misunderstood, and thus has become the subject of mythology. A battle pitting Kurita's force, led by the superbattleship *Yamato*, against six slow, unarmored, and lightly armed escort carriers, escorted only by destroyers and destroyer escorts, could have only a single outcome. But, as already outlined, this was a battle unlike any other. The result was an American victory which will always stand as an example of the tenacity and bravery of the American sailor.

In the final action, the Battle off Cape Engano, Halsey almost had his opportunity for a battle of annihilation. The Japanese carrier force was subjected to a total of 527 offensive sorties from Halsey's carriers – no other force in naval history had ever been subjected to such massive air attacks over such a compressed period. Three Japanese carriers were sunk and a fourth left crippled. In the middle of this action, Halsey began to receive calls for assistance from the escort carriers off Samar. Halsey declined to suspend his battle of annihilation until Nimitz weighed in. Only then did Halsey decide to send part of this force south to catch Kurita. But Halsey's failure to act immediately and decisively retarded his intervention until it was too late – after the Battle off Samar, Kurita turned north and escaped through San Bernardino Strait. Had Halsey decided to assist the escort carriers at the first sign of trouble, he could have caught Kurita before he escaped through the strait. There was still a chance of catching Kurita after Halsey finally turned part of his force south in the late morning, but the movement toward the strait was conducted without alacrity. The epic battle of Halsey's modern battleships facing off against *Yamato* and her escorts was never meant to be.

Unable to contend with the US Navy by using conventional tactics, by the time of the invasion of Leyte the Japanese decided to use "special" (suicide) attacks. The Battle of Leyte Gulf witnessed the first pre-planned Japanese use of this radical tactic. The first two days of suicide attacks brought undeniable success. Against two groups of escort carriers with nine carriers, kamikaze aircraft sank one and damaged five more. Suicide attacks are also part of the legacy of the Battle of Leyte Gulf.

This book requires readers to take a fresh look at the battle. That fresh look seeks to overturn decades of faulty analysis based on incorrect assumptions. Because Leyte Gulf was such a complex affair, the author has decided to treat the battle thematically instead of on a strict chronological basis. The battle is best presented by following the operations of each of the principal Japanese forces. The adventures of these forces led to the four major clashes outlined above. The Americans were mainly reactive to the Japanese, so their operations are examined in the context of Japanese operations.

Japanese names are given with surname first, as was the custom at the time.

Mark Stille
Annapolis, Maryland
June 2022

List of Illustrations

General Douglas MacArthur and Admiral Chester Nimitz, both
    theater commanders, had different visions for the direction of
    the American advance in the Pacific in late 1944. Ultimately,
    MacArthur's vision was accepted and the invasion of the
    Philippines was approved. However, the split command
    arrangement for the operations was not addressed, and this
    became a problem going into the Battle of Leyte Gulf.
Admiral William Halsey, shown on the left, was the commander of
    the Third Fleet. His aggressive actions earlier in the war had
    made him a legend in his own time. Charged with providing
    cover for the Leyte invasion against the Imperial Navy, he acted
    in his usual aggressive manner to make a decision that has been
    criticized ever since.
Vice Admiral Thomas Kinkaid, pictured here in January 1945 in
    Lingayen Gulf, commanded the Seventh Fleet during the Leyte
    operation. His actions during the battle were a contributing
    factor in allowing part of his forces to come under heavy
    Japanese attack.
Rear Admiral Jessie Oldendorf was in charge of the American forces
    at the Battle of Surigao Strait. He had the time to set up an
    elaborate ambush against the approaching Japanese, which
    proved devastatingly effective. However, his pursuit of the
    shattered Japanese was lackluster.
Rear Admiral Clifton Sprague, commander of a group of escort
    carriers known as Taffy 3, was thrust into a very unexpected and
    very desperate fight against a powerful Japanese surface force. His

quick and decisive actions turned what could have been a local defeat for the Americans into a victory.

Admiral Toyoda Soemu, commander of the Combined Fleet, was the author of the Japanese plan to defend the Philippines. The plan resulted in the destruction of the Combined Fleet as an effective force, but it provided the fleet with a chance to die fighting as desired by Toyoda.

Vice Admiral Kurita Takeo was the most controversial Japanese commander of the battle. He led the largest Japanese force with orders to break into Leyte Gulf to attack the shipping located there. When given the chance to execute these orders, he declined the opportunity to lead his fleet to destruction.

Generally seen as the most competent Japanese admiral of the war, Ozawa Jisaburo was given the unenviable task of leading a force comprised of toothless carriers to lure Halsey's Third Fleet to the north, thus allowing Kurita to attack into the gulf. He accomplished his mission, becoming the only Japanese commander to do so during the battle.

Vice Admiral Nishimura Shoji was the only Japanese commander during the battle who obeyed his orders to the letter and led his force to virtual destruction. His small force was the subject of the American ambush at Surigao Strait, which destroyed all but one of his ships.

Vice Admiral Shima Kiyohide led a small force with the grandiloquent name of the Second Diversionary Attack Force. He fought hard to get it involved in the attack into Leyte Gulf. During the actual battle, he fought indecisively and decided not to sacrifice his force.

The heart of the Third Fleet was its carriers, the most powerful of which were Essex-class fleet carriers. This is *Intrepid*, pictured in November 1944. She played a prominent role during the Battle of Leyte Gulf, conducting five major air attacks in two days.

Embedded within Third Fleet were six of the most modern battleships in the world. This is *New Jersey*, pictured in 1944. These powerful ships were an integral part of American doctrine to fight a fleet action, but because of Halsey's blundering, they never got an opportunity to engage the Japanese.

The standard American carrier fighter in 1944 was the F6F Hellcat, like this aircraft taking off from *Lexington* on October 12, 1944

during the air-sea Battle off Formosa. The Hellcat was superior to
its Japanese counterparts, and, with the benefit of radar direction,
provided American carrier task forces with a large degree of
immunity from conventional Japanese air attacks. This fact drove
the Japanese to suicide tactics.

The standard American torpedo bomber in 1944 was the TBM
Avenger, serving aboard escort, light, and fleet carriers. This
photo shows an Avenger being loaded with a Mark 13 torpedo
with the modifications that made the torpedo effective after
a series of problems earlier in the war. Torpedo bombers were
essential to sinking heavily-armored Japanese warships. Even
superbattleship *Musashi* was dispatched by the Avenger and its
Mark 13s.

The SB2C Helldiver was the standard American dive-bomber at Leyte
Gulf. After a prolonged and painful introduction, it proved to be
a rugged and effective aircraft and eventually sank more Japanese
ships than any other Allied aircraft.

The centerpiece of the Japanese plan was the First Diversionary Attack
Force under Kurita. It was built around five battleships. Three of
those, *Yamato*, *Musashi*, and *Nagato*, are shown here at Brunei
Bay before departing on their fateful voyage to Leyte Gulf.

In the week before the American invasion of Leyte, the Third Fleet
fought a major engagement off Formosa. An all-out Japanese air
offensive failed to sink or damage any of Halsey's carriers, but
did succeed in damaging two American cruisers with torpedoes.
This is light cruiser *Houston* being towed clear of the area.

The First Diversionary Attack Force pictured departing Brunei Bay
on the morning of October 22. Of the three battleships and
six heavy cruisers in view, only three of these ships remained to
return to Brunei on October 28.

The first disaster to befall the First Diversionary Attack Force was an
ambush in the Palawan Passage by two American submarines on
October 23. Achieving total surprise, the two submarines sank
two heavy cruisers and crippled a third. *Darter*, pictured here
aground on Bombay Shoal, was lost the next day as she tried to
finish off the damaged cruiser.

The Japanese conducted a series of attacks on October 23 to neutralize
the Third Fleet. This effort failed, though the light carrier
Princeton was hit by a single bomb and later sank. Failure to

neutralize the American carriers opened the First Diversionary Attack Force up to concerted air attack.

The First Diversionary Attack Force is shown here under air attack on October 24. The formation appears to be in disarray, but in fact the Japanese were using their preferred circular evasion maneuver. Kurita's force had no air cover to counter the five major air attacks launched by the carriers of the Third Fleet.

In the center of this dramatic scene, superbattleship *Musashi* comes under attack. The American aviators overconcentrated on this single target, allowing the rest of Kurita's force to emerge largely unscathed. It required a minimum of 16 bomb and at least 11 torpedo hits to force *Musashi* under the waves.

Nishimura's force was only subjected to a single air attack on October 24 as it transited toward its destruction in Surigao Strait. This is *Yamashiro* under attack. Though damage was light, the discovery of Nishimura's force on the morning of October 24 gave the Americans ample time to prepare their ambush in Surigao Strait.

Destroyer *McDermut* was part of the American force that launched a series of devastating torpedo attacks on Nishimura's force on the night of October 24–25 in Surigao Strait. Five of Nishimura's seven ships were struck by torpedoes, including three from a single salvo fired by *McDermut*.

The last battleship action in naval history occurred during the final stages of the Battle of Surigao Strait. Six American battleships, including *West Virginia* shown here, engaged a single Japanese battleship. The gunnery phase of the battle was anticlimactic, since Nishimura's formation had already been shattered by torpedo attack.

Surigao Strait was also the last major night engagement of the war. The possession of radar gave the Americans a decisive advantage at night. In this view, some of the eight Allied cruisers engage Japanese targets during the battle.

In the Battle off Samar, Kurita's fleet encountered a force of six American escort carriers, like *Kalinin Bay* shown here. All six carriers possessed no protection, limited armament, and a low top speed. *Kalinin Bay* was hit as many as 15 times but survived.

The American escort carrier force was escorted by three destroyers and four destroyer escorts. These were aggressively used to defend the slow escort carriers. The most aggressive of the escorts was destroyer *Johnston*, shown here. *Johnston* torpedoed a Japanese heavy cruiser, forcing her out of the battle, and then later forced a Japanese destroyer squadron to launch a premature torpedo attack. *Johnston* did not survive the battle, losing over half her crew.

Destroyer escort *Samuel B. Roberts* was also thrown against Kurita's heavy ships. She launched her three torpedoes at a Japanese heavy cruiser before return Japanese fire sank her with heavy loss of life.

Caught by surprise at Samar, American ships immediately began to make smoke. This was a highly effective tactic and greatly reduced the accuracy of Japanese gunnery. In this view, two escort carriers (with *Gambier Bay* in the foreground) and two destroyer escorts emit black smoke from their stacks.

Japanese gunnery was mediocre during the Battle off Samar. Four of the six escort carriers were hit during the battle, but only one was sunk. In this view, *Gambier Bay* is straddled by Japanese shells and falls behind the rest of Taffy 3. She sank after receiving at least 26 hits.

In the first 30 minutes of the battle, the six escort carriers of Taffy 3 launched 95 aircraft. This is *Kitkun Bay* conducting flight operations, with shells splashing around carrier *White Plains* in the distance. During the two hours of the Battle off Samar, over 200 aircraft from all three American escort carrier groups attacked Kurita's force.

In this view, heavy cruiser *Chikuma* lies dead in the water in the middle of a large oil slick. American aircraft accounted for three heavy cruisers during the battle, including *Chikuma*.

In this view, Ozawa's carrier force maneuvers in the initial stages of the Battle off Cape Engano. The Third Fleet flew 527 sorties against Ozawa's force on October 25, an unsurpassed effort for such a brief period. Note the antiaircraft bursts, indicating that the Japanese are using ineffective barrage fire.

Of the four carriers in Ozawa's force, three were sunk by air attack and the last crippled. Here *Zuikaku* (in center) and *Zuiho* (upper right) are attacked by Helldivers (note the aircraft on the left).

The last surviving Japanese carrier from the Pearl Harbor attack was *Zuikaku*. Her end came at Leyte Gulf after taking as many as six torpedo hits. Note the Avenger in the foreground.

One of the most iconic photos of the war shows light carrier *Zuiho* in her dramatic camouflage under air attack. Note the ship has already been damaged, as evinced by the buckled flight deck and the smoke issuing from the ship's starboard quarter. *Zuiho* later sank.

Ozawa's force included two Ise-class battleship-carriers. These featured a flight deck aft but carried no aircraft during the battle. Despite coming under heavy air attack after the four carriers were sunk or crippled, both ships survived the battle.

The last phase of the Battle off Cape Engano featured an American surface force mopping up the cripples from the preceding air attacks. In this view, light carrier *Chiyoda* burns after being subjected to cruiser gunfire. Her entire crew of some 970 men perished.

Leyte Gulf heralded the arrival of Japanese suicide tactics. Escort carrier *St Lo* was the first ship sunk by kamikazes. Here the ship's magazine explodes from fires created by an earlier suicide attack.

List of Maps

I

The Road to Leyte Gulf

In 1898, the United States defeated Spain and gained control of the Philippines in the Treaty of Paris signed that December. Situated in the Western Pacific, the Philippines were the most important American possession in the region. Being almost 4,500 nautical miles (nm) from the American naval base at Pearl Harbor in the Hawaiian Islands and separated by a series of Japanese-held islands in the Central Pacific, the Philippines would be hard to defend against a Japanese attack. In both American and Japanese war planning before the Pacific War, it was assumed that the Philippines would quickly fall to the Japanese. The United States Navy (USN) would subsequently lead an offensive to recapture the islands and subsequently bring naval pressure on the Japanese Home Islands. During this advance through the Central Pacific into the Western Pacific, both the USN and the Imperial Japanese Navy (IJN) foresaw a climactic naval engagement that would decide naval supremacy in the Pacific.

When hostilities between the United States and Japan opened in December 1941, this script remained largely true to prewar projections. There were some unforeseen twists, but the Philippines remained a major planning factor for both sides. The initial Japanese offensive focused on seizing resource areas in Southeast Asia which would permit Japan to continue the war. To support this critical effort, the IJN planned and executed a surprise attack on the USN's Pacific Fleet based at Pearl Harbor. Though actually intended by Admiral Yamamoto Isoruku, commander in chief of the Combined Fleet, as a decisive strike to cripple the Pacific Fleet and begin the process of forcing the United States to negotiate an early end to the war, the success of the attack eliminated any possibility that the Pacific Fleet could move to stop the Japanese occupation of Southeast Asia. Concurrently with the Pearl Harbor operation, the IJN commenced a series of landings in Malaya, southern Thailand, and the Philippines as the first stage of the operation to seize the resource-rich Netherlands East Indies (NEI).

Seizure of the Philippines was an important aspect of the Japanese campaign because of the islands' location astride the sea lines of communications (SLOCs) between Japan and her newly-won resource areas in Southeast Asia. In a well-planned and boldly-executed series of operations, the IJN crippled American air power in the Philippines and then executed a number of smaller amphibious operations as a precursor to the major attack on Luzon, the largest and most important island in the Philippines archipelago. The principal landing on Luzon occurred at Lingayen Gulf on December 22, 1941. Within three weeks of the war's opening, the IJN had effectively set the conditions for Japanese victory in the Philippines by eliminating American air power, forcing the USN's small Asiatic Fleet to retreat south into the NEI, and delivering a large invasion force onto Luzon.[1] There were differences between the Japanese invasion of the Philippines in 1941 and the American invasion in 1944, but both were mounted for the same basic reason and conducted with the same broad objectives. A major difference between them was that the 1941 Japanese invasion was conducted under the support of land-based air cover, and the 1944 American invasion was not. The other key difference was that the IJN was determined to massively resist the 1944 invasion, while the USN in 1941 did not have the means to do so.

While the IJN quickly accomplished its objectives in the Philippines campaign, the Imperial Japanese Army had a much tougher time. American and Filipino ground forces anchored their defense on the Bataan Peninsula and defeated the initial Japanese offensive to clean them out. After the IJA was forced to commit additional forces, the defenders of Bataan were compelled to surrender on April 9. Corregidor Island held out for an additional month and did not surrender until May 6. On May 8, all other American forces throughout the Philippines were ordered to surrender. However, the Japanese never had absolute control of the islands, on which a large and increasingly effective resistance movement took hold.

As the Japanese realized the completion of their first-phase objectives, the Philippines became a backwater. Dutch authorities in the NEI surrendered in early March and the Japanese moved on to new conquests in New Guinea and the South Pacific. In May 1942, within only days of the surrender of the American forces on Corregidor, the Japanese received their first strategic setback of the Pacific War. Planning to land an invasion force on Port Moresby in southeastern New Guinea, the IJN encountered an American carrier task force sent to stop further Japanese advances in the South Pacific. In the world's first carrier battle between May 7 and 8, 1942, the Japanese carrier force covering the landing was badly battered, forcing the cancelation of the landing. Just over a month later, Yamamoto's plan to use Midway Atoll as a lure to bring the Pacific Fleet to battle where it could be decisively defeated by the much larger Combined Fleet went seriously astray. Poor operational planning by the Combined Fleet set the conditions for the defeat in which the Japanese lost four fleet carriers and had their capabilities for future large-scale offensive operations blunted.

Japanese defeat at Midway presented the initiative to the Americans. They used it to open their first offensive of the entire war in the South Pacific with the goal of recapturing key points in the region. In the view of General Douglas MacArthur, commander of Allied forces in the Southwest Pacific, these were the first steps on the road back to the Philippines.

The initial American attack in the South Pacific focused on Guadalcanal in the southern Solomon Islands. From the American landing in early August 1942 until the final Japanese evacuation from the island in early February 1943, the campaign featured attrition of the nature that the Japanese could not afford. Both sides committed growing air, naval, and ground forces in an attempt to secure the air and waters around the island. For the Japanese, who still had a numerical edge in all ship categories, the opportunity for a decisive battle against the USN went unrecognized and therefore unrealized. Yamamoto never marshalled his available forces for a decisive strike. The struggle for Guadalcanal had similarities to the struggle for Leyte Island in the Philippines fought between October and late December 1944.

Following their capture of Guadalcanal, the Americans decided to continue up the Solomons to isolate and capture the key Japanese base at Rabaul on the island of New Britain. Not until November 1943 did the Americans reach Bougainville in the northern Solomons. By this

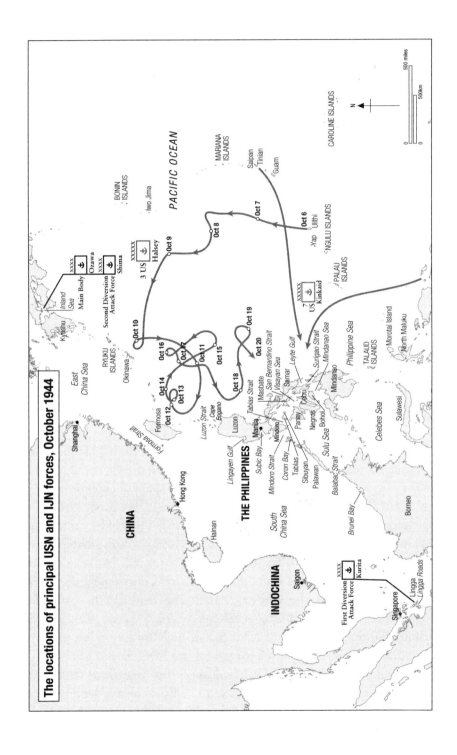

The locations of principal USN and IJN forces, October 1944

point, the original plan to seize Rabaul was replaced with a plan to isolate it.

The long slog up the Solomons was not the USN's preferred method to take the war to the Japanese. In its view, the most direct route to Japan was through the Central Pacific. While the bulk of the Pacific Fleet was tied up in the grinding battle of attrition for Guadalcanal, a second line of advance was impossible. By late 1943, the USN's growing strength allowed it to open a second front in the Central Pacific. In addition to being the shorter route to Japan, an advance in the Central Pacific was under the control of Admiral Chester Nimitz, unlike the advance in the South Pacific and New Guinea that was under the strategic direction of MacArthur.

THE AMERICANS APPROACH THE PHILIPPINES

The opening of the second front against Japan accented the divided American command structure in the Pacific. Overall strategic direction was provided by the Joint Chiefs of Staff (JCS) in Washington. The Pacific was divided into two separate theaters. The Southwest Pacific Area (SWPA) was placed under command of MacArthur on March 18, 1942. This included Australia, New Guinea, the NEI, and the Philippines. The remainder of the Pacific comprised the Pacific Ocean Area under the command of Admiral Chester W. Nimitz, who assumed his position on April 3, 1942. Because these were two separate commands, any conflict between them could only be resolved by the JCS.[2]

Approval for the USN's preferred two-front offensive against Japan was gained at the Trident Conference held in Washington in May 1943. MacArthur was tasked to continue his advance along the New Guinea coast with the ultimate objective of seizing Morotai in the Moluccas. Nimitz was directed to commence his drive through the Central Pacific starting with the Gilbert Islands, followed by the Marshalls, and then the Marianas. Taking the Marianas would bring the Japanese Home Islands into range of long-range American bombers and was therefore expected to prompt a major Japanese reaction. This would likely include a major naval battle and with it a chance to destroy the Combined Fleet. After the Marianas, the next objective was the Palau Islands. Once Morotai and the Palaus had been captured, the island of Mindanao in the southern Philippines would be within air range.[3]

In accordance with this overall guidance, the Gilbert Islands were invaded in November 1943 and the invasion of the Marshalls followed in January and February 1944. On April 22, 1944, MacArthur made a major advance landing at Hollandia on New Guinea.

The rivalry between MacArthur and Nimitz grew more heated as the pace of the American advance accelerated. In a February–March planning conference in Washington, MacArthur's staff advocated for their advance along northern New Guinea to continue into Mindanao. Admiral Ernest J. King (Chief of Naval Operations and Commander in Chief, US Fleet) and Nimitz wanted their Central Pacific drive as the primary focus. During the conference, Nimitz proposed a timetable for future operations. His operational plan called for an invasion of Saipan in the Marianas by June 15 and landings in the Palaus on October 1. The resulting JCS directive issued on March 12, 1944 combined Nimitz's short-term schedule and MacArthur's longer-term goal of invading Mindanao. The invasion of the Marianas was set for June 15 and the operation against the Palaus for September 15. The attack against Mindanao was given a target date of November 15. The toehold in the Philippines at Mindanao would support the capture of Formosa scheduled for February 15, 1945. On the important question of whether to attack Luzon, the JCS left open the possibility that such an operation might be conducted to support the capture of Formosa.[4]

In the largest amphibious operation of the Pacific War to date, US Marines stormed ashore at Saipan on June 15. Being within their "absolute defense zone," the Japanese mounted a major fleet operation to defeat the invasion. The Japanese expected an invasion of the Marianas and had plans in place to conduct a decisive battle to defeat the Pacific Fleet and turn the tide of the war. For the first time since October 1942, the Japanese committed their carrier fleet. This force had been built up to nine carriers and over 400 embarked aircraft. Large numbers of land-based aircraft were also earmarked to take part in the operation. However, the level of training of Japanese pilots, carrier-based and land-based, was low and this proved to be the critical weakness in Japanese hopes for victory.

By this point in the war, the USN's Fast Carrier Task Force had grown to 15 fleet and light carriers with almost 900 embarked aircraft. Despite this marked superiority, Admiral Raymond A. Spruance decided to fight a very conservative battle to eliminate any possibility that the Japanese could attack the landing force. Using a well-developed air defense doctrine and superbly-trained fighter pilots, the American carrier force crushed a series of large Japanese air attacks on June 19 at little cost to itself. The following day, the Americans were able to launch a strike at the retreating Japanese fleet. The air attack was delivered hurriedly at dusk and accounted for only one Japanese carrier. The battle had been disastrous for the Japanese, but the full scope of the disaster was unknown to the Americans. Two more Japanese carriers had been sunk by submarine attack, and the entire Japanese carrier fleet returned with only about 35 aircraft.

The Battle of the Philippine Sea, the largest carrier battle of the war, was decisive, but not in the way the Japanese had planned. Their defeat was so comprehensive that the Combined Fleet's carrier force would not be ready by the time the Americans attacked the Philippines. Nevertheless, the battle felt like an incomplete victory to many American admirals, since the Japanese fleet had been allowed to escape. The inability of the Japanese to reconstitute its carrier force had a huge impact on its planning for the Battle of Leyte Gulf, while the Americans were determined to finish the Japanese carrier force should such a chance be offered in the future.

While both Nimitz and MacArthur concurred that Mindanao was a necessary foothold in the Philippines, the question of the next target after the capture of Mindanao was left unresolved by the JCS's March directive. The goal of cutting Japan off from its resource areas in Southeast Asia was clear, but the approach to achieve it was anything but. MacArthur wanted to follow the Mindanao operation with a landing on Leyte in the central Philippines on November 15, followed by an attack to recapture Luzon. In his view, the United States had an obligation to liberate the Filipinos and Luzon was a better location for supporting the final advance on Japan than Formosa. For MacArthur there was also the question of seeking revenge for his earlier defeat in the Philippines.[5] This question of his personal prestige should not overshadow the fact that MacArthur's plan had strategic merit and was ultimately the plan selected for execution.

King and Nimitz did not favor slogging through the Philippines after Leyte was secured. In their view, the goal of cutting off Japan from the resource areas in the south was better served by taking Formosa and key locations on the Chinese coast. Events in China undermined the prospects for King's Formosa–China option. The Imperial Army conducted a major advance in China in May 1944 that made it painfully obvious that Chinese forces would not be able to assist in securing a lodgment on the Chinese coast. Formosa had been part of the Japanese empire since 1895 and was well defended. American planners estimated that a successful invasion of Formosa would require nine divisions. This was the death knell of King's Formosa strategy, since a force of this size could not be assembled until mid-1945.

Both MacArthur and Nimitz had a chance to present their strategic visions to President Franklin D. Roosevelt on July 28, 1944 when the president visited Oahu. As dramatic as this meeting was with both men personally making their cases to Roosevelt, there was no final decision. Roosevelt seemed to prefer MacArthur's plan to invade Mindanao and then Leyte as a precursor to landing on Luzon, but he did not rule out an invasion of Formosa.[6] It would take the JCS to make a final decision.

The JCS met again on September 1 to provide clarity on the long-term strategy to defeat Japan. The question whether to invade Luzon or Formosa was again left unresolved, but they did approve MacArthur's plan to occupy Leyte, with a target date of December 20.[7] The landing on Leyte would be preceded by an invasion of southern Mindanao in November. The operation to invade Leyte was to be a joint effort of MacArthur's and Nimitz's forces.

It did not take long for this timetable to change, and the change was dramatic. On August 28, Nimitz's carrier force, designated Task Force 38 under Admiral Halsey's Third Fleet, departed its advanced fleet anchorage at Eniwetok in the Marshalls. Halsey's mission was to reduce Japanese land-based air power that might interfere with the planned invasions of Morotai off northwestern New Guinea and Peleliu in the Palaus. TF 38's initial raids on the Palaus on September 6–8 and Mindanao on September 9–10 were unopposed. Halsey shifted his focus to the Visayas in the central Philippines on September 12–13. Flying some 2,400 sorties over those two days, American aviators claimed 200 Japanese aircraft destroyed in the air or on the ground, in addition to wreaking damage on shipping and infrastructure. It seemed to Halsey that Japanese air power in the region had been neutralized. Based on this belief, the always aggressive Halsey made a momentous recommendation to Nimitz that the preliminary landings on Morotai, Yap, Peleliu, and Mindanao be canceled and the forces used for a landing on Leyte as early as October 20.[8]

Halsey's proposal was indeed bold – it moved up the invasion of Leyte by two months. Nimitz quickly agreed that the intermediate operations to seize Yap and Mindanao could be canceled, but he ultimately decided to proceed with the operation to seize the Palaus. MacArthur and his staff also agreed that the opportunity to speed up the pace of operations could be supported and quickly gave the proposal their support. On September 15, the idea reached the JCS in Quebec where the Combined Chiefs of Staff were in conference. Since MacArthur and Nimitz both agreed with the revised and more aggressive timetable, there was little debate. After only 90 minutes, they approved the new plan and sent the requisite orders to the theater commanders. The invasion of Leyte was on, with a target date of October 20.[9] As will be seen in the next chapter, the Japanese had already discerned that the Philippines and specifically Leyte would be the next American target, and they were already planning yet another decisive battle to defeat it.

In retrospect, the decision to move the invasion of Leyte up by two months contained an element of risk, but it was not a rash move. It may not have surprised the Japanese, but it gave the Imperial Army little time to move forces into the central Philippines from Luzon and the IJN insufficient time to complete the training of new carrier air groups. Most importantly, it avoided a lengthy campaign on Mindanao. The risk was that it was MacArthur's first invasion beyond the range of land-based air power. In fact, Japanese air power in the Philippines was not as weak as Halsey assessed, since the Japanese were withholding their remaining air units in anticipation of the impending American invasion.

Landing on Leyte without the benefit of intermediate operations to gain airfields was only possible because of the proven excellence of Halsey's carriers in defeating Japanese air attacks against Allied shipping. The carriers would have to remain on station until sufficient airfields were made operational on Leyte to accommodate MacArthur's land-based air force. This became a real problem since the soil on the eastern side of Leyte was unsuitable for development into airfields during the monsoon season.[10] Monsoon weather was worst from October to December, which meant the carriers would have to remain tied to Leyte for a prolonged period. This was a factor as early as the immediate aftermath of the invasion when Halsey detached his largest carrier task force for rest and replenishment, making it miss most of the battle.

THE AMERICAN PLAN TO INVADE LEYTE

Whatever MacArthur's emotional ties were to return to the Philippines and liberate its people, there was sound military logic driving an attack on the islands. The Philippines occupy a critical location in Southeast Asia. The largest and most populous island of Luzon dominates the Luzon Strait between Luzon and Formosa. This critical chokepoint was used by most Japanese trade to and from Japan and the resource areas in Southeast Asia. If the Americans could control those waters, Japan would be threatened with economic strangulation and its ability to continue the war would be jeopardized. The first step to seizing Luzon was to gain a toehold in the central Philippines at Leyte.

Leyte was the best location in the central Philippines for an amphibious attack for several important reasons. The east coast of Leyte presented a direct and undefended approach from the Philippine Sea. Once made secure, Leyte Gulf offered a large anchorage suitable as a staging point for future operations. Once Surigao Strait had been secured, Leyte Gulf would be an excellent jumping off point for operations into the Visayas and ultimately to Luzon itself. Another major attraction of Leyte was its eastern valley plain, which was flat and well-suited (except during the monsoon, as already noted) for development into airfields. Aircraft based on Leyte could cover central Luzon, the Visayas, and all of Mindanao.

There were only five weeks available to prepare the invasion plan between JCS approval and the target date of October 20. Seizure of Leyte was the responsibility of the Sixth Army. Four divisions were landed in the initial assault with two more in reserve. MacArthur believed that the entire operation hinged on the ability of the USN to keep the Japanese from attacking the invasion force or reinforcement and resupply convoys while denying the movement of Japanese reinforcements to Leyte.[11] Vice Admiral Thomas C. Kinkaid's Seventh Fleet was given the responsibility for moving MacArthur's forces to Leyte and providing them with antisubmarine and air defense. It was also tasked to prevent Japanese reinforcements from reaching the island.[12] In fact, the Seventh Fleet was capable of providing local security to the invasion but was incapable of preventing Japanese reinforcement of Leyte. As MacArthur had feared, this prolonged the battle considerably.

By agreement of Halsey's and MacArthur's staffs, the Third Fleet had responsibility for supporting the invasion by reducing Japanese air power in the region and defeating any attempt by the Combined Fleet to intervene. These tasks were broken down into several phases. From October 10 to 13, the carriers would strike Okinawa, Formosa, and northern Luzon to reduce Japanese air power. From October 16 to 20, as the landings approached, the TF 38 would shift its attention to Leyte and the central Philippines. After the landings, TF 38 would operate in "strategic support" by being ready to destroy Japanese air and naval forces that threatened the invasion.[13]

Since the divided American command structure became such a major factor in the forthcoming battle, it is worth looking into Nimitz's operation plan. It was in compliance with MacArthur's intent, except for one possible exception. Third Fleet was tasked to support MacArthur's forces and to destroy Japanese air and naval forces threatening the landing. This was standard tasking for the carriers in an amphibious operation. What was not standard was the insertion of the clause:

> In case opportunity for destruction of major portion of the enemy fleet is offered or can be created, such destruction becomes the primary task.[14]

Such a clause was not part of Admiral Raymond A. Spruance's orders for the invasion of the Marianas. Accordingly, he decided that his primary mission was the support of the amphibious invasion, not the destruction of the enemy fleet. In the aftermath of Philippine Sea, Nimitz gave Halsey orders that his main task was to aggressively go after the Japanese fleet. It is unlikely that Halsey needed any prodding to seek out the Japanese fleet and bring it to battle, but Nimitz left no doubt in the matter. Halsey's own operations order issued on October 3 mirrored his new primary task. Halsey interpreted Nimitz's orders as a blank check to disregard the standard, but more passive, task of protecting the invasion force for an aggressive option more to his liking. Halsey also directed that TF 38 would concentrate off Samar after refueling on October 19 to be in position to support the landings the following day in coordination with Kinkaid's forces. His orders emphasized that TF 38 task groups attack Japanese forces within range and that the battleships within TF 38 would play a major role in operations. Halsey believed the need to cooperate with the Seventh Fleet did not preclude offensive operations by his carriers.

Though the insertion of additional tasking in Nimitz's orders may appear to be confusing, it did not change Halsey's overall mission. The focus on Nimitz's adjustment to Halsey's orders misses the key point that Halsey's mission was to support MacArthur's forces, and more specifically, the invasion. The additional orders from Nimitz to focus on the Japanese fleet did not overrule the original task of covering the landing. The mission of destroying the Japanese fleet was dependent on it contributing to the mission of supporting the landing.[15] In any event, the inclusion of the additional tasking from Nimitz had the potential to cause confusion if conditions required that Halsey make a choice about competing priorities. For Halsey, though, it just reinforced his natural inclination to seek battle with the IJN whenever it was possible. Nimitz must have known this.

The divided American command structure and the fact that MacArthur's and Nimitz's intents with regard to Halsey's Third Fleet were at variance was bound to cause problems. At the very least, the result would be a slow reaction if the Japanese mounted a major operation to intervene with the invasion. In addition, the divided command structure posed problems for intelligence, logistics, air searches, and submarine deployments. In a worst case scenario, there was the real potential for miscommunication between Halsey and Kinkaid. The two primary commanders now believed they had different primary missions – Kinkaid's to protect the landing and Halsey's to attack the Japanese fleet. Combined with the communications problems between forces under the command of different theaters, the American beachhead's vulnerability to attack was greatly increased. How Halsey would interpret his orders would be a major part in the upcoming battle.

AMERICAN COMMUNICATIONS AND INTELLIGENCE

As a result of the divided command structure, American naval communications were difficult. The sheer amount of forces and the high level of communications activity made basic communications difficult from commanders down to subordinates. Even more difficult were communications that crossed theater boundaries. MacArthur, always mistrustful of the USN, did not want the Third and Seventh Fleet communicating directly. Therefore a direct, secure, and high-speed communications link did not exist between Halsey and Kinkaid.

In the days preceding the largest naval battle of the war, senior American leaders did not expect the Imperial Navy to make a major effort to defend the Philippines. MacArthur's intelligence assessments even went as far as to state that no more than 70–80 Japanese fighters and bombers would be employed to defend the Philippines. Adding to this very poor analysis was the assessment that no air reinforcements would be sent to the region and that the Japanese carrier fleet would not make an appearance. MacArthur's intelligence was no better when it came to the Japanese naval situation. The estimates of the Combined Fleet's order of battle were in error both in numbers of units (especially carriers) and their location. The existence of a Japanese naval plan to defend the islands had been detected, as had the existence of a First and Second Diversionary Attack Force. However, there were no insights into the Combined Fleet's operational planning to defend the islands, and no major Japanese reaction was expected.[16] Seventh Fleet intelligence analysts were also sanguine regarding the prospects for a Japanese naval reaction to the invasion. They flatly stated that the Japanese fleet was not expected to react to the Leyte operation. Overall, American intelligence support for planning the Leyte operation was very weak. It totally underestimated Japanese naval and air capabilities. Most importantly, it totally missed Japanese intentions. American intelligence analysts fell into the classic trap of assessing IJN intentions instead of its capabilities. The Japanese fleet would not conduct a large-scale reaction because, in the view of the rational analysts sitting in Melbourne, it was simply too risky for the Japanese to initiate a fleet action.[17]

Analysts at Nimitz's Joint Intelligence Center Pacific Ocean Area (JICPOA) did a better job discerning Japanese capabilities for the upcoming battle but were also wrong about actual Japanese intentions. In early September, the JICPOA assessed that the Combined Fleet was focused on rebuilding its strength, and that this process would take until December. Later that same month, JICPOA provided a revised estimate that the Combined Fleet would only be able to employ a single carrier division with some 175–200 aircraft and that the carrier force had been separated from the bulk of the surface fleet.[18] JICPOA also provided assessments relating to the use of decoy forces by the Japanese. These insights were accurate as far as they went, but they failed to give a complete picture of Japanese intentions. The fact that the centerpiece of the Japanese plan was a large force of battleships and heavy cruisers based near Singapore was never made clear. Most importantly, the timing of the Japanese plan to disrupt the invasion was unknown. Halsey had no reason to believe that the Japanese would mount a major operation to attack the invasion force, and his initial deployments on October 20 reflected this belief.

THE AMERICAN COMMAND STRUCTURE
AND COMMANDERS

The invasion of Leyte required MacArthur's and Nimitz's forces to focus on the same objective. As Supreme Commander of the Southwest Pacific Area, MacArthur commanded the ground and air forces committed to the operation. Also under his command was the Seventh Fleet. Since November 1943, the Seventh Fleet had been under the command of Vice Admiral Kinkaid. Though MacArthur did not inspire confidence in many because of his overarching ego, it is fair to point out that he did not meddle in naval affairs. Kinkaid and MacArthur were able to work closely together and Kinkaid had successfully stood up against his boss when required.[19]

The Seventh Fleet had grown into a huge force of some 550 ships by October 1944. It was divided into two attack forces, with each responsible for landing one of the two corps of Lieutenant General Walter Krueger's Sixth Army on the eastern coast of Leyte. The Seventh Fleet also included its own force of escort carriers, a group of motor torpedo boats, seven submarines tasked to directly support the invasion, and a large number of logistical units. Appendix 1 provides a detailed review of the Seventh Fleet's principal combat units.

The commander of the Seventh Fleet played a large role in the battle. Kinkaid's background was as a surface warfare officer. Right after the start of the Pacific War, he was given command of a division of heavy cruisers and assigned to carrier task force escort duties. He and his cruisers saw action at the Battles of Coral Sea and Midway; because of his familiarity with carrier operations, Kinkaid was given command of a carrier task force during the Guadalcanal campaign. His performance at the Battle of Santa Cruz was not good. Placed into an unsupported position by Halsey, he lost one of his carriers and saw the other damaged. Kinkaid was the last surface admiral to command a carrier task force in combat during the war.

In the aftermath of Santa Cruz, Kinkaid maneuvered his carrier task force far to the south of Guadalcanal, making it difficult for him to be in the position desired by Halsey to defeat the last major Japanese offensive against Guadalcanal beginning on November 13.

As a result, the fast battleships Halsey needed to counter a Japanese surface bombardment of the airfield on the island were out of position. This was a "great disappointment" to Halsey, and it came on top of Kinkaid's poor performance at Santa Cruz. There is no doubt a level of professional friction existed between Halsey and Kinkaid in 1942 and it is unlikely that this was forgotten by 1944.[20]

After his South Pacific performance, in January 1943 Kinkaid was sent to a back-water command in the North Pacific and was ordered to improve relations with US Army commands in the area. Kinkaid's ability to work with the Army resurrected his career. Kinkaid led the recapture of Attu and Kiska in the Aleutians. This set him up for the much more important billet as Commander, Allied Naval Forces Southwest Pacific Area and Commander of the Seventh Fleet. The Seventh Fleet became known as "MacArthur's Navy" because of its string of successful amphibious operations in the New Guinea area. In addition to dealing well with MacArthur, Kinkaid was respected by his subordinates. He routinely sought advice from them and delegated authority and responsibility to them. However, Kinkaid had no experience with major fleet operations like those he faced in the Leyte operation.

Direct air cover for the invasion was the responsibility of Task Group 77.4, the Escort Carrier Group. This was under command of Rear Admiral Thomas L. Sprague, who was also in direct command of one of the groups of escort carriers designated by its radio call sign as "Taffy 1." Sprague was an experienced naval aviator who had commanded fleet carrier *Intrepid* before taking over a division of escort carriers before the invasion of the Marianas. "Taffy 2" was under the command of Rear Admiral Felix B. Stump. He was also an experienced naval aviator who had commanded fleet carrier *Lexington* before gaining flag rank and assuming command of a division of escort carriers. The last group of escort carriers, known as "Taffy 3," was thrust into a central role during the battle. It was under the command of Rear Admiral Clifton A. F. "Ziggy" Sprague. Of all the naval commanders during the battle, Sprague was the most impressive. He was also an experienced aviator (by law, USN naval aviation commands were required to be under the command of a naval aviator) and had commanded the fleet carrier *Wasp* before assuming command of an escort carrier division in July.

The Northern and Southern Attack Forces were each responsible for delivering one of MacArthur's corps to the invasion beaches on Leyte.

The Northern Attack Force was commanded by Rear Admiral Daniel E. Barbey and the Southern Attack Force by Vice Admiral Theodore S. Wilkinson. Both were experienced amphibious commanders expert at getting the landing force ashore and quickly withdrawing the assault ships. This was important in any amphibious operation conducted within range of enemy air power, and this was no less vital at Leyte. Supporting the landings was the Bombardment and Fire Support Group under Rear Admiral Jesse B. Oldendorf. Early in the war he was given assignments in the Atlantic Theater, but in January 1944 he was placed in command of Cruiser Division 4 and saw action in a number of Pacific invasions throughout the year. As the most senior of Kinkaid's admirals commanding surface combatants, he was assigned responsibility for planning how to contend with a Japanese surface force attempting to interfere with the landing. Oldendorf's principal subordinates were Rear Admiral G. L. Weyler and Rear Admiral R. S. Berkey.

While MacArthur was in overall charge of the Leyte operation, the Pacific Fleet provided support for the landing with its main battle fleet. Overall American naval strategy and force allocation was under the ultimate direction of Admiral King in his duel capacities as Commander in Chief, US Fleet and Chief of Naval Operations. Nimitz was his direct subordinate. After a rough start in 1942 when Nimitz first assumed command of Pacific operations, King and Nimitz had reached a position of mutual respect.

Nimitz was directly involved in the battle in his capacity as Commander in Chief, Pacific Fleet. By 1944, Nimitz had gained a well-earned reputation as a calm but determined leader. As a strategist, he was aggressive and decisive. He got along well with MacArthur and respected him to the point that he never let his staff criticize MacArthur.[21] Nimitz was calm and polite with his subordinates and gained their respect by keeping his meddling in their operations to a minimum so they could get on with their assigned tasks. However, he closely supervised major operations and occasionally sent them messages with operational recommendations.

Two of Nimitz's forces were assigned to support the Leyte operation. The first was the Third Fleet under Admiral William F. Halsey. The Third Fleet contained the Navy's fast carriers and in October 1944 was the most powerful naval striking force in the world. It was comprised of four subordinate task groups and a large logistical support element.

Halsey was the key command figure in the upcoming battle, so his background and experiences must be fully detailed. After spending his early career on torpedo boats and destroyers, in 1934 the Chief of the Bureau of Aeronautics, Ernest King, offered him command of carrier *Saratoga*. Since carrier commanders had to be qualified naval aviators, Halsey attended a 12-week aviation course for senior commanders and earned his aviator's wings in May 1935 at the age of 52. Halsey believed in the potential of naval aviation and became a well-regarded carrier commander.

By the start of the war, Halsey was the USN's senior carrier commander. Always known for his aggressive tactics, Halsey achieved legendary status by leading his carriers on several early-war raids against Japanese-held islands. These series of raids culminated in the raid on Tokyo in April 1942. Because of the Tokyo raid, he barely missed a chance to lead his two carriers against the Japanese at Coral Sea. Adding to this frustration, Halsey missed the Battle of Midway because of a serious skin disease. After his recovery, Nimitz placed him in command of the faltering Guadalcanal campaign in October. Halsey was at his best during his stint as Commander, South Pacific Ocean Area. He injected much-needed energy into the American effort at Guadalcanal and willingly committed all his available resources to support the Marines on the island. Though Nimitz thought him to be aggressive but not foolhardy, his boldness verged on rashness. At the Battle of Santa Cruz in October, he committed his only two operational carriers beyond the range of land-based air support against a larger Japanese carrier force. The result was the only Japanese victory in a carrier battle during the war; had Halsey lost both carriers, the result would have been catastrophic. The following month, he committed his only two operational modern battleships to a night battle in the confined waters around the island. The result was a key victory. While the Combined Fleet failed to muster its numerically superior forces for a decisive blow, Halsey's bold actions provided the margin of victory.

After victory at Guadalcanal, Halsey directed naval operations as the Americans fought up the Solomons during 1943. In another risky operation, he sent two carriers protected only by land-based air cover to attack a large force of Japanese heavy cruisers in Rabaul preparing to attack the American beachhead on Bougainville Island in the northern Solomons. Again, Halsey's boldness paid off and the beachhead was spared an attack.

Nimitz had the utmost confidence in Halsey, and in March 1943 Halsey was given command of the Third Fleet. In June, the carrier force under Admiral Spruance witnessed what many officers, especially the naval aviators, thought was an incomplete victory against the Japanese fleet. Had Halsey been in charge, he would have unquestionably engaged the Japanese carrier force in the most aggressive manner possible. In October 1944, Halsey was a complex and flawed commander. He still retained his desire to take the fight to the Japanese whenever possible. But he was also known for his lack of attention to details and his staff did not always cover this weakness. Much had changed in the art and practice of carrier warfare since Halsey led a couple of carriers in hit-and-run raids against isolated Japanese islands and then Tokyo in the early months of 1942 until 1944 when the Third Fleet had become a juggernaut able to project power and successfully defend itself against land-based air attack. Despite his lack of recent carrier experience, Halsey still saw himself as a carrier commander at heart. He therefore had little need to ask for advice from other more experienced carrier commanders.[22]

The Third Fleet's carrier force was designated Task Force 38 (TF 38). This huge force, consisting of four task groups, was commanded by Vice Admiral Marc Mitscher. At this point, Mitscher was the premier practitioner of carrier warfare in the world, having led the Fast Carrier Task Force through the invasion of the Marshalls, the neutralization of Truk in February 1944, and the Battle of the Philippine Sea. Despite his undoubted expertise in all aspects of large-scale carrier operations, Mitscher and Halsey had an uneasy relationship. Halsey and his staff often took it upon themselves to act as the task force, rather than the fleet, commander. This tendency to micromanage undermined Mitscher's responsibilities and reduced his initiative. When Halsey assumed tactical command of TF 38, which happened often, Mitscher would give recommendations to Halsey but sulked when they were not taken.

In addition to Mitscher, other experienced commanders directed the operations of TF 38's four subordinate task groups. Task Group (TG) 38.1 was under Vice Admiral John S. McCain; TG 38.2 was led by Rear Admiral Gerald F. Bogan; TG 38.3 by Rear Admiral Frederick C. Sherman; and TG 38.4 was commanded by Rear Admiral Ralph E. Davison. The last major command figure in TF 38 was Vice Admiral Willis A. Lee. A surface warfare officer, Lee was considered the USN's leading gunnery expert and was the victor of the only battleship clash of the war to date. He did not command any part of TF 38 on a routine basis, but Pacific Fleet doctrine called for the formation of a separate battle line in a major fleet engagement. Commanded by Lee, this powerful force included all the battleships in TF 38 with a large cruiser and destroyer escort. When formed, this force was designated Task Force 34.

The second force from the Pacific Fleet operating in support of the Leyte operation was a large force of fleet submarines designated as Task Force 17. The 22 submarines were under the command of the very capable Vice Admiral Charles A. Lockwood, who had molded the submarine force into a formidable weapon.

The Japanese Plan Another Decisive Battle

If the American command structure for the Leyte invasion was convoluted, then the Japanese command structure for the upcoming battle bordered on dysfunctional. While the USN and the United States Army often found themselves in bitter disagreement over strategy and command arrangements, these issues were worked out without extreme rancor affecting present and future operations. The rivalry between the Imperial Navy and the Imperial Army went to extremes. Mutual distrust and outright antagonism were the norms. In regard to strategy, the only joint coordinating body was Imperial General Headquarters, which included representatives from both services. As a joint headquarters, it was only marginally effective; however, when it came to planning the defense of the Philippines, the extreme danger to Japan forced both services to be more receptive to the other's views than was the case earlier in the war.

The Naval General Staff, under the direction of Admiral Oikawa Koshiro, doubled as the navy section of the Imperial General Headquarters and had the responsibility of providing strategic guidance for naval operations. The most important IJN operational entity was the Combined Fleet under the command of Admiral Toyoda Soemu. He had his headquarters in a suburb of Tokyo after he decided to disembark from his flagship in September. The Combined Fleet had always controlled most of the IJN's combat units, but after a reorganization in August 1944 it assumed command of all naval forces in China, the forces assigned to protect shipping, and all naval districts and local guard forces. Thus, by the start of the Leyte battle, Toyoda controlled all Japanese naval assets and all combat naval air forces.

Admiral Toyoda was considered by his peers to be an experienced and intelligent officer. He was a conservative strategist who had opposed Japan's decision for war against the United States. Like most of his fellow officers, he distrusted the Imperial Army.[1] He had not held a combat or sea-going command since the start of the war, but his seniority and lack of a better candidate meant he was still selected to assume command of the Combined Fleet after the death of Admiral Koga Mineichi in March 1944 from an aircraft crash. Toyoda assumed command of the Combined Fleet on May 3, 1944 and immediately was tested when the Combined Fleet attempted to fight a decisive battle in defense of the Marianas the following month. Using the plan devised by Koga, the Combined Fleet suffered a catastrophic defeat. Now Toyoda was forced to plan an even more desperate defense of the Philippines with a crippled fleet. Though he had no good options, the plan he developed was fatally flawed and resulted in the destruction of the Combined Fleet as an effective force.

The Battle of the Philippine Sea was fought by the Combined Fleet's principal operational command, the First Mobile Force. In mid-September, this entity was redesignated Mobile Force, Main Body and remained under the command of Vice Admiral Ozawa Jisaburo. The Main Body was built around the old Third Fleet, which was the IJN's carrier force. By the start of the Leyte battle it consisted of three carrier divisions and three divisions of escort ships. By October 1944, Ozawa was the Navy's most capable and experienced officer. Before the war, he had been an air power advocate and had also held the job as Combined Fleet chief of staff. When the war began, he was entrusted with the vital task of conquering the resource areas of Southeast Asia. After successfully completing this mission, he led forces into the Indian Ocean in April 1942. In November 1942, he assumed command of the Third Fleet. As commander of the First Mobile Force at Philippine Sea, he fought an intelligent battle but his carriers were outclassed by American technical and numerical superiority. Though given a mission at Leyte Gulf to sacrifice his remaining carriers, he conducted his role as professionally as possible. After the war, he made the most favorable impression of all the Japanese admirals interrogated by the Americans.[2]

Effective in August, the Combined Fleet's other primary commands were placed under Ozawa's command. The most important of these was the First Diversionary Attack Force under the command of Vice Admiral Kurita Takeo. This was the old Second Fleet, which traditionally contained the bulk of the Combined Fleet's heavy cruisers. By October Kurita's force included three battleship divisions, three heavy cruiser divisions, two destroyer squadrons, and one destroyer division. Totaling 42 ships, this was the cream of the Imperial Navy and was the centerpiece of Toyoda's plan for the defense of the Philippines. Kurita was an experienced commander and had been involved in almost every major battle of the war to date. In light of his later controversial decision at Leyte, it is worth looking at his war record in detail. At the start of the Pacific War, he was in command of a division of four heavy cruisers. These ships supported the invasion of Malaya and later the NEI. In the last stage of the campaign, Kurita's force was covering the invasion of western Java and was surprised by two Allied cruisers. Kurita's ships reacted slowly but sank the Allied ships (including the American heavy cruiser *Houston*); in the process they also torpedoed and sank five Japanese transports. In April 1942, Kurita led his cruisers into the Indian Ocean. He was also present at Midway where he suffered defeat for the first time. His cruisers were ordered to proceed to Midway Atoll without air cover and shell the airfield there. This was a foolish order, as evinced when his ships came under American air attack. One of his cruisers was sunk, and a second (*Mogami*, later to see action at Leyte) was heavily damaged. Kurita's other two cruisers left the scene and were undamaged. In July 1942, Kurita assumed command of a battleship division of two Kongo-class battleships. He was given orders again to take his ships to shell an American airfield, this time Henderson Field on Guadalcanal. Using battleships in the restricted waters around Guadalcanal was controversial and risky, but after a protest Kurita carried out his orders. On the night of October 13, Kurita conducted the most successful Japanese battleship action during the entire war when he unleashed a devastating bombardment of Henderson Field that temporarily neutralized the airfield. Even in this moment of triumph, Kurita decided to break the bombardment off 15 minutes early to avoid any American counterattack. Building on this success, Kurita was next given command of the Second Fleet. As part of the First Mobile Force, Kurita commanded one of Ozawa's carrier task groups at the Battle of the Philippine Sea. After the first day of disastrous air attacks, Kurita advised Ozawa to retire before the Americans could launch a retaliatory air strike. Ozawa ignored this advice and was struck late the next day, losing a carrier and two oilers. When the Second Fleet was sent south to the Singapore area and renamed the First Diversionary Attack Force, Kurita retained command.

Kurita's personality did not make him the best choice to command the most important Japanese naval force in the most desperate operation of the war. His war record and observations from other officers indicated that Kurita was a dogged and highly experienced commander – he was certainly no coward. But he was clearly a cautious commander and cannot be called aggressive. He was a taciturn man, even being viewed as dim by some of his contemporaries. Kurita was known to show concern for his men and this sometimes clouded his thinking. He mistrusted the Combined Fleet staff. Above all, he was a realist.[3] All of these traits were evinced during the battle. Since he never really explained his thinking during the battle after the war, Kurita remains a controversial and mysterious figure to this day.

The First Diversionary Attack Force was split into three sections. Kurita retained direct command of the first two, but the Third Section was given to Vice Admiral Nishimura Shoji. This was a scratch force of seven ships, including two old battleships, tasked to proceed independently to support the main attack of Kurita's force. Nishimura also played a controversial role in the battle, so his background is also important. Originally an expert in navigation, he switched his area of expertise to torpedoes. Nishimura was a true "sea dog," spending the vast majority of his career at sea and detesting shore tours. From 1936 to 1938, he attended the Naval Staff College and was allowed to take the exams necessary for promotion to flag rank without completing all the classes. After his Naval Staff College experience, Nishimura was even more disdainful of "armchair strategists" and remained more comfortable at sea.

During the Pacific War, Nishimura gained extensive combat experience. As commander of a destroyer squadron, he suffered defeat and embarrassment at the Battle of Balikpapan in February 1942 when the invasion force he was charged to protect was attacked by a force of four American destroyers. The bold American attack sank several transports and the attacking ships escaped unscathed. In October 1942, Nishimura commanded a force of heavy cruisers that conducted an ineffectual bombardment of Henderson Field during a critical point in the campaign. In spite of his mixed combat record, he was promoted to vice admiral. After a brief period ashore, Nishimura was given command of Battleship Division 2 in September 1944. This unit consisted of battleships *Fuso* and *Yamashiro* that later became the heart of the First Diversionary Attack Force's Third Section.

During the Battle for Leyte Gulf, Nishimura exhibited a determined and fatalistic attitude. He has been accused by most historians of simply rushing headlong into his death and pointlessly sacrificing the men under his command. Nishimura knew his small command was expendable and probably faced annihilation, but he was determined to carry out his mission if it contributed to Kurita's success. Instead of being a rash fool, by all accounts from both subordinates and superiors he was a serious and studious man who considered all options during planning.[4]

Also directly subordinate to the Combined Fleet was a geographic command responsible for the Philippines known as the Southwest Area Force. It was led by veteran commander Vice Admiral Mikawa Guinichi. Though he commanded few forces, he played an important role in the planning for the defense of the Philippines. Mikawa began the war as the commander of battleships in the IJN's carrier force. Next, he was assigned as the commander of the Eighth Fleet in Rabaul and played a central role in the Guadalcanal campaign. He personally led a cruiser force in reaction to the initial American landings on Guadalcanal; the resulting Battle of Savo Island was one of the worst American naval defeats of the war.

The last major IJN force in the battle was the Second Diversionary Attack Force under the command of Vice Admiral Shima Kiyohide. This was the former Fifth Fleet, which was renamed and reassigned to Ozawa's command in August 1944. Shima was an Etajima classmate of Nishimura and was slightly senior to him. Unlike Nishimura, Shima was not a sea dog, having spent most of his career on staffs with a specialty in communications. During the war, he commanded two cruiser divisions before being promoted to vice admiral in May 1943. Shima assumed command of the Fifth Fleet in February 1944. While his actions during the battle were not as controversial as those of Ozawa or Nishimura, they still came in for criticism from Japanese officers. One of his contemporaries stated that Shima was a gentle man well suited to staff work, but as a fleet commander he was found wanting, especially in chaotic night battles. Another stated that Shima possessed a forceful character.[5] Both descriptions were accurate in October 1944. Also under Mikawa's command was a small force designated the Southwest Area Guard Force and charged with conducting a reinforcement mission to Leyte (this was described by the Japanese as a "counterlanding" operation). Vice Admiral Sakonju Naomasa commanded this force. He was convicted of war crimes for the execution of Allied prisoners in March 1944 and was hanged after the war.

Land-based air forces were an important aspect of most Imperial Navy operations. Two formations participated in the defense of the Philippines. The First Air Fleet (redesignated the Fifth Base Air Force by the start of the battle) was subordinate to Mikawa's Southwest Area Force and was commanded by Vice Admiral Onishi Takijiro. Onishi was one of the IJN's principal air power advocates and was known as an aggressive commander. He initiated deliberate suicide attacks during the battle. The Second Air Fleet (later the Sixth Base Air Force) was commanded by Vice Admiral Fukudome Shigeru effective June 1944. He was an influential and controversial figure, being the Combined Fleet's chief of staff in 1943–44. In the same incident that killed Admiral Koga, Fukudome's plane crashed and he was captured by Philippine guerrillas. He was able to escape the stain of being captured and assumed command of the Second Air Fleet. On October 22, he flew to the Philippines with all his available aircraft to reinforce Onishi's command.

All Combined Fleet submarines were subordinate to the Sixth Fleet headquartered in Kure, Japan. This formation, down to some 13 operational submarines in October 1944, was commanded by Vice Admiral Miwa Shigeyoshi.

SHO-GO COMES TO LIFE

Defeat at the Battle of the Philippine Sea, followed by the fall of Saipan and other islands in the Marianas, made Japan's position perilous. The attempt to fight a decisive battle in defense of the Marianas resulted in a decisive defeat. Not only was the Combined Fleet brushed aside, but Japan's "absolute" defensive line had been penetrated. Because the Battle of the Philippine Sea marked the effective end of the Combined Fleet's carrier force, the ability of the IJN to conduct subsequent operations was fatally compromised. Nevertheless, since the next American advance threatened Japan with economic strangulation, the IJN was determined to conduct an all-out response, whatever the odds of success were.

Loss of the Marianas, combined with MacArthur's advance up the coast of northern New Guinea, forced the Japanese to fall back to their inner defense line. This extended from the Kuriles, through the Japanese Home Islands, then to the Ryukyu Islands and Formosa, to the Philippines, and down to the NEI. Defense of the inner line was sufficiently important to prompt the planning of another decisive battle. The Japanese identified the Philippines as the linchpin in this defense, as it connected Japan with the resource areas in the south.[6]

As the Americans debated whether and when to land in the Philippines, the Japanese had no doubts that the Philippines would be next. In March 1944, Imperial General Headquarters assessed that the American advances in the Central Pacific and through the Southwest Pacific would soon converge on the Philippines. This view was supported by MacArthur's April invasion of Hollandia on New Guinea and Nimitz's landing on Saipan in June. The Japanese possessed no intelligence regarding future American plans. Instead, they considered American capabilities and projected their most likely next moves. Using this commonsense approach, the Japanese deduced that the Philippines were the next American target. They were unsure as to what island in the Philippines would be struck first, though Mindanao was suspected as the most likely initial target. Probable time for the initial landing in the Philippines was assessed to be mid-November.[7] This was a very solid piece of deduction and correctly reflected the initial American target and landing date for their return to the Philippines.

The Imperial Army and Navy did not agree on much, but they did agree that defense of the Philippines was critical to Japan's ability to continue the war. Accordingly, the two services concluded the Army-Navy Central Agreement on July 24, 1944 to prepare for a "decisive battle." In spite of this agreement, no joint plan for defense of the Philippines, or any other area in the inner defense zone, was ever prepared. Both the Imperial Army and Navy prepared their detailed plans for the defense of the Philippines separately.[8] An example of this parallel planning was the lack of coordination for air operations. Though the Army's Fourth Air Army and the Navy's Fifth Base Air Force signed an agreement to cooperate in their attacks against American carrier forces, no Army assistance was ever forthcoming. Despite the Imperial Army's identification of Leyte as the likely location of the American landing, only one division was on the island when the Americans arrived in late mid-October.

If the inner defense line consisting of the Home Islands, the Ryukyus, Formosa, the Philippines, and the NEI could be held, Japanese war industry would continue to receive the resources required to produce essential war materials. If this defense line was penetrated, the war would be lost since oil and other vital resources could not reach the Home Islands. Without oil, the Combined Fleet's surface ships and submarines would be worthless. The highest priority in their inner defense line was the Philippines, since this was assessed to be the Americans' next target. Accordingly, Imperial General Headquarters gave the Philippines top priority for preparations for the anticipated decisive battle. The plan for the decisive battle was designated *Sho-Go* (Victory Operation). American invasions of the Philippines, Formosa-Ryukyus, Honshu-Kyushu and Hokkaido-Kuriles were given separate variants of the *Sho* plan. *Sho-1* was the plan for the Philippines and was the one the Japanese expected to employ.

On August 19, Imperial General Headquarters formally presented *Sho-Go* to the prime minister and the Emperor at a meeting of the Supreme War Guidance Council. Prime Minister Koiso Kuniaki, appointed after the loss of the Marianas, pressed the leaders of the Army and Navy to use all available resources to fight the decisive battle. Having received a promise of fighting the battle "with a firm conviction of victory," the plan was approved.[9]

Planning the naval component of *Sho-1* was the responsibility of the Combined Fleet under Admiral Toyoda. He was totally convinced that the IJN had no choice but to do everything possible to defend the Philippines. In his view, if the Philippines were lost and the SLOCs between Southeast Asia and Japan were severed, the fleet would become "a white elephant" through lack of oil. Toyoda admitted after the war that the plan he devised was contrary to accepted wisdom, but he felt he had no choice but to commit the remaining strength of the Combined Fleet before it became irrelevant.

Toyoda had more than a few problems to consider as he began to plan *Sho-Go*. In the aftermath of the defeat in the Philippine Sea, the Combined Fleet's carrier force returned to Japan to train new aviators. This process was expected to take until mid-November. Until then, the principal striking power of the Combined Fleet would be its heavy surface ships. Because fuel stocks in Japan were inadequate to support the entire fleet, the heavy surface ships were forced to go to Lingga Roads near Singapore to be near fuel sources in the NEI. Thus, the remaining strength of the Combined Fleet was geographically divided by some 2,500nm. This was a huge handicap since it forced the main fleet elements to fight separately and increased the difficulty of force synchronization.

Toyoda and his staff quickly drew up the naval plans necessary for *Sho-Go*. Combined Fleet Top Secret Operations Order No. 84, issued on August 1, provided the outline of operations and the groupings of naval forces. More detailed force employment directions were presented on August 4 in Combined Fleet Top Secret Operations Order No. 85.[10] The completed plans were presented to the subordinate commanders at a conference in Manila on August 10. The primary objective was to destroy the American landing force before it could deliver its men and supplies ashore. The force tasked to do this was the First Diversionary Attack Force coming up from Lingga to attack the invasion force in the Mindanao area, which at this point was where the Japanese expected the invasion to fall. The First Diversionary Attack Force would depart from Lingga, execute a refueling stop at Brunei, and still arrive in Davao Bay off Mindanao in order to attack the invasion force before it landed. If the First Diversionary Attack Force was unable to attack the invasion force before it began landing operations, then it would arrive at the invasion site within two days of the beginning of the landing. Supporting the main attack by the First Diversionary Attack Force was the Mobile Force, Main Body (with all eight of its carriers and two hybrid battleship-carriers) and the Second Diversionary Attack Force. Operating together, these forces would depart from the Inland Sea and proceed south to attack American carrier task forces in the area east of Mindanao. It is noteworthy that at this point the Main Body was not acting as a decoy force to draw the American carrier force away from the invasion area. Japanese land-based air forces in the central and southern Philippines, reinforced by additional units staging through Formosa and Luzon, would also attack American carrier formations. Attacks by land-based air forces were scheduled for the day before the First Diversionary Attack Force would storm into the invasion anchorage. Also coordinated with the attack of the First Diversionary Attack Force was the movement of Imperial Army reinforcements to the threatened spot.[11]

This first draft of *Sho-1* was modified extensively up until the start of the battle, but its overall scheme of maneuver was essentially unchanged and it provided the basis for the Combined Fleet's last major battle. There were assumptions incorporated into the plan that glossed over major problems critical for the plan's success. The most obvious was the requirement that the place and time of the American landing be deduced early enough to allow the First Diversionary Attack Force time to attack the invasion force before it could disembark its troops. This assumption was not totally based on wishful thinking, since the Japanese planned to conduct air searches out to 700nm from the Philippines. If these were successful in detecting approaching American forces, this would provide several days' warning of the invasion. The biggest assumption was that the First Diversionary Attack Force would be able to approach the invasion area without effective air cover while being subjected to American air attack. At this point it was envisioned that the First Diversionary Attack Force would operate as a single entity. This huge force of seven battleships, 12 heavy cruisers, three light cruisers, and 20 destroyers had the primary mission of brushing aside American surface forces on its way to attack the invasion fleet. Its secondary mission was to mop up American carrier forces damaged by air attack.

From the very beginning, there was friction between planners on the Combined Fleet staff who devised *Sho-1* and the officers of the First Diversionary Attack Force who were charged to execute it. At the August 10 conference in Manila to review the plan, Kurita's chief of staff presciently asked if he could attack an American carrier force if the opportunity presented itself and then return to attack the invasion force. The Combined Fleet representatives agreed that this would be acceptable, but the angst felt by officers of the First Diversionary Attack Force who were being ordered to attack transports instead of fighting a decisive battle would only grow. In their view, the enemy's carrier force should be the primary target, since if it was destroyed the American advance could be stopped. Destruction of the invasion fleet would only result in a temporary delay to American plans.

The worst fear of Kurita's chief of staff, and no doubt that of Kurita himself, was that Japanese air reconnaissance would fail to detect the invasion force far enough away from its objective to provide adequate warning for the First Diversionary Attack Force to attack it before the landing was begun. In this worst case scenario, the cream of the

Imperial Navy would be committed to attack empty transports and probably be annihilated by relentless air attacks from an intact American carrier force. According to Kurita's chief of staff, the intent by the First Diversionary Attack Force to engage in a fleet engagement with the American carrier force if given the opportunity was fully understood by Combined Fleet headquarters.[12]

Sho-1 underwent an important modification in early September. It was at this point that the Mobile Force, Main Body, clearly lacking the means to conduct effective attacks against the American carrier force, began to be considered as a possible decoy force responsible for diverting the American carrier force to the north. It is not clear exactly when this shift in mission for Ozawa's force took place. His chief of staff indicated after the war that the shift was done quickly in conjunction with Combined Fleet headquarters: "By telephone we decided. It was planned on the spur of the moment."[13] The new mission for the Mobile Force, Main Body required it to coordinate with the First Diversionary Attack Force in order to divert the American carrier force to the north in the two days prior to the First Diversionary Attack Force reaching and attacking the American invasion force. The Main Body would move to a position northeast of the Philippines and launch attacks on the American carrier force to draw attention to itself. The composition of the force was also modified. Ozawa insisted that the force be reduced to the minimum required to conduct its decoy mission. Instead of the eight carriers the Main Body possessed on paper, only four were required to steam to their probable destruction. Another variant of the plan shifted a carrier division from the Main Body to strengthen the First Diversionary Attack Force. Carrier Division 1, with its two new Unryu-class fleet carriers, was expected to join the Main Body at the end of December following the completion of the training for their air groups.[14]

The limited striking power of the carriers of the Main Body thrust an even greater responsibility on the land-based air forces. In the case of *Sho-1*, the Fifth Base Air Force in the Philippines would be reinforced by the Sixth Base Air Force from Formosa. Together, these would wait until the day before the First Diversionary Attack Force was scheduled to penetrate the invasion area to mount all-out attacks against the Americans. Carriers were the top priority, followed by the amphibious force. In the case of *Sho-2*, the defense of Formosa, the same timing and target prioritization applied, but the Fifth and Sixth Base Air Forces would be reinforced by the Seventh Base Air Force based on Kyushu and the elite Imperial Navy and Army combined T-attack Force.[15]

SHO-I IN DETAIL

Despite the reservations of the officers of the fleet, the First Diversionary Attack Force prepared extensively for its role in *Sho-1*. Having unlimited fuel from the nearby facilities at Palembang, Sumatra, the fleet trained hard. Knowing that his force would have to proceed to its objective under heavy air attack, Kurita ordered that antiaircraft drills and evasive maneuvering under air attack be rehearsed. Another area of emphasis was night combat training. Torpedo drills were incessantly practiced and gunnery exercises using star shells and radar were conducted. The final focus area was penetration of an enemy anchorage, since this was not an operation the IJN had previously conducted. Three likely landing areas were studied – Lamon Bay in southern Luzon, Leyte Gulf, and Davao Gulf off Mindanao.[16]

Training was conducted at a relentless pace until mid-October, when Kurita decided that the American invasion was imminent. Accordingly, on October 15 he ordered training to cease, replenished his ships, and ordered that all preparations be made to depart Lingga.[17]

On three occasions (September 4–6, September 9, and September 14–16), Kurita's commanders conducted wargames using Davao Gulf as the target. The first detailed plan of the attack was completed on September 18. In this iteration, the First Diversionary Attack Force would be kept together as one large force.[18]

After the American invasion force was detected off Leyte and *Sho-1* was activated, Combined Fleet headquarters issued the sortie order for those units participating in the operation. The order included the routing of the First Diversionary Attack Force through the Philippines and the tentative day for the penetration into Leyte Gulf. Using the San Bernardino Strait, Kurita's force would enter Leyte Gulf early on October 24. Ozawa's Mobile Force, Main Body would arrive off eastern Luzon one or two days before to perform its decoy function. The Second Diversionary Attack Force and the three ships of Cruiser Division 16 from Kurita's force were assigned to the Southwest Area Force and ordered to prepare for the counter-landing operation.

The selection of the day and time of the penetration into Leyte Gulf was vital not only because it determined how quickly the American

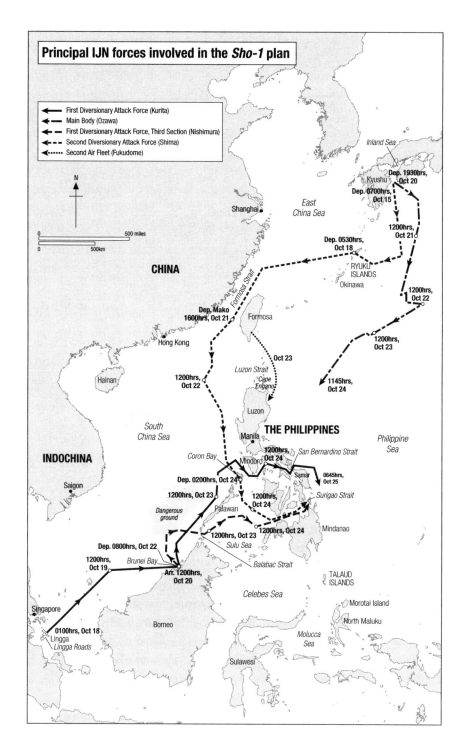

Principal IJN forces involved in the *Sho-1* plan

First Diversionary Attack Force (Kurita)
Main Body (Ozawa)
First Diversionary Attack Force, Third Section (Nishimura)
Second Diversionary Attack Force (Shima)
Second Air Fleet (Fukudome)

N

0   500 miles
0   500km

CHINA

Shanghai

East
China Sea

Inland Sea

Kyushu

Dep. 1930hrs,
Oct 20
Dep. 0700hrs,
Oct 15

1200hrs,
Oct 21

Dep. 0530hrs,
Oct 18

RYUKU
ISLANDS
Okinawa

1200hrs,
Oct 22

Formosa Strait

Dep. Mako
1600hrs, Oct 21

Formosa

1200hrs,
Oct 23

Hong Kong

Oct 23

Luzon Strait
Cape
Engano

1200hrs,
Oct 22

Hainan

1145hrs,
Oct 24

Luzon

South
China Sea

THE PHILIPPINES

Philippine
Sea

Manila

1200hrs,
Oct 24   San Bernardino Strait

INDOCHINA

Coron Bay
Mindoro

Samar

0645hrs,
Oct 25

Saigon

Dep. 0200hrs, Oct 24

1200hrs, Oct 23
Palawan

1200hrs,
Oct 24

Surigao Strait

Dangerous
ground

1200hrs, Oct 23

1200hrs, Oct 24

Mindanao

Dep. 0800hrs, Oct 22

Sulu Sea

1200hrs,
Oct 19   Brunei Bay

Balabac Strait

Arr. 1200hrs,
Oct 20

TALAUD
ISLANDS

Celebes Sea

Morotai Island

Singapore

North Maluku

0100hrs, Oct 18
Lingga
Lingga Roads

Borneo

Molucca
Sea

Sulawesi

invasion could be attacked, but because it provided the central action that all other Combined Fleet forces had to synchronize with. It was quickly realized that the tentative selection of October 24 as penetration day was unrealistic.

Even at this very early point, *Sho-1* began to crumble, primarily due to sloppy staff work. While the First Diversionary Attack Force had been brought to a high state of readiness, this was not the case with other commands participating in *Sho-1*. None of the submarines of the Advance Expeditionary Force were ready to depart their bases in Japan; all required at least 48 hours before they could sortie. Ozawa indicated that he would need until the afternoon of October 20 to load aircraft and depart.[19]

The biggest problem was with fuel. Even though it was long planned that the First Diversionary Attack Force would proceed to Brunei to refuel before heading to the Philippines, the Combined Fleet's staff failed to make the necessary arrangements for tankers. Only two tankers had been originally requested, which was clearly inadequate for Kurita's force. On the evening of October 18, four more tankers were requested at the expense of the Imperial Army. This prompted the comment from Army planners that their Navy counterparts had committed a major misstep.[20]

After confirming the location of the American invasion and rectifying the fuel situation, the Combined Fleet finally issued the final plan for *Sho-1* on the morning of October 20. Kurita's attack into Leyte Gulf was set for the morning of October 25 – the operations of the other naval forces were adjusted to this. The air offensive by the Fifth and Sixth Base Air Forces was set for October 24. The Mobile Force, Main Body had to be positioned to execute its mission by the same day.[21]

Toyoda's plan centered on the First Diversionary Attack Force and its ability to enter Leyte Gulf to attack the American invasion force. The detachment of Cruiser Division 16 to support the counterlanding operation left Kurita with considerable firepower in the form of seven battleships, 11 heavy cruisers, two light cruisers, and 19 destroyers. Later on the morning of October 20, Combined Fleet headquarters sent Kurita a "suggestion" on how to execute his attack. Combined Fleet assessed that the attack into Leyte Gulf would be better conducted as a pincer attack instead of as a single thrust. In typical Japanese style, the suggested change in the plan was not worded as an order but as a preference. This was not a suggestion that Kurita could refuse, so it was adopted and Kurita split his force into two groups. The main attack, conducted by Sections A and B with five battleships, ten heavy cruisers, two light cruisers, and 15 destroyers, would transit the San Bernardino Strait and attack Leyte Gulf from the north. A supporting attack would be made from the south through Surigao Strait with Section C, consisting of two battleships, one heavy cruiser, and four destroyers. The main attack force would be under Kurita's personal command, while responsibility for the supporting attack went to Vice Admiral Nishimura.

The advice from Combined Fleet headquarters was in keeping with the propensity of Japanese planners to conduct attacks from multiple axes. By dividing his force into two, Kurita increased the possibility of creating confusion and gaining surprise. Kurita viewed Nishimura's small force as a decoy which might reduce the pressure on his main force. There were also tactical reasons for detaching the seven ships of Section C. The heart of Nishimura's force was the two Fuso-class battleships. These were the slowest ships in the entire First Diversionary Attack Force; by detaching them, Kurita was increasing the speed that his main force could use, therefore increasing his operational and tactical flexibility. Since the two battleships were the least protected, Kurita thought their actual combat power was marginal and that he lost little by detaching them. Also, the staff and communications of the staff of Nishimura's Battleship Division 2 was considered weak.[22] Overall, Kurita probably considered the two old battleships as an impediment. He readily detached them and provided them with as small an escort as possible.

Having decided to split his force, Kurita now had to select the route his main force would use to get from Brunei to San Bernardino Strait. This was a critical choice because Kurita wanted to avoid detection from American aircraft or submarines for as long as possible. Underpinning everything was the fuel factor. The route chosen would determine the distance and speed required to meet the deadline of arriving at Leyte Gulf on the morning of October 25. The route selected would impact the fuel condition of Kurita's destroyers, which had the shortest endurance.

Kurita's staff came up with three possible routes. The first route was the most direct. It used the Balabac Strait and then ran south of Palawan Island before entering the Sibuyan Sea and continuing to Leyte Gulf. It had the attribute of requiring the least fuel, but was considered to be the most exposed to detection and attack by American land-based aircraft.

The second route went well north of Palawan through the Dangerous Ground and then through the Mindoro Strait into the Sibuyan Sea. Because it was the longest route, it would have required a refueling of the destroyers on the way. The final route ran from Brunei along the Palawan Passage north of Palawan, and then into the Mindoro Strait. Kurita rejected the first route because of the air threat. The second route was rejected because of the extra fueling requirement. Despite the fact that the route through the Palawan Passage had the greatest submarine threat, this is the one chosen by Kurita.

This was a poor selection by Kurita on two accounts. One was the increased submarine threat. The selected route was in an area where American submarines were known to be operating. The second factor was the exposure not to long-ranged bombers (all three routes were within range of B-24s flying from Morotai), but to aircraft from TF 38. Using this route placed Kurita's force within the morning search range of the TF 38 carrier task group operating off southeast Luzon. Detection by the morning search meant a full day of strikes; had the detection been delayed until TF 38's afternoon search, the time of exposure to air attack would have been reduced.

OZAWA'S ROLE

Kurita estimated that he had a 50 percent chance of reaching his objective.[23] If he was to have any chance, Ozawa's Mobile Force, Main Body had to perform its mission well and hope that Halsey took the Third Fleet north. The success of *Sho-1* depended on finding a way to neutralize the Third Fleet. Toyoda's preferred method was to neutralize the American carriers with a direct attack from land-based air power based in the Philippines. This offered little chance of success, as even Toyoda assessed. Realizing that his land-based air forces were too weak to neutralize the American carriers, Toyoda's primary plan for dealing with the Third Fleet was using the Mobile Force, Main Body to lure Halsey's carriers to the north. This would open the door for Kurita to break into the Philippine Sea via the San Bernardino Strait and then head south to Leyte Gulf.

Ozawa had to scramble to get his force ready to play its critical role. In the aftermath of the disastrous attempt by land-based Japanese air forces to attack TF 38 off Formosa, Ozawa had to quickly assemble some scratch air groups for his carriers. Most of his carrier air groups were committed by Toyoda to reinforce the strikes against TF 38, and losses to these precious assets were heavy. Ozawa was able to assemble some scratch air groups by the morning of October 20. To conduct its mission, Ozawa planned to be northeast of Luzon by October 23 or 24 to support Kurita's planned attack on October 25. At this point, the Second Diversionary Attack Force was still under Ozawa's command. He ordered it to move to a position east of Luzon by October 23. Ozawa planned to use Shima's force as an advance guard and to have it send out false radio messages to deceive the Americans.[24] If conditions permitted, the large destroyers and two battleships from the Mobile Force, Main Body would join with the Second Diversionary Attack Force to engage American "remnants" after Ozawa's air strikes.

This plan did not survive long. On October 21, Combined Fleet took the Second Diversionary Attack Force from Ozawa and assigned it to the Southwest Area Force. Without his advance guard, Ozawa planned to take the Mobile Force, Main Body to a position some 275nm northeast of Cape Engano by the morning of October 24. He planned to make a morning and an afternoon search to find the American carriers. Once the location of the American carriers had been confirmed, an all-out strike was planned. If the aircraft were faced with a dusk or night landing, which was beyond the capabilities of the poorly-trained aircrews, surviving aircraft would be ordered to land on Luzon. In the meantime, his ships would issue radio messages to increase the possibility of being detected by the Americans. If this failed to draw the American carriers north, the back-up plan was to form an advance guard and send it south to draw the Americans' attention.[25]

THE ROLE OF THE LAND-BASED AIR FORCES

The Combined Fleet placed great importance on the role of its land-based air forces in the forthcoming decisive battle. Even though the massive effort to destroy TF 38 off Formosa had just failed, Fifth and Six Base Air Forces were tasked to try again in the days before the First Diversionary Attack Force was scheduled to attack into Leyte Gulf. Toyoda ordered the base air forces to start their attacks against TF 38 on October 24. Accordingly, Fukudome planned to move almost the entire Sixth Base Air Force from Formosa to various bases in the Philippines to reinforce Onishi's battered Fifth Base Air Force. The move from Formosa was scheduled for October 22. Because of expected bad weather on October 24, the massive air strike was moved up to October 23.[26]

The perilous state of Japanese air power made many Japanese officers advocate for the adoption of special attack tactics. This was a euphemism for deliberate suicide attacks by bomb-laden aircraft onto the decks of American ships. One of the most vocal advocates of this tactics was Vice Admiral Onishi, the newly-appointed commander of the Fifth Base Air Force. He immediately established the first Special Attack Corps. Blessed by Vice Admiral Mikawa, the first units were set up using the 201st Air Group as a basis. Using unconventional tactics, Onishi hoped to smash the decks of American carriers and render them inoperative. If possible, this was to occur by October 25.[27]

SHIMA'S AND NISHIMURA'S CONFUSION

Another indication of the fatuous nature of Combined Fleet planning for *Sho-1* was the planning for and operations of the Second Diversionary Attack Force. Shima's force appears to have been an afterthought in the planning process, having its mission and orders changed several times in the week before the battle. Shima's force was originally assigned to Ozawa's Mobile Force, Main Body. Ozawa planned to use it as the advance force for his carrier fleet when it headed south on its decoy mission. Before *Sho-1* was even activated, Shima's force had a brush with annihilation. The Second Diversionary Attack Force, with its two heavy cruisers, one light cruiser, and seven destroyers, departed the Inland Sea and headed south in the early hours of October 15. Shima was under orders to mop up cripples from TF 38 believed to be east of Formosa and rescue downed Japanese aviators. Using Shima's small force for such a mission was utterly quixotic and provided another example of the muddled thinking at Combined Fleet headquarters. Whatever damage suffered by TF 38 from Japanese air attack, it would still dwarf Shima's force.

Despite the claims of Japanese aviators who reported massive damage to TF 38, Japanese air searches on October 16 indicated that Halsey's force was largely intact. This unfortunate truth was brought home to Shima when his ships came under American air attack that afternoon. He wisely decided to steam north out of range. After stopping briefly at Amani-O-Shima on October 17, Shima departed the next morning for Mako in the Pescadores (located between China and Formosa). While on the way to Mako on October 18, Shima received orders detaching him from Ozawa's command and moving the Second Diversionary Attack Force under the command of Mikawa's Southwest Area Force. Shima's force was directed to go to Manila, where it would join Cruiser Division 16 which had just been detached from Kurita's fleet. Under Shima's command, the combined force would assume a new mission of escorting the transports carrying ground forces conducting counterlanding operations on the western side of Leyte. Shima resented the escort mission – his force would be better used to break into Leyte Gulf to attack the American invasion fleet. He began a campaign to get his force into the fight, supported by Mikawa who assessed that the counterlanding mission could be accomplished without the assistance of the Second Diversionary Attack Force. Mikawa went as far as to inform Shima on the afternoon of October 19 that his force was not required to support the counterlanding.[28]

Based on Mikawa's orders, Shima was already planning how to use his force to support the attack into Leyte Gulf. When Mikawa informed him that his force was not required for the counterlanding, Shima was quick to propose that his force cooperate with Kurita's force to storm into Leyte Gulf on October 25. Shima planned that his attack would be through Surigao Strait and would be conducted independently but in cooperation with Kurita. At this point, it is unclear if Shima was aware of the Combined Fleet's suggestion that Kurita conduct a pincer attack into Leyte Gulf.[29]

Early afternoon on October 21, the Combined Fleet again ordered Shima to take part in the transport mission and ordered his force to Manila. At this point, two forces were assigned to the counterlanding operation with a total of five cruisers and eight destroyers. This was a very questionable use of the Combined Fleet's limited resources. Mikawa proved to be tenacious in his desire to release Shima's force for a more appropriate mission. Twice on October 21 he sent Combined Fleet headquarters a blunt message that Shima should be assigned the mission of supporting Kurita's attack into Leyte Gulf. At 0900 the following morning, Toyoda relented – the Shima force was ordered to assist Kurita's force in its attack into Leyte Gulf.[30]

As Mikawa and Combined Fleet headquarters debated how best to use Shima's force, Nishimura's force had already received orders to use Surigao Strait for its attack into Leyte Gulf. Kurita was unaware that Shima's force would also be ordered to take the same approach route into the gulf. The only authority aware of this was Combined Fleet headquarters, and it made no attempt to coordinate the operations of the two forces.

Shima's force departed Mako at 1600 on October 21. Finally cleared to take part in the attack into Leyte Gulf, Shima arrived at Coron Bay to refuel at 1800 on October 23. When he found no tankers waiting for him, he was forced to refuel his destroyers from his two heavy cruisers. At 0200 on October 24, the Second Diversionary Attack Force departed Coron and headed to Surigao Strait. The movement of Shima's force was, by design, never coordinated with Nishimura's. Shima's intent was to operate independently from Nishimura's force and to attack through Surigao Strait separately and arrive at the area of the American beachhead at 0900 on October 25.[31] The original interval between the two forces was five hours, but Shima reduced it to an hour by the time his force began to enter the strait. This delay between the two forces ordered to attack through Surigao Strait was known to Toyoda, but he was content to let Shima plan his own battle. As a matter of course, the commander in chief of the Combined Fleet did not meddle in the operational plans of his principal subordinates. But, if there was ever a case when he should have, it would have been here.

The final plan for Nishimura's force was simple but was still controversial. From Brunei, Nishimura's force was routed into the Sulu Sea, then the Mindanao Sea, and was scheduled to arrive in Leyte Gulf at dawn on October 25. Nishimura was scheduled to arrive off the beachhead at 0430 and Kurita's main force at 0600. Kurita was content with this sequencing since it set up Nishimura's force as a diversion before the arrival of the main force. He also stated after the war that the delay was to avoid congestion with two forces attacking the same objective at the same time.[32] It is almost certain that Kurita viewed Nishimura's force as nothing more than a sacrificial decoy. A force as small as Nishimura's could be nothing else. This is almost certainly also how Nishimura viewed his role and explains why he was so intent on maintaining his schedule. Some of the survivors from Nishimura's ships were also clear on their role. One of the few surviving crewmen from *Fuso* recalled after the battle that his ship was on a "surface special attack" mission.[33]

With the role of Shima's force settled, the Combined Fleet's four main surface forces and two base air forces were ready to execute Toyoda's decisive battle plan. Timing was critical for the success of *Sho-1*.

The Mobile Force, Main Body's diversion mission had to be accomplished in time to save the First Diversionary Attack Force from coming under concerted American air attack as it transited the Sibuyan Sea. Ozawa's force departed its base in the Inland Sea on October 20 and exited the Bungo Strait that evening undetected by American submarines. Kurita's force had departed earlier, leaving Lingga at 0100 hours on October 18. From Lingga, it headed for Brunei Bay for refueling and a final pre-attack conference. After refueling, it departed Brunei at 0800 on October 22 and began its fateful track to Leyte Gulf. Nishimura's section departed Brunei the same day at 1500. Just behind Nishimura's force was Shima's Second Diversionary Attack Force. If all went according to plan, the three surface forces would storm into Leyte Gulf on the morning of October 25. Presaging the final approach of the Japanese forces, the land-based forces in the Philippines would make an all-out attack on the American carriers on October 24. Speed was of the essence, since the American landing had occurred on October 20 and with each passing day the hope for crippling the invasion receded.

ASSESSMENT OF *SHO-I*

The Combined Fleet's plan to defend the Philippines led to the largest naval battle in history. It also resulted in the destruction of the Imperial Navy as an effective force. Was this the result of the plan itself? If so, why did the Japanese even attempt it?

Toyoda felt he had no choice but to commit the remaining strength of the Combined Fleet to a desperate attempt to defend the Philippines. In his words:

> If we are beaten at the Philippines and even if the fleet remained to us, the southern sources of supply would be isolated. When it returned to Japanese waters the fleet could not be refueled: left in the south it could not be supplied with arms and ammunition. It would be pointless therefore, to lose the Philippines and save the fleet.[34]

This mindset of desperation was present throughout the planning for *Sho-Go*. In Imperial General Headquarters, the Navy admitted to the Army that the plan was an "all-or-nothing" operation. Even the Army advised against rashness and warned that the loss of the fleet would open the Home Islands to invasion.[35] It cannot be denied that there was a fatalistic strain in the Combined Fleet's planning for the battle. The battle for Leyte might be the Combined Fleet's last opportunity to die with honor. Going down to defeat was preferable to the fate of surrendering the fleet, as was the case of the German Imperial Navy in 1918 and the Royal Italian Navy in 1943. The sentiment of allowing the fleet to die with honor was put succinctly by Rear Admiral Nakazawa Tasuku, chief of the Navy's Operations Section, when talking to his Army counterpart: "Please give the Combined Fleet the chance to bloom as flowers of death. This is the navy's earnest request."[36] The *Sho-1* plan reflected this desire much more than it represented a serious chance for victory in a decisive battle. Again, in Toyoda's own words:

> Since without the participation of our Combined Fleet there was no possibility of the land-based air forces in the Philippines having any chance against (American) forces at all, it was decided to send the whole fleet, taking the gamble. If things went well, we might obtain unexpectedly good results: but if the worst should happen there was a chance we might lose the entire fleet. I felt the chance had to be taken.[37]

Thus, the planning basis for *Sho-1* was simple and utter desperation. If the plan was bad and disaster ensued, this was better than the alternative of having to surrender the fleet. Such assumptions did not provide a sound starting point for planning.

The first issue with *Sho-Go* was the Japanese assumption that they could still fight a decisive battle in October 1944. For the Imperial Navy, the notion of a decisive battle was a cherished element of strategy. Even this late in the war, Toyoda clung to the notion that a decisive battle was possible. Against an opponent with the resources of the USN, the idea that any one battle could be decisive was never viable. By this point in the war, the Combined Fleet simply lacked the capabilities to fight a battle that could in any sense be considered decisive. The divergence in strength was simply too great. The idea that *Sho-1* provided the opportunity for a decisive victory was strategic lunacy.

Even if you grant to Toyoda his assumption that it was better to risk the fleet than to see it wither on the vine, the plan he and his staff devised did not provide the best chance of success. Of all the faults with *Sho-1*, the most grievous was that the plan could not achieve its stated objective – defeating the invasion fleet before it had a chance to land its invasion force. If the First Diversionary Attack Force had any chance of attacking the American invasion fleet before it landed on Leyte, adequate warning of the exact time and place of the landing was essential. This was the Achilles heel of *Sho-1* – there were no prospects that such warning would be provided.

To provide the necessary warning, long-range air reconnaissance was an essential element of the *Sho-1* plan. The fundamental weakness of the Fifth Base Air Force and its inability to provide adequate warning jeopardized the entire plan. Knowing this, Toyoda meddled in the formulation of air search plans. His air reconnaissance plans for the Philippines called for searches up to 650nm from Manila, Davao, and Legaspi in southern Luzon. There was also an agreement with the Imperial Army to supplement the long-range Navy searches with short-range searches. Nevertheless, the Japanese air search plan totally failed to provide advance warning of the movement of American forces toward Leyte. The reason for this has to do with the general shortage of aircraft following Halsey's strikes in September, a lack of fuel, and the movement of the surviving aircraft to bases further west to provide some measure of protection.[38] Thus, the first warning of the invasion did not come until October 17, when the American advance force appeared off the approaches of Leyte Gulf.

Even the seemingly definitive warning of an invasion fleet being spotted off Leyte Gulf was not sufficient for Toyoda to act. There was a significant period of time between the first sighting on October 17 and the landings on October 20. If the Combined Fleet was on alert, why didn't the Japanese use these three critical days to their advantage? The answer lies in the precarious Japanese logistics supporting the operation. Toyoda had to be absolutely sure this was the invasion, because if it wasn't and he initiated operations the result would have been catastrophic for the Japanese.

Without adequate warning, Kurita's force could not attack the American amphibious operation in its most vulnerable phase, but would only arrive days later. Compounding this fatal flaw was a further delay brought on by the inability of the Combined Fleet to arrange fueling arrangements for Kurita's force. In its final form, *Sho-1* called for the First Diversionary Attack Force to arrive at the beachhead on October 25, an incredible five days after the landing on Leyte. By this point, the invasion fleet had come and gone, as had the first reinforcement group, and the second reinforcement group had already placed its men and supplies ashore.

On October 25, the invasion of Leyte was already an American success, and the temporary appearance of a Japanese surface force off the beachhead was not going to reverse that. This meant that the Combined Fleet was being risked for no strategic purpose and that even if Kurita had pressed his attack and lost his fleet, the Japanese would have gained little, if any, advantage. Kurita's worst fears would have been realized. He was attacking against heavy odds just for the opportunity to attack transports of the follow-up reinforcement echelons, not to crush the landing force before it got ashore. Kurita and his staff saw this clearly and before the battle advocated a modification to the base plan that would allow the fleet's primary objective to shift to fighting the American carrier fleet if it came within striking distance. This was a much better use of the Combined Fleet's remaining strength instead of a pointless death attacking empty transports.

The heart of *Sho-1* called on getting a large force of surface ships 1,160nm to an attack objective in the face of submarine and air attack. On the face of it, this seemed like sheer recklessness. Nevertheless, it came close to success. Had Kurita actually pressed into Leyte Gulf, another weakness of *Sho-1* would have become painfully apparent. Once Kurita's force entered the gulf, there was no hope or any realistic plan to get it back out through the two easily-blocked exits from the gulf. The First Diversionary Attack Force would have been trapped between the Seventh Fleet and Third Fleet, each of which was more powerful than Kurita's force. The combined strength of the Third and Seventh Fleets would have totally crushed Kurita's remaining ships. Since the entire *Sho-1* plan was nothing more than an acceptable method for the Combined Fleet to go down fighting, this oversight was of no great importance to Toyoda.

If *Sho-1* did have a clever aspect to it, this was the use of Ozawa's carriers as a lure to draw the American carrier force north. This aspect of the plan was fully successful and has served to overshadow all the other illogical and faulty parts of *Sho-1*. Yet the Japanese stumbled upon the use of Ozawa's force as a decoy. In an interview after the war, Toyoda stated that the decoy was not part of the original plan but was adopted after the invasion of Leyte.[39] Despite mythology surrounding the battle, the decoy was not prepared for the over-aggressive Halsey. None of the principal Japanese officers who planned and executed the operation even mentioned that they knew who was in command of the American carrier force and none described the decoy plan as being aimed at Halsey in particular. Their assumption, which was valid, was that the Americans had viewed the Japanese carriers as the principal threat throughout the war and that this would not suddenly change in October 1944.

The fact that the Japanese get too much credit for the successful decoy operation is backed up by the fact that there was no apparent thought given to what happened after the American carriers crushed the decoy force.

The diversion may have succeeded in taking the Third Fleet away from Leyte temporarily, but there was no plan how to contain it after it annihilated the Mobile Force, Main Body. Following the destruction of Ozawa's toothless force, Halsey was free to return south. His forces could have easily blocked access to the San Bernardino Strait and if necessary continued south to trap Kurita in Leyte Gulf.

The operations of the other surface forces ordered to penetrate into Leyte Gulf were also unsound. Nishimura's force was clearly too weak to accomplish its mission. The refusal to coordinate the actions of Nishimura's and Shima's forces even though they were operating in the same restricted waters and were pursuing the same objective staggers the imagination.

Another weakness of the plan was the dismissal of the weakness of Japanese land-based air power. Without significant assistance for the base air forces, the operations of the surface forces faced little prospects of success. In spite of the proof that Japanese air power was impotent against TF 38 provided off Formosa only a week before the American landings, *Sho-1* unfolded with very limited assistance from Japanese land-based air forces.

Still another serious flaw with the plan was the high level of coordination required among forces spread over a massive geographic area. As with almost all Combined Fleet plans during the war, *Sho-1* was an intricate plan that featured different forces attacking from different directions to surprise and confuse the enemy. Unless communications were flawless, the necessary synchronization of forces was easily disrupted. The operations and schedule of the First Diversionary Attack Force was central to the entire plan, but each of the other forces played an important supporting role. If the timetable for any of the principal forces was disrupted, the entire plan was jeopardized.

In summary, *Sho-1* had no prospects of strategic success. The disparity in strength between the IJN and the USN in October 1944 precluded any outcome that looked like a Japanese victory. *Sho-1* was conceived under the conditions of near total impotence by Japanese carrier and land-based air power. This forced the inclusion of the dubious premise that Japanese surface forces could operate without air cover and move significant distances under air attack and still achieve their objectives. Toyoda and his staff glossed over the fact that *Sho-1* required a very high level of coordination from forces spread over a wide area. The fact that *Sho-1* did not contain any method to neutralize the Third Fleet, only to temporarily divert it, meant that even if Kurita's force had succeeded in reaching Leyte Gulf it would have been caught between the Seventh and Third Fleets and almost certainly annihilated. Most damning is the fact that had *Sho-1* gone largely to plan and Kurita had attacked into the gulf on October 25, any result promised no strategic gain for Japan. Examined objectively, *Sho-1* had no chance of reversing the course of the war and had a much higher chance of bringing about the complete destruction of the Combined Fleet. It was more about providing the IJN with a glorious opportunity to go down fighting, thus defending its peculiar brand of honor, than an opportunity to affect the outcome of the war.

WAS THERE A BETTER ALTERNATIVE TO *SHO-1*?

Obviously, Japan's situation in October 1944 precluded any realistic prospects of defeating a major American military operation. But was there a better alternative to the deeply flawed *Sho-1*? Toyoda was right about one thing – the Combined Fleet did have to fight for the Philippines or the fleet would wither on the vine as its fuel tanks ran dry. But this did not mean that the fleet should be sacrificed in a battle without real hope. Fighting a battle without any real hope of victory is reckless. While time was not on Japan's side in late 1944, October was not the best time for Toyoda to commit the Combined Fleet to a decisive battle. The weaknesses of its carrier fleet and land-based air forces guaranteed bitter defeat.

Another alternative to fighting a hopeless battle for Leyte was to hold the Combined Fleet in reserve until it had a chance to rebuild its air strength. Fighting a decisive battle for Luzon in December or January with the prospect of employing a more effective air force was preferable to fighting a hopeless battle for Leyte in October. With a rebuilt carrier force available by the end of 1944, the Combined Fleet could have been united. This would have meant the surface force would have operated with some degree of air cover. Greater Japanese air strength brought to bear in the defense of Luzon could have posed a real challenge to the Americans, especially if the Japanese had actually coordinated Imperial Army and Navy air operations and if the massive Japanese air attacks directed at the invasion fleet included suicide attacks. Ideally, suicide attacks would not have been conducted piecemeal as scattered units were activated, but held in abeyance until massed attacks on a surprised defender could be conducted.

In this hypothetical battle of Luzon in 1945, a massive American invasion force makes its way from Leyte Gulf to Lingayen Gulf in western Luzon. This was the actual American invasion plan executed in January of that year. The Japanese unleash massive conventional and suicide attacks on the invasion force. The Combined Fleet, still based at Lingga, would have almost certainly have had much greater warning time of an American invasion fleet headed for Lingayen Gulf; combined with a shorter transit time to strike the invasion fleet, the First Diversionary Attack Force would have had a much greater chance of interdicting the invasion fleet before it reached the area. Much greater air cover could have been provided to Kurita's force, increasing its chances for success.

The problem of handling TF 38 would have been much easier with a more effective land-based air force and with the shock value from the first massed use of suicide attacks. To provide protection to the invasion fleet, TF 38 would probably have been positioned in the South China Sea, making itself vulnerable to air attacks from multiple axes.

Another factor making defense of Luzon more attractive for the Japanese was the greater capacity of the Imperial Army to mount a defense there. Fighting the decisive battle on Leyte had proved disastrous since, predictably, any forces sent there could not be sustained. This would not have been a problem on Luzon, where the Imperial Army could have fought a prolonged battle against MacArthur's ground forces as they did historically. Prolonged resistance would also have provided additional opportunities for Japanese air and naval forces to strike American reinforcement and resupply convoys. Dragging out resistance on Luzon and making it even more costly for the Americans would have been a far greater contribution to the Japanese war effort than a fairly brief period of resistance on Leyte. Using the fleet to prolong resistance on Luzon would have been preferable to an impossible attempt to win a decisive victory at Leyte.

If the Japanese could have conserved their air, ground, and naval forces to fight a battle for Luzon in 1945, this would have been a much bloodier battle for the Americans. Just as in January 1945, it is unlikely that the American invasion would have been turned back, but a massive air-sea battle, followed by a prolonged ground campaign, would have been the bloodiest battle of the Pacific War to date for both sides. The Imperial Navy would still probably have suffered a catastrophic defeat, but it might have been a defeat that gave the Americans pause, since a staunch defense of the Philippines would have provided a preview to the bloodbath of future invasions against the Ryukyus and then the Home Islands.

3

Two Navies, Two Different Directions

At the start of the Pacific War, the IJN possessed a significant edge over the USN in almost every category of combatants. This was particularly true in terms of naval aviation, where the Japanese possessed a much larger carrier force and a much larger and more capable land-based air force. Japanese naval land-based air forces provided a decisive edge during their advance into Southeast Asia. In addition to its numerical advantages, the IJN deployed a force that was highly trained and capable of outperforming Allied forces in most warfare areas. Using these advantages, the IJN had little trouble accomplishing its initial objectives. By February 15, 1942, the British situation in Southeast Asia was fatally compromised by the surrender of Singapore. Within just weeks, Allied forces in the NEI were also routed, leading to the Dutch surrender in early March.

While the Japanese moved to secure the vital resource areas, they also attempted to destroy the USN's Pacific Fleet. The first attempt was at the very start of the conflict. Led by the strongest naval force in the Pacific, the six fleet carriers of the Striking Force, the Japanese caught the Pacific Fleet by surprise at Pearl Harbor and inflicted heavy losses. Of the eight battleships present, five were sunk or heavily damaged. Only three fleet carriers were available to the Pacific Fleet when hostilities opened, and two of these were in the Central Pacific on December 7, 1941. Neither was caught by the Japanese attack, but the attack on Pearl Harbor affirmed that naval air power was going to play a decisive part in the Pacific War.

Had the Japanese kept the Striking Force together as a single operational entity, it would have been difficult for the Americans to counter. Instead, Yamamoto acquiesced to dividing it up to achieve multiple objectives. This proved successful until May 1942, when the two fleet carriers committed to support the planned invasion of Port Moresby on New Guinea were roughly handled by two American carriers in the first carrier battle of the war. Though one American carrier was lost in the Battle of the Coral Sea, both Japanese fleet carriers were unable to participate in the next carrier battle of the war fought the following month.

The Battle of Midway was Yamamoto's second attempt to fight a decisive battle against the Pacific Fleet. His intent was thwarted by poor operational planning that forced his commanders to carry out an overly complex plan. The same plan negated Yamamoto's numerical advantage. At the tactical level, the Striking Force fought indecisively. All four of its carriers were lost in exchange for a single American fleet carrier. This was not the end of the Combined Fleet's carrier force, but Midway did mark the end of Japanese offensive operations in the Pacific War at the strategic level.

Using his newly-won initiative, Admiral King thrust the Pacific Fleet into its first offensive of the war. The target selected was Tulagi and Guadalcanal in the southern Solomons. The Americans took both places on August 7, but an immediate Japanese counterattack marked the beginning of a six-month campaign. During this period, American and Japanese naval forces fought five major surface actions and two carrier battles. The fulcrum of the entire campaign was the airfield on Guadalcanal that the Americans quickly brought into service and that the Japanese were never able to fully neutralize. Control of the airfield meant the Japanese could never bring sufficient troops and supplies to the island to expel the Marine garrison. By February 1943, when the Japanese were forced to evacuate their remaining men from the island, both sides had suffered heavily. In total, 25 American surface combatants were lost (including two fleet carriers), while Japanese losses totaled 18 surface combatants, including a light carrier and two battleships. The Japanese had displayed superiority in night fighting (all five surface battles were fought at night), but American air power proved decisive. At the end of the campaign, the grinding attrition had crippled the IJN's carrier force and its land-based air force. Over just the first four months of the campaign, the land-based 11th Air Fleet lost 241 aircraft and over 800 irreplaceable aircrew. Combined with the losses in the Solomons campaign through November 1943, the IJN's cadre of highly trained and effective prewar aviators was destroyed; never again would the IJN's air force play a decisive part in Pacific War battles.

Heavy Japanese naval and air losses at Guadalcanal and the Solomons left them unable to contest the Americans' Central Pacific drive when it began in November 1943. Japanese garrisons in the Gilberts and Marshalls fought bravely when attacked, but the outcome of these battles was preordained when the Combined Fleet failed to support them. Not until the Americans threatened the Marianas did the Japanese commit the Combined Fleet to another attempt to turn back the American advance.

The Japanese operation during the Battle of the Philippine Sea was their third attempt of the war to fight a decisive battle against the USN. The plan revolved around using the rebuilt carrier fleet, supported by a large land-based air force, to destroy the Pacific Fleet's carrier force. Once this was accomplished, the Combined Fleet could destroy the American invasion force off Saipan. The plan was noteworthy for the central role of the Japanese carrier force and the vital supporting role of land-based air forces. Often overlooked is the Combined Fleet's weak strategic mobility. A lack of firm intelligence, combined with a minimal fuel and tanker situation, meant that the fleet could not be committed until the target of the American operation was beyond doubt. This forced a late start for the Combined Fleet, with the result that the decisive battle could not occur until the American invasion had already been conducted. Before the Combined Fleet made its appearance after the location and timing of the American invasion had been confirmed, Japanese land-based air forces would have to extract significant attrition on American naval forces. The Japanese plan to defend the Marianas had been carefully considered, extensively rehearsed, and the forces designated to conduct it rebuilt to the greatest possible extent over many months. Even so, it was a spectacular failure.

THE NAVAL BALANCE, OCTOBER 1944

By October 1944, the Pacific Fleet was superior to the Combined Fleet in every measure. As the once-mighty Japanese carrier Striking Force had been reduced to impotence, the Pacific Fleet's Fast Carrier Task

Force had grown into a weapon able to project power at a strategic level. The Pacific Fleet's surface force, once overmatched by the Japanese in night battles, had developed equipment and tactics that stripped the Japanese of their advantages at night and made it another area of American naval superiority. American amphibious forces had grown in power and sophistication and were now able to deliver large invasion forces in any threat environment. Not only did the Pacific Fleet outpace the Japanese in all warfare areas, but the size of American naval forces had also become overwhelming. Given this numerical edge, and the stream of additional aircraft and ships coming from American factories and yards, there was no possibility that a single engagement, however well it developed for the Japanese, could turn the tide of war. Backing up the growing torrent of American naval power was a massive logistical effort capable of sustaining an offensive of growing intensity. The table below illustrates the growing disparity of the two sides, but these numbers do not convey the Pacific Fleet's growing qualitative edge.

Total Forces Employed at Leyte Gulf		
	IJN	USN
Air Power		
Fleet Carriers	1	8
Light Carriers	3	8
Escort Carriers	0	18[1]
Total Carrier Aircraft	116	1,500
Land-based aircraft	Approximately 260 operational on October 24	0[2]
Surface Combatants		
Battleships	9	12
Heavy Cruisers	14	13
Light Cruisers	7	15
Destroyers	35	147[3]
Destroyer Escorts	0	14[4]
Total Combatants	69	235

The Japanese total does not include one old destroyer and the six escort ships assigned to the supply unit of the Mobile Force, Main Body.

THE UNITED STATES NAVY

The Third Fleet

The Pacific Fleet's carrier force operated under a dual command arrangement. When the Fast Carrier Task Force was under the command of Admiral Spruance in his capacity as commander of the Fifth Fleet, it was designated TF 58. When under Halsey's Third Fleet, the designation changed to TF 38. The only difference was the fleet commander and his staff; Mitscher and his staff remained in place.

Under Mitscher's direction, the Fast Carrier Task Force had revolutionized naval warfare in the Pacific. By massing carrier air power, the Fast Carrier Task Force had become an offensive weapon of unparalleled power. The first dramatic evidence of this was provided in February 1944 when Mitscher's carriers assaulted the Combined Fleet's principal anchorage at Truk Atoll. Over the space of two days, the Americans conducted 1,250 sorties against Truk. The Americans quickly seized control of the air over the atoll and destroyed 250–275 Japanese aircraft in the air and on the ground. Though the Combined Fleet had departed days before, damage to Japanese shipping was considerable. A total of 45 ships of all types totaling some 220,000 tons were sunk. Only 17 American aircraft were lost in combat over the two days.[5] The Japanese air response was tepid, but they did manage to torpedo fleet carrier *Intrepid*, forcing her out of the war until August.

Intrepid's damage at the hands of Japanese torpedo bombers was a rare event. Between January and June 1944, she was the only TF 58 ship damaged by Japanese aircraft. The radar-directed Hellcat fighters made it difficult for Japanese aircraft to attack TF 58 during the day, so most attacks were conducted at dusk or at night. This was the case when *Intrepid* was damaged in February. American fleet air defense doctrine received its biggest test yet during the Battle of the Philippine Sea in June 1944.

Using fighter control directors at the task group and even task force level, Hellcats could be pooled and then vectored to deal with prioritized threats. American radars could detect large groups of Japanese aircraft flying at altitude at distances up to 125nm. Interceptions at Philippine Sea were also conducted at extended ranges up to 60nm from the nearest TF 58 task force. This gave the Hellcats time to break up even large formations. At Philippine Sea, four major Japanese raids were mounted, with a total of 373 aircraft. Of these, 243 aircraft were shot down, the vast majority by Hellcats. The final factor in the ineffectiveness of Japanese air power was the poor tactical skills of Japanese aviators. Despite the efforts of the Hellcats, several large groups of Japanese aircraft broke through American defenses and were in a position to attack TF 58's capital ships. However, only one direct hit was gained, on battleship *South Dakota*. It hit one of the most heavily armored parts of the ship and caused minimal damage. Two near misses were scored against carriers *Wasp* and *Bunker Hill*, but damage was again minimal and the ships remained in action.

On August 26, Halsey assumed command of the Fast Carrier Task Force which became TF 38. This force contained all the USN's fast carriers and most modern battleships. It was organized into four task groups. In Mitscher's own words:

> The ideal composition of a fast-carrier task force is four carriers, six to eight support vessels and not less than 18 destroyers, preferably 24. More than four carriers in a task group cannot be advantageously used due to the amount of air room required. Less than four carriers requires an uneconomical use of support ships and screening vessels.[6]

By October 1944, the flood of new ships arriving in the Pacific allowed Mitscher to fill out his vision. Ships were constantly being shuttled from one task group to another, so the composition of task groups was not static. On October 23, TF 38 was organized in this manner:[7]

TG 38.1 (Vice Admiral John McCain)
Fleet carriers *Hancock, Hornet, Wasp*
Light carriers *Cowpens, Monterey*
Heavy cruisers: 3
Destroyers: 21

TG 38.2 (Rear Admiral Gerald Bogan)
Fleet carrier *Intrepid*
Light carriers *Cabot, Independence*
Battleships *Iowa, New Jersey*
Light cruisers: 3
Destroyers: 18

TG 38.3 (Rear Admiral Frederick Sherman)
Fleet carriers *Essex, Lexington*
Light carriers *Langley, Princeton*
Battleships *Massachusetts, South Dakota*
Light cruisers: 4
Destroyers: 9

TG 38.4 (Rear Admiral Ralph Davison)
Fleet carriers *Enterprise, Franklin*
Light carriers *Belleau Wood, San Jacinto*
Battleships *Alabama, Washington*
Heavy cruisers: 2
Destroyers: 15

TF 38 was built around its large force of aircraft carriers, but it also contained many of the USN's most powerful surface warships. American admirals sought methods to maximize the potential of these surface forces. Accordingly, it was doctrine for a battle line to be formed around the Fast Carrier Task Force's battleships when a fleet action seemed imminent. The battle line would operate in advance of the carrier task groups to place it in position to engage the Japanese fleet should circumstances permit. At the very least, the battle line could be used to destroy Japanese ships crippled by air attack. Spruance used this tactic at Philippine Sea. Though the battle line was never in a position to engage Japanese surface ships, it proved a success by drawing Japanese air attacks upon itself instead of against the carriers. Halsey intended to form the battle line again as part of his plan to crush the Japanese fleet. When formed, the battle line was designated TF 34 and was placed under Vice Admiral Willis Lee. Any decision to form TF 34 had real implications, since it stripped the heavy escorts from the screens of the carrier task groups and thus compromised their antiaircraft protection. When formed, it would exhibit this organization:[8]

TF 34 (Vice Admiral Willis Lee)
Battleships *Alabama, Iowa, Massachusetts, New Jersey, South Dakota*
    Washington
Heavy cruisers: 2
Light cruisers: 5
Destroyers: 18

The Ships

Eight fleet carriers operated with TF 38 during the battle. Seven of these were Essex-class ships. These were the most powerful ships of the entire war; their arrival in the Pacific, beginning in May 1943, provided the backbone of the American advance during the last two years of the war. Essex-class carriers were massive ships at 37,000 tons full load and possessed a fine balance of offensive striking power, protection, and endurance. With a design emphasis on operating a large air group of 90–100 aircraft, they possessed massive offensive capabilities. Their offensive potential was combined with a top speed of 33 knots, endurance of over 15,000nm, and a protective antiaircraft battery of 12 5-inch/38 guns and as many as 72 40mm and 58 20mm guns. These ships proved to be resistant to damage, with crews well trained in damage control. None were lost during the war. The last fleet carrier operating with TF 38 was the veteran *Enterprise*. She was slightly smaller and less capable than the Essex-class carriers but still carried an air group of 90 aircraft.

Complementing the fleet carriers were eight Independence-class light carriers. A total of nine Cleveland-class light cruisers were converted into light carriers. This successful program provided the Fast Carrier Task Force with fast and well-protected ships. After conversion, the 15,000-ton full load displacement hulls were large enough to embark a useful air group of 34 aircraft. Usually light carrier air groups were focused on fleet air defense, allowing the fleet carriers to concentrate on offensive operations.

A big part of Halsey's plans to crush the Japanese fleet was to unleash TF 34. Only once before during the war, during the attack on Truk, had the escorts of the Fast Carrier Task Force engaged Japanese surface forces. After being restricted to providing antiaircraft protection to the carriers, the sailors aboard TF 34 ships were certainly itching for a chance to engage the Japanese. Because it never had an opportunity to engage the Japanese with its full combat power, it is hard to realize how much firepower TF 34 possessed.

The centerpiece of TF 34 was its battle line of six battleships, all commissioned in 1941 or after. All six ships carried 16-inch guns and the best fire control systems available to any navy. This was combined with heavy protection, high speed, and the best level of antiaircraft protection available. This balance made the USN's modern battleships the most powerful in the world. TF 34 included three classes of modern battleships. *Washington* was one of two North Carolina-class ships mounting nine 16-inch/45 guns and 20 5-inch/38 dual purpose guns with a top speed of 28 knots. *Alabama, Massachusetts,* and *South Dakota* were three of the four ships of the South Dakota class. They carried the same main battery of nine 16-inch/45 guns but were better protected than the North Carolina class. They were also slightly slower. *Iowa* and *New Jersey* were the first two ships of the Iowa class. The four ships of this class were the only USN battleships built without restrictions from prewar naval treaties. Unlike prior USN battleships that emphasized protection, the Iowa class emphasized speed (top speed 33 knots). At over 57,000 tons full load displacement, they were also large enough to carry heavy protection and a main battery of nine 16-inch/50 guns.

Halsey and his admirals wanted to give their battleships a crack at the Japanese because they were convinced of the superiority of American battleships. In particular, the USN's 16-inch naval rifle was thought to be a devastating weapon and its fire control was proven to be highly effective. In fact, the advantage conferred on USN battleships by their superior fire control systems was immense. American battleships augmented their optical rangefinders with radar. The Mark 8 radar, introduced in 1943, was capable of blind fire (important in night or low visibility conditions), and could track a battleship-sized target at 40,000 yards and a smaller target at up to 31,000 yards. Using their long-range fire control capabilities and superior protection, modern American battleships should have dominated older Japanese battleships. Only the two Yamato-class ships possessed comparable capabilities. Against these ships, the superior fire control systems aboard American battleships gave them a significant advantage.

Two types of heavy cruisers were embedded in TF 38. Five prewar "Treaty" cruisers were present. These ships carried powerful 8-inch main batteries, but their design incorporated compromises in protection to meet tonnage restrictions. The second type of heavy cruiser was the Baltimore class, the first few ships of which had entered service. These were much larger than the Treaty cruisers, with a full load displacement of over 17,000 tons. The Baltimore class was a balanced design with good protection, high speed, and heavy main, secondary, and antiaircraft batteries. Early in the battle, Baltimore-class cruiser *Canberra* was torpedoed off Formosa but survived. On balance, the Baltimore class was the finest class of heavy cruiser built during the war.

Light cruisers assigned to TF 38 included three Atlanta-class ships. These were small cruisers without heavy armor but carried a heavy 5-inch/38 battery and were well suited for antiaircraft duties. Wartime production also provided a large number of 10,000-ton Cleveland-class light cruisers – six operated with TF 38 during the battle. These ships mounted a formidable main battery of 12 6-inch guns with radar-directed fire control and a high rate of fire. These ships also carried significant antiaircraft capabilities. *Houston* took two torpedoes in the early part of the battle but was saved by her crew. The Cleveland class was the best light cruiser of the war.

TF 38's destroyer force included a mix of prewar and war-built destroyers. The most important class of destroyers was the Fletcher class. These large destroyers of some 2,500 tons full-load displacement possessed high speed, a main battery of five 5-inch/38 guns, and ten torpedo tubes. In a surface engagement, the destroyer's most powerful weapon was the torpedo. The standard USN destroyer torpedo was the Mark 15. Early in the war, the Mark 15 experienced severe problems that restricted its effectiveness. These had finally been addressed by late 1943. During the Solomons campaign USN destroyers used new tactics and radar direction for their torpedoes. This combination made American destroyers formidable surface warfare ships.

Carrier Air Groups and Aircraft
The primary weapon of TF 38 was its carrier air groups. Essex-class carrier air groups were formidable offensive weapons. In early 1944, an Essex-class air group was comprised of a 36-aircraft fighter squadron, a 36-aircraft dive-bomber squadron, and a torpedo squadron with 18 aircraft. On July 31, 1944, authorization was given to reduce the dive-bomber squadron from 36 to 24 aircraft and increase the size of the fighter squadron up to 54 aircraft.[9] Also embarked was a detachment of four radar-equipped night fighters and usually some photo-reconnaissance Hellcats. The size of the torpedo squadron was unchanged. In the short period before the Battle of Leyte Gulf, Essex-class air groups were transitioning to this new structure. The Independence-class light carrier embarked an air group of 25 fighters and nine torpedo planes.

The arrival of Essex-class carriers in mid-1943 was accompanied by the introduction of new aircraft to operate off their decks. The standard USN carrier fighter at this period of the war was the Grumman F6F-3

Hellcat. Upon entering combat service in summer 1943, the Hellcat immediately proved its superiority over its Japanese counterpart, the Mitsubishi A6M "Zero" fighter. The Hellcat possessed important advantages in protection, speed, and firepower by virtue of its tough and armored airframe, armament of six .50-caliber machine guns, and its powerful Pratt & Whitney R-2800 engine. The Zero retained an advantage in maneuverability, so Hellcat pilots were instructed to avoid dogfights with it. In addition to flying a superior airplane, USN fighter pilots were much better trained and more experienced than all but a very few of their Japanese adversaries.

The Hellcat was used in fleet air defense and air superiority roles. It also operated occasionally during this period of the war as a fighter-bomber. However, the primary offensive weapons in a fleet carrier's air group were its dive-bombers and torpedo bombers. By October 1944, the only carrier dive-bomber was the Curtiss SB2C Helldiver. After an excessively long gestation period, the SB2C-3 version successfully addressed a series of lingering problems and was approved for fleet service. The Helldiver was an improvement from the much-loved Douglas SBD Dauntless. The new aircraft was faster (with a top speed of almost 300mph), more rugged, and had a payload of 2,000 pounds carried internally. Against unarmored ships, a 1,000-pound bomb could be deadly, but even the armor-piercing version of this weapon was unable to sink heavily-protected battleships.

Torpedo bombers could sink any size ship. Early in the war, USN torpedo bombers were ineffective through a combination of poor aircraft and unreliable torpedoes. After the Battle of Midway, the USN's standard torpedo bomber was the Grumman TBF/TBM Avenger. It was so versatile that it was embarked on fleet, light, and escort carriers. The Avenger proved reliable in service, was able to absorb severe punishment, and performed as both a torpedo and conventional bomber. By October 1944, the Avenger carried an effective and reliable torpedo. Since 1938 the standard USN air-launched torpedo was the Mark 13. This weapon proved chronically unreliable during the first part of the war; its problems took two years to completely address. Not until 1944 could the Avenger take a fully functional torpedo into combat. The Mark 13 could be employed at speeds up to 270mph and at an altitude of up to 800 feet. If it hit its target, its warhead of 600 pounds of the explosive Torpex was devastating. This warhead could defeat the side protection system of battleships, including the Yamato class. Avengers could also operate as conventional bombers with a typical load of four 500-pound bombs.

Carrier Air Group Doctrine

By October 1944, TF 38 employed an effective and well-practiced doctrine. Each carrier task group conducted morning and afternoon searches in accordance with Mitscher's overall reconnaissance plan. The maximum search range of USN carrier aircraft was about 325nm under normal operational conditions. The typical strike range of a carrier air group was much less because of the requirements to carry a heavy payload and to spend time assembling and then flying in attack formation. Based on a range of tactical requirements, the standard attack range was 200–250nm.

TF 38's air groups trained intensively to conduct attacks on ships, but in the months before the battle most of TF 38's strike operations had been directed against land targets. The result was an atrophy of the skills required to attack maritime targets. Intense operations created a much more serious problem – aircrew fatigue. In the middle of the battle (October 23), fleet carrier *Bunker Hill* was detached from TF 38 because her air group was too exhausted to continue. For the remaining air groups, fatigue grew during the hectic period from October 23 to 26 when aircrews were ordered to fly two or three missions per day. The resulting fatigue had a direct impact on aircrew effectiveness.

By October 1944, TF 38 air groups possessed a proven doctrine for attacking Japanese naval targets. The days of USN carrier air strikes being rendered ineffective by poor tactics, poor communications, and an unreliable torpedo were a thing of the past. Each carrier air group conducted its attack separately. Targets were assigned by an overall strike coordinator, who was responsible for ensuring that all key targets were attacked and that overconcentration in a single target was avoided.

A successful attack at the air group level depended on coordination between the fighters, dive-bombers, and torpedo planes to overwhelm the target's defenses. Existing doctrine called for the Helldivers to attack first, using a standard dive-bombing profile consisting of a shallow approach from 20,000 feet followed by a steep 65–70-degree dive from between 15,000 and 12,000 feet. The Helldivers released their 1,000-pound bombs 1,500–2,000 feet above the target. If the entire squadron was present, it was divided into divisions of six aircraft to enable attacks on different targets or to overwhelm one target from several different directions. When possible, the Helldivers attacked a target along its longitudinal axis, since this presented the largest target possible. This preference was noted by the Japanese, who devised an evasion tactic of steering a complete circle to present the dive-bomber pilots with a constantly changing target axis. If attacking large ships, the Helldivers executed their attacks first with the purpose of reducing its defenses by causing topside damage or simply by drawing fire from the more vulnerable torpedo bombers.

Hellcats were used to suppress target defenses by conducting low-level strafing attacks to kill antiaircraft gun crews. The last aircraft to attack were the Avengers. Coming in against a target at low attitude increased their vulnerability to antiaircraft fire. Where tactical conditions permitted, the Avengers were divided into two sections to conduct an "anvil" attack from both bows of the target. If correctly executed, an anvil attack made it difficult for the target to maneuver without exposing itself to attack from at least one of the sections. For both dive-bomber and torpedo bomber pilots, it was extremely challenging to hit a maneuvering target. Add in the fact that the target was trying to shoot down the attacking aircraft, and both bravery and skill were required for a successful attack.

TF 38 Fleet Air Defense

TF 38 was subjected to concerted Japanese air attack during the battle. Unlike during the four carrier battles of 1942 when Japanese aviators had inflicted severe punishment on American carrier task forces, by October 1944 USN fleet air defense had improved to such an extent that carrier task forces had achieved a large degree of immunity against conventional Japanese air attack. The main reason was the lack of tactical proficiency on the part of Japanese aviators. Against heavy USN fighter and antiaircraft defenses earlier in the war, Japanese aviators had pressed home their attacks and skillfully conducted damaging attacks. However, the increasing toll extracted by American defenses eventually reduced Japanese naval aviation to impotence.

One of the bedrocks of effective fleet air defense was early radar warning of approaching threats. USN cruisers, battleships, and carriers were fitted with the SK radar that could regularly detect formations of Japanese at high altitudes out to 100nm and sometimes beyond if atmospheric conditions were favorable. If detection was gained this early, it was more than adequate for marshalling an effective fighter interception. The SM radar fitted aboard carriers provided height information of incoming threats that was critical for fighter direction officers (FDOs). By this point in the war, FDOs were routinely successful in vectoring Hellcats onto approaching Japanese raids. However, even the most successful interception could never account for every incoming enemy aircraft, and invariably "leakers" got through the CAP.

Dealing with those aircraft that escaped interception was the responsibility of the task force's inner defense layer – its antiaircraft guns. American warships were fitted with long-range, intermediate-range, and short-range antiaircraft guns. Incoming Japanese aircraft would have to fly through all these layers to deliver an attack on a high-value target at the center of the formation. Carrier task groups deployed in a circular formation in the face of air attack with the carriers in the center.

The outer zone of antiaircraft fire was provided by the 5-inch/38 gun; using radar control it was effective out to 10,000 yards. Every ship in the formation, including destroyers, carried these accurate and fast-firing weapons. The 40mm Bofors gun provided intermediate-range protection. This weapon possessed a high rate of fire and a fire control director capable of delivering effective fire out to about 3,000 yards. It was fitted in dual and quadruple mounts on board almost all destroyers and all larger ships. The final layer of defense was constituted by the 20mm Oerlikon gun fitted in single mounts. When fitted with the Mark 14 gyro-sight, the Oerlikon was effective out to about 1,500 yards.

The overall quality of American antiaircraft fire was formidable. It accounted for many approaching Japanese planes and, just as important, it affected the pilot's aim, causing many misses. Finally, its lethality soared against exactly those Japanese aviators who pressed home their attacks.

Seventh Fleet

Though not expected to play the primary role in defeating a major Japanese effort to defeat the Leyte invasion, the Seventh Fleet fought two of the four major engagements during the battle. Some 130 principal combatants (destroyer and above) were assigned to the Seventh Fleet, about twice as many as the total number of Japanese warships in the battle. Seventh Fleet planners believed that this force could protect the invasion force from Japanese cruisers and destroyers, but not from the Combined Fleet's main effort.

The Seventh Fleet was allocated a large number of heavy warships from the Pacific Fleet to provide naval gunfire support, which had become a staple of American amphibious operations. Until this point, Kinkaid and his staff lacked experience with large-scale fleet operations. The centerpiece of the Seventh Fleet's surface force was its six old battleships. Of these, five had been present at Pearl Harbor on December 7, 1941, and two of the five had been sunk. All six old battlewagons had been modernized since the start of the war. These extensively modernized ships possessed firepower capabilities against both surface and air targets virtually equal to the modern battleships assigned to TF 38.

However, all older battleships were deficient in speed and possessed deficiencies with underwater protection.[10] Another potential problem was a flawed assessment by Seventh Fleet planners that the heavy ships did not need their full allotment of armor-piercing (AP) shells. For the Leyte operation, the mix was set at 75 percent high-capacity (high explosive shells for shore bombardment) and 25 percent AP for engaging heavily-armored enemy warships.[11]

Seventh Fleet battleships were a mixed bag. Three had been virtually rebuilt, but three were only lightly modernized. *Maryland* and *West Virginia* were two of the three ships of the USN's first class of 16-inch battleships. After suffering minor damage at Pearl Harbor, *Maryland* was only lightly modernized before October 1944. *West Virginia* had been severely damaged by torpedoes during the Pearl Harbor attack. She had settled on an even keel, so was raised and rebuilt. *Tennessee* and *California* were also damaged at Pearl Harbor (*California* actually sank after progressive flooding) and were also rebuilt along the same lines as *West Virginia*. The main difference between *Tennessee* and *California* and the earlier *West Virginia* was that the first two ships were fitted with a main battery of 12 14-inch guns. All three ships retained their original main batteries, but had their fire control capabilities dramatically upgraded with the addition of two Mark 34 main battery directors, each with the Mark 8 fire control radar. To augment their antiaircraft capabilities, the old casemate-mounted secondary battery was removed and replaced with a battery of 16 dual-purpose 5-inch/38 guns. Underwater protection was significantly improved by the addition of a torpedo blister and more internal longitudinal bulkheads. Horizontal protection was also much improved.

Mississippi was one of the three New Mexico-class ships and also carried a main battery of 12 14-inch. All three ships were heavily modernized between the wars and possessed the best underwater protection of the USN's old battleships by the start of the Pacific War. Even this underwater protection system would have been inadequate against the IJN's powerful Type 93 torpedo, however. The last of the Seventh Fleet's battleships, and the oldest, was *Pennsylvania*. Launched in 1916, she was fitted with a main battery of 12 14-inch guns. During the war, she received significant enhancements to her antiaircraft fit but remained severely deficient in underwater protection. *Maryland*, *Mississippi*, and *Pennsylvania* carried the older and less capable Mark 3 fire control radar for their main batteries. It was capable of providing target ranges from 15,000 to 30,000 yards, but lacked the beam definition required to distinguish between the target and nearby shell splashes. This often resulted in fire control personnel targeting the shell splashes instead of tracking the target.

In addition to its six battleships, the Seventh Fleet was assigned 11 heavy and light cruisers. These included three Treaty heavy cruisers, all carrying a main battery of nine 8-inch guns. The Royal Australian Navy (RAN) contributed two County-class heavy cruisers, each carrying eight 8-inch guns, also designed to Treaty limitations. Like USN Treaty cruisers, they were not well protected from shells and torpedoes. The fleet's six light cruisers were all modern and powerful ships, with superior firepower and protection than the Treaty heavy cruisers. In total, four Brooklyn-class ships began the battle; they carried a formidable main battery of 15 6-inch/47 guns each capable of pumping out as many as 12 rounds per minute. However, *Honolulu* was torpedoed on the first day of the invasion and knocked out of the battle. *Nashville* was also unavailable since MacArthur refused to disembark from her, making the ship and her cargo too valuable to risk in a naval battle. The two Cleveland-class ships available carried a main battery of 12 6-inch guns, but in addition mounted a secondary battery of 12 5-inch/38 dual purpose guns capable of firing as many as 20 rounds per minute. All USN cruisers carried modern fire control radars for use against surface and air targets.

Some 62 destroyers were allocated to the Seventh Fleet. The most capable were the Fletcher-class ships, which, as has been discussed, were powerfully armed and fast ships with formidable surface warfare capabilities. Their modern radars made them very capable night-fighting assets, and USN night-fighting doctrine gave destroyers and their radar-guided torpedo barrages a central role.

The invasion of Leyte included the largest concentration of escort carriers yet seen in the war. A maximum of 18 were initially available, but two were detached on the afternoon of October 24, leaving 16.[12] Escort carriers had the responsibilities to provide local air defense, conduct antisubmarine patrols, and fly close air support missions for the troops ashore. Two types of escort carriers were assigned to the Escort Carrier Group. By far the most capable was the Sangamon class; four were present at Leyte. These were converted from oilers and had a full load displacement of almost 24,000 tons. Their size and tanker hull made them resistant to damage. The same cannot be said about the Casablanca-class escort carriers, which were mass-produced conversions from merchant hulls.[13]

Escort carriers were forced to operate in large groups to compensate for their inadequate armament and small air groups. For the Leyte invasion, the 18 escort carriers were organized into three groups of six. The total number of aircraft embarked on these 18 ships was impressive. Sangamon-class ships embarked a fighter squadron with up to 22 Hellcats (one carrier retained a fighter squadron of 24 older FM-2 Wildcat fighters) and a squadron of nine Avengers. The smaller Casablanca-class carriers carried a composite air group with a mix of up to 16 Wildcats and 12 Avengers. The actual number of aircraft available in each air group varied depending on operational and combat losses and the availability of replacement aircraft. However, the nominal aircraft strength of the Escort Carrier Group was over 500 aircraft – equal to five Essex-class fleet carriers. Escort carrier air groups were trained and equipped to conduct maritime strikes, though they rarely had a chance to conduct such missions. Each escort carrier task unit was allotted three Fletcher-class destroyers and four or five Butler-class destroyer escorts.

American submarines were expected to play a major role during the Leyte operation. Primary among their tasks were to interdict and report the movements of Japanese surface forces. Many submarines were also assigned to act as lifeguards for downed aircrews. Both the Pacific Fleet and the Seventh Fleet deployed submarines to support the invasion. By pulling submarines off antishipping patrols, a large number of submarines were made available to directly support the invasion. For the Seventh Fleet, this included 14 boats on patrols and another seven on lifeguard duties. Even these were not enough, and there were too few to cover all the western approaches to the Philippines. In addition, none were available to cover the Lingga–Singapore area, where the heaviest concentration of Japanese warships was located.[14] Pacific Fleet submarines were assigned to TF 17 – a total of 27 boats conducted patrols in direct or indirect support of the operations, with another two assigned to lifeguard duties. These submarines were deployed in the Luzon Strait, the Ryukyus, and off the Japanese Home Islands. Halsey was concerned that TF 17's deployment of the submarines was faulty and might allow an IJN force to depart the Home Islands and enter the Philippine Sea without being detected.[15] In fact, this is exactly what happened during the battle.

By October 1944, American submarines were not just deadly against Japanese shipping, but also against Japanese fleet units. The problems with the unreliable Mark 14 torpedo had been rectified, ineffective skippers had been weeded out, and code breaking of Japanese naval codes provided actionable intelligence to boats on patrol. American fleet boats were the best submarines used by any navy during the war. The standard Gato- and the Balao-class boats possessed long range, a high surface speed, an excellent radar suite, and carried up to 24 torpedoes. Using their radar effectively, especially in night attacks, aggressive American submarine skippers were able to attack Japanese convoys and even fleet formations with a high expectation of success. As the effectiveness and confidence of American submariners grew, Japanese antisubmarine weaponry, tactics, and training failed to keep pace.

Logistical Support
Another area of significant American superiority was in naval logistics. Because of the extensive resources devoted by the USN to logistics, TF 38 was capable of projecting power over prolonged periods. The level of effort to maintain USN forces at sea was unequaled by any other navy. The Third Fleet's logistics train was designated TG 30.8 and was comprised of over 100 ships. Operating out of the new advanced fleet anchorage at Ulithi after October 1, 9–12 oilers were stationed close to TF 38 (but at the edge of Japanese air range) to provide refueling services to the carrier task forces. Every third or fourth day, three new oilers would replace those that were nearly empty.

Each oiler group also had an attached escort carrier to provide replacement aircraft.[16] Typically, each carrier task force was replenished every 3–5 days, depending on the pace of operations. At-sea replenishment included provisions for fuel, ammunition, and replacement aircraft. A total of 34 oilers were assigned to TG 30.8. Underway replenishment of various types of munitions was not highly developed at this point in the war, but six ammunition ships were available to provide new stocks of primarily aircraft ordnance. In addition to the three escort carriers used to provide replacement aircraft, eight more were assigned to provide CAP and antisubmarine protection. Ten fleet tugs were available to conduct salvage operations of damaged ships. Third Fleet's logistics force was a critical component of its operations, but the Japanese never identified its importance or attempted to attack it. Had they done so, the Americans devoted considerable assets to protect it. In addition to the escort carriers, a total of 17 destroyers and 26 destroyer escorts were assigned to its screen.[17] TG 30.8 could not provide everything TF 38 required, so each of TF 38's task forces were periodically sent to Ulithi for full replenishment and a short period of crew recreation.

Seventh Fleet logistics were stretched to the utmost when the fleet was heavily reinforced before the Leyte operation. The fleet's primary logistics base was at Manus in the Admiralties. Compared to the wealth of tankers enjoyed by the Third Fleet, the Seventh Fleet only possessed six oilers capable of underway replenishment. The fleet was provided with fuel, munitions, and other provisions through a system of periodic supply convoys run from Manus and other bases into Leyte Gulf.[18]

THE IMPERIAL JAPANESE NAVY

For reasons already explained, Toyoda felt he had no choice but to commit all remaining ships of the Combined Fleet to *Sho-Go*. To gather as many ships as possible, the Kuriles were abandoned, which allowed the reallocation of the Fifth Fleet. Battleship Division 2, on training duties in the Inland Sea, was assigned operational duties, and Toyoda even gave up his flagship and moved his headquarters ashore. By such means, 69 ships were made available and organized into several disparate forces. This was an impressive number that included all of the Combined Fleet's still formidable force of heavy ships.

However, looking at the force in detail, its weaknesses immediately become apparent. Toyoda's biggest problem was the condition of his carrier force. When the Americans landed on Leyte, the carrier force was still in the process of being rebuilt, and this was not expected to be complete for several more months. While the carrier force was in deplorable shape, the Combined Fleet's surface force was still powerful. Even after almost three years of war, most of the fleet's heavy units were still in commission. The IJN began the war with ten battleships and commissioned two more during it; nine were still available in October 1944. Of the 18 heavy cruisers that the Japanese began the war with, 14 were still afloat when the battle began. Of 22 light cruisers commissioned by the Japanese before or during the war, ten were left afloat by October 1944. Of these, two were unavailable. One had just been commissioned and the other was in a dockyard undergoing repair to battle damage. Seven of the eight available light cruisers were committed to *Sho-Go*.

While still impressive in terms of heavy ships, the Combined Fleet had a deficit of destroyers and submarines. Traditionally, destroyers were an important component of the Combined Fleet and had a vital role to play in a decisive battle. These ships carried the best torpedo of the war, the 24-inch Type 93, which had been used with devastating effect on many occasions earlier in the war. Skillful torpedo attacks, especially in a night battle, were an essential part of any conflict, since they could compensate for any numerical disadvantage on the part of the Combined Fleet. Destroyers were also essential for screening heavy units against submarine attack, which by 1944 had become a real threat to Japanese surface forces. The Combined Fleet's destroyers had fought in every battle since the start of the war and had borne the brunt of losses, especially during the Guadalcanal and Solomons campaigns in 1942–43.

Production of new ships was entirely inadequate to keep up with losses. As a result, the IJN's destroyer force was in dire straits in October 1944. Of the 96 modern destroyers available before the war or built during it, only 35 were available in late October 1944. All of these were committed to *Sho-Go*, but this number was clearly not enough, as events demonstrated. To make up for their heavy destroyer losses, the IJN began construction of the Matsu class in August 1943. At 1,262 tons standard displacement, capable of only 28 knots, and carrying only three 5-inch guns and four torpedo tubes, these ships were closer to destroyer escorts in capability. Four were assigned escort duties as part of *Sho-Go*. Another 14 old destroyers were also available, but these were suited for escort duties only; just one was committed to the operation.

Adding to Toyoda's list of problems, the Combined Fleet was experiencing a severe fuel shortage by this point of the war. By necessity it was split in two in October 1944. The carrier force was in the Inland Sea rebuilding its carrier air groups, but there was not sufficient fuel in the Home Islands to base the surface fleet there as well. Because of the low fuel stocks in Japan, the bulk of the surface fleet was based in the Lingga area, where fuel was much more easily obtained from sources in the NEI. The division of the Combined Fleet was forced on Toyoda by dire circumstances. Following the disaster at Midway, the Combined Fleet had combined its heavy surface forces with its carrier force to provide mutual support. This was the way Toyoda wanted to fight the next decisive battle. As soon as the new carrier air groups could be trained, Toyoda intended to move the carriers south to join the main surface force. Even if things went smoothly, this was not anticipated until mid-November.[19]

Combined Fleet Organization

In the months before *Sho-Go*, Toyoda reorganized the Combined Fleet in preparation for the upcoming decisive battle. The first move took place on August 1 and affected many of the key units slated for *Sho-Go*. The Second Fleet, traditionally comprised of the Combined Fleet's heavy surface units, was redesignated as the First Diversionary Attack Force. Land-based air forces also underwent a redesignation – the First, Second, and Third Air Fleets became the Fifth, Sixth, and Seventh Base Air Forces, respectively. Also in August, the Fifth Fleet, the force responsible for defending northern Japan, was pulled back to the Inland Sea, placed under the First Mobile Fleet, and redesignated the Second Diversionary Attack Force. Both the First and Second Diversionary Attack Forces were subordinate to the First Mobile Fleet.[20]

In mid-September, the First Mobile Fleet was redesignated Mobile Force, Main Body. Even though the First Diversionary Attack Force had been sent south, it remained subordinate to the Main Body which remained in Japan.

The Carrier Force

Known as the Main Body, the Combined Fleet's carrier force was a shadow of its former self in October 1944. On paper, it looked formidable, with eight aircraft carriers and two converted battleships capable of carrying attack aircraft. In reality, it was a force with almost no striking power. The first two ships of the Unryu class (*Unryu* and *Amagi*) comprised Carrier Division 1, but having just been completed in August, neither was fully operational. The third Unryu-class carrier, *Katsuragi*, was completed in October, so was obviously not yet available for operations. Carrier Division 3 included veteran fleet carrier *Zuikaku* and three light carriers. Before 1943 and the arrival of the American Essex class, the two Shokaku-class ships (*Shokaku* and *Zuikaku*) were the best carriers in the world, with a combination of striking power (an air group of 75 aircraft), protection, speed, and range. Following *Shokaku*'s loss at Philippine Sea, only *Zuikaku* remained. She was also the last of the six carriers that had participated in the Pearl Harbor attack. The light carriers included the veteran *Zuiho* and newer sister ships *Chitose* and *Chiyoda*. All had been converted from auxiliaries and could embark a small air group of 30 aircraft. They were useful ships but possessed no protection.

Carrier Division 4 was a mix of converted carriers *Junyo* and *Ryuho* and battleship-carriers *Ise* and *Hyuga*. *Junyo* was a conversion from a large passenger liner. Able to embark over 50 aircraft, she proved an important addition to the IJN's carrier fleet when she was commissioned in 1942. However, she had a marginal top speed of 26 knots. Being a converted merchant, she lacked effective protection – her sister ship *Hiyo* was lost for this reason at Philippine Sea. *Ryuho* was the worst of the IJN's light carrier conversions, having a top speed of only 26 knots and light construction marked by no armor and inadequate internal subdivision.

The two battleships were part of the IJN's efforts to reconstitute its carrier force after the defeat at Midway. In what can only be called an act of desperation, the two old Ise-class battleships were removed from service in May 1943 and slated for conversion into hybrid battleship-carriers. This concept required extensive work. The two aft 14-inch gun turrets were removed and replaced with a hangar and a 230-foot-long deck. This deck was too small to launch or recover aircraft. A total of 22 aircraft could be embarked (a mix of conventional and floatplanes), which were launched from two catapults. Since the aircraft could not return to their ships, they would recover on a conventional carrier or at a nearby island base. On paper, this looked like a viable method to increase the fleet's striking power by 44 aircraft. In reality, the entire scheme was impractical, and proved unworthy of the time and resources devoted to it. After being converted, neither ship ever embarked a single aircraft for combat operations. Even though *Ise* and *Hyuga* were useless as hybrid carriers, they still remained useful as battleships since they retained eight 14-inch guns. Both ships also carried a very heavy antiaircraft battery.

A weak screen comprised of three light cruisers and eight destroyers was allocated to the Main Body. *Oyodo* was the newest and largest of the light cruisers. Originally designed as a flagship for submarine flotillas, she was a "white elephant," so was used by Toyoda as Combined Fleet flagship. After Toyoda took the Combined Fleet headquarters ashore in September, *Oyodo* was made available for fleet work. The 8,534-ton ship carried a main battery of six 6-inch/50 guns and was lightly protected. The other two cruisers, *Isuzu* and *Tama*, dated from 1921 to 1923 and were designed as destroyer flotilla leaders. As such, they were lightly protected and carried a weak main battery of 5.5-inch guns. They were significantly weaker than USN light cruisers. *Isuzu* was better suited as an escort, as she had been converted into an antiaircraft cruiser and carried six 5-inch dual-purpose guns and 50 25mm guns.

The best IJN destroyers of the war were the Akizuki class. These large ships were designed for carrier escort duties and carried the excellent Type 98 3.9-inch gun that possessed a better range than the standard USN destroyer 5-inch/38 gun. They also retained four torpedo tubes and four reloads. Four Akizuki-class ships were available for operations with the Main Body. To provide more escorts, a division of four Matsu-class destroyers was assigned to Ozawa's force.

Japanese Carrier Air Groups

Throughout the war, the Combined Fleet's carrier force had been its primary striking arm. The Battle of the Philippine Sea resulted in the almost total destruction of the Combined Fleet's carrier air groups. Reconstitution of these critical assets was not expected to be completed until mid-November at the earliest.

Plans to complete the training of the carrier air groups and to unify the Combined Fleet were dealt a severe blow during the great air-sea battle off Formosa. Seeing an opportunity, the Japanese committed the air groups of Carrier Divisions 3 and 4 to support the attacks by the land-based air fleets. The almost-trained carrier air groups suffered heavy losses during this battle. Of the 300 carrier pilots in training that began the battle, less than half remained afterwards. As a senior Combined Fleet staff officer admitted after the war, these were bad airmen but were good enough to act as decoys.[21] By October 20, those remaining pilots and aircraft capable of carrier operations were loaded by crane onto the four carriers of Carrier Division 3. Such was the state of training of these pilots that it was thought unadvisable to fly the aircraft onto the carriers. Since there were no aircraft available for the two conventional carriers of Carrier Division 4, Ozawa decided that it was unnecessary that they participate in the Main Body's decoy operation.

After loading their air groups, the four carriers embarked a total of 116 aircraft. This was only about 75 percent of their regular aircraft capacity and roughly equivalent to one of the fleet carriers in TF 38. These aircraft included 52 A6M5 "Zero" fighters, 28 older A6Ms equipped to carry a 550-pound bomb and act as fighter-bombers, seven D4Y2 "Judy" dive-bombers, and a total of 29 torpedo bombers, broken down into 25 B6N2 "Jills" and four older B5N2 "Kates" (the last four were probably radar-equipped reconnaissance aircraft). Of these, 65 were embarked on *Zuikaku* (28 A6M5 "Zero" fighters, 16 A6M fighter-bombers, seven D4Y2 "Judy" reconnaissance aircraft, and 14 B6N2 "Jill" torpedo bombers). The balance of 51 aircraft was divided among the three light carriers, with *Zuiho* carrying 17, *Chitose* 18, and *Chiyoda* 16.[22] The level of training for the aircrew aboard Ozawa's four carriers was extremely low. This was evinced by the fact that after a single combat sortie on October 24, only 29 aircraft remained (19 Zero fighters, five Zero fighter-bombers, four Jills, and a single Judy), because after making their attacks they were ordered to recover at land bases rather than attempt to land back aboard their ships. Among Ozawa's escort ships, *Oyodo* carried two reconnaissance floatplanes.[23]

The First Diversionary Attack Force

The heart of *Sho-1* was the First Diversionary Attack Force under the veteran Vice Admiral Kurita. To conduct his mission, Kurita was assigned most of the Combined Fleet's heavy surface units. With five battleships, ten heavy cruisers, two light cruisers, and 15 destroyers, it was the largest surface force yet assembled by the Japanese for a single mission and among the largest such concentrations of the entire war.[24]

After its arrival at Lingga Roads on July 22, Kurita began to drill his force relentlessly. The IJN had always valued intense training, but Kurita's exercise program broke all records. A typical exercise was practicing attacking into a defended anchorage with the First Diversionary Attack Force divided into two parts, each led by *Yamato* or *Musashi*. As usual, the Japanese placed special emphasis on night fighting.[25] Antiaircraft combat was another point of emphasis, since the fleet was expected to reach its objective without air cover. Throughout most of the war, Japanese surface ships conducted combat operations without the benefit of radar. By October 1944, every major Japanese warship carried some sort of radar, and in some cases up to three different types of radar. The arrival of radar gave the Japanese renewed confidence and great efforts were made to incorporate radar into gunnery drills. Because of their low power and poor definition, no Japanese radar possessed the capability to perform effective control of gunnery.[26] Japanese radar was useful for assisting gunnery, but by no means was capable of guiding it. Japanese air warning radars could detect aircraft flying at altitude at up to 55nm (sometimes more under ideal conditions) and the primary surface radar could detect a large target at up to 13nm.

To maximize its firepower, the First Diversionary Attack Force was allocated the most powerful of the Combined Fleet's remaining battleships. Principal among these were superbattleships *Yamato* and *Musashi*, built at immense cost to the nation but which had yet to engage an enemy surface target during the war. The two Yamato-class ships were designed to achieve a qualitative overmatch against any conceivable American battleship and possessed the highest levels of firepower and protection ever placed on a battleship. However, their main battery of nine 18.1-inch guns possessed only a small range advantage over the American 16-inch battleship gun, and the Japanese guns were handicapped by inferior fire control equipment.

The two ships of the Nagato class were the heart of the Combined Fleet's battle line before the arrival of the Yamatos. In October 1943, only *Nagato* remained. Laid down in 1917 but modernized between 1934 and 1936, the ship carried eight 16-inch guns but was relatively slow, with a 25-knot maximum speed. Kurita's last two battleships were the aged *Kongo* and *Haruna*. Originally launched in 1913 and 1915 respectively as battlecruisers, they underwent extensive modernization between 1927 and 1936. Both ships carried a main battery of eight 14-inch guns and were the fastest Japanese battleships at 30 knots. But even after modernization, their protection was comparatively weak.

Perhaps the most important component of Kurita's force was its ten heavy cruisers. Heavy cruisers were an integral part of Japanese night fighting tactics and had proved themselves to be deadly opponents earlier in the war. These ships were fast, heavily armed, fairly well protected, and crewed by well-trained and experienced men. All heavy cruisers carried a main battery of between eight and ten 8-inch guns. Unlike American heavy cruisers, Japanese heavy cruisers mounted a heavy torpedo battery of between 12 and 16 torpedo tubes, with additional torpedoes available for reload. The principal Japanese torpedo was the incomparable Type 93. It possessed the astounding maximum range of 43,746 yards and carried a huge 1,082-pound warhead. While inclusion of a torpedo battery on Japanese cruisers gave them tremendous offensive potential, it was also a vulnerability if the torpedoes were hit while still on board; in fact, five Japanese heavy cruisers were lost in this manner during the war. Two light cruisers were allocated to Kurita's force. Though modern ships completed during the war, they were designed as destroyer leaders and were not as heavily armed or protected as USN light cruisers.

The Japanese expected much from their destroyers in any surface action. Because of heavy destroyer losses earlier in the war, only 15 were available for the First Diversionary Attack Force. Japanese destroyers had performed brilliantly in many night actions during the war and had proven masters at torpedo combat. Japanese destroyers were designed to be superb torpedo platforms, but they were much less capable as antisubmarine and antiair warfare platforms. The two destroyer squadrons assigned to screen the 17 major warships of the First Diversionary Attack Force were clearly unable to provide adequate antisubmarine protection due to a lack of sufficient destroyers and their weak antisubmarine capabilities.

First Diversionary Attack Force, Third Section
The First Diversionary Attack Force was divided into the First, Second, and Third Sections (also referred to by the Japanese as A, B, and C Forces). The Third Section was given an independent mission from the remainder of Kurita's force and placed under Vice Admiral Nishimura. As already discussed, this was a small force with a decoy mission. Accordingly, the heavy ships comprising Nishimura's small fleet were second rate. This was a scratch unit, as none of Nishimura's ships had worked together and their commanding officers were unfamiliar to each other.[27]

The force was built around battleships *Fuso* and *Yamashiro*. These were the IJN's least modernized battleships and were too slow to keepup with Kurita's main force. *Fuso* had yet to see action during the war. *Yamashiro* was designated as a training ship for midshipmen in September 1943, but was brought back into front-line service in September 1944 when Toyoda scraped the bottom of the barrel looking for ships to conduct *Sho-Go*. Being only lightly modernized between the wars, both battleships possessed weak protection, particularly underwater protection against torpedoes. They were viewed as expendable, as shown by the fact they were sent into battle with an inadequate screen and by serious consideration of a June 1944 scheme to send them to Saipan on a one-way mission to reinforce the garrison after the American invasion of the island.

The two battleships were provided with a clearly inadequate screen to carry out their mission. These ships were also second-rate. Heavy cruiser *Mogami* was converted into an aircraft-carrying cruiser in 1943 and had lost two of her 8-inch turrets. At least she was well-protected and retained a battery of 12 torpedo tubes plus reloads. Kurita assigned only four destroyers to his Third Section, and these were the oldest of his destroyers. The four ships included *Shigure*, the last remaining Shiratsuyu-class destroyer, and three remaining Asashio-class ships. Though all were commissioned before the war, they were powerful surface warfare platforms with eight torpedo tubes and eight reloads.

The Second Diversionary Attack Force

This force, under Vice Admiral Shima, was formerly the Fifth Fleet responsible for defending the northern approaches to Japan. Since this was a secondary theater, the force possessed minimal capabilities. The centerpiece of Shima's force was its two Myoko-class heavy cruisers. As with the heavy cruisers assigned to Kurita's fleet, these were fast, heavily armed, and operated by well-trained and veteran crews. Light cruiser *Abukuma* was the flagship of Destroyer Squadron 1. Modernized before the war, she carried a torpedo battery of eight torpedo tubes with the Type 93 torpedo. A total of seven destroyers was assigned to Destroyer Squadron 1 from three different classes. Each of Shima's destroyers carried between six and nine torpedo tubes filled with more Type 93s, with reloads.[28]

IJN Antiaircraft Capabilities

Toyoda and his principal commander understood that the success of *Sho-Go* depended on the ability of Japanese surface ships to reach their objectives while under heavy air attack. Since the First Diversionary

Attack Force had been split from the carriers of the Main Body, and the IJN's land-based air forces were too weak to provide air cover, Kurita's force would be very much on its own to defend against what was expected to be concerted American air attacks as it headed to Leyte Gulf. In fact, the First Diversionary Attack Force was subjected to the most intensive air attacks in naval history during the period of October 24–26. Over only three days, over 1,000 sorties were flown against Kurita's force. Ozawa's carrier force also came under devastating air attack on October 25. Even Nishimura's and Shima's small forces received the attention of American naval aviators. The ability of Japanese naval forces to withstand air attack was a key factor in deciding the battle.

After the Battle of the Philippine Sea, Toyoda oversaw a significant effort to upgrade the Combined Fleet's antiaircraft capabilities. This rested on augmenting the antiaircraft batteries of all combatants, from destroyers up through battleships and carriers. For the most part, this meant increasing the number of light antiaircraft guns. The IJN's standard short-range antiaircraft weapon was the Type 96 25mm gun. It was used in single, twin, and triple mounts. Wherever ships had a clear arc of fire, and within permitted stability limits, all Japanese surface combatants received huge numbers of Type 96 guns. In Kurita's force, *Yamato* and *Musashi* led the way with 152 and 130 respectively; heavy cruisers carried up to 66, and destroyers up to 28. A similar situation developed in Ozawa's force; *Ise* and *Hyuga* each carried 104 25mm guns, *Zuikaku* 96, and the light carriers between 46 and 68. Smaller ships also received significant augmentation to their light antiaircraft batteries, with light cruiser *Isuzu* embarking 50 25mm guns and the Akizuki-class destroyers almost 40.

This augmentation program was impressive on the surface, but the Type 96 25mm gun was a mediocre weapon in every respect. Even the Japanese recognized that the Type 96 was hampered by its inadequate training and elevation speeds, low sustained rate of fire, and excessive blast which affected accuracy. The single mount was almost worthless, since it had only an open-ring sight for fire control, could not handle high-speed targets, and was difficult to handle. Twin and triple mounts could be controlled by the Type 95 Short-Range High-Angle Director, but this was unable to track high-speed targets. Another factor inhibiting the Type 96 gun was its effective range of only 1,635 yards. Even when the Type 96 hit its target, its 9-ounce shell was too small to ensure damage against the robust Helldivers and Avengers.

The standard Japanese long-range antiaircraft weapon was the Type 89 5-inch High-Angle Gun dating from 1932. The Japanese liked this weapon because it was reliable, possessed high elevating speeds and a high muzzle velocity, and fired a large shell. While the gun itself was satisfactory, it relied on an inferior fire control system. The Type 94 High-Angle Firing Control Installation was complex and too slow to provide fire control solutions on high-speed targets. Taking some 20 seconds to track a target and then another 10–12 seconds to produce a fire control solution meant that it was unable to deal with American carrier aircraft.[29] Accordingly, Japanese doctrine was to use their 5-inch heavy batteries to conduct barrage fire instead of the much more effective aimed fire at specific targets.[30] These issues limited the use of the Type 89, as Japanese records of the rounds expended during air attacks indicate. In another attempt to increase the antiaircraft potential of heavy ships, the Japanese developed incendiary antiaircraft shells for their battleship main guns. These essentially turned the 14-, 16-, and 18.1-inch guns into huge shotguns. Though spectacular when employed, they were totally ineffective in service.

The inadequacies of Japanese air defense weapons and their fire control systems meant the Combined Fleet was vulnerable to air attack. The effort to increase the fleet's antiaircraft protection succeeded in producing an impressive volume of fire, but was ineffective at shooting down American aircraft in any significant numbers. The main defense against air attack was the inherent difficulty aircraft had in hitting a moving target at sea. A ship conducting adept evasive maneuvers and throwing up antiaircraft fire at approaching aircraft, even if it failed to hit the aircraft, increased the level of difficulty.

Logistical Support

The Combined Fleet operated under a severe lack of strategic mobility by October 1944. Toyoda stated after the war that lack of tankers in June 1944 was the greatest hindrance to his operational planning even before the Battle of the Philippine Sea. The lack of fuel and tankers reduced the Combined Fleet's striking range to 2,500nm by early 1944.[31]

As planning for *Sho-Go* proceeded, the fuel problem was even more of an issue. This was exacerbated by the Combined Fleet's reduced ability to conduct replenishment at sea. From May to September 1944, the IJN lost 18 tankers to air and submarine attack, making it difficult to bring fuel to the fleet. This problem forced the First Diversionary

Attack Force to move to Lingga Roads, since it was close to fuel sources on Borneo and Sumatra. The IJN also lifted the requirement that all fuel used in its ships had to be processed. This allowed light oil from Tarakan on Borneo to be burned in ship's boilers without refining. This short-term fix came at a cost – the unprocessed fuel had a heavy sulfur content that could damage boilers and was highly volatile.

Getting the First Diversionary Attack Force from Lingga to Leyte was not a simple problem. The distance involved required that the heavy ships refuel at least once and because fuel would be used at an alarming rate once battle was joined, destroyers would require two refuelings. Kurita was constantly concerned about his fuel status and this influenced his operational freedom. The lack of fleet oilers and trained crews precluded underway refueling, so any refueling had to be done on a protected bay.[32] To support Kurita's force, the Japanese assembled eight tankers. Several were sent to Brunei Bay in northwestern Borneo to top the fleet off before it departed for Leyte. Even with full bunkers, Kurita's force faced fuel challenges during the upcoming battle. In particular, the destroyers faced fuel issues that restricted their operational freedom. Steaming at 18 knots, a destroyer had a 5,000nm range. It was 1,400nm from Brunei to Leyte Gulf using the San Bernardino Strait. In addition, fuel expenditure would rise exponentially if the destroyers were forced to steam at high speed to avoid air attack or during a surface engagement. Given this, the First Diversionary Attack Force could only make it to Leyte and then directly back. The fuel state of Kurita's destroyers on October 26 demonstrated the perilous state of his logistics. Many were down to only a few tons of fuel and barely made it to Coron Bay in the Calamian Group where a tanker was waiting.

Overall, the Combined Fleet's fuel problem was insoluble. It was so short of fleet oilers capable of performing refueling at sea that only the Main Body was capable of receiving such support. Fuel supplies were continually tight, and even sending the heavy surface ships to Lingga posed problems, since the shortage of tankers made it difficult to get fuel from facilities in the NEI to the fleet. Kurita could not move his force until a sufficient number of tankers had been diverted from other duties. After its journey to Leyte, Kurita's fleet would require at least two months to accumulate enough fuel for a subsequent operation. For the Main Body operating out of Japan, where fuel supplies were critically low, there was insufficient fuel for another operation.[33] While the USN could maintain a huge invasion fleet on station for an extended period, the Combined Fleet possessed only enough fuel to act as a raiding force capable of sporadic operations.

Land-based Air Forces

A critical component of *Sho-Go* was the IJN's land-based air forces. With the Combined Fleet's carrier force reduced to impotence, the burden of striking American forces and providing cover for the First Diversionary Attack Force was left to the land-based air forces. *Sho-Go* included plans for two land-based air formations to participate in the defense of the Philippines. The First Air Fleet, redesignated the Fifth Base Air Force on August 1, was headquartered at Clark Field near Manila under the command of Vice Admiral Onishi. Though the Japanese made efforts to increase the strength of the Fifth Base Air Force before the battle, its strength kept fluctuating due to Halsey's efforts to reduce Japanese air strength in the Philippines before the landing on Leyte.

On September 1, the Fifth Base Air Force had some 410 aircraft available, of which about 250 were operational. After a brief increase in strength as aircraft returned to service, its operational strength fell to 190 aircraft on September 16 after Halsey rampaged through the southern and central Philippines. This was further reduced when Halsey's aviators struck Manila on September 21 and 22. Reinforcements increased the Fifth Base Air Force's overall strength to about 340 aircraft in early October. Of these, about 200 were operational, including 115 Zero fighters and 21 bombers, probably Judy dive-bombers and Jill torpedo bombers.[34] The continual losses and influx of new aircraft meant that the overall level of training was poor. It was in this condition that the Fifth Base Air Force began the Air Battle off Formosa. Following this encounter with TF 38, not more than about 100 aircraft were operational on October 20.[35] The Imperial Army had about 400 aircraft in the Philippines on October 10 under the command of the Fourth Air Army. These were not trained for overwater operations and played no part in the battle.

Much more important was the Sixth Base Air Force (formerly the Second Air Fleet) based in Kyushu, the Ryukyus, and Formosa under the command of Vice Admiral Fukudome Shigeru. In August, Fukudome moved his headquarters to Takao on Formosa and concentrated most of his aircraft on the island. In September, the force was ordered to readiness in expectation of executing its role in *Sho-Go* of attacking

TF 38. On October 10, just before Halsey appeared off Formosa, the Sixth Base Air Force possessed a seemingly impressive total of 737 aircraft including 233 fighters. Of these about 440 aircraft were operational. As will be detailed in a subsequent chapter, the Combined Fleet saw an opportunity to neutralize TF 38 on October 10 and ordered another 690 aircraft to reinforce Fukudome's command.[36]

After being mauled by TF 38 during the Battle off Formosa, the Sixth Base Air Force was still responsible for reinforcing the Philippines. Accordingly, Fukudome flew to Manila on October 22, followed by his remaining operational aircraft the next day. It is impossible to get a firm number for the total operational aircraft present in the Philippines on October 23 when *Sho-1* began in earnest, but the total operational strength of both the Fifth and Sixth Base Air Forces at the start of the battle was between 200 and 250 aircraft.[37]

4

Toyoda's Opening Gambit Fails and MacArthur Returns

During September, the Americans laid the foundation for the invasion of the Philippines the following month. TF 38 was the principal force responsible for softening Japanese defenses. According to plan, Halsey's aviators ravaged Japanese facilities in the southern and central Philippines in mid-September. On September 9, airfields on Mindanao were struck; TF 38 aviators claimed 68 aircraft destroyed on the ground and in the air. Three days later, airfields in the Visayan Islands were targeted and another 200 Japanese aircraft were claimed destroyed. Strikes continued the next day against Japanese air reinforcements that arrived in the Visayas. Another 135 aircraft were claimed destroyed on the ground and 81 more in the air. By September 14, no Japanese air opposition was reported, leading Halsey to make his assessment that Japanese air power had been neutralized. In total, the Americans believed that some 500 of the almost 900 Japanese aircraft in the Philippines had been destroyed.[1] Seeing the feeble Japanese response prompted Halsey to recommend that the landing on Mindanao be canceled in favor of a much earlier landing on Leyte. On September 15, MacArthur's forces landed a division on lightly-defended Morotai Island in the Moluccas. By October 4, air bases on the island were in operation. From Morotai, long-range aircraft (but not fighters) could strike targets in the southern and central Philippines. Despite Halsey's recommendation that the Palaus also be bypassed, Nimitz decided it was too late to cancel the invasion scheduled for September 15. The invasion ran into heavy Japanese defenses and it took until late

November to secure Peleliu Island. These two operations convinced the Japanese that the Philippines were the next American objective.

With the earlier invasion of Leyte approved and scheduled for October 20, the Americans intensified their air campaign to isolate the Philippines. Some of this work was done by bombers flying from Morotai, Biak Island, and other airfields in New Guinea against targets in the NEI and the Philippines. The bulk of the damage to the Japanese was again done by TF 38. Using a severe weather front and radio silence, TF 38 executed a high-speed run to a point only 70nm east of central Luzon on September 20. Having reached the launch point undetected, Halsey sent waves of aircraft to attack airfields in the Manila area and shipping in Manila Bay and along the western coast of Luzon. When TF 38 struck Manila on September 21, Japanese fighters mounted a strong defense but were brushed aside by the Hellcats. Another day of severe Japanese losses ensued with the Americans claiming 110 aircraft destroyed in the air and 95 more on the ground. This left only 350 Japanese aircraft in the Philippines, according to MacArthur's intelligence estimates. In addition, 27 Japanese merchant ships of all types and sizes were sunk in a single day, along with three destroyers. This was in addition to an estimated 105 merchants lost to all causes in the central and southern Philippines from September 1 to 15.[2] On September 24, TF 38 struck targets in the Visayas and at Coron Bay (a known Japanese anchorage) before departing for a brief respite at the new advanced fleet anchorage at Ulithi.

THE AIR BATTLE OFF FORMOSA

Though largely unknown, the largest air-sea battle in history up to that point was fought in the period immediately before the invasion of Leyte. It has been overshadowed by the Battle of Leyte Gulf that followed, but deserves recognition as an important event in its own right. The great air-sea battle off Formosa marked the true beginning of the Battle of Leyte Gulf. Its implications were immense. Once again, TF 38 demonstrated that it was largely immune to serious damage from Japanese land-based air power using conventional tactics, however large that air force was. After the failure of Japanese air power to inflict any serious losses on TF 38, it would not be an exaggeration to state that the outcome of the Battle of Leyte Gulf, fought only a week later, was already a foregone conclusion.

Half of TF 38 (TG 38.2 and TG 38.3) departed Ulithi Atoll on October 6. The following day, they rendezvoused with the rest of TF 38 some 375nm west of the Marianas. The entire fleet spent October 8 refueling in heavy weather. For the planned attack on Formosa, TF 38 had nine fleet and eight light carriers – much stronger than it would be for the actual Battle of Leyte Gulf. Halsey's intent was to weaken Japanese air power just before the invasion and cut off the flow of potential air reinforcements to the Philippines by attacking airfields in the Ryukyus and Formosa. Formosa played a key role in Japanese air operations, since its 30 airfields were within easy staging range of Luzon located just 200nm to the south. Halsey planned to follow up his attacks against the Ryukyus and Formosa with another round of attacks on airfields on Luzon and the Visayas. Nimitz hoped that the strikes planned on the inner Japanese defense zone would entice Toyoda to commit the Combined Fleet. If the opportunity was presented, TF 38 could destroy a big part of the Japanese fleet just before the Leyte invasion.[3] Whether or not the Combined Fleet made an appearance, the Americans expected a major engagement, since operating in Japan's inner defenses put TF 38 within range of aircraft from Luzon, Formosa, and the Ryukyus, and within easy reinforcement range of Japanese aircraft based on the Home Islands and eastern China.

The battle began on October 10 with TF 38 making attacks throughout the Ryukyus, including targets on Okinawa. A total of 1,396 sorties were flown throughout the day in the form of a fighter sweep followed by four major air strikes. The haul for such an intensive effort was not great – a handful of merchants and auxiliaries (the most important of which was submarine tender *Jingei*) were sunk and 111 aircraft claimed as destroyed. American losses were light at 21 aircraft.[4]

TOYODA'S RESPONSE

Japanese intelligence suggested that TF 38 was planning a major series of strikes in early October. Exact targets were unknown, but when the Americans began strike operations on October 10, all Japanese forces in the region were placed on alert. Despite this, Toyoda had inexplicably decided to leave his headquarters and make a morale-building tour of Japanese forces in the Philippines. After arriving in Manila on October 7, he planned to be back in Japan by October 10.

The first American attacks on the Ryukyus kept Toyoda from returning to his headquarters near Tokyo. They also confirmed his suspicion that a major American operation was imminent. With Toyoda stuck on Formosa, his aggressive chief of staff, Rear Admiral Kusaka Ryunosuke, issued a flurry of orders in Toyoda's name. At 0925 on October 10, he ordered the activation of the land-based air units earmarked for *Sho-1* and *Sho-2*. This order was in keeping with Toyoda's intent and was made after consultation with the Navy section at Imperial General Headquarters. Nevertheless, Toyoda's absence during these critical days was a contributing factor in what became a disjointed Japanese response.[5]

Given the level of American air operations against Japanese forces and facilities, Kusaka really had no choice but to activate the land-based air forces in the region. He and Fukudome were confident that by massing air power and fighting a battle close to Japan, they had an excellent chance of victory against TF 38.

Japanese air power in the region was considerable. Fukudome's Sixth Base Air Force had some 740 aircraft, of which approximately 440 were operational. Of these, 270 were based on Formosa, 245 on Kyushu, and only 40 remained in the Ryukyus. Also under his command was the T-Attack (Typhoon) Force with about 190 aircraft. This was a joint Army-Navy unit consisting of long-range twin-engine medium bombers. It had received extensive training for maritime attacks and was considered an elite unit. It was the only Japanese unit capable of night operations. Fukudome thought he could operate 230 fighters over Formosa at one time, which he believed gave him a numerical advantage over an attacking American force.

Given what he thought was a real opportunity to inflict serious losses on TF 38, Toyoda sent reinforcements to Fukudome. The most important of these were the best pilots and aircraft from Ozawa's carrier fleet. One hundred and seventy-two aircraft (97 of which were fighters) were sent to Formosa. This was the bulk of the 634th and 653rd Air Groups. The order to strip Carrier Divisions 3 and 4 of their aircraft was issued at 1019 on October 10 and caught Ozawa by surprise, but he dutifully sent orders to his air groups to move south on October 12.[6]

After additional aircraft were dispatched from the Home Islands and China, and with the addition of the 200 Imperial Army aircraft on Formosa that were placed under Fukudome's tactical control, the total number of aircraft available reached 1,425. This impressive force was in reality about 860 aircraft, given that only 60 percent were typically operational.[7]

Fukudome realized that his aviators were poorly trained in even basic skills and lacked training to attack in large formations. Nevertheless, he placed his hopes on mounting large-scale attacks with the maximum number of attack aircraft and the strongest possible escort to overwhelm American defenses. He placed extra importance on the T-Attack Force. It could operate at night or in bad weather, thus minimizing the possibility of being intercepted by Hellcats. Two squadrons of Army bombers were assigned to the T-Attack Force, but only one was fully qualified for night operations. Both Army and Navy pilots were very weak on ship recognition.[8]

Fukudome was given one more day to prepare his forces after Halsey spent October 11 attacking Aparri Airfield on northern Luzon. This small strike of 61 aircraft, all fighters, was conducted by TG 38.1 and 38.4. It encountered no air opposition; American aviators claimed 15 Japanese aircraft destroyed on the ground. TF 38 spent the rest of the day taking on 61 replacement aircraft from three escort carriers and moving into position to attack targets on Formosa beginning on the morning of October 12.[9]

On October 11, Japanese search aircraft detected TF 38. Fukudome knew that TF 38 would strike Formosa the following day. Given time to prepare, he positioned his 230 fighters in two groups over two key air bases and ordered all other aircraft to be dispersed. The T-Attack Force, along with other attack aircraft based on Kyushu, were ordered to attack TF 38, staging through the Ryukyus.[10]

The first day of the showdown between TF 38 and the Sixth Base Air Force did not go as Fukudome expected. TF 38 moved to a position only 50–90nm east of Formosa to launch a series of strikes on October 12. The first wave was a fighter sweep launched before dawn. Following the fighter sweep, four large air strikes were planned; between the strikes, two mid-morning fighter sweeps were inserted. Each of the task groups had an assigned area: TG 38.2 took northern Formosa; TG 38.3 was responsible for central Formosa; TG 38.1 was assigned targets in southern Formosa; and TG 38.4 attacked the Takao area (location of a major airfield, port, and Fukudome's headquarters).

The initial fighter sweep consisted of 203 Hellcats, including four photographic aircraft. Despite Fukudome's confidence that his fighters would put up a stout defense, the results shocked even him. Half of the Japanese fighters were assigned to defend Takao. As the air battle unfolded above him, Fukudome observed his fighters attacking the Americans. Soon, many burning aircraft, which Fukudome took as American, were observed falling to earth. This prompted him to exclaim, "Well done! Well done! A tremendous success!" Soon it became apparent that the fallen aircraft were Japanese and that the fighters remaining overhead were American. According to Fukudome, one-third of the Japanese fighters were lost in these initial encounters with the Hellcats. When the second American attack wave appeared, only 60–70 defending fighters were left to oppose them. By the third wave, no Japanese fighters rose in defense.[11]

The weight of the attack against Formosa was the heaviest that the Fast Carrier Task Force mounted up until this point in the war. After the fighter sweep, the first attack of 314 aircraft (115 Hellcats, 107 Helldivers, and 92 Avengers) roared in. Only a few of the Avengers carried torpedoes. The second attack consisted of 273 aircraft (98 Hellcats, 101 Helldivers, and 74 Avengers); the third of 283 aircraft (116 Hellcats, 90 Helldivers, and 77 Avengers); and the last wave totaled 275 aircraft (121 Hellcats, 92 Helldivers, and 62 Avengers). With the two smaller sweeps and some searches, the total sortie count from TF 38 was 1,378. It was simply an unprecedented display of naval air power.[12] This onslaught faced heavy opposition, both from Japanese fighters and antiaircraft fire. Losses were heavy during the day – 25 Hellcats, 14 Helldivers, and nine Avengers.

Expecting a Japanese riposte, Mitscher kept a strong CAP (Combat Air Patrol) over TF 38 throughout the day. Each task group was continually protected by 12–16 Hellcats. During the day, intercepting Hellcats claimed 15 Japanese aircraft. The main event was the T-Attack Force mounting dusk and night torpedo attacks. According to Japanese sources, 101 sorties were flown. Reports from the attacking aviators were optimistic, indicating that four carriers were sunk (this was reduced the next day to two carriers). TG 38.2, located to the north and the closest to Formosa, was the target of these night torpedo attacks. Altogether, TF 38 claimed 12 aircraft destroyed by antiaircraft during the night, nine by TG 38.2. The Japanese admitted to losing 42 aircraft.[13]

Halsey kept up the pressure on October 13 with 974 more sorties. Launching the new series of raids began at 0614 some 70nm east of Formosa. This time, the morning fighter sweep of 135 Hellcats was followed by three major air strikes with 287, 222, and 290 aircraft, respectively. Of course there was no surprise, but opposition was less than expected. Only 12 aircraft were lost. The CAP was busy all day, claiming 21 Japanese aircraft. Mitscher canceled the planned fourth strike in order to prepare for the possibility of strong Japanese air attacks at dusk.[14]

The Japanese did return to strike TF 38, and again featured the T-Attack Force making dusk attacks with 43 sorties. This was the best time to attack because the approaching aircraft, flying at low altitude to evade radar, were difficult to spot and because they could still use the last bit of light to silhouette their targets. Against TG 38.1, the torpedo aircraft successfully escaped radar detection and were not detected until they were spotted by lookouts on heavy cruiser *Wichita*. Eight B6N2 "Jill" aircraft made the attack; five were shot down by antiaircraft fire, but one gained a torpedo hit on heavy cruiser *Canberra* at 1835. Damage to both engine rooms brought her to a stop. Against TG 38.4, ten torpedo bombers threatened the task group for over 40 minutes. Six were shot down, but the aircraft penetrated the screen to launch torpedoes at carriers *Franklin* and *San Jacinto*. All missed, but at 1831, one of the G4M "Betty" bombers crashed on *Franklin*'s flight deck, doing only superficial damage. In total, the Japanese admitted to losing 20 aircraft that night. During the day, a major strike of 170 Imperial Navy and Army aircraft from the Philippines miscarried when it failed to find a target.[15]

Damage to *Canberra* was serious. The single torpedo hit left her without power and dead in the water. Halsey decided not to scuttle her, but to tow the cruiser clear of the area. This was a bold decision, since she lay only 90nm off Formosa. Halsey assessed he could save the cruiser and still carry out his assigned air attacks on Luzon and the Visayas on October 16–17. Supporting the crippled *Canberra* and the tow ship *Wichita* were three light cruisers and four destroyers. TG 38.1, TG 38.2, and TG 38.3 were ordered to conduct a third day of unscheduled strikes on Formosa. TG 38.4 was ordered to move south and attack airfields on Luzon.[16]

On October 14, most of TF 38 operated about 120nm east of Formosa to cover the withdrawal of *Canberra*. To reduce the effectiveness of potential air strikes against *Canberra* and her escort group, one large strike was conducted against airfields on Formosa. This consisted of 146 Hellcats and 100 Helldivers. Despite very little opposition being reported, losses from all causes were fairly heavy – 23 aircraft.

Meanwhile, TG 38.4 carried out its orders to strike airfields on northern Luzon. From a position about 120nm north of Aparri, 48 Hellcats were launched at two airfields. No air opposition was encountered, and only five aircraft were reported destroyed on the ground.[17]

The Japanese mounted their biggest effort against TF 38 on October 14, with over 400 sorties in several waves. From about 1500 and lasting until 2330, all three task groups east of Formosa were subjected to continual air attacks. A total of 360 daylight sorties were flown from Formosa. The first wave failed to find a target, and the third wave was recalled and failed to attack. The second wave ran into the CAP of TG 38.2 and TG 38.3. Since air attacks were expected, a heavy CAP was maintained throughout the day – 76 Japanese aircraft were claimed by the Hellcats. At 1523, carrier *Hancock* suffered minor damage from a near miss by a 550-pound bomb. The only bright spot for the Japanese was another twilight attack by the T-Attack Force by 52 aircraft against TG 38.1. Ten aircraft were claimed shot down, but four Jills broke through to attack light cruiser *Houston*. Three were shot down, but at 1841 the last succeeded in placing a torpedo in a vulnerable spot that flooded the engineering spaces and caused the loss of all power. The ship was almost abandoned but was eventually taken in tow. In addition to the losses extracted by CAP, TF 38 claimed another 21 aircraft destroyed by antiaircraft fire.

Now Halsey had another decision to make. He was scheduled to make strikes on Japanese airfields on Luzon and on the Visayas on October 16 and 17 in final preparation for the Leyte landings on October 20. The crippled *Houston* was sitting just 150nm from Formosa and potential salvage operations threatened TF 38's ability to meet its more important mission. Halsey decided to continue efforts to salvage both *Canberra* and *Houston* and gave TG 38.1 the mission of protecting them. The rest of TF 38 could continue to pound the Philippines.

All this changed on the morning of October 15 when Nimitz provided Halsey information on Japanese intentions. According to intelligence, the Japanese believed that TF 38 was withdrawing after being seriously damaged. Further air attacks were expected and the Second Diversionary Attack Force had been ordered to complete the annihilation of Halsey's force.[18] In Halsey's mind, this was an opportunity to destroy a segment of the Combined Fleet. In keeping with his orders that if an opportunity arose to destroy the Japanese fleet this became his primary mission. Halsey prepared for a fleet action and informed Nimitz and MacArthur that no further strikes on Philippine airfields would be conducted other than those already planned.

To entice the Japanese into believing that the Third Fleet had in fact been routed, Halsey developed a plan with the crippled cruisers and their escorts (designated TG 30.3) posing as the remnants of TF 38. The four carrier task groups were deployed to the east out of the range of most Japanese aircraft based on Luzon and Formosa. The decoy group began to transmit urgent dummy radio messages to suggest their desperate condition. By the afternoon of October 15, TG 30.3 had grown to the two crippled cruisers, escorted by light carriers *Cabot*, *Cowpens*, one heavy cruiser, three light cruisers, and 13 destroyers.

Exaggerated reports of success from his aviators led Toyoda to order further attacks. Almost 200 sorties were flown on October 15 from bases on Luzon, Formosa, and Okinawa. The strikes from Luzon consisted of some 90 aircraft targeted against TG 38.4. From 1022 to 1047, TG 38.4 came under heavy air attack. *Franklin* was hit by a bomb on her deck edge elevator that did little damage; 19 Japanese aircraft were claimed as destroyed. Two raids in the afternoon were broken up by Hellcats and never reached the task group.[19] TG 38.1 was attacked by approximately 80 aircraft. The CAP destroyed 52 and antiaircraft fire one more. Only three Hellcats were lost.[20] TG 38.2 and 38.3 were undetected during the day and were not subjected to any attack. TF 38 also managed to execute some offensive actions. TG 38.4 was able to carry out its mission to conduct strikes on targets in the Manila area. Starting just before 0900, two attacks were launched consisting of 72 and 45 aircraft respectively. An estimated 50–60 Japanese fighters rose to challenge the attackers; the Hellcats claimed 44 Japanese aircraft.

On the afternoon of October 16, the Japanese directed their attacks on TG 30.3. Hellcats from light carriers *Cabot* and *Cowpens* did great execution against a Japanese formation of over 100 aircraft. However, three Jills penetrated the screen and put another torpedo into *Houston* at 1348. The ship had some 6,300 tons of water on board, but the cruiser's crew refused to let her sink. These were the last Japanese attacks before the two crippled cruisers finally pulled out of air range.

As indicated by American intelligence, Toyoda did send the Second Diversionary Attack Force to mop up the remnants of TF 38. During the afternoon of October 16, Shima's force was approaching the location where the Japanese believed what was left of TF 38 was operating. At 1430 a search aircraft from *Bunker Hill* reported Shima's force about 200nm north of TG 30.3. The report was badly garbled by communications relay aircraft. Instead of reflecting Shima's weak force built around two heavy cruisers, the information received indicated that the Japanese force included three carriers.[21] The delay required to clarify the report cost TF 38 the chance to launch a strike before it was too late in the day. After being spotted, Shima changed course to the north. The Second Diversionary Attack Force had lived to fight another day.

The all-out effort by Japanese land-based air forces between October 12 and 16 to crush the Third Fleet was the biggest air-sea battle of the war to date. For the Japanese, the effort was a total failure. Damage to two cruisers did not even come close to neutralizing TF 38 and the invasion of Leyte remained on schedule. Fukudome had been unable to mass his air power. Japanese attacks were conducted piecemeal against the numerically superior CAP protecting TF 38. Radar-directed Hellcats had made quick work of the formations of poorly-trained Japanese aviators. During the battle, TF 38 claimed it destroyed 278 aircraft on the water or ground and 377 in the air. Aerial losses were broken down as 216 over Formosa, 112 near TF 38, 46 by antiaircraft fire, and three by TF 38 search aircraft. In addition, 18 merchants of all sizes, one medium transport, and six submarine chasers were claimed sunk, with many other ships recorded as probably sunk or damaged. These claims were excessive; a review of Japanese records indicated only seven small merchant ships and two patrol craft had been sunk. Damage to airfields and other installations was also extensive.[22]

Japanese efforts against TF 38 included a total of 761 offensive sorties. Of these, 321 aircraft were lost, according to Japanese sources. The Japanese admitted to the loss of 492 total aircraft, which was not too far from TF 38's claims of 655. Almost all of these were Imperial Navy aircraft, with the Imperial Army losing half of its 200 aircraft on Formosa. In return, USN losses were 76 aircraft in combat and 13 due to operational causes. In exchange for their heavy losses, the Japanese claimed a great victory with 11 American carriers sunk and many other ships sunk or damaged. In reality, only the two cruisers were damaged. Such a massive exaggeration was explained by the fact that the attacks took place at night by poorly-trained aviators with negligible ship recognition skills. Japanese commanders recognized at once that the claims were inflated, but even Fukudome thought that his T-Attack Force units had sunk at least a third of what they had claimed.[23] Japanese air reconnaissance on October 16 revealed that TF 38 had survived intact, so Japanese commanders realized that the invasion of the Philippines could be expected any day.

MACARTHUR RETURNS

In the immediate period before the landing on Leyte, the Allies made only a cursory effort to deceive the Japanese regarding the location of the next Allied target. An American cruiser force shelled Marcus Island on October 9 in the hopes that it might convince the Japanese that the Bonin Islands were a landing target. The Royal Navy's Eastern Fleet conducted a large raid on the Nicobar Islands in the Indian Ocean between October 17 and 21 to make the Japanese consider a threat to their western flank. Both diversions failed to make an impression on the Japanese.[24]

As the landings approached, Halsey held the bulk of TF 38 northeast of Luzon through October 19 to provide escort for the two crippled cruisers. TGs 38.1 and 38.4 fueled on October 21 and then were ordered to head to Ulithi the following day. As it became apparent the Japanese were mounting an operation to oppose the landing, Halsey ordered TG 38.4 to turn back toward Leyte on October 23, but TG 38.1 continued until being recalled on the 24th.

The first echelon of the invasion force departed Manus in the Admiralties and Hollandia on New Guinea in order to be in the approaches to Leyte Gulf on October 17. There are two entrances into Leyte Gulf from the east. These are bracketed by Samar Island to the north and Dinagat Island to the south, with the small islands of Suluan and Homonhon in the center. The first indication that the Japanese had of the upcoming storm was when their garrison on tiny Suluan spotted the American minesweeping force beginning its work to clear the channel to the island at 0650 on October 17. By 0820, men of the 6th Ranger Battalion stepped ashore on Suluan, making them the first Americans to return to the Philippines. A landing on undefended Dinagat followed later in the morning.

After securing the approaches of Leyte Gulf, clearing them of mines could begin on October 18. A small number of moored and floating mines were encountered, but a preparatory bombardment of the southern invasion beaches went ahead in the afternoon. In the very early hours of October 19, destroyer *Ross* struck two mines in quick succession south of Homonhon Island. The ship was towed to safety and survived. Later in the morning, the attack groups for both the southern and northern beaches began a heavy bombardment of suspected Japanese defenses.

At 1000 on October 20, the invasion of Leyte began to unfold. At two different locations, a corps of two divisions landed against sporadic opposition. The northern landing took place near the city of Tacloban under the command of Rear Admiral Daniel Barbey. Gunfire support was provided by battleships *Maryland*, *Mississippi*, and *West Virginia*, four cruisers, and ten destroyers. Aircraft from Rear Admiral Sprague's escort carriers joined the attack at 1000 as the landing craft made their final runs to the beaches. Japanese opposition was weak, with only some 50 American casualties recorded on the northern beaches. Overall, the landing went off better than could be expected and by midafternoon the rapid unloading of men and supplies was under way. The beach was safe enough for MacArthur to temporarily go ashore from light cruiser *Nashville* during the afternoon.

Barbey and his commanders were veterans of many previous landings. Seventh Fleet doctrine called for assault ships to be loaded with only enough supplies so that everything could be unloaded by the end of the day, allowing the ships to depart and avoid any Japanese counterattack. In accordance with this doctrine, all of Barbey's assault ships completed unloading at 1735 and were prepared to depart at 1800.[25]

The southern attack force was under the command of Vice Admiral Theodore Wilkinson, another expert in amphibious warfare. Opposition on the southern beaches was also sporadic and by noon most of the assault force was ashore. The only unplanned event was when a single Japanese torpedo bomber gained complete surprise and placed a torpedo in light cruiser *Honolulu* at 1602. The torpedo brought the ship to a stop and temporarily created a 13-degree list, but the Pearl Harbor survivor was saved by efficient damage measures. Sixty men were killed, however, and a valuable ship was out of the fight.

The assault ships on the southern beaches were more heavily loaded than those in the north. Wilkinson's command was from the Pacific Fleet, where the doctrine of unloading by the end of the first day was not seen as necessary. The lack of intensive Japanese air attacks from October 20 to 23 meant that unloading was completed on schedule. Overall, the landings on Leyte had been a great success, and the operation transformed as planned into a ground campaign.

The build-up phase was also successful and was largely unmolested by Japanese air attacks. However, around dawn on October 21, a Japanese aircraft crashed into the foremast of Australian heavy cruiser *Australia*. The captain and 19 other men were killed, and another valuable ship was forced to leave the battle for repairs. On October 24, the scale of Japanese air attacks increased. The escort carriers were fully occupied flying CAP over the invasion area. Of the estimated 150–200 Japanese aircraft active near the beachhead, the escort carriers claimed 66 and prevented all but a few from making an attack. Tacloban Airfield had been captured on the first day of the invasion and engineers worked furiously to make the airfield operational. This was no easy task, since the airfield sat on a very shallow water table. By October 25, the airfield was suitable as an emergency airfield for the escort carriers, though a quarter of the landings proved fatal for aircraft attempting them. Dulag Airfield to the south was also available as a divert strip for carrier aircraft, but its soft condition made aircraft operations perilous.

It is important to trace the movements of American assault shipping during October 20–25. On the northern beaches, the assault ships were quickly unloaded and departed by evening on October 20. The first reinforcement echelon arrived on October 22 and finished unloading that same afternoon. Reinforcement Group 2 arrived on October 24. This was a large force of 33 LSTs, 24 Liberty ships, and ten support ships escorted by four destroyers and two frigates. Of these, most were still present on October 25 and were ordered to wait inside the gulf until the battles that day were concluded.

In total, 80,900 men and 114,990 tons of supplies were ashore before October 25. Between October 20 and 24, 37 assault ships and 80 LSTs had unloaded and departed.[26]

On the southern beaches, the unloading had not gone as quickly due to the heavy loading of the assault ships and the lack of personnel to unload supplies ashore. Eighteen ships had unloaded and left the gulf by October 21, 11 more the next day, seven more on October 23, and eight on October 24. In addition, 38 LSTs and 37 smaller craft had departed. Some 51,500 men and 85,000 tons of supplies had been moved ashore through the southern beaches. The fact that 132,400 men and just under 200,000 tons of supplies were already safely ashore at Leyte made it impossible for *Sho-1* to achieve its objective of thwarting the American landing.

The Japanese had observed American amphibious operations for over two years and knew that American amphibious doctrine stressed the rapid unloading and departure of amphibious shipping. It is utterly unbelievable that Toyoda would endorse a plan in which his principal attack against the invasion force would not take place until five days after the landing. At midnight on October 24, American shipping inside Leyte Gulf consisted of three amphibious flagships, one assault transport, 23 LSTs, two medium landing ships, and 28 Liberty ships, most of which were empty.

SHO-1 IS ACTIVATED

For the Japanese, the warning provided by the small garrison on Suluan Island at 0650 on October 17 confirmed their assessment that the Philippines were under direct threat. At 0809, Toyoda issued the alert order for all units with a role in *Sho-1*. However, Toyoda had to be absolutely sure that the Allied operations east of Leyte were the main attack before activating the *Sho* plan.

The next morning at 1110, Toyoda decided the situation was clear enough that he could issue the execute order. This put in motion the widely scattered forces tasked to repel the American invasion. After some confusion, October 25 was selected as the climactic day when Kurita's and Shima's surface forces would crash into Leyte Gulf and annihilate the American invasion fleet. Four submarines of the Sixth Fleet departed Japan after receiving the alert order and seven more would soon follow. At 0100 on October 18, the First Diversionary Attack Force departed Lingga and headed to Brunei for refueling. This majestic sight of the bulk of the Imperial Navy's remaining heavy warships steaming together must have given all who witnessed it full confidence in victory. Cruiser Division 16 – heavy cruiser *Aoba*, light cruiser *Kinu*, and destroyer *Uranami* – was ordered to detach from Kurita's command and head to Manila. The Shima force was already under way, with its exact mission still under debate. Vice Admiral Fukudome prepared to move what was left of his command from Formosa down to the Philippines to have another crack at TF 38 in support of Kurita's main attack. Finally in Japan, Ozawa regrouped his Mobile Force, Main Body and prepared to depart on its sacrificial mission. Toyoda had cast the dice on the Imperial Navy's last attempt to engage the United States Navy in a decisive battle. The largest battle in naval history was ready to begin.

5

The Adventures of the First Diversionary Attack Force

The First Diversionary Attack Force departed Lingga at 0100 hours on October 18 and headed to Brunei Bay on the north coast of Borneo. Kurita's force arrived without incident at Brunei on the morning of October 20. Because the two tankers dispatched to refuel the force had not arrived, Kurita ordered the heavy cruisers to refuel the destroyers and then for the battleships to refuel the cruisers. Eventually, tankers *Hakko Maru* and *Yuho Maru* showed up to refuel the larger ships. The entire process of refueling took until 0500 on October 22.[1]

While this was occurring, Kurita received his final orders from Toyoda and the advance routes for the First Diversionary Attack Force were decided. With this done, Kurita called a conference for his senior officers and ship captains on his flagship *Atago* between 1700 and 2000 on October 21. When Kurita outlined the final plan, there was disbelief and dissent from the officers present. Nothing about the role of the First Diversionary Attack Force made sense to many of Kurita's officers. Tactically, the orders for the force to attack into Leyte Gulf in the morning hours of October 25 seemed foolish given the Combined Fleet's prowess in night combat and the fact that they had just spent the last weeks training for a night attack. The strategy of sending the Kurita force to attack days after the landing also seemed dubious, since the invasion force would be long gone. If the fleet was to fight a decisive battle, it needed to be directed at the enemy's main fleet. Others were offended that the commander of the Combined Fleet did not see fit to lead the cream of the fleet personally into this decisive battle. In response to those who believed they were embarking on an operation without hope, Kurita made an eloquent plea:

> I know that many of you are strongly opposed to this assignment. But the war situation is far more critical than any of you can possibly know. Would it not be a shame to have the fleet remain intact while our nation perishes? I believe that Imperial General Headquarters is giving us a glorious opportunity. Because I realize how very serious the war situation actually is, I am willing to accept even this ultimate assignment to storm into Leyte Gulf.
>
> You must all remember that there are such things as miracles. What man can say that there is no chance for our fleet to turn the tide of war in a decisive battle? We shall have a chance to meet our enemies. We shall engage his task forces. I hope you will not carry your responsibilities lightly. I know you will act faithfully and well.

After this emotional appeal to lay down their lives for a bad plan with faint hopes of success, the "assembled officers leaped to their feet, inspired by the Admiral's determination, [and] filled the room with resounding shouts of 'Banzai!'"[2]

Whatever their doubts, the crews and ships of the First Diversionary Attack Force departed Brunei at 0800 hours on October 22 and made a course toward the Palawan Passage. Nishimura's Third Section watched as Kurita's force departed and then steamed out of Brunei Bay at 1500 hours, making a course for the Balabac Strait.

AMBUSH AT THE PALAWAN PASSAGE

Before sailing, Kurita sent almost all his cruiser and battleship floatplanes (some 45 in total) to San Jose Airfield on Mindoro. His reasoning was that once they were launched it would be impossible to stop and recover them as the formation was under the threat of submarine and air attack. This removed these valuable aircraft from Kurita's effective control. Their absence reduced his ability to perform antisubmarine screening, reconnaissance of nearby American forces, and even to perform spotting for gunnery in a major engagement.

The absence of Kurita's floatplanes was soon felt. Combined with a number of other shortcomings, it set the stage for the first disaster to befall the First Diversionary Attack Force during the battle. As has already been discussed, after careful analysis Kurita decided to take the most direct route to the Sibuyan Sea, which was along the west coast of Palawan through the Palawan Passage. This was a curious choice, since it was an area where American submarines were known to operate. Even more difficult to explain was that Kurita made no special preparations for submarine defense as he approached the passage. Kurita divided his force into two sections. The lead section consisted of the three most powerful battleships and six heavy cruisers, escorted by the destroyers of Destroyer Squadron 2. The second section was about four miles behind with the two Kongo-class battleships and four heavy cruisers, escorted by the destroyers of Destroyer Squadron 10. The heavy ships of both sections were arranged in two columns. Flagship *Atago* was the lead ship of the left column of the First Section. During the afternoon of October 22, there were three reports of submarines, all false alarms. That night, Kurita reduced his speed to 16 knots and ceased zigzagging. At daybreak on October 23, the formation's speed was increased to 18 knots and zigzagging resumed.

Aside from the lack of aircraft flying antisubmarine patrols as daylight developed, the First Diversionary Attack Force lacked adequate destroyers to properly screen a force of 17 heavy warships. The 15 destroyers that were available were inadequate for the job and Kurita compounded this by not correctly deploying the destroyers he did possess. No destroyers were deployed at the front of the formation nor were any positioned in advance of the formation as an antisubmarine picket to clear the way through waters known to be submarine infested. Even worse for the Japanese was the inferior quality of their radar. Though all of Kurita's ships carried some sort of radar, none detected the American submarines in the area even though they were on the surface near the First Diversionary Attack Force for a prolonged period. In contrast, the radars on American submarines were excellent, allowing submarine commanders to detect targets and then maneuver into the best firing position.

It should have been obvious to Kurita that it was almost certain that American submarines would be positioned in the southern entrance of the Palawan Passage. In fact, two submarines were waiting there, *Darter* and *Dace*. Both were under the tactical control of *Darter's* skipper, Commander David H. McClintock. Commander Bladen D. Claggett commanded *Dace*. At 0116 on October 23, *Darter's* radar picked up the approaching Japanese 15nm distant. As was the practice for USN submarines in 1944, they aggressively moved on the surface (in this case at over 20 knots) to close the contact. The two submarines raced up the 30nm wide Palawan Passage to get ahead of the Japanese. They soon gained visual contact on Kurita's armada and sent the first of three contact reports. These were passed to Halsey and Kinkaid with a final estimate that the large task force contained 11 heavy ships and six destroyers.

Darter's contact reports were picked up by Japanese radio intelligence personnel in the First Diversionary Attack Force, prompting Kurita to order his ships to be extra vigilant for submarines. He still failed to send any destroyers to clear the route for his force. *Darter* and *Dace*, still moving on the surface, outpaced Kurita's formation and at 0525 reached a position in front of the Japanese. Both submarines submerged at 0609 and gained perfect attack positions – *Darter* to attack the port column of heavy ships led by *Atago*, while *Dace* lay in wait to strike the starboard column. At 0632, as dawn broke and the Japanese formation began to zigzag, McClintock fired his six bow tubes from a range of 980 yards. After maneuvering his boat 180 degrees, McClintock fired his four stern tubes just as the first of the bow torpedoes found their mark.[3]

The first torpedoes struck *Atago* at 0633, just as Kurita was having morning tea with his chief of staff. Four torpedoes hit the cruiser, dooming her instantly. Nineteen officers and 341 sailors went down with the ship. Kurita and his staff were thrown into the water and had to swim for their lives. Two destroyers saved 710 crewmembers, among them the principal members of Kurita's staff. Kurita himself was picked up by destroyer *Kishinami*. Of note, half of the fleet communications personnel were lost when the destroyer that picked them up went to Brunei. Their loss was made up by using communications personnel from *Yamato*, which Kurita and his staff was finally able to board at 1540 after a series of false submarine alarms.[4]

Darter's second salvo hit heavy cruiser *Takao* at 0634. Steaming in column behind *Atago*, two torpedoes hit the ship. These inflicted massive damage – the rudder and one screw were destroyed, and three boiler rooms were flooded. Thirty-two crewmen were killed and 30 wounded. Although an emergency rudder was rigged, the crippled cruiser could only make six knots and was largely unsteerable. *Takao* was ordered to return to Brunei under the escort of destroyers *Asashimo* and *Naganami*. *Takao* was not only out of the battle, but after she finally reached Singapore on November 12, she was deemed unrepairable.[5]

On *Dace*, Claggett observed *Darter's* devastating attack. Claggett identified a Kongo-class battleship for attack and began his approach. Six torpedoes were fired from a range of 1,800 yards toward the target, which was actually heavy cruiser *Maya*. At 0557, the cruiser took four hits on her port side and sank in a mere eight minutes, taking with her 16 officers and 320 men; 769 men were saved.[6]

Both submarines went deep and survived ineffective counterattacks from Japanese destroyers. *Darter* attempted to finish off *Takao* but was unable to get close enough for another attack. As *Darter* stalked *Takao* that night, she was running at 17 knots on the surface when she went hard aground on Bombay Shoal. After an attempt by *Dace* to tow her off failed, it was decided to abandon *Darter*. This took two hours, after which *Dace* tried unsuccessfully to destroy the helpless *Darter* with four torpedoes and 30 rounds of 5-inch shellfire.

This brilliant attack by *Darter* and *Dace* not only reduced Kurita's force by three powerful cruisers, but it removed two destroyers when Kurita dispatched them to escort the crippled *Takao* back to Brunei. Given that Kurita's force was on a mission vital to the survival of the Japanese Empire, it seemed unnecessary to lose two destroyers to escort a crippled ship back to base. Perhaps more importantly, the Americans knew a major Japanese naval operation was under way.

HALSEY STUMBLES

At 0620 on October 23, Halsey received the first sighting report from *Darter*. Now he had no doubt the Japanese were mounting a major operation to oppose the invasion. Halsey has been bitterly attacked for his actions during the battle. This criticism centers on his actions on the night of October 24–25 when he decided to take the Third Fleet north, leaving San Bernardino Strait unguarded, to attack Ozawa's toothless carriers. As debatable as this action still remains, what is not debatable is how poorly Halsey handled his force between October 21 and 24. On October 22, after the landings had been successfully accomplished, Halsey detached TG 38.1 and TG 38.4 to Ulithi for rest and replenishment. After receiving the initial reports of a major Japanese reaction on October 23, Halsey recalled TG 38.4. He failed to recall TG 38.1 until the following day. TG 38.1 was the largest of TF 38's four task forces, with three fleet carriers and two light carriers. This powerful force was 625nm to the east of Samar when Halsey finally called them back. This tardy response meant these five carriers contributed very little to the American effort on October 24.[7] With the detachment of *Bunker Hill* on October 23 to Ulithi, this meant that TF 38 fought for most of October 24 with only 11 of the 17 carriers it had when it pummeled Formosa.

On the morning of October 24, as the first full day of the Battle of Leyte Gulf began, Halsey's forces were spread out to the east of the Philippines. TG 38.3 with fleet carriers *Essex* and *Lexington*, and light carriers *Princeton* and *Langley* under Rear Admiral Sherman, was positioned east of Luzon to cover the movement of any Japanese forces from the north. TG 38.2, under Rear Admiral Bogan, having just detached *Bunker Hill*, was now the weakest of TF 38's task groups with only fleet carrier *Intrepid* and light carrier *Cabot*. Light carrier *Independence* was also assigned to Bogan's task group, but her air group was specially trained for night operations so did not fly day sorties. Bogan's task group was assigned to cover San Bernardino Strait. TG 38.4, commanded by Rear Admiral Davison, was deployed to the south watching Surigao Strait. His force consisted of fleet carriers *Franklin* and *Enterprise*, and light carriers *Belleau Wood* and *San Jacinto*.

This deployment had the effect of leaving the weakest carrier group, TG 38.2, with the main burden of combating the strongest Japanese force, the First Diversionary Attack Force, as it entered the Sibuyan Sea headed for San Bernardino Strait. TG 38.3 in the north came under heavy Japanese air strikes during the morning, forcing Sherman to suspend offensive operations to concentrate on CAP. It lost a light carrier during the course of these attacks and was not able to attack Kurita's force until the afternoon. In the south, TG 38.4 spent the morning attacking Nishimura's secondary force; again, it was not until the afternoon that any strikes were flown against the primary Japanese force. The net effect of this dispersed effort was dramatic. Whereas when TF 38 was massed it flew almost 1,400 sorties against Formosa on October 12, on October 24 it was only able to mount just over 250 sorties against the First Diversionary Attack Force. This failure by Halsey to bring his full offensive power to bear allowed Kurita to penetrate into the Philippine Sea and set up the Battle off Samar.

Halsey's detachment of two carrier task groups on October 21 before he had solid intelligence on whether the Japanese were going to mount a major naval effort to disrupt the landing and from what direction that effort would come from was a major error.[8] It is true that his aviators had been in action for a prolonged period and that periodic rest was a vital concern, but the schedule Halsey imposed for these moves was extremely ill-timed. It also speaks of the failure of American intelligence that it did not provide Halsey with an accurate assessment of Japanese intentions.

JAPANESE AIR ATTACKS AGAINST TF 38

Air activity by both sides was very heavy on October 24. Japanese air operations against TF 38 will be covered first. On October 23, Fukudome moved his operational aircraft from Formosa to the Philippines. Upon arriving in the Philippines, Fukudome conferred with Onishi about the next day's operations. It was decided that only a token effort would be made to provide direct support to Kurita (a total of ten fighters were seen by the American aviators over Kurita's force during the day). Instead, all available aircraft would be sent to attack TF 38 to provide indirect support to Kurita. It was crucial that the American carriers be neutralized, since Kurita's and Ozawa's forces would come within range of TF 38 on October 24.

Bad weather restricted Japanese search operations on October 23, but during the night of October 23–24 Japanese aircraft were in constant contact with an American carrier group east of Luzon. This was TG 38.3 with its four carriers, which was the closest American task group to the airfields on Luzon. Accordingly, all Japanese attacks on October 24 were directed against TG 38.3. The main attack force of the Fifth and Sixth Base Air Forces mustered 199 operational aircraft at Clark Field – 126 fighters, 63 strike aircraft, and ten Judy dive-bombers.[9] This was inadequate to mount the massive effort necessary to neutralize TF 38. Hoping for the best, Fukudome and Onishi launched an all-out strike in three attack waves.[10]

At 0600 radar aboard the ships of TG 38.3 held contact on five Japanese aircraft in the area. TG 38.3 had been shadowed most of the night and Sherman knew that his group would come under attack in the morning. The weather in the area of his task group was marked with rain squalls interspersed with clear weather. Ceiling was limited, with broken clouds at 2,000 feet. American ships could use the squalls to hide from air attack during the day, but the clouds could also hide approaching aircraft.

TG 38.3 had sent out a number of search groups in the morning; each group had four Hellcats and four Avengers. In addition, Sherman had been ordered to send 20 Hellcats to conduct a fighter sweep against airfields in the Manila area. This was a significant drain on his resources. After TG 38.2's morning search reported Kurita's force in the Sibuyan Sea, Sherman was preparing to launch a large strike at this lucrative target. This plan was set aside when radars detected a large group of Japanese aircraft approaching the task force from Luzon. Within minutes, two more groups were detected behind the first, with the third group larger than the first two. Sherman was forced to cancel the strike and use the Hellcats assigned to provide strike escort to reinforce the CAP. All available Hellcats were scrambled to engage the incoming threat. Eventually, the 12 Hellcats on CAP from the light carriers were joined by 53 more Hellcats.[11]

The Japanese attack began just after 0830 and lasted for about an hour. The first American fighters to intercept the approaching Japanese were the eight Hellcats from *Princeton* as part of the original CAP. These were joined by seven Hellcats from *Essex* which were scrambled and made contact only about 30nm from the carriers. The *Essex* aircraft were led by Commander David McCampbell, *Essex*'s air group commander. McCampbell methodically proceeded to shoot down nine Japanese aircraft, for which he was awarded the Congressional Medal of Honor. His wingman claimed six more. The ill-trained Japanese were virtually helpless against McCampbell and the other Hellcat pilots.

Once under attack, the Japanese aircraft scattered and the fighters went into a defensive circle instead of trying to protect the dive-bombers and torpedo aircraft. By 0845, the second Japanese attack group had been broken up. Altogether, aviators from *Essex* were credited with 24 downed enemy aircraft and fighters from *Lexington* 13; only one Hellcat was lost in return. The light carriers also scored heavily, with *Princeton*'s air group issuing claims for 34 aircraft and *Langley*'s fighters claiming five.[12] It was an air battle reminiscent of the "Marianas Turkey Shoot" of the previous June. The Japanese admitted the loss of 67 aircraft, which is remarkably close to the total number of claims submitted by the Hellcats. No Japanese aircraft got through to the carriers, and no attacks were reported as Sherman kept his ships hidden by squalls.

Despite the Hellcats' success against the hapless Japanese aviators, fleet air defense could never be airtight. At the conclusion of the aerial melee, radar indicated no Japanese aircraft in the area. This allowed Sherman to bring his force out of a rain squall and commence recovering the CAP aircraft. At 0938, as the recovery was winding down, one Judy dive-bomber using cloud cover made a skillful attack against light carrier *Princeton*. Despite being engaged by antiaircraft fire, the dive-bomber's pilot placed his 551-pound bomb in the middle of the flight deck some 75 feet forward of the aft elevator. The bomb penetrated several decks to the ship's bakery and exploded. The resulting blast reached the hangar deck, where six fully armed and fully fueled Avengers were soon engulfed in flames. When these aircraft inevitably exploded, the blasts were so powerful that both of the ship's elevators were thrown into the air. Water pressure was knocked out, making fire-fighting difficult and allowing the flames to spread from the carrier's island to its stern. Another large explosion at 1010 prompted an order that all non-essential personnel abandon ship; ten minutes later, all but fire-fighting personnel were ordered to leave.[13]

As more explosions racked *Princeton*, escort ships were ordered to aid in fighting the fires. This was made difficult by the inability of the smaller ships to keep station along the carrier, now dead in the water, and by smoke and intense heat from the fires. At about 1055, light cruiser *Birmingham* came alongside and 38 of her crew went over to the carrier to assist in fighting the fires. With progress being made, Sherman decided to tow the carrier to Ulithi. However, a persistent fire near the stern resisted efforts to extinguish it, and it gained strength when *Birmingham* was forced to cast off at 1212 when a Japanese submarine contact was reported. At 1330, reports of Japanese aircraft in the area further delayed salvage operations. The cruiser came back at 1445 to resume the fight, but by this time the fire near the stern had gained more strength. *Birmingham* was closing to rig a tow line when at 1523 the fires reached the torpedo magazine aft. The resulting huge explosion shattered *Princeton*'s stern and destroyed her after flight deck.[14] Positioned alongside, *Birmingham* suffered massive devastation topsides. Personnel losses were extremely heavy – 229 crewmen killed and 420 wounded (219 seriously).[15] Damage to *Birmingham* and the loss of over half her crew forced the cruiser to go to Ulithi for repairs.

Princeton's fate was sealed by the latest explosion. Since no other ship in the task group was able to rig a tow line and the fires on the carrier raged unchecked, it was decided to abandon the carrier at 1600. Sherman was forced to give the order to scuttle the ship after he was instructed by

Mitscher that TF 38 was headed north. Efforts by a destroyer to scuttle her with torpedoes failed, so light cruiser *Reno* fired two more torpedoes at the burning hulk at 1746. The first hit the carrier's forward aviation fuel storage tanks and created a huge explosion; in under a minute, *Princeton* was gone. Total losses were light in view of the punishment inflicted on the carrier – seven killed, 101 missing, and 190 wounded. *Princeton* was the first carrier lost by the Fast Carrier Task Force and the first fast carrier lost since October 1942. She was also the last fast carrier sunk in the war.

The ordeal of TG 38.3 was not over. After the morning attack, Sherman launched his first raid against Kurita's force just before 1100. At 1245 a new group of Japanese aircraft was detected to the northeast. Based on their direction of approach, these could only be from Japanese carriers.

In fact, this was the Imperial Navy's last carrier strike of the war. Ozawa planned to use his meager striking power to assist in the effort to neutralize TF 38 on October 24. Ozawa's morning search failed to detect any part of TF 38, but multiple contacts were reported by Japanese land-based aircraft on a USN carrier task force east of Luzon. Ozawa knew he had only enough aircraft for a single strike and that once he launched his strike aircraft they were too poorly trained to land back on board their carriers. Knowing from experience the unreliability of contact reports, Ozawa declined to launch his strike until he could confirm the enemy's location with one of his own search aircraft. This crucial information was received at 1115 with a report of an American carrier task group only 180nm to the southwest of the Main Body.[16] It was incredible that at this point in the war a Japanese carrier force could steam to within 180nm of one of TF 38's task groups without being detected. Ozawa's aviators had located TG 38.3, which was focused on searching to the west and defending against air attacks and was simply unable to cover its northern flank.

Ozawa did not have the capability to make Sherman pay for his carelessness, but he launched an all-out strike at 1145 consisting of 62 aircraft. *Zuikaku* contributed the most with ten Zero fighters, 11 Zero fighter-bombers, six torpedo bombers, and two reconnaissance aircraft.[17] From the three light carriers came 20 Zero fighters and nine Zero fighter-bombers, and four Jill torpedo bombers.[18] The strike group was ordered to proceed to Nichols Field on Luzon if bad weather made it impossible to return to the carriers. This was a concern, since the morning search missions reported bad weather in the area of the American carrier force.[19]

As the strike headed toward TG 38.3, it was detected by radar at a range of about 105nm. This provided plenty of time to vector an interception by Hellcats from *Langley* and *Essex*. The Hellcats tore into the Japanese formation and accounted for 19 aircraft – eight from *Zuikaku* and another 11 from the light carriers. It is unclear if the surviving aircraft pressed their attack against TG 38.3's carriers; if they did, the attacks were tentative and went unnoticed by the Americans. Following the encounter with the Hellcats, 39 aircraft flew on to Luzon, with a single Zero from *Zuikaku* flying all the way to Formosa. Three aircraft, from *Chitose* and *Chiyoda*, returned to their carriers.[20] The Imperial Navy's final carrier-borne strike inflicted no damage to the Americans. But the attack did have some significance, since from its seaward origin and by the fact that the aircraft were reported to have tailhooks, the Americans knew for the first time that Japanese carriers were lurking to the north.[21] What the Americans could not know was that Ozawa's carriers had expended all their offensive power in a single totally ineffective strike. By the end of October 24, Ozawa possessed just five strike aircraft and 24 fighters.[22]

Though *Princeton*'s demise was undeniably a Japanese success, the massive air strike planned by Fukudome, Onishi, and Ozawa to neutralize TF 38 ended in failure. Only TG 38.3 had been attacked. This only delayed the launching of a strike by Sherman's task group against Kurita's force until late in the morning. Failure to inflict serious damage on TF 38 left Kurita's force exposed to a series of attacks on October 24.

THE BATTLE OF THE SIBUYAN SEA

The first of the four great battles that made up the collective engagement known as the Battle of Leyte Gulf was the air-sea battle in the Sibuyan Sea that occurred during the late morning and afternoon of October 24. Most accounts of the Battle of the Sibuyan Sea focus on the sinking of the superbattleship *Musashi* and how she was literally battered to a hulk by innumerable torpedo and bomb hits. In spite of this spectacular American success, the fact of the matter was that the battle was a tactical victory for the Japanese. For the loss of *Musashi* and the crippling of a heavy cruiser, the First Diversionary Attack

Force, operating with no air cover, was able to transit the Sibuyan Sea and proceed to San Bernardino Strait on its way to Leyte Gulf. This constituted nothing less than a failure by TF 38 to defeat, or even seriously weaken, the primary Japanese force. This failure had significant implications. It forced Halsey to decide between making further attacks on the First Diversionary Attack Force or going north to deal with the newly-discovered Japanese carrier force. It also led directly to the Battle off Samar the following day, when the First Diversionary Attack Force was given the opportunity to engage the Seventh Fleet's escort carrier force off Samar.

As previously outlined, Halsey had already put himself in a bad position when Kurita's force was spotted on the morning of October 24. Of the 11 carriers in TF 38, only two were in position to launch immediate attacks on Kurita. The air groups of these two carriers were the mainstay of efforts to attack Kurita throughout the day. In addition to having only a fraction of his striking power in immediate position to attack Kurita, the air groups of all three TF 38 task groups were further weakened by the diversion of almost 100 Hellcats and 58 Helldivers to conduct the aggressive searches that Halsey ordered for the morning of October 24.[23]

The First Diversionary Attack Force regrouped after the debacle in the Palawan Passage and proceeded toward the Mindoro Strait. An American submarine spotted Kurita's force after midnight on October 24, but could not make an attack. At 0820, a Helldiver from *Intrepid* detected a large group of ships south of Mindoro. The pilot closed the formation to make a visual inspection of its composition. He reported that the force was composed of four battleships, eight cruisers, and 13 destroyers. This was very close to Kurita's actual strength of five battleships, nine cruisers (seven heavy and two light), and 13 destroyers. This information clearly indicated that a major Japanese effort was under way.

Within minutes of the initial contact on Kurita's force, Halsey issued a string of orders to deal with this new threat. Davison's TG 38.4 was directed to move north and join with Bogan's TG 38.2. These two groups and Sherman's TG 38.3 were ordered to attack the huge Japanese force entering the Sibuyan Sea. McCain's TG 38.1 was ordered to turn around from its transit to Ulithi.[24] Of the three task groups ordered to attack, only TG 38.2 was able to launch a strike immediately. Sherman's task group was busy dealing with Japanese air attacks and Davison's task group was unnecessarily tied up attacking Nishimura's force in the Sulu Sea.

With only *Intrepid* and *Cabot* available, TG 38.2 launched the initial strikes against Kurita's force. The Battle of the Sibuyan Sea began at 0853 when *Intrepid* turned into the wind at 25 knots and the first strike aircraft lifted off. From *Intrepid* came eight Avengers, all carrying torpedoes, 12 Helldivers (with 1,000-pound bombs; four each general purpose, semi-armor piercing, and armor piercing), and 11 Hellcats. *Cabot* contributed five Avengers (all with torpedoes) and eight fighters.[25] The strike was under the command of Commander William E. Ellis, commander of *Intrepid*'s air group. Flying into the Sibuyan Sea, the Americans spotted the First Diversionary Attack Force at 1020 through a break in the clouds. The lead group of Japanese ships included the huge *Yamato* and *Musashi*. Ellis decided to make them the focus of his attack. Of the two, *Musashi* was nearest, so Ellis selected her as the main target. He split the Helldivers into two six-aircraft divisions to attack both battleships with their 1,000-pound bombs. The two nearest large ships were the targets for *Intrepid*'s Avengers. Two were ordered to go after the heavy cruiser shielding the battleship (this was *Myoko*), and the others were directed against *Musashi*. These were divided into two three-plane sections in order to execute an anvil attack. The Avengers from *Cabot* were allocated against *Yamato* in the center of the formation. Since there were no Japanese aircraft present, the Hellcats were ordered to suppress the antiaircraft defenses by conducting strafing attacks.[26]

After being spotted at 0810 by American search aircraft, Kurita ordered his formation to increase speed to 24 knots and prepare for air attack. The First Diversionary Attack Force was divided into two sections. The lead section was the largest and had the biggest targets, so it received the bulk of attacks during the day. In the center of the formation was *Yamato* with Kurita on board. On her starboard quarter was *Musashi*; *Nagato* was on her port quarter. Arrayed around the battleships were three heavy cruisers, *Myoko*, *Haguro*, and *Chokai*. Light cruiser *Noshiro* was stationed in the front of the circular formation of the heavy ships around *Yamato*, and seven destroyers watched the flanks of the formation. Trailing the lead formation was the Second Section with battleships *Kongo* and *Haruna*, heavy cruisers *Chikuma*, *Tone*, *Suzuya*, and *Kumano*, light cruiser *Yahagi*, and six destroyers.

When no air attack developed after the initial detection, Kurita ordered the formation to reduce speed and to resume zigzagging. A series of radar contacts on aircraft and a periscope sighting were reported over the next two hours. At 1000 a radar contact was gained on a large aircraft formation to the east. Then at 1025, aircraft were sighted to the south, off the starboard beam of the lead section. TG 38.2's first strike of the day had arrived. At 1026, the Japanese opened fire with long-range antiaircraft guns.[27]

One of the main themes of the battle was the general ineffectiveness of Japanese antiaircraft defenses. American pilots remarked on the ferocity of the antiaircraft fire, from multi-colored 5-inch bursts to the streams of tracers from the multitudes of 25mm guns. The Japanese also used Type 3 incendiary shells from 18.1-inch and 16-inch battleship main battery guns. The giant Type 3 shells were spectacular but proved totally ineffective; no American aircraft were damaged or destroyed by them. Japanese records indicate that fairly few 5-inch shells were fired during the five attacks (for instance, *Musashi* fired only 203 even though she was the principal target of the American attacks[28]), indicating that the fire control systems servicing the 5-inch mounts were taking too long to generate targeting solutions. The most effective weapon was the ubiquitous 25mm gun. While many American aircraft were damaged, only 18 were shot down. Though the numbers confirm the ineffectiveness of IJN antiaircraft fire in shooting down aircraft, it cannot be stressed enough that American aviators displayed great courage pressing home attacks through what they described as an impenetrable wall of fire. Even Japanese observers commented on the tenacity of the American aviators.

Starting with the first attack and lasting for most of the subsequent attacks, the impressive size of *Musashi* drew the most attention. Once she was damaged, she became an irresistible target for the American aviators. *Musashi*'s ordeal began with the first six Helldivers from *Intrepid*. According to Japanese sources, one of the Helldivers placed a bomb on the roof of the main battery Turret Number 1. Damage was negligible thanks to the turret's thick armor. Four other Helldivers scored near misses, two on the starboard side and two to port. This was not inconsequential, as bomb splinters penetrated the hull plating and caused flooding.[29] The flooding was worst in the bow. The large compartments in the bow of the Yamato class represented a design flaw, as they allowed severe flooding. As the vulnerable Avengers began their torpedo runs, Hellcats strafed the length of the battleship.

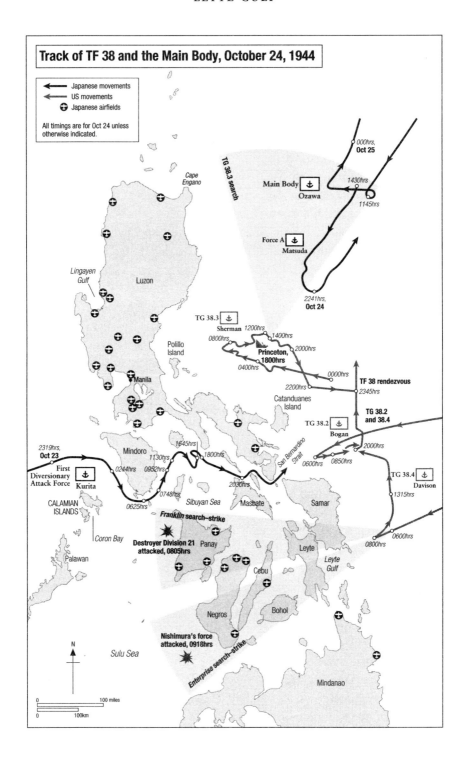

Track of TF 38 and the Main Body, October 24, 1944

Japanese movements
US movements
Japanese airfields

All timings are for Oct 24 unless otherwise indicated.

TG 38.3 search

Cape Engano

Main Body
Ozawa

000hrs, Oct 25

1430hrs

1145hrs

Force A
Matsuda

Lingayen Gulf

Luzon

2241hrs, Oct 24

Polillo Island

TG 38.3
Sherman

1200hrs
0800hrs
1400hrs
Princeton, 1800hrs
2000hrs
0400hrs

0000hrs

Manila

2200hrs

Catanduanes Island

TF 38 rendezvous
2345hrs

TG 38.2
Bogan

TG 38.2 and 38.4

San Bernardino Strait

0600hrs
0850hrs
2000hrs

TG 38.4
Davison

2319hrs, Oct 23

First Diversionary Attack Force
Kurita

Mindoro

1645hrs
1130hrs
0244hrs
0952hrs
1800hrs

0748hrs

0625hrs

1315hrs

CALAMIAN ISLANDS

Coron Bay

Palawan

Sibuyan Sea

2030hrs

Masbate

Samar

0800hrs

0600hrs

Franklin search–strike

Destroyer Division 21 attacked, 0805hrs

Panay

Leyte

Leyte Gulf

Cebu

Nishimura's force attacked, 0918hrs

Negros

Bohol

Sulu Sea

N

Enterprise search–strike

Mindanao

0   100 miles

0   100km

At 1030 *Musashi* took her first real blow when an Avenger placed one torpedo amidships slightly abaft the bridge on the starboard side. Due to a design fault in the belt armor, flooding began in two adjacent boiler rooms. *Musashi* took on some 3,000 tons of water, which created a 5.5-degree list. This was quickly reduced to a single degree by pumps in the affected boiler rooms and counterflooding on the opposite side. The damage could have been worse, since two more torpedoes were seen to pass under the battleship amidships. Facing *Musashi*'s intact antiaircraft defenses, one Avenger was shot down before it launched its torpedo and a second went down after dropping its weapon.[30]

Only two Avengers attacked *Myoko*, but these aircraft made a big impact. One torpedo hit the heavy cruiser at 1029 on her starboard side aft. The subsequent flooding knocked out an engine room and the aft generator room. This in turn brought the two starboard shafts to a halt, reducing speed to 15 knots. The cruiser fell astern of the formation.[31] Kurita decided to send her back to Singapore for repairs without destroyer escort. Since *Myoko* was the flagship of Cruiser Division 5, at 1100 the division commander transferred to cruiser *Haguro*. *Myoko* limped back to Singapore but never returned to service. With the departure of *Myoko*, Kurita had lost four of ten heavy cruisers before they had a chance to engage an American ship.

The attack on *Yamato* was less successful. None of *Intrepid*'s Helldivers scored a direct hit and only one near miss was recorded, near the battleship's bow. *Yamato* successfully evaded all weapons dropped from *Cabot*'s torpedo aircraft; one of the aircraft was lost to antiaircraft fire.[32] The entire attack was over by 1050.

Following TG 38.2's opening attack, the First Diversionary Attack Force continued through the Tablas Strait and entered the Sibuyan Sea. At 1053, Kurita ordered that zigzagging be resumed as no further air attacks appeared to be imminent. However, this respite was brief. The second American strike, launched from TG 38.2 at 1045, was already in the air. This attack consisted of 14 Hellcats, 12 Helldivers and nine Avengers.[33] Except for five fighters from *Cabot*, all were from *Intrepid*. The follow-on strike was launched at 1045, detected by Japanese radar at a range of 50nm, and sighted by the Japanese at 1203. The battle opened at 1207 when the Japanese opened fire and ceased only eight minutes later.[34] In that short period, the well-coordinated assault inflicted severe additional damage on *Musashi*.

The new strike leader took the advice of Commander Ellis to concentrate solely on *Musashi*.[35] As a result, all the dive-bombers and torpedo bombers went after her. Diving through intense fire, the Helldivers again opened the attack. The 12 bombers scored two direct hits and five near-misses. One 1,000-pound bomb hit forward and passed through *Musashi*'s bow without exploding. The second hit just to the port side of the stack and penetrated two decks before exploding against the middle armor deck. The resulting explosion in a crew space created a fire that reached the Number 2 Engine Room and two boiler rooms. Number 2 Engine Room was never re-manned, so *Musashi* was down to three shafts. By increasing revolutions of the other three shafts, speed was temporarily maintained.[36] Bomb splinters damaged steam lines; adding to the chaos, *Musashi*'s steam siren was damaged, and it sounded off and on for the remainder of the action.[37] Five Helldivers scored near misses, all forward, but these caused only minor flooding.

This attack featured better coordination between the dive-bombers and the torpedo bombers. On the heel of the dive-bombers, *Intrepid*'s nine Avengers deployed to conduct an anvil attack. Of the nine aircraft, eight were able to drop their Mark XIII torpedoes. Three of these hit *Musashi*'s port side. One hit near the stack on the junction of the outboard port engine room and the port hydraulic machinery space; it caused additional flooding, but little else. Another hit forward of the armored citadel and caused massive flooding into several large compartments. The final torpedo hit abaft Turret Number 2. This additional beating created another five-degree list, but this was also corrected to one degree by flooding some starboard voids. At this point, though, *Musashi* was down over six feet by the bow.[38] In spite of this beating, *Musashi* was in no danger of sinking. Because she was operating on three shafts, her top speed was reduced to 22 knots.

Musashi put up a storm of antiaircraft fire during the brief attack. Her gunners forced one Avenger to ditch some 15 miles away and shot down two Helldivers.[39] Japanese records indicate nine Type 3 shells were fired from her main battery during the attack. American pilots were impressed that they were being engaged at 25,000–30,000 yards from the target, but no aircraft were damaged. After two attacks, *Musashi* had accounted for four Avengers and two Helldivers. For the entire battle, *Musashi*'s gunners claimed 30 aircraft destroyed and another 15 probably shot down.[40]

In exchange for just six aircraft, TG 38.2 had inflicted serious damage on Kurita's force. Heavy cruiser *Myoko* was forced to retire and *Musashi* was in serious, but by no means fatal, condition. The battleship's well-trained damage control crews had prevented the ship from sinking and had kept her top speed at a respectable 22 knots. But her condition was becoming a serious problem for Kurita. To allow *Musashi* to maintain her place in formation, Kurita ordered that the First Diversionary Attack Force reduce speed to 20 knots. However, keeping *Musashi* in formation restricted Kurita's operational and tactical options. Kurita's main concern was the certainty his force would be subjected to additional air attacks. Since he had received no information on the efforts of the land-based air forces and had no indication whether Ozawa's diversion mission had been successful or not, it must have seemed to him like the First Diversionary Attack Force was fighting the Americans alone. This fear was reflected in his 1315 message addressed to Ozawa and Mikawa: "We are being subjected to repeated enemy carrier-based air attacks. Advise immediately of contacts and attacks made by you on the enemy."[41] Poor communication kept Kurita from knowing that the land-based air forces had failed in their mission to neutralize TF 38 and that Ozawa had not even been spotted by the Americans. The First Diversionary Attack Force would have to endure many more attacks on October 24.

After countering the morning air attacks from land-based Japanese aircraft, Sherman's TG 38.3 was ready to go on the offensive. A full strike was spotted on the flight decks of *Essex* and *Lexington*. Each big carrier would launch 34 aircraft – eight Hellcats, ten Helldivers, and 16 Avengers. However, the air groups flew their missions with very different payloads. *Essex* fitted 500-pound bombs to her Hellcats, 1,000-pound bombs on the Helldivers, and all the Avengers carried Mark XIIIs. *Lexington's* air group was not armed with weapons suitable to attack heavily-armored ships. Because the ship's air officer, and later the ship's captain, did not want to open the magazines to rearm the aircraft for fear of ending up like *Princeton*, all of *Lexington's* aircraft carried smaller bombs suitable for attacking land targets.[42]

TG 38.3's first strike commenced launching at 1050. Adding to the problems with arming *Lexington's* aircraft, the air groups were separated by heavy weather. When the air groups were reunited over Mindoro, *Lexington's* group was missing five Helldivers and five Avengers. After finding the Japanese, the strike commander, Commander Hugh Winters from *Lexington*, ordered his remaining aircraft to attack the lead section and for *Essex*'s air group to attack the rear section.[43] The lightly-armed aircraft from *Lexington* had no capability to seriously damage any of the battleships in Kurita's First Section.

Japanese radar detected the approach of the third attack; in response, Kurita ordered an increase in speed to 24 knots. This was quickly reduced to 22 knots after it became apparent that *Musashi* could not keep up. Even at this reduced speed, *Musashi* gradually fell behind the formation.[44]

The attack did not go as Winters had intended. Most of the aircraft selected *Musashi* for attack. According to Japanese sources, she was under attack from 1331 until 1350 from two waves of aircraft. Five Helldivers from *Essex* ended up attacking the first section in addition to the *Lexington* Helldivers. In the first wave of attacks against *Musashi*, the dive-bombers scored two near misses aft, but these caused little damage. *Musashi* was also hit by a torpedo forward on the starboard side, flooding several large compartments. Many crewmen were poisoned by carbon monoxide which filled the forward sick bay.[45] Other Helldiver pilots selected *Yamato* for attack. One of the *Essex* Helldivers scored a hit forward on the port side near Turret Number 1 at 1350.[46] As was often the case when a bomb hit the forward section of a Yamato-class battleship, several large compartments were flooded. For some reason, five *Essex* Helldivers selected light cruiser *Yahagi* in the second section as their target. One bomb landed in the aft crew compartments and another started a small fire in the chain locker, opening a hole in her starboard bow. *Yahagi*'s speed was temporarily limited to 22 knots.[47]

The second wave of attacks on *Musashi* was much more deadly. At least four bombs hit the ship. The first three all hit forward near Turret Number 1 and exploded in unoccupied crew accommodation spaces below. No fires resulted, and damage was light. The fourth bomb exploded on contact after hitting the starboard side of the stack. Again, no fires resulted and damage was limited.[48] However, the explosion devastated many nearby 25mm triple gun mounts and caused heavy casualties among the gun crews.

Damage from Helldivers did not pose real problems for *Musashi*'s survival, but torpedo damage inflicted by Avengers was another story. In the second wave of the third attack, *Essex* Avengers scored three more Mark XIII hits, bringing the total of torpedo hits on *Musashi* to seven. Two struck forward of the armored citadel on either side of the bow.

The design flaw of having comparatively little compartmentation in the unarmored bow section led to massive flooding. The torpedo explosions forced the hull plating outward, creating what looked like a huge plow throwing water up as the ship moved forward.[49] Another torpedo struck *Musashi*'s starboard side close to the previous starboard side hit. This increased flooding and forced the abandonment of the starboard hydraulic machinery room. A possible fourth hit was reported by some witnesses near the forward 6.1-inch triple turret on the starboard side. Japanese sources dismiss this hit as doubtful.[50]

American losses from the third attack were again light. Japanese antiaircraft fire accounted for one Helldiver that was damaged and could not return to its ship and three Avengers (two from *Essex* and one from *Lexington*). Another Helldiver was lost to a fighter attack within sight of its carrier.[51]

The addition of three more torpedo hits from the third attack made *Musashi*'s situation perilous. In total, she had taken seven torpedo and six bomb hits – this level of damage would have been mortal for any other battleship. Even after taking such abuse, *Musashi* was in no immediate danger of sinking, since there was no progressive flooding. The excellent work of her damage control personnel reduced the two-degree list to starboard to a single degree, but the counterflooding required to do so used up almost all the ship's reserve buoyancy.[52] A bigger issue was the bow trim; the original freeboard of 32.8 feet on the bow was down to 19.6 feet. *Musashi*'s top speed was reduced to 16 knots, and this was further reduced by the ship's captain to 12 knots for fear that his ship could suddenly plunge by the bow.[53] As *Musashi* was unable to maintain formation, at 1500 Kurita ordered her to proceed to the west with destroyers *Shimakaze* and *Kiyoshimo*. At 1507, Vice Admiral Suzuki Yoshio, leading the Second Section, detached heavy cruiser *Tone* to defend *Musashi* against torpedo bomber attacks.[54]

At 1259 TG 38.3 began launching its second strike of the day. This consisted of 12 Helldivers carrying 1,000-pound bombs and eight Hellcats fitted with 500-pound bombs, all from *Essex*.[55] According to Japanese records, the fourth attack against the First Diversionary Attack Force occurred between 1426 and 1450. The American aviators passed up the obviously struggling *Musashi* and went after the other two battleships in the First Section. At least three bombs hit *Yamato* forward. One penetrated the bow and exploded below the waterline. Flooding by 3,000 tons of seawater created a five-degree list to port.

Counterflooding reduced the list to one degree. *Yamato* was slightly down by the bow, but her speed was unaffected. The other two bombs hit near Turret Number 1 but neither caused significant damage.[56]

The next American strike group to launch was the first (and only) attack from TG 38.4. Beginning at 1313, *Enterprise* sent a 33-aircraft strike consisting of 16 Hellcats armed with 5-inch rockets, nine Helldivers (each carrying two 1,000-pound bombs instead of the usual one), and eight Avengers.[57] Fifteen minutes later, *Franklin* sent an even larger strike composed of 34 aircraft. These included 12 Hellcats (eight with rockets), 12 Helldivers each with two 500-pound bombs, and ten torpedo-armed Avengers.[58]

When the latest strike arrived in the area of Kurita's force, *Musashi* was just beginning to carry out Kurita's order to proceed to Coron Bay. She was defended only by *Tone* and destroyer *Kiyoshimo*. As the *Enterprise* strike group turned to the north, the First Section took a similar course in order to present their sterns to the approaching American aircraft. This left *Musashi* and her small group of escorts by themselves. The leader of the *Enterprise* strike selected *Musashi* for attack.[59]

This attack against *Musashi* began at 1515 and ended 15 minutes later. By this point, *Musashi* was unable to defend herself. She had a top speed of 12 knots and could barely maneuver. Only about a fourth of her antiaircraft guns remained in action. While the Hellcats suppressed the escorting destroyers, the Helldiver and Avenger pilots pressed their attacks against the wallowing giant. Bombing results against the near-defenseless battleship were devastating. Of the nine *Enterprise* Helldivers that dove on *Musashi*, seven claimed hits and the other two near misses. Against a much-diminished level of antiaircraft fire, *Enterprise*'s Avengers also did great execution. The eight *Enterprise* Avengers conducted an anvil attack and observed two, and possibly three, hits. None of the *Enterprise* aircraft were lost.[60]

Right on the heels of the *Enterprise* strike, *Franklin*'s air group arrived on the scene. *Franklin*'s fighters conducted suppression attacks in support of the Helldivers and Avengers; two destroyers were damaged by rockets. Seven Helldivers selected *Nagato* for attack. She was hit by two bombs and near missed by three more. The bomb that struck the boat deck destroyed or damaged five 5.5-inch casemate guns and jammed one of the Type 89 5-inch dual-purpose mounts. Damage to one of the boiler room air intakes caused a temporary loss of speed to 22 knots.[61]

Two *Franklin* Helldivers dove on *Tone*. Dropping their weapons from the usual altitude of 2,000 feet, they inflicted only minor damage on the heavy cruiser. According to Japanese records, the ship was subjected to two near misses, and bomb hits that caused minor fires. One bomb penetrated the upper deck above Boiler Room Number 2 but was stopped by the main armored deck without exploding.[62] *Tone*'s speed and fighting capabilities were unimpaired.

Three *Franklin* Helldivers reported attacking *Musashi*, as did all her Avengers. Of the ten Avengers, nine delivered attacks, approaching the ship from both beams. Even though *Musashi*'s light antiaircraft battery had been much reduced, she continued to fight back at her tormentors. The group of five Avengers coming at the battleship from the north was hit hard, with two shot down and the other three damaged. The surviving torpedo bombers dropped from long range, 4,000–6,000 yards away.[63]

The final attack of the day came directly on the heels of the *Franklin* strike. This was TG 38.2's third strike of the day. Led by Commander Ellis flying his second mission, it included 16 Hellcats, 12 Helldivers, and the last five operational Avengers from *Intrepid*'s torpedo squadron.[64] Half of the Helldivers selected *Musashi* for attack, together with all the Avengers.[65]

Because the attacks occurred in quick succession, Japanese accounts do not separate the damage to *Musashi* caused by the *Enterprise* dive-bombers, the trio of *Franklin* dive-bombers, or the last attack by *Intrepid*'s Helldivers. The Japanese do confirm a total of ten bomb hits. One bomb hit forward of Turret Number 1 and added to the damage on the bow from earlier bombs. Another bomb hit the roof of Turret Number 1 but failed to penetrate its thick roof armor. Another hit to the starboard side of the same turret and penetrated two decks before exploding against the main armor deck. Two bombs hit together between the forward 6.1-inch turret and the superstructure, exploded on contact, and did minimal damage. Another two hit just to port in the same general area, penetrated two decks, and exploded on the main armored deck without penetrating. The eighth bomb hit the port side of the massive superstructure and exploded on contact, causing devastation to nearby 25mm gun mounts and their crews. Another projectile hit the top of the superstructure and destroyed the main battery fire control director and its rangefinder. The resulting explosion caused significant personnel casualties on the bridge and operations room, totaling 78 killed and wounded. Among the killed were five senior officers, and the ship's captain, Rear Admiral Inoguchi Toshihira, was wounded. The final hit landed abaft the superstructure but caused only minor damage. None of the 1,000-pound projectiles penetrated the main armor deck, but topside damage was extensive and many 25mm gun mounts were knocked out.[66] Of these ten hits, *Enterprise* Helldivers probably accounted for four, *Franklin* Helldivers another two, and *Intrepid* Helldivers the last four, including the devastating hit on the bridge.

Japanese accounts also do not distinguish between the torpedo hits scored by *Enterprise, Franklin, Intrepid,* or *Cabot* aircraft. From 1515 to 1530, the Japanese recorded 11 torpedo hits, of which two failed to explode. All but two of these were on the port side. Both *Musashi's* executive officer and the chief engineer survived the attack. Using their accounts, the US Naval Technical Mission to Japan performed postwar analysis of the original Japanese account. In spite of the close scrutiny given to this action, the number of torpedo hits suffered by *Musashi* remains a matter of debate until this day. Of the five torpedoes the Japanese claimed hit the ship forward, only two were verified, one to port and one to starboard. The confirmed hit to port caused the flooding of the magazines for Turret Number 1. Another confirmed hit to port caused immediate flooding to a boiler room and slow flooding in another. Two more hits were confirmed amidships on the port side. One of these caused flooding in the two port-side engine rooms. This left only the two starboard-side shafts still functioning. As the last American aircraft left the scene, *Musashi* was listing ten degrees to port. Counterflooding reduced this to six degrees. The bow continued to settle until sea water was washing over it. Top speed was down to six knots and the ship could no longer be steered.[67]

After taking a minimum of 16 bomb and at least 11 (and possibly as many as 15) torpedo hits, *Musashi* was clearly doomed. Her list increased to 12 degrees, prompting the chief engineer to order the flooding of the three starboard-side boiler rooms. This held the list at 12 degrees but reduced the ship to a single shaft. *Musashi* could barely move on her last operational shaft and the flooding continued unchecked. At 1715 she was ordered to beach herself on nearby Sibuyan Island. This proved impossible – severely down by the bow, the ship would not answer to her helm and so circled slowly. By 1800 the last boiler room was abandoned due to flooding, leaving the ship without power.[68]

Musashi's demise was now only minutes away. By 1900 the list increased to 15 degrees and water had reached Turret Number 1. By 1920 the list reached a dangerous 30 degrees. Finally, the executive officer (now acting as captain) gave the order to abandon ship. Minutes after the order was issued, *Musashi* began a slow roll to port. At 1935 the ship turned bottom up and then slid under bow first. Destroyers *Kiyoshimo* and *Hamakaze* picked up 1,376 survivors, but another 1,023 were lost. The process of rescuing this many men went on until 0215 the following morning.[69] Inoguchi elected to go down with his ship. Considering the damage inflicted on *Musashi*, the number of survivors was amazing. They were taken by the two destroyers to Corregidor and later played an unsavory role in the battle for Manila in 1945.

As *Musashi* went through her death throes, Kurita was taking stock of his situation. He had suffered five major air attacks and more seemed likely. Given the scale of air attacks, it was apparent that the land-based air forces had accomplished little. He still had no information on the operations of Ozawa's force. Instead of taking the next series of expected air attacks in the more restricted waters of the eastern Sibuyan Sea, at 1530 Kurita decided to head west and retreat to the open waters of the central Sibuyan Sea. At 1600, he sent a message to Toyoda explaining his decision. It was also addressed to Onishi and Fukudome:

> Originally the main strength of the First Diversion Attack Force was intended to force its way through San Bernardino Strait about one hour after sundown, coordinating its moves with air action. However, the enemy made more than 250 sorties against us between 0830 and 1530, the number of planes involved and their fierceness mounting every wave. Our air forces, on the other hand, were not able to obtain even expected results, causing our losses to mount steadily. Under these circumstances it was deemed that were we to force our way through, we would merely make ourselves meat for the enemy, with very little chance of success. It was therefore concluded that the best course open to us was temporarily to retire beyond the reach of enemy planes and reform our plans. At 1600 we were… on course 290 speed 18 knots.[70]

As Kurita headed west to give Japanese land-based air forces more time to strike the enemy, no further American air attacks were forthcoming. At 1630, Kurita ordered a change of course to the north and at 1648 again headed west. Still, no American aircraft appeared overhead, so at 1714 Kurita again changed course to the east and resumed the advance to San Bernardino Strait. After Kurita had already resumed his advance, Toyoda responded to Kurita's 1600 message. At 1813, Toyoda issued a terse order, "All forces will dash to the attack trusting in divine assistance." By the time this was received on *Yamato* at 1915, the First Diversionary Attack Force was already headed east.

The Battle of the Sibuyan Sea was the largest air-sea battle in history up to that point. Kurita's force had been subjected to a series of attacks over the span of five hours by over 250 carrier aircraft. The star performer was *Intrepid*, whose air group conducted 96 sorties in three strikes.[71] Aboard the six carriers that had conducted the strikes, aviators made extravagant claims of losses inflicted on the Japanese. The overconcentration on *Musashi* did not stop TF 38's aviators from claiming much greater success. TG 38.2 claimed to have damaged three battleships and three heavy cruisers; TG 38.3 claimed three battleships, four heavy cruisers, and two light cruisers damaged; TG 38.4 issued claims for one light cruiser and one destroyer sunk, one battleship and one destroyer probably sunk, and damage to two battleships, one light cruiser, and four destroyers.[72] Even given that some of these claims were duplicative, it appeared that both Yamato-class battleships had been crippled with one probably sunk, *Nagato* was hit and badly damaged, and a Kongo-class battleship was crippled. Four heavy cruisers, two light cruisers, and six destroyers were reported sunk or damaged. The only reasonable assumption following the day's attacks was that the First Diversionary Attack Force had been rendered combat ineffective.

In fact, the opposite was true. The First Diversionary Attack Force had been battered but was still a formidable threat. *Musashi* had sunk, but the damage to *Yamato* and *Nagato* was minor and their fighting capabilities were unimpaired. Battleships *Kongo* and *Haruna* were undamaged. Of the seven heavy cruisers, only *Myoko* had been damaged and forced to retire. Damage to *Tone* was minor, leaving Kurita with six fully-functional heavy cruisers. Both light cruisers were fully operational, as the damage to *Yahagi* in no way impaired her capabilities. Destroyers *Kiyoshimo* and *Hamakaze* were damaged and subsequently ordered to handle *Musashi*'s survivors, leaving Kurita with 11 destroyers. By any reasonable measure, Kurita's force had fared well. The fact that the First Diversionary Attack Force had survived the best that TF 38 could throw at it and remained on track to its objective with most of its combat power intact made this battle a tactical victory for the Japanese. This was largely due to the ability of *Musashi* to withstand a fearsome pounding and the willingness of the Americans to focus the majority of their efforts on a single target.

The apparent decimation of the First Diversionary Attack Force set up the most dramatic decision of the battle. Having sighted the Japanese carriers at 1640, and with the threat from the Japanese force in the Sibuyan Sea seemingly removed, Halsey decided to move north during the night and attack Ozawa's force. The reasons behind this controversial decision will be covered later, but with Halsey focused on a new target, Kurita was free to continue his trek to Leyte Gulf.

Kurita adjusted his plans in the aftermath of his delayed advance toward Leyte Gulf. At 2145 he sent a message with his new timetable. The reduced but still potent First Diversionary Attack Force with its four battleships, six heavy cruisers, two light cruisers, and 11 destroyers would transit San Bernardino Strait at 0100 on October 25, head down the east coast of Samar, and arrive at Leyte Gulf at about 1100.[73] The First Diversionary Attack Force approached the strait at 20 knots and went to general quarters expecting a fight. As the Japanese passed through on a clear, moon-lit night, no American ships contested their passage. After entering the Philippine Sea at 0037, Kurita changed course to the south and headed to Leyte Gulf.

6

Execution at Surigao Strait

Of the four major actions that made up the Battle of Leyte Gulf, the engagement known as the Battle of Surigao Strait was the least important. However, the action is noteworthy since it was the last battleship engagement in naval history. Despite the fact that the Americans and Japanese operated large numbers of battleships during the war, it was extremely rare for them to meet each other in battle. Surigao Strait was only the second (and last) time battleships encountered each other during the Pacific War. The first clash of battlewagons took place during the climax of the Japanese effort to expel the Americans from Guadalcanal in November 1942. In this instance the Japanese battleship *Kirishima* encountered two more modern and powerful American battleships, *South Dakota* and *Washington*. Though *South Dakota* was knocked out of action early in the battle, *Washington* used her superior fire control system to pummel *Kirishima* with 16-inch shells; the outmatched Japanese battleship was sunk, with *Washington* suffering no damage. At the Battle of Surigao Strait, the result was even more lopsided, with an American force built around six battleships nearly annihilating a Japanese force led by two old battleships. In addition to employing radar-directed gunnery, the Americans also used radar to mount a series of devastating torpedo attacks. In the last major night action of the war, the Americans demonstrated that they had definitively surpassed the Japanese in night fighting. The only blemish on the American victory was that several Japanese ships escaped destruction because of a tepid American pursuit.

THE ADVANCE OF THE THIRD SECTION

The seven ships of Nishimura's force departed Brunei Bay at 1500 on October 22 and headed for the Sulu Sea by way of the Balabac Strait. Nishimura's objective of forcing Surigao Strait and storming into Leyte Gulf was very unlikely to be realized unless he could somehow gain surprise. Otherwise the Americans could use their superior forces to block any Japanese attempt to move through the strait.

Another daunting challenge for Nishimura was to transit the Sulu Sea without friendly air cover in the face of potential American carrier attacks.

In order to retain the element of surprise by avoiding detection by American aircraft, Nishimura had to carefully gauge his track to stay out of the search range of American carriers operating to the east of Leyte for the longest period of time. Though he could have easily surmised the general location of the American carriers and was well aware of their usual search range, Nishimura decided to advance at 18 knots while transiting outside American search range. This meant he was 110nm further along his track than he should have been when the Third Section was first spotted at 0905 by TG 38.4.[1] When they spotted the Japanese, the American aircraft were at the edge of their search pattern. Had Nishimura employed a slower initial cruising speed, his force would have been outside the range of TG 38.4's morning searches on October 24. Had the Japanese avoided being detected in the morning, it is possible that they could have transited the Sulu Sea undetected, since TG 38.4 was ordered north later in the morning to assist TG 38.2 in attacking Kurita's force in the Sibuyan Sea. Nishimura's early detection opened his force up to air attack, and more importantly it provided more than ample time for Kinkaid to prepare to mount the strongest possible defense of the Surigao Strait.

Of TF 38's three task groups, TG 38.4 was operating east of Leyte and was given responsibility to cover the distant approaches to Surigao Strait. Under command of Rear Admiral Davison, TG 38.4 included fleet carriers *Enterprise* and *Franklin* and light carriers *Belleau Wood* and *San Jacinto*. The fleet carriers launched a search and attack mission at 0600 to cover the Sulu Sea. Davison employed a large number of aircraft in this mission – 32 Hellcats and 24 Helldivers (each loaded with two 500-pound bombs). Under perfect weather conditions, the four separate search groups took off and headed west.

Enterprise's air group was responsible for covering the southern sector of the Sulu Sea. A total of 28 *Enterprise* aircraft comprised two search groups each with six Helldivers carrying bombs and eight Hellcats. At 0855 radar on *Yamashiro* detected approaching American aircraft. *Enterprise*'s aviators sighted Nishimura's force at 0905. Not only had the Americans gained first contact on a new Japanese force transiting the Sulu Sea, but the initial contact report provided the exact composition of Nishimura's force – two Fuso-class battleships, one Mogami-class cruiser, and four destroyers.

The commander of the search group making the initial contact radioed *Enterprise*'s second search group and waited for its arrival in order to make a coordinated attack. The second group arrived at 0840, and the attack began. Each of the two groups selected one of Nishimura's battleships for attention. Against what was described as fairly accurate antiaircraft fire, including Type 3 incendiary shells from the 14-inch main batteries on the battleships, the Hellcats led the attack with strafing runs. *Yamashiro* suffered only a near miss on her starboard side that ruptured her anti-torpedo bulge. The ensuing flooding caused a brief five-degree list which was quickly corrected by counterflooding. Strafing caused the deaths of 20 crewmen.[2] *Fuso* suffered more extensive damage. A 500-pound bomb hit near Turret Number 2, penetrated to the main armor deck, and exploded. Damage was moderate, but about ten crewmen were killed. Much more dramatic were the results of a bomb that struck the fantail by the aircraft catapult. The fuel tanks from the ship's two floatplanes caught fire, destroying both aircraft and creating thick black smoke. *Fuso* was staggered and temporarily left formation. By 1100 the fire had been extinguished, the floatplanes jettisoned, and full speed restored.[3]

Mogami was also attacked. She suffered only three near misses and minor damage to her flight deck from strafing.[4] Destroyer *Shigure* was also strafed, but she did not suffer a bomb hit on her forward 5-inch mount, as is often stated.[5] The entire attack lasted 20 minutes. Only a single Hellcat was lost to antiaircraft fire.

Franklin's air group was assigned the northern sector of the Sulu Sea. Its search-strike group was comprised of 28 aircraft with the same composition as *Enterprise*'s. At about 0800, *Franklin*'s aircraft spotted a group of three Japanese ships south of Panay. Though misidentified by the Americans, these were the three Hatsuharu-class destroyers of Destroyer Division 21. These ships had been detached from Shima's force at 1200 on October 21 to proceed from Mako to Takao to move Sixth Base Air Force ground equipment and personnel from Formosa to Manila. After completing this mission, they were scurrying to rejoin Shima's force.[6] One of the last *Franklin* aircraft to attack succeeded in hitting the frantically maneuvering *Wakaba* at 0813. The direct hit at the mainmast penetrated deep into the ship and exploded. The destroyer came to a halt and took a list to port. Within 45 minutes *Wakaba* sank with the loss of 30 crewmen. The other two destroyers rescued the survivors and continued south to join Shima. These were the target of a follow-up strike from *Franklin*. The attack group of 12 Hellcats and 11 Helldivers commenced a fresh attack at 1152. One bomb hit *Hatsushimo* but failed to fully detonate and did little damage. The Japanese officer commanding the two destroyers decided that he had had enough. At 1445, he broke off his mission to join Shima and took a course north to Manila to unload *Wakaba*'s survivors. Even more inexplicable than his decision to decline to play any further role in a decisive battle was his decision not to notify Shima of his actions.[7] Destroyer Division 21 was out of the battle, but it had absorbed the bulk of *Franklin*'s sorties for October 24.

The attacks from TG 38.4 failed to impair the speed or fighting capabilities of Nishimura's Third Section, but had forced Shima's Destroyer Division 21 to retreat to Manila. At 1024 TG 38.4 was ordered to move north to join the attack on Kurita's force in the Sibuyan Sea. This meant the end of air attacks against Nishimura's force on October 24. The movement of these forces through the Sulu Sea had provided a useful diversion since they had absorbed much of TG 38.4's offensive strikes during the day, thus lessening the pressure on Kurita.

Shima's Second Diversionary Attack Force was not subjected to air attack on October 24. However, it was spotted by a B-24 bomber south of the Cagayan Islands at 1155. The Army Air Force aircraft issued a generally accurate contact report.[8] This report reached Kinkaid at 1435 but was confused by the same aircraft issuing a subsequent contact report which included battleships. The second report probably reflected a sighting of Nishimura's force. Even though all three Japanese forces operating in the Sulu Sea on October 24 had been spotted, and two of them were attacked, the Americans failed to develop an accurate picture of the Japanese forces headed for Surigao Strait.

OLDENDORF'S GRAND AMBUSH

Early detection of Nishimura's force on October 24 gave Kinkaid ample time to prepare. His obvious conclusion was that a strong Japanese force would attempt to force Surigao Strait on the night of October 24–25. But there was still doubt in Kinkaid's mind as to the actual intentions of the Japanese and real confusion regarding their strength. Based on the morning searches, Kinkaid and his staff concluded that the Japanese force headed toward the strait consisted of two battleships, four heavy and four light cruisers, and ten destroyers. Of course, this was greater than the combined strength of Nishimura's and Shima's forces. There was also reason to believe that the Japanese force could include up to four battleships. Kinkaid also had concerns that the Japanese were conducting a "Tokyo Express"-type mission to move reinforcements to Leyte. The possibility of a transport mission was included in his 1343 message to Halsey.[9]

Since the most dangerous Japanese course of action was to attack through Surigao Strait into the gulf, Kinkaid had to guard against this above any other eventuality. At 1443 he directed Rear Admiral Jesse Oldendorf to prepare for a night battle. His order included the best estimate of the size of the oncoming Japanese force and a directive to use the PT boats in the lower strait. Though Japanese strength had been overestimated, Oldendorf had more than adequate forces to conduct his mission. Under his command were six battleships, four heavy and four light cruisers, and more than two dozen destroyers. Some 40 PT boats were also available, but these remained under Kinkaid's command.

Kinkaid's basic battle plan, fine-tuned by Oldendorf, created a set-piece battle that virtually eliminated any chance that any portion of Nishimura's force could slip into the gulf. The battle line under Rear Admiral Weyler was ordered to steam back and forth between a point east of Hingatungan Point to a point north of Hibuson Island. The battleships were positioned to seal the northern portion of the strait while still retaining maximum sea room. From this position, they could fire broadsides down the strait at the approaching Japanese. South of the battle line by 2.5 nm were two groups of cruisers. Oldendorf took command of the left flank cruiser group with three heavy and two light cruisers; Rear Admiral Berkey commanded the right flank unit comprised of one heavy and two light cruisers. Light cruiser *Nashville* was forced to remain out of harm's way when MacArthur refused to leave the ship and join Kinkaid on his flagship.

The only major concern for Kinkaid and Oldendorf was the fact that some ships were low on ammunition, and especially in armor-piercing (AP) projectiles. Since it was known that the Japanese force included battleships, AP shells were essential to tackle heavily-armored ships. The situation was most marked on the six battleships. In anticipation of bombarding Yap Island, later changed to Leyte, the battleships had been loaded with a predominate mix of high explosive shells (77 percent high explosive and 23 percent AP). As the clash with the Japanese loomed, the six battleships carried a total of 1,637 AP shells and 1,602 high explosive shells.[10] To make the best use of the available AP shells, it was planned that the battleships would not open fire until the Japanese had closed to between 17,000 and 20,000 yards. The heavy cruisers were also deficient in AP rounds, having been loaded with 66 percent high explosive and 34 percent AP. The destroyers had full loads of torpedoes but only 20 percent of their 5-inch rounds remaining. No replacement torpedoes were available. The available ordnance was sufficient for one battle, but if a second had to be fought the ammunition problem would become an issue.

Positioned south of the cruiser groups were two groups of destroyers tasked to conduct torpedo attacks against the oncoming Japanese before the cruisers and battleships were unleashed. The right flank destroyers were ordered to attack first, followed by the left flank destroyers. Radar-directed torpedo attacks were expected to exact significant attrition on the Japanese. The destroyers were ordered to keep to the sides of the strait when not making their torpedo attacks. This would degrade the performance of Japanese radar, which would have problems picking out the destroyers against the islands in the background, while also minimizing the possibility that the destroyers could be confused for the advancing Japanese. An improvised division of six destroyers was retained to screen the battleships.

The destroyer force received a late reinforcement when Captain J. G. Coward, commanding Destroyer Division 54, inserted himself into Oldendorf's battle plan with a message at 1950 announcing his intention to make a torpedo attack. Oldendorf approved Coward's plan, which added five more destroyers to the mix. Because it was considered possible that the Japanese might try to slip light forces into the gulf to the east of Hibuson Island (located in the middle of the strait), Oldendorf made his left flank stronger than his right flank.

The last part of Kinkaid's plan was the aggressive employment of torpedo boats. Of the 45 PT boats that deployed to Leyte Gulf, the 39 operational boats were deployed in sections of three at 13 positions in the southern approaches to the strait. This was an ideal opportunity for these fast and heavily armed boats (each carried four torpedoes) to conduct hit-and-run attacks on Japanese units. Lying silently so as not to betray their presence with a wake, and with the benefit of radar, their orders were to report all contacts and then conduct independent attacks.[11]

On the night of October 24–25, all remaining shipping inside Leyte Gulf was moved into San Pedro Bay in the northern part of the gulf. Keeping them out of the way was crucial to avoid confusion in a night battle. At sunset, all movements in and out of the gulf were stopped.[12]

Before he issued his orders for the upcoming battle, Oldendorf brought Weyler and Berkey to his flagship, heavy cruiser *Louisville*, to discuss the plan. Oldendorf wanted to make sure his principal commanders understood their roles in the battle. American naval officers knew from hard-won experience gained from night battles earlier in the war that confusion was rampant in a night action and that the Japanese were expert night fighters. Superior numbers did not guarantee victory at night. Oldendorf's careful force disposition and attention to reviewing the plan left as little as possible to chance. As Oldendorf stated after the battle, "My theory was that of the old-time gambler: Never give a sucker a chance. If my opponent is foolish enough to come at me with an inferior force, I'm certainly not going to give him an even break."[13] Never before had the Americans planned a night battle so carefully and brought such overwhelming force into play. Once these factors were combined with the massive advantage of superior radar technology, there was absolutely no doubt as to the outcome. Surigao Strait was to be a naval execution more than a battle.

NISHIMURA'S APPROACH

The approach phase of the battle went largely as Kinkaid and Oldendorf planned; in fact, it went better than they hoped, since by the time Nishimura's force reached the northern part of the strait and encountered the Allied battle line, his already inadequate force had been shattered and fought the last stage of the battle with only three of its seven ships.

Since neither Nishimura nor any member of his staff survived the battle, little is known about Nishimura's thinking as he approached the strait. What is known is his intention to arrive off Tacloban at 0430 on October 25 in accordance with Toyoda's master plan that had Kurita's force arriving off the American beachhead a short time later. As *Sho-1* began to unravel on October 24, Nishimura made every effort to stick to the plan. At around 1830 Nishimura received Kurita's message that he was under heavy attack in the Sibuyan Sea and was turning west to relieve the pressure. At 2013 Nishimura sent a message to Toyoda and Kurita that he now planned to be off Dulag at 0400 the next morning. Dulag was the location of the southern American landings on Leyte, so this did not constitute a major change in plan. At 2200 Nishimura received Kurita's change of plan that he would not arrive in the gulf until 1100 on October 25.[14] This had huge implications for Nishimura, but he did not see fit to change his plans. We can only speculate why Nishimura stuck to his original plans. The delay in Kurita's schedule meant that Nishimura would be on his own. Against the larger American forces in the gulf, this was a recipe for certain annihilation. Judging by his actions, Nishimura was determined to maintain his original schedule and attack before Kurita, hopefully drawing American forces away from Kurita's main attack. It is also likely that Nishimura preferred a night battle, since a day battle against superior forces in the confined waters of the strait offered no hope of success. According to *Shigure's* captain, who survived the battle, Nishimura was an old school admiral who preferred a night engagement over a day one.[15] In any event, it is fair to assume that Nishimura entered the battle with a sense of fatalism. By sacrificing his small force, he hoped to improve the chances for Kurita to accomplish his mission.

First to encounter Nishimura's force were the PT boats operating in the Mindanao Sea. The 13 PT boat sections were deployed starting with a skirmish line in the Mindanao Sea between Bohol and Camiguin Islands and extended all the way up to the southern part of Surigao Strait between Leyte and Dinagat Islands. Tasked with conducting independent attacks, the PT boats had an even more important function of providing early warning of the Japanese approach.

Nishimura expected to meet PT boats and made plans to counter them. He detached *Mogami* and three destroyers and sent them ahead as a scouting unit. The two battleships and destroyer *Shigure* trailed behind and took a more northern course along Bohol Island. At 2236 one of the boats from Section 1, *PT-131*, gained radar contact on Nishimura's main force. *PT-131* was joined by *PT-130* and *PT-152*, and the three boats attempted to close for a torpedo attack. The Japanese never detected them on radar, but at 2252 *Shigure* spotted the oncoming Americans and took them under fire. Two boats were slightly damaged. The Americans were not able to launch torpedoes but did issue a contact report that eventually reached Oldendorf at 0026 on October 25.

The Japanese scouting group centered around *Mogami* passed through Section 2 undetected but was sighted by Section 3 at 2350. *PT-151* and *PT-146* each fired a torpedo at *Mogami* at 0015 but missed.[16] By 0100 the two parts of Nishimura's force reunited. About the same time, *Mogami* was hit by a 6-inch shell from *Fuso*, clearly demonstrating the difficulty of distinguishing friend from foe at night. The "friendly" shell did not explode, but it still killed three men.[17] Section 6 was the next to attack. Advancing through heavy fire, *PT-134* closed to within 3,000 yards of *Fuso* and fired three torpedoes at 0205. The bravery of the boat's crew was not rewarded as all torpedoes missed. At 0207, Section 9 fired four torpedoes at the destroyers in the van of Nishimura's formation. One of three boats, *PT-490*, closed to within a mere 400 yards of *Michischio* before launching its weapons. Despite this almost suicidal display of courage, all the torpedoes missed. In return, Japanese gunfire hit *PT-490* twice and *PT-493* three times. The former was run aground after losing two men killed; the latter sank after also running aground. The last boats to attack were those of Section 8. *PT-523*, *PT-524*, and *PT-526* fired six torpedoes at a target identified as a Mogami-class cruiser before withdrawing at 0213. Again, none of the torpedoes hit its target. Section 11 detected Nishimura's force on radar at 0225 from a range of 10nm, but before it could make an attack it was warned to clear the area by American destroyers commencing their attack.

Nishimura had successfully run the gauntlet of torpedo boats without suffering any major damage and without his force losing cohesion. During these actions, and later against Shima's force as it ventured up the strait, the PT boats performed their mission well. Of the 39 boats, 30 contacted the Japanese and launched a total of 34 torpedoes. None of Nishimura's ships were hit, but Shima's force was not as lucky. Ten of the PTs were hit, but only one was lost. Personnel casualties were light, with three dead and 20 wounded.[18] Though they were unable to exact any attrition on Nishimura, the PTs provided invaluable information on the location of the approaching Japanese.

Though he had survived the PT boat threat without damage, Nishimura now faced a much more formidable threat in the form of Fletcher-class destroyers each carrying ten torpedoes directed by radar. It is possible that, based on information from one of *Mogami's* scout aircraft on the location and numbers of American ships inside the gulf, Nishimura believed that the main action would occur inside Leyte Gulf and not in Surigao Strait. It was not a rational assumption that the Americans would not use favorable geography to their advantage. Perhaps this mistaken assumption contributed to the subsequent disaster befalling Nishimura, but more important was the poor performance of Japanese lookouts and radar. The Japanese were totally unprepared for the series of American destroyer attacks that followed, and they paid a very high price for this unpreparedness.

The first destroyer attack was the deadliest. It was delivered by the five destroyers from Destroyer Division 54 under the command of the aggressive Coward. Two other destroyers from Coward's unit were left on picket duty and did not take part in the torpedo attack. The five destroyers conducting the attack were deployed on both bows of the approaching Japanese formation, with *McDermut* and *Monssen* attacking from the west and *Remey*, *McGowan*, and *Melvin* from the east. Coward's plan was to approach at 30 knots, track the Japanese by radar and launch torpedoes based on radar data, while not using their 5-inch guns so as not to disclose their positions. Once the torpedoes were in the water, Coward's destroyers would head north along the coast to clear the area and reduce the possibility of a friendly fire incident. This plan went off like clockwork.

The eastern group of Coward's destroyers gained first radar contact at a range of 18nm at 0240. The western group gained radar contact at 0254 at almost 15nm. *Shigure* spotted the American destroyers, but they were still able to maneuver unmolested into ideal firing positions. Only after Coward's destroyers had launched their torpedoes did the Japanese open fire. Inexplicably, even with this warning and after having engaged enemy destroyers, Nishimura failed to order any evasive maneuvers against possible torpedo attack. Coward's three eastern destroyers fired a barrage of 27 torpedoes just after 0300 at ranges between 8,200 and 9,300 yards. After they had launched their weapons, the destroyers were subjected to heavy Japanese fire, but none of Coward's ships were hit. At 0308 the first serious damage of the battle was recorded when two torpedoes from *Melvin* hit *Fuso*.

As Coward's eastern destroyers conducted their attack, the two western destroyers were also able to track the approaching Japanese and get into ideal launching positions. Between 0310 and 0311, *McDermut* and *Monssen* launched a full salvo of ten torpedoes each. This time Nishimura ordered evasive maneuvers, but he failed to hold the new course long enough to let the American torpedoes clear the area. When he resumed his original heading, his screening destroyers were directly in the path of *McDermut*'s salvo of ten torpedoes. At 0319, these weapons began to wreak havoc. Three torpedoes hit *Yamagumo* – within two minutes she sank with the loss of all but two of her crew.[19] Another *McDermut* torpedo hit *Michishio* amidships and flooded the engine room. The destroyer lost all power and went dead in the water. According to her commanding officer (one of only four survivors), the ship sank in 15 minutes.[20] *McDermut* scored yet again when a single torpedo hit *Asagumo* on her bow. With her bow gone, *Asagumo* was left to struggle with a top speed of 13–15 knots. *McDermut* almost gained a clean sweep of Nishimura's destroyers, but three other torpedoes passed just ahead of *Shigure*. The salvo from *McDermut* was the most effective American destroyer torpedo strike of the entire war.

Monssen also scored with her salvo. One of her torpedoes hit *Yamashiro* on her port quarter at 0322. As a precaution, the ship's captain ordered the flooding of the magazines to Turrets Five and Six.[21] This put the two aft 14-inch turrets out of action, reducing the battleship's firepower by a third. As *Yamashiro* was absorbing her first of several torpedo hits, *Fuso* was in her death throes. The two torpedoes from *Melvin* had begun a chain of events that proved fatal. One torpedo hit abreast Turret Number 1 and the second hit aft, flooding a boiler room and causing a fire. *Fuso* lacked modern underwater protection and that weakness was immediately apparent. The wounded battleship fell out of formation and developed a starboard list. Even with speed reduced to 12 knots, the ship's captain ordered the advance up the strait be resumed. This was abandoned at 0320 when *Fuso* changed course to the south and slowed to ten knots. The forward torpedo hit had caused massive flooding and the forecastle was awash. Counterflooding had reduced the starboard list, but unchecked progressive flooding doomed the ship. Accordingly, the abandon ship order was passed. According to her few survivors, the battleship sank by the bow at about 0345. Oil from the ship rose to the surface and caught fire, immolating many survivors in the water. From a crew of 1,630 officers and men, only about ten ever saw Japan again.[22] This version of *Fuso*'s demise, provided by the few survivors and confirmed by the recent discovery of the wreck still in one piece, contradicts the generally accepted one that torpedoes blew *Fuso* into two parts with each remaining afloat.

Even Nishimura was ignorant as to the full destruction caused by Coward's brilliant torpedo attack. At 0330 he reported the loss of two of his destroyers and the damage to *Yamashiro* in a message to Kurita and Shima. He indicated that *Yamashiro* could continue her mission. He was totally unaware that *Fuso* had already fallen out of formation and would soon sink.

The second torpedo attack was delivered by Destroyer Squadron 24 with its five Fletcher-class destroyers and the Royal Australian Navy Tribal-class destroyer *Arunta*. By this point, only *Yamashiro*, *Mogami*, and *Shigure* remained in formation. The six Allied destroyers, split into two groups of three, approached what was left of Nishimura's force from the west by moving along the coast of Leyte. At 0323, the first group (*Beale*, *Killen*, and *Arunta*) began to launch a total of 17 torpedoes at ranges between 6,500 and 6,800 yards. At 0331, one of *Killen*'s torpedoes hit *Yamashiro* port side amidships. This strike caused additional flooding in her machinery spaces which temporarily reduced her speed to five knots.[23] The second group of destroyers (*Bache*, *Hutchins*, and *Daly*) launched 15 torpedoes between 0329 and 0336. By this point damage control crews on *Yamashiro* had restored her speed to 18 knots; none of the torpedoes found its target. *Yamashiro* engaged the destroyers with her secondary battery of 6-inch guns, but her fire was ineffective. The American destroyers directed 5-inch fire at *Yamashiro*, *Mogami*, and probably *Asagumo* before clearing the area.

Next up were the nine ships of Destroyer Squadron 56 from the left flank of Oldendorf's formation. They made their attacks as the deluge of shells from the Allied cruisers and battleships roared overhead. The first two sections, each with three destroyers, attacked Nishimura's reduced force from both bows. The three ships approaching from the east (*Robinson*, *Halford*, and *Bryant*) each fired a half-salvo of five torpedoes, beginning at 0354. Launched at long range, none of the weapons found a target. Minutes later the section approaching from the west (*Edwards*, *Leutze*, and *Bennion*) launched their weapons at *Yamashiro* and *Shigure*. The Japanese ships conducted evasive maneuvers and all the torpedoes missed. Gunfire from the Japanese ships also failed to score. The final section (*Newcomb, Leary, Albert W. Grant*) approached the Japanese from dead ahead and pressed their attack to 6,200 yards before launching 13 torpedoes commencing at 0404. One of these, either from *Albert W. Grant* or possibly from the salvo fired earlier by *Bennion*, hit *Yamashiro* on her starboard engine room at 0407. Two more torpedoes from *Newcomb* hit the battleship at 0411 on her starboard side.

The final group of destroyers had made its attack while the gunnery duel was in full swing. Positioned between Japanese and Allied forces, it came under fire from both. The first two destroyers escaped without damage, but at 0407 the rearmost destroyer, *Albert W. Grant*, was hit by the first of many shells. Light cruiser *Denver* had been tracking *Shigure* and opened fire at 0406 from a range of 7,700 yards. The same target was already being engaged by *Louisville's* secondary battery. Actually, both ships were firing at *Albert W. Grant*, which had been confused with the previous radar track of *Shigure*. Unfortunately for the American destroyer, both *Denver* and the secondary battery aboard *Yamashiro* were on target. Eventually 11 shells from *Denver* and five from *Yamashiro* hit the ship. *Albert W. Grant* was pulled out of danger in near-sinking condition by *Newcomb*, but not before 34 of her crew were killed and another 94 wounded.[24]

THE FINAL BATTLESHIP CLASH

The effectiveness of the destroyer attacks made the gunnery phase of the battle anticlimactic. American radar from the cruisers and battleships in the northern portion of the strait detected the approaching Japanese at 0323 and steadily tracked their progress north. Every advantage was in the hands of Oldendorf. Possession of radar gave him excellent situational awareness, opposed to Nishimura's very incomplete knowledge of his own forces and those of the enemy. Only three Japanese ships had survived the destroyer gauntlet and now faced six battleships and eight cruisers. And the Americans had managed to create the much-sought and rarely-attained tactical advantage of capping the Japanese T, that is being able to fire full broadsides while the Japanese could only use their forward weapons.

Having gained radar contact at 33,000 yards, Admiral Weyler ordered his battleships to fire at 26,000 yards. This was beyond the range agreed before the battle, but Weyler did not want to squander his advantage against the seemingly oblivious Japanese.

Yamashiro was proving much tougher than her sistership *Fuso*. By 0337 she had restored speed to 18 knots. *Mogami* trailed *Yamashiro* by 3,000 yards and *Shigure* took up position on the battleship's starboard quarter. As his force neared the northern part of the strait, Nishimura ordered a reduction in speed to 12 knots. His last message at 0352 instructed *Fuso* to make her top speed to join the fight.

The last major gunnery duel in naval history opened at 0351 when Oldendorf ordered his cruisers to open fire at the lead Japanese ship at a range of 15,600 yards. He would have preferred to wait until Destroyer Division 56 completed its torpedo attack, but the rapidly-reducing range forced him to delay no longer. Two minutes later Weyler's battle line joined the fray from 22,800 yards. The three battleships equipped with the Mark 8 fire control radar were the first to open fire and the ones firing the most during the action. For some 30 minutes before the order was given to open fire at 0353, gunnery crews on *West Virginia* had been tracking the Japanese and had already gained a fire control solution for the first salvo.[25] The same was true aboard *California* and *Tennessee*, as these ships also carried the Mark 8. *California* fired her first salvo at 0355 from 20,400 yards, followed by *Tennessee* at 0356. Three of Weyler's battlewagons carried the much less capable Mark 3 fire control radar; these ships struggled to develop a fire control solution and consequently played a lesser role in the battle. *Maryland* opened fire at 0359 by ranging on the shell splashes around *Yamashiro*. *Mississippi* fired only a single salvo at 0412 from 19,790 yards. *Pennsylvania* was unable to find a target, so did not fire a single salvo.

All of the battleship salvos were directed at *Yamashiro*. The effects of the hurricane of fire will never be precisely known. *West Virginia* shot 93 16-inch rounds. *California* and *Tennessee* shot 63 and 69 14-inch rounds respectively. To conserve their limited supply of AP rounds, they used six-gun half salvos. *Maryland* shot 48 rounds of 16-inch shells. *Mississippi's* single 14-inch salvo was 12 rounds. Hers was the last battleship salvo fired during the battle and the last big-gun salvo directed at an enemy warship in naval history.[26] The cruisers used their much greater rates of fire to add to the weight of fire directed at the Japanese. Initially, all five of Oldendorf's cruisers directed their fire at *Yamashiro*. Even before the battleships opened up, hits were observed on Nishimura's flagship. In all, the five left flank cruisers fired a total of 3,100 6- and 8-inch shells. Light cruiser *Columbia* accounted for an incredible 1,147 rounds in 18 minutes. This meant she was dispatching a full 12-gun salvo every 12 seconds.[27]

The right flank cruisers also opened up at 0351, firing 1,077 6- and 8-inch AP shells and 104 high-explosive rounds. Most of these were from *Phoenix* and *Boise* with their 15 6-inch guns. Both opened up on *Yamashiro* at 16,600 yards and were soon firing four full salvos per minute. *Shropshire* began firing at 0356 after some radar fire control issues were resolved, but she shot slowly and deliberately.[28]

The gunnery phase of the battle lasted only 18 minutes. For the first seven minutes, *Yamashiro* was the only target – hundreds of 6-, 8-, 14-, and 16-inch shells splashed around her. *West Virginia*'s first salvo hit *Yamashiro*'s forward superstructure. Nishimura was not wounded and remained on the bridge until the ship capsized. The number of actual hits suffered by *Yamashiro* will never be known, but by 0356 *Yamashiro* was observed to be burning amidships, aft and in her bridge area. *Yamashiro* was able to maintain 12 knots and put up a brave fight using her two forward 14-inch turrets and secondary battery.[29] At 0356 hours she targeted *Phoenix;* at 0359 hours, *Columbia* was subjected to near misses from 14 salvos.[30] At 0401, she straddled *Shropshire* with several salvos. *Yamashiro* conducted a turn to unmask her two middle 14-inch turrets and proceeded to engage *Denver*, achieving a straddle at 0407. Given the storm of fire she was being subjected to, her shooting was remarkedly good. However, no American ships were actually hit by any of *Yamashiro*'s 14-inch shells. *Yamashiro*'s secondary battery was also active, engaging enemy destroyers. Its accurate gunfire contributed to the damage inflicted upon *Albert W. Grant*.

As American gunfire ravaged *Yamashiro*'s topside, it was the final three torpedo hits on her starboard side from the destroyers of Destroyer Division 56 that proved mortal. After it was apparent his destroyers were being subjected to "friendly" fire, Oldendorf ordered a ceasefire at 0409 hours. *Yamashiro* used this lull to turn south and increased speed to 14 knots. After the final two torpedo hits at 0411, *Yamashiro* came to a stop and developed a severe list. Her captain ordered the crew to abandon ship. *Yamashiro*'s brave but futile fight came to an end at 0419 when she capsized to port. Both Nishimura and her captain went down with the ship. Only three survivors of the approximately 150 men in the water chose to be picked up by an American destroyer. In what was another disaster, only ten of the 1,636 men aboard saw Japan again.[31]

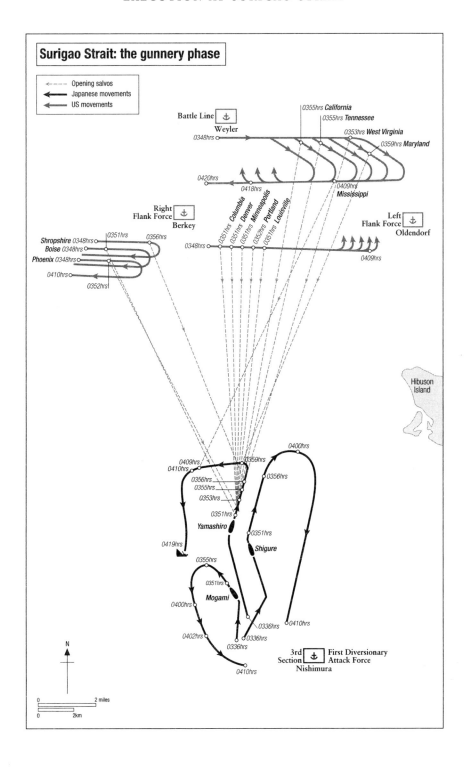

Surigao Strait: the gunnery phase

Opening salvos
Japanese movements
US movements

Battle Line
Weyler
0348hrs

0355hrs *California*
0355hrs *Tennessee*
0353hrs *West Virginia*
0359hrs *Maryland*

0420hrs
0418hrs
0409hrs
Mississippi

Right Flank Force
Berkey

Columbia
Denver
Minneapolis
Portland
Louisville
0351hrs 0351hrs 0351hrs 0352hrs 0351hrs

Left Flank Force
Oldendorf

Shropshire 0348hrs
Boise 0348hrs
Phoenix 0348hrs
0351hrs 0356hrs
0348hrs
0409hrs

0410hrs
0352hrs

Hibuson Island

0400hrs
0409hrs
0410hrs
0359hrs
0356hrs
0356hrs
0355hrs
0353hrs
0351hrs
0351hrs
Yamashiro
Shigure
0419hrs

0355hrs
0351hrs
Mogami
0400hrs
0336hrs
0410hrs
0402hrs
0336hrs
0336hrs
0410hrs

N

3rd Section
Nishimura
First Diversionary Attack Force

0   2 miles
0   2km

Mogami also took tremendous punishment. In the early phase of the battle, she took several 5-inch hits from destroyer *Bache*. More 5-inch hits followed at 0354 from American destroyers that were mistaken for Japanese ships. Starting at 0358, the Allied cruisers shifted their fire from *Yamashiro* to *Mogami*. Damage from 8-inch shells immediately ensued; one knocked out Turret Number 3 and another hit the starboard engine room air intakes, creating a fire and forcing one of the engine rooms to be evacuated. The ship was reduced to three operational shafts. *Mogami* turned to the west to unmask her torpedo battery and at 0400 fired four torpedoes at gun flashes from enemy ships to the north. These were spotted by an American destroyer, prompting Weyler to order evasive action by his battleships. *Portland* found the range at 0402 – two 8-inch shells hit the bridge, killing the captain and the executive officer. Two more rounds knocked out two more engine rooms, leaving the ship with a single operational shaft. The acting captain ordered the ship to withdraw, which she did at 8 knots.[32] On this new course, the battered *Mogami* encountered the Second Diversionary Attack Force.

ENTER THE SECOND DIVERSIONARY ATTACK FORCE

At 0200 on October 24, the Second Diversionary Attack Force departed Coron and headed to Surigao Strait. Shima's force was detected by aircraft during the day as it transited the Sulu Sea, but was not attacked. Shima did not coordinate his movements with those of Nishimura and planned his advance so that his force would attack separately from Nishimura's. The gap between the two forces was originally five hours, but Shima reduced this to two hours by increasing speed twice by the time his force began to enter Surigao Strait. At 0101 Shima informed all other commanders of his precise intentions. In this message, he stated his intent to enter the southern part of Surigao Strait at 0300, bypass the southern beachhead at Dulag, and then proceed to the northern beachhead at Tacloban where his force would attack American shipping. Following this, the Second Diversionary Attack Force would withdraw by way of Surigao Strait and arrive at its southern approaches at 0900.[33] As his force entered the strait, Shima had no real idea regarding the fate of Nishimura. Though Nishimura had issued status reports during the first phase of the battle, which Shima received, when he met serious resistance the reports stopped. The only information available to Shima were gunfire flashes in the distance and pieces of radio traffic from Nishimura's embattled ships.

The first firm indication that a second Japanese force was approaching the strait was a contact report on Shima's force from the PT boats at 0038. Oldendorf now knew he was dealing with two widely-spaced Japanese forces. Against Nishimura the PT boat attacks had proven to be just a nuisance; the story was different against Shima's force. The action opened at about 0315 when *PT-134* mounted an ineffective torpedo attack.

Disaster struck Shima's force ten minutes later. As Shima's force steamed off the southern tip of Panaon Island in the southern approaches to the strait, *PT-137* crept to within 900 yards of one of the Japanese destroyers and launched a torpedo attack. The torpedo passed underneath the destroyer but continued toward light cruiser *Abukuma*. It struck the ship in its forward boiler room. The explosion killed 30 men and reduced *Abukuma*'s speed to ten knots, forcing her to leave Shima's formation.[34]

Shima's remaining two cruisers and four destroyers increased speed to 28 knots. Shima was still oblivious of Nishimura's fate, but sighting ships on fire prompted him to assume that Nishimura's attempt to force the strait had not been successful. *Shigure* emerged out of the darkness and continued to head south at high speed. *Nachi*'s radar picked up contacts 13,000 yards away, and Shima ordered his two cruisers and four destroyers to prepare for gun and torpedo action. Without Shima's approval, his chief of staff ordered the two cruisers to maneuver for a torpedo strike against the distant and indistinct radar contacts. Shima decided not to countermand the order, so at 0422 *Nachi* and *Ashigara* each fired eight Type 93 torpedoes at the radar contacts. The targets of this attack were heavy cruisers *Louisville* and *Portland*. Though the Japanese had gained surprise, and no evasive action was taken by the American ships, none of the Japanese torpedoes found a target.

Immediately after firing her torpedo broadside, *Nachi* faced disaster. The burning *Mogami* had loomed out of the darkness minutes before. *Nachi*'s skipper failed to see that *Mogami* was advancing at a slow speed, rather than being stationary, and he failed to take proper measures to avoid the damaged cruiser. When *Nachi* failed to pass forward of *Mogami*, the two ships side-swiped each other at 0423. Frantic last-second maneuvers lessened the impact of the collision, but the result was still dramatic. *Nachi* took the brunt of the collision, suffering a large gash in her bow at the waterline on her port side. This serious damage reduced her top speed to 18 knots.

Shima's four destroyers advanced at high speed to the north in search of targets for their torpedoes. Since the American ships had ceased fire, there were no flashes of gunfire visible indicating potential targets. At 0435 Shima gave his destroyers orders to break off and head south. As his damaged flagship worked up to 18 knots, Shima contemplated his options. Senior officers on his staff advised that he suspend the attack, fearing they were headed for certain destruction. Without much debate, Shima agreed. Well after the war, he stated that his withdrawal was driven by a desire not to fall into a trap. Unable to gauge the enemy's strength, and having seen the destruction of Nishimura's force, Shima's decision was eminently logical. A short message to Mikawa indicated his plans: "This force has concluded its attack and is retiring from the battle area to plan subsequent action." Just like Kurita would do several hours later, Shima declined the opportunity to condemn his men to a pointless death.

OLDENDORF'S LACKLUSTER PURSUIT

Surigao Strait was obviously an American victory, but the lack of an aggressive pursuit allowed Shima's force to escape. As *Nachi* was running into *Mogami*, Oldendorf ordered his forces south to finish off the fleeing Japanese. Since the battleships were too valuable to risk in the dark, confined waters of Surigao Strait, Oldendorf only committed cruisers and destroyers. *Denver*, one of the left flank cruisers, reported three large contacts (the three Japanese heavy cruisers) 14nm to the south. Oldendorf tasked his last six destroyers with a full torpedo load to lead the pursuit. These were from an improvised unit called Destroyer Division X-Ray under an inexperienced commander. Oldendorf's order for them to head south was issued at 0432, but the six destroyers did not leave their screening position near the battleships until 0500. In addition to Destroyer Division X-Ray, both the left and right flank cruisers belatedly headed south at a leisurely 15 knots accompanied by seven destroyers from Destroyer Division 56.

With as many as eight cruisers and 13 destroyers, Oldendorf possessed a much superior force compared to Shima and the remnants of Nishimura's force. In spite of this, Oldendorf never pressed his advantage. He chose to fight a very cautious battle, primarily because he was uncertain as to the size of the force he was facing and because pre-battle intelligence suggested there could be additional Japanese forces operating in the area. This abundance of caution resulted in Shima making good his escape. At 0441 Shima instructed the surviving ships from Nishimura's force to follow him south. The escape of Nishimura's survivors looked uncertain even given the uncertain American pursuit. *Mogami* could only make 15 knots, so she fell behind Shima's force by 3,000 yards. Without her bow, *Asagumo* could not keep up and fell some 6,000 yards behind Shima's cruisers. With a top speed of about nine knots, her escape looked most doubtful. Only *Shigure*, still able to steam at top speed, looked likely to make an escape.

Given her position and large radar signature, *Mogami* was the first ship encountered by Oldendorf's pursuing cruisers. At 0529 *Portland* opened fire with her 8-inch guns from 19,500 yards (though her target may have been nothing more than a pool of burning oil).[35] Within minutes, *Louisville* and light cruisers *Denver* and *Columbia* also opened fire, targeting *Mogami*'s real radar return. This resulted in at least ten more hits on the battered cruiser that created fires amidships and on the aft flight deck. *Minneapolis* gained contact on *Asagumo* at 0533 and hit the destroyer's stern with an 8-inch shell, resulting in a fire and a reduction in speed to seven knots. Shima saw *Mogami* come under fire but continued to head south. He had abandoned *Mogami* and *Asagumo* to their fates.

The retreating Japanese were given a respite when Oldendorf ordered his cruisers to head north at 0537 to avoid possible torpedoes from *Mogami*. This was followed by a cease fire order at 0539. During the few minutes the cruisers had engaged *Mogami*, 197 8-inch and 356 6-inch shells were expended. The profligate expenditure left *Minneapolis* with a mere 15 AP rounds and *Denver* with only 113.[36] The cease fire provided another reprieve for *Mogami*. Incredibly, she was able to restore speed and continue south. She fought off an attack by *PT-491* at 0600 with her two remaining 8-inch turrets. At 0610, *Mogami* sighted Shima's cruisers ahead.[37] Against all the odds, it looked as if *Mogami* would reach safety. But just minutes later, three more PT boats (*PT-150*, *PT-190*, and *PT-491*) appeared and began their attack runs. Against the combined firepower of Shima's force, the Americans broke off the attack at 0637. Subsequently, *Mogami* faced another PT boat at 0645 and three more just five minutes later. These were driven off with the assistance of destroyer *Akebono* that Shima had detached to escort the wounded cruiser to either Coron Bay or Cagayan.

Oldendorf's decision to cease fire and turn his cruisers north essentially brought the pursuit to an early and unsatisfying end. Shima's force was now out of radar range and suffered no more attacks from American surface units. Belatedly, Oldendorf turned south again at 0617 and at 0643 ordered two light cruisers and three destroyers to finish off any Japanese cripples still in the area.

The last ship sunk by American surface forces was *Asagumo*. At 0600 the ship's captain decided to stop the destroyer's engines and abandon ship. With fires raging on board and dawn approaching, there was no hope of saving his ship. *PT-323* attacked the destroyer as the crew was abandoning ship, and one of her torpedoes struck *Asagumo* aft at 0702. *Denver*, *Columbia*, and an eventual total of eight destroyers arrived and took *Asagumo* under fire just minutes later. The Japanese ship replied with her aft 5-inch turret before sinking at 0721. Most of her crew – 191 men – perished, but 39, including her commanding officer, got ashore and were later turned over to the Americans.[38] As *Asagumo* slipped under, hundreds of survivors were left in the water. American destroyers were also coming across other groups of Japanese survivors, including a large number of those from *Yamashiro*. Oldendorf instructed the destroyers to pick up survivors as long as the destroyers did not become overloaded. These efforts were largely in vain, as few Japanese accepted rescue. Only three *Yamashiro* sailors were brought out of the water. Some of those refusing to be rescued eventually reached the shore, where they were most often killed by vengeful Filipinos. Only a handful survived to be handed over to the Americans. Later in the morning, when one of Oldendorf's destroyer skippers asked at 0735 what to do with the hundreds of men still in the water, Oldendorf simply replied, "Let them sink."[39] By this time Kinkaid and Oldendorf had much more pressing concerns than the fate of Japanese sailors that refused rescue.

Just before 0700, Kurita's First Diversionary Attack Force encountered the most northern of Kinkaid's three escort carrier groups off Samar. This was "Taffy 3" under Rear Admiral Clifton Sprague, who almost immediately issued requests for help. Oldendorf recalled his units in the southern part of Surigao Strait at 0723 to prepare to move north to render assistance. As the pressure on Sprague grew and his pleas became more urgent, Kinkaid ordered Oldendorf to bring his entire force north at 0847. Accordingly, Oldendorf formed a task force of

General Douglas MacArthur and Admiral Chester Nimitz, both theater commanders, had different visions for the direction of the American advance in the Pacific in late 1944. The split command arrangement became a problem going into the Battle of Leyte Gulf.

Admiral William Halsey, shown on the left, was the commander of the Third Fleet. Charged with providing cover for the Leyte invasion against the Imperial Navy, he acted in his usual aggressive manner to make a decision that has been criticized ever since.

Vice Admiral Thomas Kinkaid, pictured here in January 1945 in Lingayen Gulf, commanded the Seventh Fleet during the Leyte operation. His actions during the battle were a contributing factor in allowing part of his forces to come under heavy Japanese attack.

Rear Admiral Jessie Oldendorf was in charge of the American forces at the Battle of Surigao Strait. He had the time to set up an elaborate ambush against the approaching Japanese, which proved devastatingly effective. However, his pursuit of the shattered Japanese was lackluster.

Rear Admiral Clifton Sprague's quick and decisive actions turned what could have been a local defeat for the Americans into a victory.

Admiral Toyoda Soemu was the author of the Japanese plan to defend the Philippines.

Vice Admiral Kurita Takeo was the most controversial Japanese commander of the battle.

Ozawa Jisaburo, generally seen as the most competent Japanese admiral of the war.

Vice Admiral Nishimura Shoji was the only Japanese commander during the battle who obeyed his orders to the letter and led his force to virtual destruction.

Vice Admiral Shima Kiyohide fought hard to get his fleet involved in the assault on Leyte Gulf. Like Kurita, he declined to lead his force to total destruction.

The heart of the Third Fleet was its carriers, the most powerful of which were Essex-class fleet carriers. This is *Intrepid*, pictured in November 1944. She played a prominent role during the Battle of Leyte Gulf, conducting five major air attacks in two days.

Embedded within the Third Fleet were six of the most modern battleships in the world. This is *New Jersey*, pictured in 1944.

Left The standard American carrier fighter in 1944 was the F6F Hellcat, pictured here taking off from *Lexington* on October 12, 1944, during the air-sea Battle off Formosa. The Hellcat was superior to its Japanese counterparts.

Above This photo shows an Avenger being loaded with a Mark 13 torpedo, modified for greater efficacy following a series of problems earlier in the war. Torpedo bombers were essential to sinking heavily armored Japanese warships.

Left After a prolonged and painful introduction, the SB2C Helldiver proved to be a rugged and effective aircraft, eventually sinking more Japanese ships than any other Allied aircraft. Pictured is a Helldiver from *Intrepid* during the battle.

Top In the week before the American invasion of Leyte, the Third Fleet fought a major engagement off Formosa. An all-out Japanese air offensive succeeded in damaging two American cruisers with torpedoes. This is light cruiser *Houston* being towed clear of the area.

Above The centerpiece of the Japanese plan was the First Diversionary Attack Force under Kurita. It was built around five battleships. Three of those – *Yamato*, *Musashi*, and *Nagato* – are shown here at Brunei Bay before departing on their fateful voyage to Leyte Gulf.

Below The First Diversionary Attack Force pictured departing Brunei Bay on the morning of October 22. Of the three battleships and six heavy cruisers in view, only three of these ships remained to return to Brunei on October 28.

The first disaster to befall the First Diversionary Attack force was an ambush in the Palawan Passage by two American submarines on October 23. *Darter*, pictured here aground on Bombay Shoal, was lost the next day as she tried to finish off a damaged cruiser.

The Japanese conducted a series of attacks on October 23 to neutralize the Third Fleet. Though they sank light carrier *Princeton*, shown exploding in this view, their failure to neutralize the American carriers opened the First Diversionary Attack Force up to concerted air attack.

The First Diversionary Attack Force is shown here under air attack on October 24. The formation appears to be in disarray, but in fact the Japanese were using their preferred circular evasion maneuver.

In the center of this dramatic scene, superbattleship *Musashi* comes under attack. It required a minimum of 16 bombs and at least 11 torpedo hits to force *Musashi* under the waves.

Nishimura's force was only subjected to a single air attack on October 24 as it transited toward its destruction in Surigao Strait. This is *Yamashiro* under attack.

Destroyer *McDermut* was part of the American force that launched a series of devastating torpedo attacks on Nishimura's force on the night of October 24–25 in Surigao Strait.

Top The last battleship action in naval history occurred during the final stages of the Battle of Surigao Strait. Six American battleships, including *West Virginia* (shown here), engaged a single Japanese battleship.

Above Surigao Strait was the last major night engagement of the war. Possession of radar gave the Americans a decisive advantage at night. In this view, some of the eight Allied cruisers engage Japanese targets during the battle.

Below In the Battle off Samar, Kurita's fleet encountered a force of six American escort carriers, like *Kalinin Bay* shown here. All six carriers were built on cargo ship hulls and possessed no protection, limited armament, and a low top speed.

The American escort carrier force was escorted by three destroyers and four destroyer escorts. These were aggressively used to defend the slow escort carriers. The most aggressive was destroyer *Johnston*, shown here.

Destroyer escort *Samuel B. Roberts* was also thrown against Kurita's heavy ships. She launched her three torpedoes at a Japanese heavy cruiser before return Japanese fire sank her with heavy loss of life.

In this view, two escort carriers (with *Gambier Bay* in the foreground) and two destroyer escorts emit black smoke from their stacks, a highly effective tactic that greatly reduced the accuracy of Japanese gunnery.

In the first 30 minutes of the battle, the six escort carriers of Taffy 3 launched 95 aircraft. This is *Kitkun Bay* conducting flight operations, with shells splashing around carrier *White Plains* in the distance.

Overall, Japanese gunnery was mediocre during the Battle off Samar. In this view, *Gambier Bay* is straddled by Japanese shells and falls behind the rest of Taffy 3. She sank after receiving at least 26 hits.

In this view, heavy cruiser *Chikuma* lies dead in the water in the middle of a large oil slick. American aircraft accounted for three heavy cruisers during the battle, including *Chikuma*.

In this view, Ozawa's carrier force maneuvers in the initial stages of the Battle off Cape Engano. Note the antiaircraft bursts, indicating that the Japanese are using ineffective barrage fire.

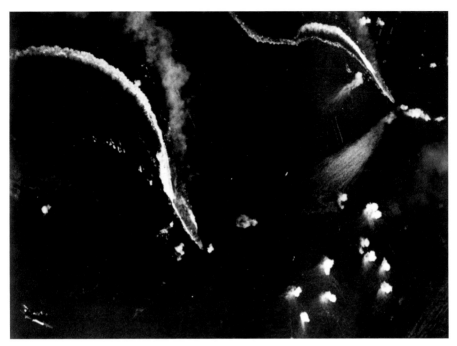

Of the four carriers in Ozawa's force, three were sunk by air attack and the last crippled. Here *Zuikaku* (center) and *Zuiho* (upper right) are attacked by Helldivers (left).

The last surviving Japanese carrier from the Pearl Harbor attack was *Zuikaku*. Her end came at Leyte Gulf after taking as many as six torpedo hits. Note the Avenger in the foreground.

One of the most iconic photos of the war shows light carrier *Zuiho* in her dramatic camouflage under air attack. Note the ship has already been damaged, as evinced by the buckled flight deck and the smoke issuing from the ship's starboard quarter.

Ozawa's force included two Ise-class battleship-carriers. These featured a flight deck aft but carried no aircraft during the battle. Despite coming under heavy air attack after the four carriers were sunk or crippled, both ships survived the battle.

The last phase of the Battle off Cape Engano featured an American
surface force mopping up the cripples from the preceding air attacks.
In this view, light carrier *Chiyoda* burns after being subjected to cruiser gunfire.
Her entire crew of some 970 men perished.

Leyte Gulf heralded the arrival of Japanese suicide tactics. Escort carrier *St Lo* was the
first ship sunk by kamikazes. Here the ship's magazine explodes from fires created by an
earlier suicide attack.

battleships *California*, *Tennessee*, and *Pennsylvania* because they had the most armor-piercing shells remaining. The battleships were escorted by three heavy cruisers and 20 destroyers with a total of 165 torpedoes. While Kinkaid was begging Halsey for intervention by TF 38, his orders to Oldendorf demonstrated a lack of alacrity.

FINAL BLOWS AGAINST SHIMA

Of Kinkaid's three escort carrier groups, the one located furthest to the south was Taffy 1 under Rear Admiral Thomas Sprague. After two of his escort carriers departed for replenishment at Morotai on the afternoon of October 24, Sprague was left with four carriers – *Sangamon*, *Suwannee*, *Santee*, and *Petrof Bay*.[40] Each carried between 26 and 31 aircraft. Though Taffy 1 carried the burden of conducting missions against Japanese remnants in the strait and in the Mindanao Sea, Taffy 2 under Rear Admiral Felix Stump was also able to contribute a small number of additional sorties. However, the majority of Taffy 2 sorties were devoted to the support of Taffy 3 after it came under heavy attack from Kurita's force. During the night word of the clash in Surigao Strait had reached the escort carriers, and assignments were made for the following day. Preparations for attacking Japanese ships included loading torpedoes on the Avengers. Four Avengers from *Petrof Bay* were launched at 0552, but larger strikes from *Santee* and *Sangamon* had already begun to depart their flight decks at 0545.

The four aircraft from *Petrof Bay* were the first to find the Japanese. They passed up attacking Shima's force and instead settled on *Mogami* and *Akebono* at 0741. The cruiser put up a strong barrage of antiaircraft fire from her remaining guns, and all the aircraft missed with their bombs.

At around 0840, *Nachi*, *Ashigara*, and destroyers *Shiranui* and *Kasumi* were attacked by Avengers and Hellcats from carriers *Santee* and *Sangamon*. *Santee* contributed nine Avengers and four Hellcats, with another two Avengers and six Hellcats coming from *Sangamon*. The Avengers all carried torpedoes. The aviators decided to go after Shima's two cruisers, which were misidentified as Fuso-class battleships. *Mogami* and her escorting destroyer were also spotted but were left undisturbed. The attack on *Nachi* and *Ashigara* was not well conducted. *Santee*'s nine Avengers attacked the ships from astern, so launched their weapons from unfavorable angles. Even in her damaged condition,

Nachi successfully evaded all the torpedoes aimed at her. One of the Avengers from *Santee* was shot down. The two *Sangamon* torpedo bombers came in from *Nachi's* port bow and pressed their attacks to about 1,000 yards before dropping their weapons. Despite the pilots seeing columns of water around the cruiser, these were also evaded by *Nachi*.[41] The only damage suffered was to destroyer *Shiranui*. She was heavily strafed by the Hellcats and suffered nine dead and 25 wounded.

Mogami and her sole escort were the target of the next attack by the escort carriers. A force of ten Avengers (each with two 500-pound bombs) and five Wildcats had launched from *Ommaney Bay* (part of Taffy 2) at 0650. At 0859, they began their attack against *Mogami*. The Avenger pilots claimed five hits on the cruiser; in fact, only three bombs struck the ship. New fires broke out on the ship and the last turbine ceased to function. When the Americans departed at 0910, *Mogami* was dead in the water and the fires were out of control. One bomb started a fire near the forward 8-inch turret barbette. The acting captain tried to flood the magazine, but the valves necessary to do so were damaged. A potential explosion of the forward 8-inch magazine put the entire crew in danger. Not wanting to jeopardize his crew, at 1030 the acting captain gave the order to abandon ship. Destroyer *Akebono* came alongside, braving the possibility of a magazine explosion, and took off the remaining crew. The destroyer then proceeded to fire a single Type 93 torpedo to scuttle the cruiser. *Mogami* sank at 1307 with the loss of 192 men (including one civilian), but 700 were rescued by *Akebono*. Four more wounded *Mogami* crewmen later died of injuries.[42] *Mogami* had put up an epic fight. In spite of the fact she had been hit by an estimated 100 shells, suffered an explosion of her own torpedoes, taken three bomb hits, and collided with *Nachi*, casualties had been relatively light.

Shigure was the only ship of Nishimura's force to survive. During the gunnery phase, her small radar signature allowed her to escape attention. However, being close to *Yamashiro* did not allow her to entirely escape damage during the first minutes of the American barrage; the destroyer was buffeted by near misses. At 0358, she was targeted directly and took a single 8-inch hit aft that knocked out equipment, making navigation temporarily impossible. Her commanding officer decided to retreat and never ordered a torpedo attack though there were targets only 12,000 yards distant, well within the range of the Type 93.[43] After withdrawing, *Shigure* was subjected to a PT boat attack at 0445 but used her 5-inch guns and her limited maneuverability to escape damage. Her skipper decided to bypass a refueling stop at Coron Bay and head straight to Brunei Bay, where the destroyer arrived at 1700 on October 27.

The remnants of Shima's force – two heavy cruisers and two destroyers – had survived a major surface action and a series of air attacks to make good their escape on October 25. But the fate of *Abukuma* was not decided until the next day. After getting hit by the PT boat torpedo early in the battle, the cruiser had restored speed to 20 knots and headed north to rejoin the fight. At 0515 she spotted Shima's force headed south and was ordered to join his formation. In her damaged condition, *Abukuma* was ordered to head to Cagayan escorted by destroyer *Ushio* at 0830. The cruiser was diverted at 2230 to the small port of Dapitan on northwest Mindanao, where the crew made repairs throughout the night. At sunrise the next morning, *Abukuma* and *Ushio* departed for Coron Bay. After only four hours of undisturbed transit, they were spotted by a group of 21 B-24 heavy bombers from the Fifth Bomb Group, 13th Air Force. Trying to hit maneuvering ships from the usual operating altitude of heavy bombers was hopeless, so on this occasion the B-24s conducted their attack from about 6,500 feet altitude. This made a huge difference in accuracy. Two bombs hit the cruiser at 1006 – one in the bridge area and another aft. Even greater damage was done by a series of near misses. A second group of 22 B-24s from the Fifth Air Force's 22nd Bomb Group immediately followed. These scored two more hits, one near the bridge and a second that penetrated into the aft engine room. The bombs created fires which raced along the deck. The captain ordered that the Type 93 torpedoes be jettisoned, but damage to one of the torpedo mounts prevented it from being trained, leaving four torpedoes in the mount. When the fires reached the area of the torpedo mounts, four of the huge Type 93s exploded at 1037. The resulting explosion destroyed the forward engine room, bringing the ship to a halt. A third B-24 attack at 1044 only accounted for more near misses. *Abukuma* was beyond saving, but remained afloat long enough for 283 of her crew to be rescued by destroyer *Ushio*. The veteran cruiser, part of the Pearl Harbor attack force, sank at 1242 with the loss of 220 men (added to the loss of 37 from the torpedo hit from the PT boat). During the action, *Abukuma* and *Ushio* shot down three of the low-flying bombers.[44] *Akebono* brought the survivors to Manila.

Surigao Strait was the last major night surface battle of the war. Predictably, it resulted in a decisive American victory. Nishimura's diversionary force was almost entirely destroyed, save for a single destroyer. Using radar and better tactics, the Americans defeated the Imperial Navy at its own game – a night surface engagement. Nishimura's force fought bravely, but almost totally ineffectively. After the battle, Japanese survivors believed that PT boats, not destroyers, were responsible for the many successful torpedo attacks, indicating the Japanese never understood what they were facing. Perhaps most puzzling was the lack of aggressiveness displayed by both Nishimura's and Shima's forces. Destroyer *Shigure* left the battle with all her torpedo tubes full, as did Shima's four destroyers. The performance of Nishimura's two old battleships was mixed, with *Fuso* sinking after taking only two torpedoes and *Yamashiro* taking a sustained pounding before succumbing. The toughness displayed by *Mogami* confirmed the courage of Japanese sailors, but even this display of tenacity made no contribution to victory.

The decision by Shima to avoid destruction and retreat foreshadowed Kurita's almost identical decision later in the day. After fighting hard to get the Second Diversionary Attack Force into the fight, Shima did almost nothing with the opportunity he had worked to create. His decision to retreat and avoid destruction was certainly the correct one. Sacrificing his men would have contributed nothing toward a Japanese victory.

Kinkaid and Oldendorf fought a cautious battle that left little room for error. Their plan maximized superior American firepower and used geography to full advantage. The key to victory was superior use of radar. It provided the Americans with superior situational awareness and critical targeting data for torpedoes and guns. Only the lackluster pursuit of Shima's force tarnished the American victory. An aggressive pursuit could have caught Shima's retreating units and likely destroyed them, but in the process Oldendorf's ships would have been exposed to a high-level torpedo threat in the confined and dark waters of Surigao Strait.

The Misunderstood Battle off Samar

The Battle off Samar is the most important of the four major engagements that made up the Battle of Leyte Gulf. It is certainly the least understood. In a battle pitting Kurita's force against a group of slow, unarmored, and lightly armed escort carriers, protected only by light units, the outcome was surely preordained. In fact, the Battle off Samar was an event unique in naval history. For the first and only time, a force of heavy surface combatants was faced with a situation in which it had to engage an enemy surface force while also contending with persistent air attack. The inclusion of American air power into the equation made the battle far from a predictable Japanese walkover. With the addition of uncertain Japanese leadership, combined with decisive American leadership, the result was an American victory against what seemed impossible odds. The Battle off Samar will always stand as an example of the tenacity and bravery of the American sailor, but its outcome should not surprise anybody who examines the action in detail with an analytical rather than an emotional mind.

The Battle off Samar was set up by Halsey's decision to go after Ozawa's carrier force. This key decision will be examined in a subsequent chapter.

TF 38 finally located Ozawa's carriers at 1640 on October 24. With this discovery, Halsey had to make a choice. He could defend San Bernardino Strait against what he thought was a crippled Japanese force that had taken a pounding for much of October 24 in the Sibuyan Sea, or he could move to the north and attack the newly-discovered Japanese threat from that direction. Given the immense resources at his disposal, he also had the option of doing a combination of both. As was almost inevitable, he decided to attack the Japanese carriers. Since Kinkaid also had made no provisions for guarding or even watching the key strait, it was undefended. This allowed the First Diversionary Attack Force to transit the strait around midnight. From there, Kurita headed south and headed to Leyte Gulf with a planned arrival time of 1100 on October 25. With four battleships, six heavy cruisers, two light cruisers, and 11 destroyers still at his disposal, it looked as if Toyoda's intention of getting the Combined Fleet's heavy units into a position to wreak havoc inside the gulf would be realized.

The question of how San Bernardino Strait, one of only two chokepoints leading from Philippine waters to Leyte Gulf, was undefended needs to be addressed. Obviously, control of the strait was critical to the success of the American invasion of Leyte. If control was not possible, it absolutely had to be monitored to ensure the American naval forces operating to the east of the Philippines weren't surprised. Despite this, neither the Third Fleet nor the Seventh Fleet ensured that the critical function of guarding or monitoring the strait was performed. Third Fleet left the strait totally unwatched by surface ships to attack what Halsey believed was a greater Japanese threat. He has been roundly criticized for this ever since. Nevertheless, there was another force with responsibility for defending the amphibious forces inside Leyte Gulf – the Seventh Fleet. Kinkaid had been monitoring Third Fleet communications throughout October 24. These seemed to indicate that Halsey was creating a force (the heavy units of TF 34) to guard the strait. In fact, Halsey only issued a preparatory order to make formation of TF 34 an option, and he never issued the "execute" order to formally create TF 34 on October 24. So Kinkaid was guilty of assuming, rather than ensuring, that a vital avenue of approach into Leyte Gulf was covered. The responsibility of leaving San Bernardino Strait undefended is almost always left on Halsey's doorstep, but Kinkaid rightfully shares the blame.

Kinkaid did make some arrangements for at least monitoring San Bernardino Strait, but these proved inadequate. At 0155 Kinkaid issued orders to Rear Admiral Thomas Sprague, commander of the Escort Carrier Group, to execute three searches, one extending 135nm north from Suluan Island in the eastern approaches to Leyte Gulf. This would have covered the strait. Sprague gave this responsibility to Taffy 2 at 0330. This order was received by Rear Admiral Stump, commander of Taffy 2, at 0430. In turn, he gave the responsibility of flying the search mission to *Ommaney Bay* in an order at 0509. Preparing for this mission was not easy on the small deck of an escort carrier, especially in dark and rainy conditions. This resulted in the ten-aircraft mission not being launched until 0658.[1] By this time the battle between Taffy 3 and Kurita's force was already under way. A planned search of the strait by Seventh Fleet Catalina flying boats based in Leyte Gulf was also botched.

Even if Taffy 2's search had been executed as planned and had discovered Kurita's fleet sometime earlier in the morning, there still would have been a major Japanese force loose in the Philippine Sea with no American force in a position to stop it. This is where Kinkaid's placement of Taffy 3 can be questioned. Even if TF 34 was in place off San Bernardino Strait as Kinkaid believed, in a major surface engagement some or all of the Japanese force could have forced their way through or somehow leaked through unengaged. Had this happened, Taffy 3 was right in the path of a Japanese force headed to the gulf. Since the Japanese detected Taffy 3 by visual means, just a few miles difference in its placement might have been enough to prevent its detection by Kurita's force. Leaving Taffy 3 potentially exposed in this manner was another oversight by Kinkaid and his staff.

SURPRISE OFF SAMAR

Between Kurita and Leyte Gulf lay Taffy 3. As the Japanese approached, Taffy 3 was 60nm east of Paninihian Point on the island of Samar.[2] Even before dawn, Taffy 3 had begun its morning flight operations. Twelve Wildcat fighters were sent to provide CAP over the ships inside the gulf, and these were joined by four Avengers and two more Wildcats flying antisubmarine patrols inside the gulf. There were also aircraft launched to provide CAP and antisubmarine patrols to protect Taffy 3. One of these aircraft, an Avenger from *Kadashan Bay*, sighted a force of Japanese warships 20nm north of Taffy 3 at 0647. The pilot identified them as four battleships, eight cruisers, and many destroyers – an amazingly accurate report. He immediately conducted an attack on one of the cruisers and was fired upon. Rear Admiral Clifton Sprague, on his flagship *Fanshaw Bay*, first thought the pilot was attacking part of TF 38, since it was inconceivable that a Japanese force could have transited undetected to within a few miles of his force. Within minutes, though, the identity of Japanese ships was confirmed, this time by lookouts aboard his flagship. Whatever doubt there still may have been over this incredible turn of events was quashed at 0659, when shell splashes were noted astern of Taffy 3.

North of Taffy 3, the Japanese were going through a similar process of surprise. At 0644 lookouts aboard *Yamato* spotted an American force to the southeast. Within minutes, the lone Avenger made its attack. It was quickly apparent that the American formation included aircraft carriers. There are many descriptions by different Japanese observers as to what they saw, but all agreed they were looking at carriers with an appropriate screen. Kurita's operations officer put the American force at five or six carriers with a screen including four or five heavy cruisers.[3] Vice Admiral Ugaki, on *Yamato*'s bridge as commander of Battleship Division 1, finally settled on six carriers, three cruisers, and several destroyers.[4] Some reports also indicated the presence of battleships.

From the start of the action, the Japanese could never correctly identify what they were looking at. All of Taffy 3's carriers were Casablanca-class escort carriers commissioned from July 1943 on. They were so new that they were unknown to the Japanese. According to Kurita's operations officer, there were no photographs of these ships in Japanese recognition materials.[5] After deliberation, the Japanese decided they were looking at "regular" (i.e. light or fleet) carriers. No observer identified them as escort carriers. While the Japanese inability to identify the hitherto unknown Casablanca class might be understood, the misidentification of Fletcher-class destroyers and John C. Butler-class destroyer escorts as cruisers and even battleships was unexplainable. Even as the battle developed over the course of the next two hours, the Japanese never corrected their mistake, and continued to fail to identify the composition of the American force they were facing. This failure was one of many reasons leading to Kurita's defeat.

As the first reports of an American force to the southeast were received, Kurita was in the process of changing from his nighttime steaming formation of four major columns to a daytime steaming formation of a circular formation suitable for antiaircraft protection. Before the transition could be made, the discovery of the enemy carriers prompted Kurita to order "General Attack" at 0703. Such an order committed his subordinate commanders to execute an immediate attack as they saw fit. Kurita's alternative was to form a battle line and subject the enemy carriers to concentrated fire. Forming a battle line and assigning targets would have taken time. Kurita selected the immediate attack option with one thought in mind – he had to disable the flight decks of the enemy carriers as quickly as possible so as to neutralize their ability to launch aircraft. This is why the misidentification of the composition of Taffy 3 was so critical. If the correct identification of escort carriers had been made, the slow speed of those ships gave Kurita the option of fighting a more methodical battle. However, with the identification that the carriers were fleet units, Kurita had no option but to order a general attack. Had he waited to form a battle line, fleet carriers could have readily escaped, since their speed (over 30 knots) was significantly greater than Kurita's battleships (the slowest was *Nagato*, capable of only 24 knots).[6] Japanese heavy cruisers possessed the speed to chase down even fleet carriers, but in a controlled attack scenario these would have been tied to the battle line. Kurita has been criticized for his general attack orders, but under the circumstances he had no choice. In his mind, failure to attack immediately would have permitted the American fleet to escape, thus bringing the battle to an end even before it had started.

The general attack order did have significant implications. It increased the level of confusion for Kurita and his staff, and this was further exacerbated by communications issues and reduced visibility. Kurita quickly lost control of the battle and never regained it. Any pretense of coordination between the various elements of the First Diversionary Attack Force was lost. When the battle was joined, Kurita's force was split into six parts. Two of these consisted of the four battleships; *Yamato* and *Nagato* operated together for most of the battle, but the other two battleships, *Kongo* and *Haruna*, operated individually for much of it. The six heavy cruisers made up two more groups. Cruiser Division 7 started the battle operating together with *Kumano*, *Suzuya*, *Tone*, and *Chikuma*. Cruiser Division 5 with *Haguro* and *Chokai* made up the other cruiser elements.

The last two groups were composed of the two destroyer squadrons. Light cruiser *Noshiro* led the seven destroyers of Destroyer Squadron 2, and *Yahagi* led the four destroyers of Destroyer Squadron 10. Kurita kept the two destroyer flotillas to the rear. This was a serious blunder, since these powerful ships played no role for most of the battle. They were not in position to screen Kurita's heavy ships from American torpedo attack and were too far back to execute a torpedo attack against the enemy. Kurita's thinking on deploying his destroyers was undoubtedly influenced by a desire to preserve their fuel to the maximum extent possible. He probably held them back to preclude any confusion on the part of his heavy ships as they conducted their gunnery attacks on the American carriers. Once the heavy ships had shattered the American formation, Kurita probably intended to have his destroyers mop up.

As Kurita's initial orders turned the battle into a melee, Sprague's first moves were decisive and effective. His aviators correctly identified the composition of the Japanese force 15nm to the north. Four battleships and six heavy cruisers possessed the firepower to lay waste to the escort carriers unless immediate steps were taken. From 0657 Sprague began issuing orders to save Taffy 3 from destruction. He first ordered a change of course from the southwest to the east. This was done to increase the range from the Japanese and because it was in the general direction of the wind. The slow escort carriers had to conduct flight operations into the wind to get their aircraft into the air. Fortunately for the Americans, the direction of the wind allowed them to launch aircraft and not have to steam in a direction that decreased the distance to the Japanese. To open the range as much as possible, Sprague increased speed to 16 knots and then to 17.5 knots. The escort carriers could go no faster.

At this point the escort carriers were in a circular formation about 2,500 yards in diameter, with the escorts forming another circle about 6,000 yards from the center of the escort carriers. Beginning at 0655, Sprague ordered every available aircraft into the air. Every ship in Taffy 3 was ordered to lay smoke. Ships began to produce black smoke from their stacks and white chemical smoke from smoke generators. Again, the Americans benefitted from a fortunate weather condition – the hot and humid air kept the smoke on the surface of the water, ideal for concealment of anything behind it. There were also rain squalls in the area that would prove useful in concealment. Having done all that he could do, at 0701 Sprague began sending clear text messages reporting his predicament and asking for all possible assistance.

With the critical exception of air strikes from Taffy 1 and 2, Sprague was on his own. Taffy 2 was operating just to the south and Taffy 1 was approximately 130nm to the south. Thomas Sprague responded immediately to Clifton Sprague's call for help and within minutes had received Kinkaid's approval to launch every available aircraft. Taffy 2 responded by launching all aircraft, and some of the aircraft already airborne were re-tasked to come to the assistance of Taffy 3. Taffy 1 was already under orders to strike Japanese surface units retreating from the action in Surigao Strait, which limited its ability to provide immediate help to Taffy 3. The last source of potential assistance for Taffy 3 was the one farthest away. After demolishing Nishimura's force and forcing Shima to turn back, the Seventh Fleet's battle line was some 100nm away when the Battle off Samar began. Oldendorf's cruisers were farther away since they were in the middle of their uncertain pursuit of Japanese forces remaining in Surigao Strait. Given the time required to assemble a task group and the speed of the American battleships, there was no prospect that the heavy ships could offer any immediate assistance.

Contrary to myth, Taffy 3 was far from helpless. Immediate assistance was available – in the form of 95 aircraft from its own flight decks and another 35 aircraft from nearby Taffy 2. By 0730, the six carriers of Taffy 3 had launched the following aircraft:

Fanshaw Bay	1 Wildcat, 11 Avengers (10 with 500-pound bombs and 1 with depth charges)[7]
Gambier Bay	10 Wildcats, 8 Avengers (1 with a torpedo, 3 with 500-pound bombs, 2 with depth charges, 2 with no payload)[8]
Kalinin Bay	10 Wildcats, 10 Avengers (3 with 500-pound bombs and 8 5-inch rockets, 6 with 100-pound bombs and 8 5-inch rockets, 1 with no payload)
Kitkun Bay	11 Wildcats, 6 Avengers (all with 4 500-pound bombs)[9]
St Lo	15 Wildcats, 4 Avengers (2 with 100-pound bombs, 1 with no payload, 1 with an unknown payload)
White Plains	5 Wildcats, 4 Avengers (all with depth charges equipped with contact fuzes)[10]

Taffy 2 was better prepared for surface strike operations, since the night before Stump had ordered his carriers to be ready to load torpedoes at short notice in expectation of attacking retreating Japanese units in Surigao Strait. When news arrived that Taffy 3 was under attack, the deck crews worked feverishly to re-arm the Avengers with weapons suited to attacking ships. This accomplished, at 0737 Taffy 2 turned into the wind to begin its launch. Within eight minutes, 20 Wildcats and 15 Avengers were in the air. All of the Avengers carried torpedoes.[11] Taffy 2 launched a second strike beginning at 0833. It took only 11 minutes to get the eight fighters and 16 Avengers in the air. Again, all of the Avengers carried torpedoes.[12]

Despite being committed to attack Japanese units retreating down Surigao Strait, Taffy 1 was also able to contribute to the defense of Taffy 3. When the battle began, eight Wildcats from *Petrof Bay* and *Santee*, six Hellcats from *Sangamon* (all carrying 500-pound bombs), and an Avenger with 100-pound bombs were over Leyte waiting to be called to strike ground targets. These aircraft were re-tasked to fly out to assist Taffy 3. Another Taffy 1 strike was launched at 0725. It was a large effort consisting of 40 aircraft: four Wildcats and six Avengers from *Petrof Bay*, five Hellcats from *Sangamon*, seven Hellcats and five Avengers from *Suwannee*, and eight Wildcats and five Avengers from *Santee*. As the strike group was assembling, Taffy 1 came under kamikaze attack. The fighters were recalled to defend the carriers. Eleven were subsequently released to accompany the Avengers to the target. Departing at 0910, they did not arrive over Kurita's force until about 1000.[13]

The combined efforts of the three Taffys accounted for a total of 196 planned sorties during or immediately after the period encompassing the Battle off Samar. The inclusion of a handful of other aircraft already airborne and re-tasked to assist Taffy 3 brought the total number of sorties flown against Kurita during the battle to over 200. This was a considerable level of effort and had a significant impact on the battle.

THE BATTLE OPENS

The opening portion of the battle featured long-range Japanese battleship gunnery trying to neutralize the escort carriers. Beginning at 0658 with the first salvo from *Yamato*, the salvos increased in frequency and gradually in accuracy. *Fanshaw Bay* and *White Plains* were the most exposed and so came under fire first. *White Plains* was targeted by both *Yamato* and *Nagato*. The carrier was straddled by large-caliber salvos; though shaken, she suffered no critical damage. *Haruna* and *Kongo* targeted *Fanshaw Bay* with a similar lack of success. Without any weather or smoke to deal with at this point, initial Japanese gunnery was generally accurate, as evinced by the many straddles of the two carriers. Though the Japanese claimed success from the extreme range of almost 30,000 yards, no direct hits were scored. As this spectacle was unfolding, American flight deck crews worked under fire to launch aircraft.

The growing pressure from the battleship gunnery ended when Sprague took the opportunity to steer Taffy 3 into a rain squall from

0706 until 0715. This and the smoke issuing from all American ships provided about a 15-minute respite. Coming out of the squall, Sprague changed course to the south and then to the southwest, which was in the direction of any help coming from Leyte Gulf. This was a risk, since it gave Kurita a chance to close the range if he had steered directly toward Taffy 3 instead of continuing on a course almost due east. Kurita did not take the opportunity to close the range to Taffy 3; for the first hour of the engagement he thought it was more important to stay upwind from the American carriers to prevent them from turning into the wind and launching aircraft. This meant the range to Taffy 3 was actually increasing despite the speed difference between the two forces. Even after Taffy 3 was observed to leave the squall at about 0716, Kurita maintained course to the east until about 0750, when his ships were north of Taffy 3. Only at this point did he change course to the south.

The effects of the weather and smoke on Japanese gunnery should not be underestimated. Japanese gunnery was dependent on good visibility since it used optical rangefinders for ranging and direct observation to correct the fall of shells. Japanese accounts state that they used radar for range-finding purposes, but it was not good enough to direct fire. Proof of this is provided by American accounts that Japanese salvos were well wide of their targets when the carriers were concealed by weather or smoke. Kurita stated after the war that American use of smoke was "exceedingly well used tactically," and this view was shared by his operations officer.[14]

By steering to the south, Sprague had actually opened the range against the Japanese. The providential rain squall had bought some time, and the first air attacks against the pursuing Japanese had begun. More had to be done to gain additional time. The best option Sprague had was to use his screening destroyers and destroyer escorts as aggressively as possible. Three destroyers were available to Sprague: *Hoel* under Commander L. S. Kintberger, *Heermann* under Commander Amos Hathaway, and *Johnston* under Commander Ernest E. Evans. All three were Fletcher-class ships with five 5-inch guns and ten torpedoes. At 0716 Sprague ordered them to conduct a counterattack to cover the escort carriers as they emerged from the squall. The actions of these destroyers have entered naval history.

The actions of *Johnston* were particularly noteworthy. Commander Evans was a made-for-Hollywood combat leader whom history had placed in the exact right place at the perfect time. He needed no orders to attack the Japanese as aggressively as he could. As fate would have it, his ship was the nearest to the Japanese when the action began. Evans immediately charged out of formation to lay smoke and engage a column of heavy cruisers with 5-inch gunfire at 0710. The target of this attack was *Kumano*, flagship of Cruiser Division 7 with Vice Admiral Shiraishi Kazutaka embarked. *Johnston* engaged *Kumano* with some 200 rounds of 5-inch shells, of which several were observed to hit. *Johnston* was taken under fire by several heavy cruisers and soon was surrounded by a forest of 8-inch shell explosions. Having received Sprague's orders to conduct a torpedo attack, Evans headed right for *Kumano* at 25 knots. Closing to within 10,000 yards of the cruiser, all the while under fire, Evans unleashed all ten of his torpedoes. After launching his weapons, Evans prudently retreated behind his own smoke. At 0727 one of *Johnston*'s torpedoes struck *Kumano* and tore off a section of her bow. The ensuing flooding was controlled, but her speed was reduced to 12 knots.[15] This was a critical early blow in the battle. Unable to maintain speed, *Kumano* was knocked out of the action. Making matters worse for the Japanese, Shiraishi ordered heavy cruiser *Suzuya* to come and get him and his staff. By the time this was accomplished, *Suzuya* never got back into the fight. Kurita ordered the wounded *Kumano* to make for San Bernardino Strait without escort. *Johnston*'s effective counterattack brought Kurita's heavy cruiser force down to only four effective ships.

Despite the fact that Japanese gunnery was not at its best on October 25, it was inevitable that Evans would eventually pay a price for approaching so close to a mass of enemy cruisers and battleships. At 0730 three large shells from *Yamato* and three 6-inch shells from *Yamato*'s secondary battery struck *Johnston*. The huge armor-piercing shells failed to explode as they ripped through the unarmored destroyer, but damage was extensive. The aft machinery room was destroyed, which reduced speed to 17 knots. Most of the 5-inch/38 guns were knocked out, but after repairs during a providential ten-minute respite as a squall passed over, three were brought back online. Evans was wounded but remained in command. *Johnston* was damaged but was definitely not out of the fight. Engaging this target from just over 20,000 yards, *Yamato* claimed she had sunk a heavy cruiser.

Hoel also responded to Sprague's orders to go after the Japanese. Kintberger selected battleship *Kongo* for attack. The destroyer opened fire with her 5-inch guns at 14,000 yards and closed to within 9,000

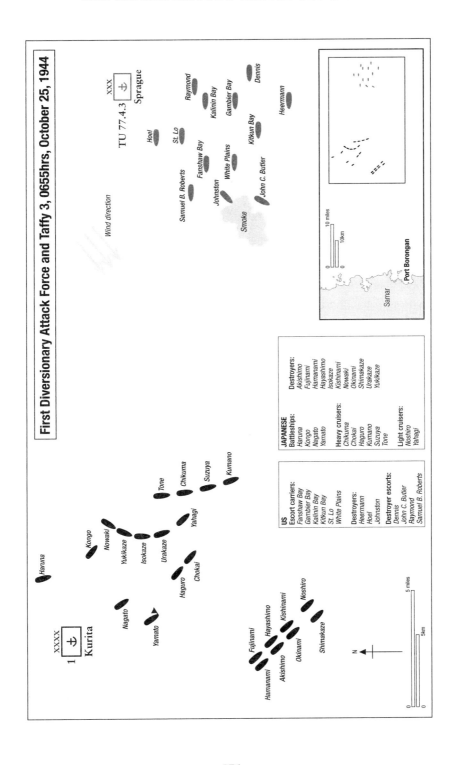

First Diversionary Attack Force and Taffy 3, 0655hrs, October 25, 1944

yards before launching five torpedoes. *Kongo* evaded the torpedoes at 0733; as *Hoel* made its approach, the battleship and heavy cruiser *Haguro* wreaked havoc on Kintberger's ship. Shells knocked out one of the two engines, three 5-inch guns, and the ship's radars. This damage did not prevent *Hoel* from responding to Sprague's order at 0742 to conduct a second torpedo attack. This time Kintberger went after heavy cruiser *Haguro*, which was leading a column of two cruisers. After closing to within 6,000 yards, he fired *Hoel's* last five torpedoes at 0750. Though the Americans were sure they had scored based on large columns of water observed around the cruiser, all the torpedoes missed.

The third of Sprague's destroyers, *Heermann*, was on the far side of the formation and did not get Sprague's 0716 order to conduct a torpedo attack. *Heermann* raced through the carrier formation to execute Sprague's 0742 order for a second attack. Hathaway joined on *Hoel* as she conducted her torpedo run against *Haguro*. At 0754 *Heermann* launched seven torpedoes at *Haguro* from about 9,000 yards, but these also missed. The cruiser took *Heermann* under heavy fire, but the destroyer was untouched. Next, *Heermann* spotted battleship *Haruna* and then *Yamato* and *Nagato* off her port bow. Hathaway went after *Haruna* with his last three torpedoes at 0800. Despite launching from only 4,400 yards, none of the torpedoes scored. The destroyer also banged away at the behemoth with 5-inch fire aimed at her superstructure. The duel between *Heermann* and *Haruna* lasted eight minutes. During this time, by using smoke and chasing shell splashes, *Heermann* was not hit by a single Japanese shell.

Hoel was the first destroyer to succumb to the Japanese barrage. After her torpedo attacks against *Kongo* and *Haguro*, she was only able to make 17 knots. This was too slow to withdraw from her exposed position with *Kongo* on one side and four heavy cruisers on the other. Skillfully maneuvering to evade the storm of shells directed against his ship, Kintberger survived for over an hour after the first hit on *Hoel* was recorded. *Hoel* took as many as 23 hits, but the actual number will never be known since many passed through the ship without exploding. At 0830 the second engine was knocked out, and the ship came to a stop. Minutes later, Kintberger ordered the crew to abandon ship as the Japanese continued to shell her. *Hoel* finally rolled over at 0855. Only 86 of her crew survived, including her skipper. Another 253 were lost either as a result of the Japanese barrage or in the water awaiting rescue.

None of Sprague's four destroyer escorts were ordered to take part in the first torpedo attack. With their slow top speed and weak armament of two 5-inch/38 guns and only three torpedo tubes, they were not suited or trained to engage enemy surface ships. Nevertheless, destroyer escort *Samuel B. Roberts*, under Lt Commander R. W. Copeland, joined *Hoel* and *Heermann* in the second torpedo attack. Using smoke she got to within 4,000 yards of the Japanese heavy cruisers to launch her three torpedoes at 0752. All missed, but *Samuel B. Roberts* used her 5-inch guns to engage another cruiser. Amazingly, the destroyer escort was unscathed by her close encounter with the quartet of Japanese heavy cruisers.

The skipper of destroyer escort *Raymond* also decided that Sprague's 0742 order for a torpedo attack applied to him. He headed toward *Haguro*, then the leading cruiser in a column north of *Raymond*. Getting to within 6,000 yards of *Haguro* through heavy fire, *Raymond* fired her three torpedoes at 0756. Again, all missed. *Haguro* fired some 15 salvos at the destroyer escort but failed to score a single hit. *Dennis* also answered the call to make a torpedo attack and also selected the Japanese heavy cruisers to the northwest as her target. At 0759, she fired her three torpedoes at *Tone* from 8,000 yards. This salvo was no more successful than the others fired by the destroyer escorts. And again, despite being under heavy cruiser fire for seven minutes, *Dennis* was undamaged as she retired with *Heermann*, *Johnston* (despite having no torpedoes left, Evans joined the second attack to provide gunfire support), and *Raymond*.

After more than an hour into the action, the Japanese had failed to deliver a crushing blow against Taffy 3. But by 0820, Sprague's position was becoming more serious. Taffy 3 remained on a southwesterly course but was under pressure from the four Japanese heavy cruisers (operating in two groups of two) to the northeast and east. Kurita's battleships were within range and targeted the carriers when visibility permitted. The most serious threat was the heavy cruisers which were on the port quarter of Sprague's carriers. At 0826 Sprague ordered three of his destroyer escorts to get between the carriers and the Japanese heavy cruisers on their port quarter. Responding to Sprague's orders, *John C. Butler* and *Dennis* moved from the starboard side of the formation to join *Raymond*, which was already engaging the cruisers with 5-inch gunfire. *John C. Butler*, the last destroyer escort to join the fray, looked to use her torpedoes but was unable to get into a favorable firing position. The destroyer escorts did engage the cruisers with gunfire, with *Raymond* closing the range to 5,900 yards. *Tone* was forced to briefly shift her fire from the carriers to deal with the brazen destroyer escort. The cost of distracting the Japanese cruisers began to mount. At 0850 *Dennis* received the first of three hits, but her speed was unimpaired. After both of her 5-inch mounts were knocked out of action, *Dennis* retreated behind smoke. *John C. Butler* also came under 8-inch fire but was not hit. As directed by Sprague, she continued to lay smoke on the port side of the carrier formation. *Samuel B. Roberts* was not so lucky. At about 0850, she took her first hit, possibly from *Chokai*. Subsequent damage was possibly caused by shells from *Nagato*. *Kongo* delivered the killing blow at 0900 when she hit the destroyer escort with two or three 14-inch shells. These turned the aft part of the ship into wreckage, tore a huge hole in the side of the ship, and knocked out all power. At least six shells of various sizes hit the ship. Copeland ordered the crew to abandon ship at 0910, but handling the many wounded meant the evacuation was not completed until 0935. At 1005, *Samuel B. Roberts* sank by the stern. Losses were heavy – of the crew of 178, more than half, 89, did not survive.

Not until late in the battle did Kurita's destroyers threaten the carriers. This attack was not ordered by Kurita, but was due to the initiative of Rear Admiral Kimura, commander of Destroyer Squadron 10. At 0845, from his flagship *Yahagi*, Kimura ordered the light cruiser to lead four destroyers into a torpedo attack. Kimura's intentions were quickly discerned by Evans on the wounded *Johnston*. He charged out of the smoke to engage the approaching Japanese with gunfire. *Yahagi* was taken under fire at 10,000 yards; as the range closed to 7,000 yards, the Americans claimed several hits on the cruiser (Japanese records indicate she was hit by a single shell forward on the starboard side that damaged an officer's stateroom.)[16] *Johnston* shifted fire to the first and then the second destroyer in column. Evans thought he had forced the Japanese ships to break off their attack when he observed they turned right 90 degrees and opened the range. In fact, the Japanese were turning to execute a torpedo attack. However, Evans' bold attack did prompt the Japanese to launch early and from an unfavorable target angle. When the torpedoes went in the water, they were 10,500 yards astern of the nearest carrier, *Kalinin Bay*, and the targets were headed away from the Japanese. *Yahagi* launched seven torpedoes at 0905, followed by three destroyers beginning at 0915 (*Urakaze* fired four, *Isokaze* eight, and

Yukikaze four). No hits were scored, though Kimura fancifully claimed three carriers and a cruiser sunk. The largest Japanese torpedo attack of the battle had ended in total failure. Earlier in the engagement, *Haguro* and *Tone* had already fired eight and nine torpedoes respectively, but without success. Failure to gain even a single torpedo hit during the battle denotes Kurita's failure to bring a critical component of his combat power to bear and was another element leading to the Japanese defeat.

After launching their torpedoes, Kimura's ships concentrated on *Johnston*. *Yahagi* and the four destroyers took *Johnston* under fire, joined by as many as three heavy cruisers. As the damage mounted and the bridge was set afire, Evans was reduced to conning the ship by yelling orders through an open hatch on the fantail to men below turning the rudder manually. With all power lost, at 0945 Evans finally gave the order to abandon ship. Japanese destroyers closed in and continued to pound the wreck. *Johnston*'s epic fight ended at 1010 when she rolled over and started to sink. Most of the crew of 327 got into the water, but 186, including Evans, were lost.

ESCORT CARRIERS UNDER FIRE

Though the Japanese were forced to deal with the counterattacks of the American destroyers and destroyer escorts, Kurita's real focus was attacking and sinking Sprague's carriers. At the start of the engagement, the carriers came under fire from Japanese battleships, and as the range closed, Japanese heavy cruisers also targeted them. This bombardment, lasting over two hours, was only marginally effective. There were several reasons for this. Foremost is the difficulty in hitting distant targets even under the best conditions. And conditions for Kurita's heavy ships were far from ideal. Their targets were obscured for much of the battle by rain squalls and smoke screens. When visibility permitted targeting of the carriers, the Japanese ships were often harassed by air and surface attack. Constant maneuvering to avoid these hazards made it difficult to formulate gunnery solutions.

The battle opened when *Yamato* fired her first salvo at 0659. This was the first time during the entire war that the pride of the Imperial Navy had fired her 18.1-inch guns at an enemy surface ship. Four more salvos followed by 0709. The second and third salvos straddled *White Plains*. *Nagato* also selected *White Plains* as her target. She fired four salvos before checking fire; no hits were registered, but the target was straddled. The carrier was shaken and all power was lost for a few minutes after some circuits tripped open.[17] The third salvo from *Yamato* was the most damaging, since it included a shell that exploded under the ship's keel. The severe shaking and the mining effect of the underwater explosion caused minor flooding and minor structural damage. Very luckily for *White Plains*, it did not hit closer to the aft engine room. Had it caused damage to the ship's machinery, *White Plains* would have most probably fallen behind the rest of Taffy 3 and been sunk.[18]

To be fair to the Japanese, *Yamato* and *Nagato* gaining straddles from between 34,000 and 36,000 yards was impressive gunnery. This accuracy was impossible to maintain as smoke covered the battle area. At 0715 both battleships shifted fire to *Johnston*, and about 15 minutes later *Yamato* hit the destroyer and claimed it sunk. At 0754 lookouts on *Yamato* spotted torpedoes which forced her captain to order a hard turn to port, taking her to the north away from Taffy 3. The battleship was forced to continue north for almost ten minutes until the torpedo tracks disappeared. This placed her at the rear of Kurita's formation and effectively took her out of the battle for a significant period. Back in the fight, *Yamato* was challenged to find targets in the midst of the ever-present smoke. At 0822 *Yamato* resumed fire and within minutes placed a six-shell straddle around *Gambier Bay*. Overall, *Yamato*'s performance was disappointing. The tough visibility conditions reduced her main battery to only sparing use, with only 100 AP rounds being expended during the entire action. Even her secondary battery fired only 127 rounds.[19]

Nagato faced the same challenges. After engaging *White Plains* at extreme range in the opening minutes of the action, her main and secondary batteries were only able to engage destroyers. She was also forced to take the same evasion course as *Yamato* at 0854 for ten minutes. Her combat log is marked by continual air attacks and references to smokescreens.[20] *Nagato* was only able to fire 45 16-inch AP and 52 high-explosive 16-inch rounds during the action, with her 5.5-inch secondary guns firing another 133 rounds.[21]

Kongo and *Haruna*, comprising Battleship Division 3, operated separately during the battle. *Haruna*, despite having her speed slightly reduced the day before from near misses in the Sibuyan Sea, had advanced the farthest south of any Japanese battleship by the end of the battle. Her first targets were carriers at 0702. After five salvos at extreme range, her main battery ceased fire. Not until 0813 was she able to resume firing at a carrier, but again this was at extremely long range. At 0854, Kurita ordered her to fire at a second group of carriers to the south (Taffy 2). This fire was totally ineffective. Only 95 14-inch AP were expended during the battle, but the 353 6-inch shells fired demonstrated *Haruna* was active in targeting Taffy 3's escorts.[22]

Kongo steamed the farthest east of any of Kurita's units during the battle. According to her combat log, it does not appear that she was able to engage any of the escort carriers until 0803. She was the most active Japanese battleship during the battle, firing 211 14-inch rounds and 272 6-inch shells.[23] At 0722 her main battery rangefinder was damaged by strafing, and repairs were not completed until 0900.[24] Her gunnery performance was mixed. At one point *Heermann* approached to within 4,400 yards of the battleships without harm, but later in the action *Kongo* inflicted fatal damage on *Samuel B. Roberts*. She claimed the destruction of one Enterprise-class carrier (cooperating with other Japanese ships) and one Craven-class destroyer (*Roberts*) during the battle.[25]

The biggest threat to Sprague's carriers were the four Japanese heavy cruisers that used their superior speed to approach Taffy 3 from its port quarter. They worked around to the port beam of the carriers, where they were in position to engage them from fairly short range while shooting through a reduced level of smoke. Late in the action, the heavy cruisers had closed the range to only 8,000 yards and were south of Taffy 3 in a position to cut off Sprague's retreat to Leyte Gulf.

Despite the best efforts of Kurita's battleships and destroyers, for almost an hour the combined efforts of Taffy 3's escorts, smoke, and air attacks had protected the carriers from severe damage. Smoke generated from all six carriers and from the destroyers and destroyer escorts on their starboard quarter succeeded in hiding the carriers from direct Japanese observation for much of the battle. During the engagement, the Japanese shot slowly and deliberately, using half (four gun) salvos. This made it easier for the carriers to use the tactic of chasing salvos – moving to the location of the last salvo to evade the corrections made for the next salvo. Nevertheless, four of the six carriers were eventually hit. Of these, only one was sunk.

As Sprague steered to the southwest, *Kalinin Bay* was in the rear of the formation. At 0750 she became the first carrier to be hit when a probable battleship shell went through the hangar deck and then out her unarmored hull.[26] As many as 13 other hits followed, all probably 8-inch rounds from the cruisers working around her port side. Damage was limited, since some of the armor-piercing shells literally went through the ship and others broke into two or three pieces and failed to detonate. The shells that did explode caused considerable chaos, including fires, flooding, and disabling the forward elevator. The damage control personnel performed well, putting out the fires and making sure the flooding did not knock out the forward engine room. It was critical to maintain speed, as falling behind would have meant almost certain destruction. The flooding did create an eight-degree starboard list, but luckily this allowed the holes on the port side to be plugged. Despite all the carnage, only five men were killed and another 55 wounded.[27] In return, *Kalinin Bay* used her aft (and only) 5-inch/38 gun to engage the heavy cruisers from a range of 18,000 yards.

Fanshaw Bay took four 8-inch hits and two near misses, all forward, that killed four men and wounded another 18. Damage included some small fires and light flooding, all of which was quickly controlled. The carrier remained capable of conducting flight operations. She too used her 5-inch gun to snap back at the Japanese cruisers.[28] *White Plains* took only a probable 6-inch hit and suffered light damage. In return, she fired back with a total of 127 rounds from her single 5-inch gun. Beginning at 0849, she opened up at a succession of Japanese cruisers which had closed to within six miles of the carrier.[29] *Kitkun Bay* was not hit but recorded several personnel casualties from the shrapnel from near misses. *St Lo* suffered no damage during the battle.

Gambier Bay was in the greatest danger, since she was located in the rear of Sprague's formation and was the closest to the Japanese heavy cruisers. She was also unprotected by smoke for an extended period; as the Japanese cruisers worked into a position on Sprague's beam, they were less impeded by smoke. Beginning at 0741, *Gambier Bay* used her 5-inch gun in a desperate attempt to ward off the cruisers. The escort carrier's captain successfully chased salvos for 30 minutes as the range fell to 10,000 yards. At 0810 *Gambier Bay* recorded her first damage when a shell struck the aft part of the flight deck and started a fire. Much worse followed at 0820 when a probable 18-inch shell from *Yamato* hit alongside on the port side and exploded underwater. The explosion ruptured the hull and water poured into the forward engine room.[30] This was a critical hit; with her speed reduced to 11 knots, *Gambier Bay* fell behind the rest of the formation and became the focus of Japanese attention. Four minutes after the deadly underwater hit, another shell hit the ship in the same area. Flooding increased and a port list developed. *Heermann* closed *Gambier Bay* at 0841 to find her burning and listing 20 degrees. After at least 26 hits from *Yamato*, *Haruna*, and several heavy cruisers, *Gambier Bay* went dead in the water at 0845 when the aft engine room was abandoned. Within five minutes her captain gave the order to abandon ship. Of her crew of 854 men, about 750 were still alive to go into the water. *Gambier Bay* capsized at 0907.

By about 0900, the last two Japanese heavy cruisers, *Haguro* and *Tone*, were off Taffy 3's port beam at a range of 8,000 yards. From this range, and largely unhindered by smoke, their fire was increasingly accurate. To deal with this threat, at 0910 Sprague ordered his remaining escorts to make another attack. Before this could be executed, *Tone* and *Haguro* ceased fire by 0917. *Haguro* was the most persistent tormentor of Taffy 3, firing 108 salvos during the battle and a total of 345 8-inch shells. Minutes later the torpedoes from *Yahagi* and three destroyers began to appear around the carriers. None hit, but some exploded prematurely nearby. Just as the Japanese appeared ready to finally close in on Sprague's carriers, Kurita called off his attack at 0911 with an order for his remaining ships to head north and join with flagship *Yamato*. This amazing turn of events was confirmed at 0925 when one of the signalmen on Sprague's flagship issued the immortal remark, "God damn it, boys, they're getting away!"

THE IMPACT OF AMERICAN AIR ATTACKS

The Battle off Samar was much more than a lop-sided fight between Sprague's escort carriers and light escorts and the heavy ships of the First Diversionary Attack Force. As the surface ships battled, there was also an air-sea battle unfolding. The scale of American air attacks on Kurita's ships from 0730 until about 0930 by over 200 aircraft was one of the heaviest onslaughts of the entire war. Unrelenting American air attacks were the main reason for the Japanese defeat.

Success by the escort carriers' aviators was achieved in spite of several constraining factors. Taffy aircrews were not highly trained for maritime attack, and the torpedoes or armor-piercing bombs needed to tackle heavily-armored ships were in short supply. From Taffy 3, most Avengers were launched with bombs instead of more effective torpedoes, for two reasons. Torpedoes took more time and preparation to load, which the deck crews on Taffy 3 did not possess. Once loaded with a heavy torpedo, Avengers could only be launched if the escort carrier steamed into the wind. Steaming to the southwest, as Taffy 3 was forced to do for most of the action, did not result in enough wind across the flight deck. Even though few Taffy 3 aircraft were properly armed to attack Japanese ships, and none of the FM-2 Wildcats carried anything more than machine guns, the pilots made unceasing strafing runs in the case of the Wildcats or dummy bombing runs in the case of the Avengers, forcing the Japanese ships to take evasive maneuvers. Because Taffy 3 could not steam into the wind while being pursued by Kurita, recovering aircraft during the battle was impossible. When Taffy 3's aircraft ran out of ordnance or fuel, they had to land on a flight deck in Taffy 2 or fly 100nm to the newly-opened airfield at Tacloban. In the eyes of the Americans, these attacks were driven by desperation and were poorly coordinated. However, the Japanese, on the receiving end of incessant attacks, saw it much differently. After the battle, Kurita and other officers in the First Diversionary Attack Force commented that the attacks were well coordinated, skillful, and aggressive. They viewed these attacks as more effective than those delivered by Halsey's aviators the day before in the Sibuyan Sea.[31]

Air attacks began as soon as 0645, when four *Fanshaw Bay* Wildcats on CAP reported that they strafed *Yamato*. Four more Wildcats strafed another battleship and a heavy cruiser. After expending their ammunition, they flew to Tacloban to rearm. At the start of the battle, Sprague ordered all available aircraft launched from his six flight decks. By 0730 all operational aircraft were airborne. This was a considerable force of 51 Wildcats and 44 Avengers. Aboard the Avengers was an assortment of weapons, but only one carried a torpedo. The first attacks by Taffy 3 aircraft were conducted in small groups. The first attacks from the newly-launched aircraft were recorded at about 0710. *Kongo* was subjected to what was described by the Japanese as a severe air attack from 0713 until 0728. Damage was light from a near miss on the port side near the stern. *Haguro* came under attack at 0717 from four *Gambier Bay* Avengers but suffered no damage. *Kalinin Bay* aircraft reported attacking two battleships and a cruiser around 0740, with the Wildcats strafing two destroyers. The first properly coordinated strike did not occur until 0830, when six Avengers and 20 Wildcats already airborne on various missions were joined by aircraft from Taffy 2.

With Taffy 3 under constant pressure, it should not be surprising that Taffy 2 mounted the most aircraft sorties during the battle. Admiral Stump ordered his aviators to cripple as many Japanese ships as possible instead of focusing on one or two. The first of six strikes consisting of 15 Avengers with torpedoes and 20 Wildcats was launched in just eight minutes. The second, launched at 0833, included 16 Avengers with torpedoes and eight Wildcats; the third mustered 12 Avengers (five with torpedoes) and eight Wildcats. The fourth, launched at 1115, was the biggest of the day with 37 Avengers and 19 Wildcats. The fifth consisted of 11 Avengers (with the last three available torpedoes) and eight fighters, and launched at 1331. The last strike, launched just after 1500, included 26 Avengers and 24 Wildcats. Total ordnance used by Taffy 2 in these strikes included 49 torpedoes, 76 tons of bombs, and 276 rockets.[32] Though it was operating just to the southeast of Taffy 3, the only time Taffy 2 came under fire was around 0854 when *Haruna*'s 14-inch guns briefly fired on the three destroyers screening the rear of Taffy 2's formation.

The incessant attacks by Taffy aircraft did more than just harass the Japanese. They were responsible for sinking three heavy cruisers and damaging many other ships. The first real damage was to *Suzuya* when at 0735 she was attacked by about ten Avengers from Taffy 3. The Avengers managed to score a near miss aft that knocked out one of the propeller shafts, reducing the cruiser's speed to 20 knots. Another attack against *Suzuya* was mounted at 1050 by as many as 30 aircraft. This time, a near-miss amidships turned deadly. Shrapnel from the bomb ignited the torpedoes in the starboard forward mount, starting a fire that caused other torpedoes to explode at 1100. The explosion caused extensive damage to the secondary battery and the machinery room located below, which left the ship unmaneuverable. For the second time that morning, Vice Admiral Shiraishi had to transfer, this time to *Tone*. When the fires reached the remaining torpedoes, a large explosion resulted at 1200. This caused the magazine of the secondary battery to explode, and soon the entire ship was an inferno. Some 620 surviving crewmen were taken off by destroyer *Okinami* after the order to abandon ship was given at 1300. At 1320 *Suzuya* sank. Two hundred forty-seven men were lost.[33]

Another of Kurita's cruisers to be sunk by air attack was *Chokai*. Her fate is difficult to retrace, since all her survivors were lost when destroyer *Fujinami* was sunk by TF 38 on October 27. Beginning at 0850, *Chokai* was hit by shellfire and crippled, then attacked by aircraft. At about 0905, she was surprised by four Avengers from *Kitkun*

Bay. Attacking against no antiaircraft fire, the American strike leader claimed the unlikely total of nine hits by 500-pound bombs.[34] Several bombs did hit the ship, causing severe damage – the forward engine rooms were knocked out and heavy fires took hold. Destroyer *Fujinami* was sent to her aid at 1018; by then the cruiser was unmaneuverable, so the destroyer took the crew off and scuttled *Chokai* with torpedoes.[35]

Chikuma was the last heavy cruiser sunk by Taffy aircraft. A group of four Avengers from Taffy 2's *Natoma Bay* caught the cruiser in an anvil attack at 0853. One torpedo hit the cruiser on her port quarter that knocked out her rudder and reduced her to a single screw and a top speed of 18 knots. When Kurita gave the order to break off the action at 0911, *Chikuma* could not comply. Kurita ordered destroyer *Nowaki* to go to her aid at 1100. Before the destroyer arrived at 1230, *Chikuma*'s condition was made much worse by two more torpedo hits in her port side in her machinery spaces. This was the result of another well-conducted anvil attack by Avengers from *Kitkun Bay*. This new damage resulted in both engine rooms being flooded and the cruiser coming to a stop at about 1110. Now dead in the water, *Chikuma* was helpless when three Avengers from *Ommaney Bay* detected her on radar through the clouds. They commenced their attack at 1415, all coming in on her port side. All three crews claimed a hit, and all three saw the cruiser capsize to port and sink stern first within ten minutes.[36] *Nowaki* was able to pick up about 100 men out of the water. The fate of *Chikuma*'s crew was equally tragic as *Chokai*'s. After picking up the crew, *Nowaki* headed north toward San Bernardino Strait. When she was sunk early on October 26, only a single member of *Chikuma*'s crew survived. The sole survivor had declined rescue by *Nowaki* and eventually reached shore to be captured by American troops.[37]

Haguro fought an aggressive battle and was also selected by Taffy aviators for attack. At about 0825 *Haguro* was hit by a 500-pound bomb from a *Fanshaw Bay* Avenger that penetrated the roof armor of Turret Number 2. The turret was knocked out, and 30 men were killed, but further damage was avoided by the quick closure of the anti-flash doors leading to the magazine. Strafing attacks disabled the main battery range-finder located above the bridge.[38] Just after 0900 the cruiser reported being strafed. After ceasing fire, she was subjected to an attack by torpedo-carrying Avengers at about 0930.

Many other Japanese ships were damaged by strafing during the battle. Among these was *Yahagi*, who incurred many casualties to her exposed antiaircraft gun crews.[39]

After Kurita broke off the action, Taffy aircraft continued to attack. The delayed strike launched by Taffy 1 at 0725 finally headed north at 0910. Not until about 1000 did they arrive in the area of Kurita's force. Now short of fuel, the strike commander ordered an immediate attack on *Yamato*. Despite five torpedo-laden Avengers setting up for an anvil attack on Kurita's flagship, no hits were scored. Other Avengers went after *Kongo* and *Haruna*, but these also failed to score. At 1240 *Kitkun Bay* Avengers attacked *Tone*. A single hit by a 500-pound bomb temporarily affected the cruiser's steering gear, but she was able to escape. *Noshiro* was attacked at 1243 by aircraft from Taffy 2 and suffered minor damage from near misses.

The weight of air power directed at Kurita's force by the escort carriers has few parallels in naval history. In total, the escort carriers flew 441 sorties on October 25 – 209 by Wildcats and 232 by Avengers. Sixty-eight of the Avengers carried torpedoes. This was more aircraft than TF 38 brought into action the previous day during the Battle of the Sibuyan Sea. In addition to sinking three cruisers and inflicting other damage on many other ships, the incessant Taffy air attacks had slowed the Japanese advance and introduced concern in Kurita's mind over the growing scale of attacks. Throughout the day, Japanese antiaircraft fire was heavy and fairly effective. Twelve Avengers and 11 Wildcats from Taffy 2 were shot down; losses from Taffy 3 are unknown, but were likely as high.[40]

THE JAPANESE VIEW OF THE BATTLE OFF SAMAR

Just as Kurita's force was shifting to an antiaircraft formation, lookouts on *Yamato* spotted masts on the horizon to the southeast. Within minutes, other ships sighted the enemy, which was recognized as "a gigantic enemy task force including six or seven carriers accompanied by many cruisers and destroyers."[41] Kurita's first estimate of the situation acknowledged mutual surprise on the part of both his force and the American task force, and assessed that the Americans would maneuver into the wind to launch aircraft. To counter this, in his after action report Kurita stated:

> So that we could take advantage of this heaven-sent opportunity, we should take after the enemy in pursuit formation and at top speed. We planned first to cripple the carriers' ability to have planes take off and land, and then to mow down the entire task force.[42]

Just as Kurita had hoped, instead of engaging empty transports, the First Diversionary Attack Force had been given a chance to engage the enemy's main task forces in decisive battle. His immediate concern was to preclude the battle against enemy carriers from becoming a one-sided action in which his force would get pounded by aircraft. This was the basis for his general attack order.

Kurita's decision to fight a pursuit battle was based on sound logic, but the execution of the attack was poor. Since the Japanese were in the process of changing formations when the battle began, there was confusion and delay in executing Kurita's plan. All of the battleships opened fire immediately. *Kongo* moved to the right flank of the formation and conducted her operations independently for the rest of the battle. The other three battleships fell behind and remained in the rear of the formation, with *Haruna*'s aggressive captain later pressing his advance. The lead elements of the attack quickly became the two cruiser divisions (with six heavy cruisers). Destroyer Squadron 10, with *Yahagi* in front, assumed a position behind the battleships. Destroyer Squadron 2, a powerful force with *Noshiro* and seven destroyers, was ordered at 0706 to assume a position in the rear of the formation. Kurita's use of his destroyers was extremely conservative during the battle. In fact, they hardly played any role at all. The reasons for this remain unclear. As always, Kurita was worried about the fuel status of his ships, especially the short-legged destroyers. Perhaps he wanted to avoid them using fuel at prodigious rates maneuvering in battle. More likely, Kurita planned to cripple the carriers with long-range battleship and heavy cruiser gunnery, and then conduct a mop-up attack with his destroyers.

However, for various reasons, the battle never developed as Kurita anticipated. Because of the smoke and squalls, the battleships could only fire at the carriers spasmodically. By 0710, *Yamato*, *Nagato*, and *Haruna* had checked fire because they lacked targets. *Kongo*, now located to the north and with a better view of Taffy 3, was able to continue firing until 0725. Thereafter, for most of the battle, the battleships were reduced to firing at "cruisers" or destroyers that emerged out of the smoke. Another factor was the beginning of American air attacks at 0710. According to Kurita's operations officer:

> The [air] attack was almost incessant, but the number of planes at any one instant was few. The bombers and torpedo planes were very aggressive and skillful and the coordination was impressive: even in

comparison with the great experience of American attack that we already had, this was the most skillful work of your planes.[43]

Added to the air attacks were the attacks by American destroyers. The observer quoted above indicated that the activities of the destroyers were effective, caused confusion, and delayed the Japanese advance.

Kurita's communications during the battle reflected the confusion endemic to the Japanese during the entire Battle of Leyte Gulf. At 0702, he sent a message to Nishimura that an engagement was under way and that he should join up. Of course, by this time Nishimura was dead, as Kurita should have surmised based on reporting from Shima. At 0730, Kurita's next message indicated that his force was engaging six carriers, including three fleet carriers. Five minutes later, he sent word that one of these carriers had been sunk.

By 0730 Kurita was already unhappy with the progress his force was making. To prevent the Americans from escaping, he ordered his six cruisers to pursue at full speed on course 110 degrees. Keeping on this course shows his determination to keep the weather gauge. About the same time he unleashed his cruisers, *Kumano* was hit by a torpedo from *Johnston* and fell out of formation. *Suzuya* went to her aid and never rejoined the fight.

An hour into the battle, the First Diversionary Attack Force was well spread out and had not delivered any decisive blows against the fleeing Americans. *Kumano* and *Suzuya* were to the west, out of the battle. Taffy 3 was now headed southwest, but Kurita was slow to react and he did not order a change of course to the south until 0750. The four remaining heavy cruisers formed the vanguard of Kurita's force. Steering south, they were for the most part clear of the smoke and located on the port quarter of Taffy 3. *Haruna* was still operating with *Yamato* and *Nagato*. *Haruna* and *Yamato* were busy engaging destroyers (identified as cruisers) from Sprague's second torpedo attack. Just before 0800, *Yamato* and *Nagato* were forced to turn to the north to evade torpedoes. This cost critical minutes and forced Kurita and his flagship seven more miles behind Taffy 3.

From about 0800 to 0830, Japanese pressure on Taffy 3 mounted. By 0810 Kurita's entire force was headed south, *Yamato* and *Nagato* having completed their torpedo evasion. *Haruna* was not forced to head north to avoid torpedoes, so she was now the closest battleship to the American carriers. After dealing with attacking American "cruisers" and destroyers, she was able to get a clear shot at the carriers and reported engaging one at about 22,000 yards. *Kongo* was now the Japanese ship farthest to the east, and she too was engaging the carriers at extended ranges. The four heavy cruisers continued to close on the carriers while firing deliberately. On the left of the formation was Destroyer Squadron 10, while Destroyer Squadron 2 remained astern of the battleships.

Had Kurita been aware of the location of his forces and had the benefit of reliable communications, this was the period he could have closed in for the kill. His cruisers were pulling ahead of Taffy 3 and were ready to cut them off from the south. His destroyers were positioned to attack from the north, and his battleships were maintaining pressure in the center. But as soon as the situation appeared to look promising for the Japanese, events changed. *Haruna* sighted Taffy 2 to the south and shifted fire onto this new target. At 0854 Kurita ordered her to pursue the new threat, which effectively took the battleship out of the effort against Taffy 3. Meanwhile, *Yamato* was struggling to get visual contact on the carriers, so was forced to engage them mainly with inaccurate fire using radar. *Kongo* remained a real threat to Taffy 3, since she was clear of the smoke and was able to engage both the carriers and their escorts; however, she was located well to the east of Taffy 3, so had failed to close the range. At 0830 the weight of air attack increased as the Americans began to coordinate their attacks. Their focus was directed against the cruisers, which were the most immediate threat to Taffy 3. Gaining surprise by coming out of a nearby squall, American aircraft succeeded in knocking out both *Chokai* and *Chikuma* by 0900. This left just *Tone* and *Haguro*, but these were scoring heavily against the carriers as the range closed. On the initiative of its commander, Destroyer Squadron 10 moved to make an attack, but was challenged by a single American destroyer and forced to launch torpedoes at fairly long range. The attack failed, though the commander of the unit reported sinking an Enterprise-class carrier, mortally wounding another, and dispatching three destroyers.

Kurita never understood the kind of battle he was fighting. The Japanese could not even decide what kind of carriers they were facing, since the silhouettes they observed were not in their recognition material. They decided they were facing regular carriers, and this assessment was supported by the fact that they had failed to gain much ground on the fleeing Americans after more than two hours of effort. This is a key point; despite the much faster speed of Kurita's ships, the Japanese had difficulty closing the range on Taffy 3. This was attributable to the combined efforts of Taffy 3's escorts and especially attacks from Taffy aircraft.

Only after the battle did the Japanese change their mind and assess that the carriers they had fought were converted (escort) carriers. The escorts were identified as cruisers and destroyers, so this was clearly a first-line American task force. Kurita essentially fought the battle blind. Given the heavy smoke hanging on the water and the intermittent squalls, he lacked reliable information beyond his line of sight. Communications with his other elements, especially the cruisers, was poor. He tried to improve his situational awareness by launching a scout aircraft from *Yamato* at 0812. Communications with this aircraft was suddenly lost at 0830. A second aircraft was launched at 0851, but after only 13 minutes it reported being chased by American fighters.[44] As a result, Kurita failed to recognize the increasingly desperate situation of Taffy 3.

KURITA BREAKS OFF THE ACTION

Kurita made more than his share of controversial decisions during the battle. His next one was made as the intensity of American air attacks seemed to increase and the American carriers seemed to be escaping. With no reliable information beyond that which he could discern from his immediate field of vision, Kurita had no way of knowing his cruisers had closed to within 8,000 yards of the American carriers and were methodically shooting them up. Photographs from the period show both American and Japanese ships in the same frame – the only time during the war this was the case. Without information to the contrary, Kurita had to assume the American carriers, estimated to be making 30 knots, had escaped.

There were other reasons why Kurita thought it was time to bring the battle to a close. A great victory had been won against a formidable enemy. Though given the opportunity to deal heavy blows to an American carrier task force, Kurita's primary mission was to penetrate into Leyte Gulf. He had to prepare his force for an expected aerial counterattack and then proceed with his primary mission. About the same time Kurita was making this decision, his battleships came under the heaviest air attack of the battle. The intensity of these attacks was only expected to grow. Regrouping his scattered force would increase its ability to withstand air attack. As always, the fuel condition of his destroyers was a concern. All these factors convinced Kurita he needed to regroup his force and assess the situation. At 0911 he began sending the message to his dispersed forces to assemble on *Yamato*, which had assumed a northerly course. With his force spread out over 25nm, it took a while for all units to respond. It was not until 0930 that *Haruna* broke off pursuit and headed north.[45]

Despite all the factors creating concern in Kurita's mind, in retrospect his decision makes little sense. His forces were locked in battle with main elements of the American fleet. Another American carrier task force had been sighted to the south but had yet to be engaged by other than long-range gunnery. In this ongoing battle, Kurita had the clear opportunity to inflict a severe defeat on the Americans. By breaking off the action against these carrier forces, the scale of air attack was certain to grow, whereas continuing the engagement had the potential to reduce it. In any event, withdrawing to regroup would not bring the First Diversionary Attack force out of air attack range. By breaking off one action, Kurita was left to pursue a much more dangerous course of action – breaking into Leyte Gulf, under air attack, while contending with other American naval forces gathering to destroy him. At this point, Kurita had gotten little, if any, rest for three days and was undoubtedly fatigued. This decision evinced his inability to mentally respond to a complex and dynamic situation. In any event, the Battle off Samar was over, and the way into Leyte Gulf seemed wide open for Kurita's force. But an even more dramatic decision was at hand.

Kurita's Decision

Kurita's order at 0911 for his ships to "Rendezvous, my course north, speed 20" essentially ended the Battle off Samar. When the order was issued, the First Diversionary Attack Force was badly dispersed and took some time to reassemble. The last to receive Kurita's orders and break off the pursuit were the heavy cruisers *Haguro* and *Tone* and battleship *Haruna*. Kurita, on *Yamato*, continued north until 1055, then came to the west and southwest until at 1147 the flagship was headed for Leyte Gulf. At 1205 Kurita informed Toyoda of his intention to penetrate into the gulf. Accordingly, at 1215 he ordered a course change to 240 degrees, which was directly toward the approaches of Leyte Gulf, now only some 45nm away.

As the First Diversionary Attack Force meandered off Samar, the Japanese tried to take stock of what they had accomplished in the just-completed engagement. It was a hard-fought action, but the Japanese were sure they had gained a major victory. At 1000 Kurita sent a message outlining the results of the battle. He claimed that two American carriers had been sunk, one of which was a large regular type, along with two heavy cruisers and some destroyers. When the results of Destroyer Squadron 10's torpedo attack were received, Kurita boosted his claims to "three or four carriers, including one of the Enterprise class."[1] In return, Kurita admitted that *Chikuma*, *Chokai*, and *Kumano* had been seriously damaged.

Even after the losses incurred in the battle against the main American carrier fleet off Samar, the First Diversionary Attack Force remained formidable. Kurita's fleet, now down to 15 ships, was built around four battleships. *Yamato* led the fleet; despite some minor damage she retained all her combat capabilities and could steam at full speed. *Nagato* had suffered damage which reduced her secondary battery, and her speed was no greater than 24 knots. *Kongo* and *Haruna* also retained their full combat capabilities, though *Haruna*'s top speed had been slightly reduced. The magazines on all four battleships were well stocked, since main battery expenditure during the battle off Samar had been relatively low. The two heavy cruisers retained their full speed, but *Haguro*'s main battery had been reduced to eight guns. *Tone*, in spite of being in the forefront of the pursuit, was essentially undamaged, but had fired 419 of her original stock of 1,000 8-inch rounds.[2] The cruisers had only used a small proportion of their torpedoes; *Haguro* had fired eight of her 34, and *Tone* had fired nine of 24. Light cruisers *Yahagi* and *Noshiro* led a force of eight destroyers, this number having been reduced after Kurita dispatched three destroyers to assist the cruisers crippled by air attack. The light cruisers were fully combat effective, but *Yahagi* had fired seven of her 16 torpedoes. The seven remaining destroyers were also in full fighting trim, but *Urakaze*, *Isokaze*, and *Yukikaze* had fired between 25 and 50 percent of their full torpedo load of 16 weapons. Considering what they had been through the last two days, Kurita's remaining ships were in good shape. Kurita did have concerns with the fuel status of his destroyers and a growing shortage of ammunition for the fleet's 25mm antiaircraft guns.

Though his force appeared in good condition to fight another battle, Kurita was obviously having doubts about his original orders to storm into the gulf. His maneuvering between 0911 and 1215, when he finally made his move toward Leyte Gulf, indicates a lack of certainty how to proceed. From the time the American carriers had been spotted, little progress had been made toward the gulf. When the Japanese first sighted Taffy 3 at 0645, Kurita's force was 64nm away from Suluan Island in the approaches to the gulf. At 0911 when Kurita ordered his force to break off the action, the distance was down to 43nm. By noon, it was still 45nm.[3]

It took Kurita a full three hours to mull his options over. When he changed course at 1215, it looked certain Kurita had decided to make a thrust into the gulf. But only 20 minutes later at 1235, the First Diversionary Attack Force dramatically changed course and headed north. By 1310 the Japanese passed the site of the battle with Taffy 3 and continued north. On the cusp of achieving his seemingly impossible mission, Kurita decided to disobey orders and break off the attack into Leyte Gulf. By doing so he eliminated the entire purpose of *Sho-1* and threw away the sacrifices of thousands of Japanese sailors that allowed the First Diversionary Attack Force to reach this position. It was almost inconceivable that a Japanese naval officer could act in this manner, especially when the stakes were so high. By not pressing the attack, Kurita eliminated any chance that the Imperial Navy would gain some sort of Pyrrhic victory in its last great operation.

In fact, Kurita had good reasons for turning back. The myth that Kurita threw away a chance for victory has survived largely intact to this day. This mythology has gone unchallenged partly because Kurita never fully explained his actions on October 25, 1944. As Kurita knew better than anybody, it was not simply a matter of storming into the gulf and achieving the objectives of *Sho-1* as laid out by Toyoda. Nevertheless, Kurita's retreat was the most controversial decision by any Imperial Navy officer during the war, with the salient exception of Admiral Yamamoto's idiotic decision to attack Pearl Harbor. As we examine Kurita's thought process on the late morning of October 25, it needs to be kept in mind that he was under extreme pressure and had been so for at least three days. It is very unlikely he got any rest during this time. After the war, he admitted to suffering from extreme mental fatigue during this period. Anybody would have been hard-pressed to successfully process the situation that faced Kurita after having experienced what he had for the last three days. On October 23 his flagship sank from under him and he was forced to swim for his life. The following day his force had come under relentless aerial bombardment which had been so fierce it forced him to temporarily abandon his mission. On the day of decision, October 25, he had been shocked to find an American carrier force barring his way to gulf. After a confused battle, during which his fatigue was already evident, he was faced with the ultimate decision. Either press on into the gulf, where he believed his force would face annihilation, or break off the attack and save his force to fight another day. He opted against annihilation. At 1236, he informed Toyoda of his decision:

First Striking Force has abandoned penetration of Leyte anchorage. Is proceeding north searching for enemy task force. Will engage decisively, then pass through San Bernardino Strait.[4]

Several key factors shaped Kurita's decision. Perhaps the most important was his assessment that overwhelming American forces were gathering to annihilate his force. A battle had just been fought with an American carrier task force; during the battle a second carrier task force had been spotted to the south. In an 1115 message, Kurita and his staff learned that American carrier aircraft were using Tacloban airbase. During the just-concluded engagement, American commanders had been active in communications, pleading in the clear for help. Kinkaid's 0940 message "Being attacked by four battleships, light cruiser and other ships. Request dispatch of fast battleships and a fast carrier air strike" was intercepted and relayed to Kurita at 1120. Another unencrypted message from Sprague requesting help be sent to Leyte at once was also intercepted and relayed to Kurita.[5]

As he struggled with his decision, Kurita was suffering from a severe lack of situational awareness. His efforts to see beyond the visual range of the massive bridge of *Yamato* had been thwarted when both search planes launched from *Yamato* on the morning of October 25 were shot down. From the time the First Diversionary Attack Force departed Brunei Bay, Kurita had not used his aircraft well. Of the 44 floatplanes available when the First Diversionary Attack Force sortied from Brunei on October 22, 36 were transferred to the 901st Air Group on Mindoro over the next three days. Five were lost when *Musashi* was sunk, and three were on *Yamato*. This left Kurita almost totally dependent on reconnaissance of Leyte Gulf by Japanese land-based aircraft, and they had failed to provide any information. The best intelligence received by Kurita of American forces inside Leyte Gulf was provided by a *Mogami* floatplane in a report received at 1400 on October 24.[6] Kurita's decision to place almost all of his floatplanes beyond his operational control was a mistake.

Communications problems and delays meant that Kurita knew little of what was transpiring with the other elements of *Sho-1*. Nothing had been heard from Ozawa. Since the success of Ozawa's decoy mission was unknown to Kurita, it made sense that the carriers he had just tangled with were part of the main American carrier force. At least Kurita was aware that his Third Section had been annihilated trying to enter Leyte Gulf that morning and that Shima had been forced to abandon his effort to penetrate into the gulf through Surigao Strait. He was also uncertain what success, if any, Japanese land-based air forces had gained. Based on what he knew, the First Diversionary Attack Force was fighting alone.

In the midst of this process, according to Kurita's battle report, sometime before noon a message was received on *Yamato*. An American task force had been located "bearing 5 degrees distance 113 miles from Suluan Light at 0945." This could only have been a report from a land-based aircraft. Kurita's staff assessed it to represent another American carrier force lurking to the north. The contact was only 60nm from the First Diversionary Task Force. Here was a chance to avoid an inglorious death against empty transports fighting a suicidal battle while trapped inside Leyte Gulf. The new contact represented a chance to sink carriers while maneuvering in the open ocean.[7]

There is a massive amount of mystery and doubt associated with the 0945 location report. No record of its origin or its receipt on *Yamato* has been found in Japanese records. There is suspicion that the message never existed among Japanese scholars and IJN veterans.[8] If it didn't exist, then why was this fiction invented? The reasons are simple – it provided an excuse to break off the advance and head away from certain destruction in the gulf. If it was just a fiction to save face, neither Kurita nor any of his staff ever confessed to it. In his later years, Kurita stated that the message came from his old Etajima (the Imperial Navy's naval academy) classmate Mikawa in order that he be given a glorious chance to die against a worthy opponent.[9] The mystery behind this key message may explain Kurita's reluctance to fully detail his decision.

Kurita and his staff had never hidden their preference to fight American fleet units rather than transports, and even worse, empty transports. The carrier force located to his north offered a chance to engage in decisive battle. There was no point trying to reengage the carrier forces to his south, since they were comprised of "regular" carriers with the speed to simply outrun him if he moved in that direction. On the other hand, the carrier force to the north probably included the fast battleships that the Japanese believed were moving toward the First Diversionary Attack Force, based on intercepts of open communications. If this was the case, then this task force would likely accept battle, giving Kurita another chance to strike a decisive blow. Whatever mental gymnastics Kurita and his staff attached to the 0945 contact report, it was fatuous to believe the First Diversionary Attack Force, steaming around blind in the Philippine Sea, could find an American task force spotted two hours earlier when even then it was three hours' steaming time away. The

Americans had been foolish enough to have their carriers surprised once by battleships, but it was unlikely that they would allow this to happen again.

According to Kurita's statements after the war, he made the decision alone to retreat from Leyte Gulf. He told his Chief of Staff of his decision and Rear Admiral Koyanagi Tomiji implemented it.[10] On the other hand, Koyanagi stated after the war that there was a conference with Kurita and that he and the entire staff decided on the plan unanimously.[11] Given the consensus-driven Japanese style of decision making, this is the more likely scenario. This is how Koyanagi put the situation:

> Under these circumstances, it was presumed that if our force did succeed in entering Leyte Gulf, we would find the transports had already withdrawn under escort of the Seventh Fleet. Even if they remained, they would've completed unloading in the five days since making port and any success we might achieve would be very minor at best. On the other hand, if we proceeded into the narrow gulf, we would be the target of attacks by the enemy's carrier and Leyte based planes. We were prepared to fight to the last man, but we wanted to die gloriously.
>
> We were convinced that several enemy carrier groups were disposed nearby and that we were surrounded. Our shore based air force had been rather inactive, but now the two air fleets would surely fight in coordination with the First Striking Force. If they could only strike a successful blow, we might still achieve a decisive fleet engagement, and even if we were destroyed in such a battle, death would be glorious.[12]

There is no doubt that Kurita held a fatalistic view of his prospects for survival under the *Sho-1* plan. Many of his officers expressed similar views. Kurita and his men did not mind dying in battle, but they wanted their deaths to count for something. Even before the departure of the First Diversionary Attack Force from Brunei, there was open discontent of having to sacrifice the fleet, which represented the cream of the Imperial Navy, for mere transports. Kurita shared this sentiment. His greatest fear, which was shared by Koyanagi, was that his force would find itself in Leyte Gulf with nothing valuable to attack, and then be trapped and annihilated by American air power and surface ships. To Kurita, his decision came down to practical matters. As he stated after the war:

> There was no consideration of fuel. There was no consideration of how to get home. We had enough ammunition.
>
> It was not a question of destruction. That was neither here nor there. It was a question of what good I could do in the Gulf.[13]

Looking at the situation from Kurita's perspective, he felt the best option was to order a retreat from Leyte Gulf. Within the context of his extreme mental and physical exhaustion, he must also be given credit for carefully analyzing the situation. From his perspective, he believed the following were true:

- There were two American carrier groups to his south.
- American carrier aircraft were operating from Tacloban airfield.
- Nishimura had been smashed and the American forces responsible for this were available to contest his entry into the gulf.
- The American invasion of Leyte had occurred five days before, thus the amphibious transports had already unloaded and departed the gulf.
- Whatever transports remaining in the gulf were empty; empty transports were not a strategic objective.
- No friendly forces were assisting him.
- American air attacks continued after he ordered his force to disengage at 0911, and the level of air attacks could be expected to increase.
- An enemy carrier force was located to his north, possibly with fast battleships.
- American naval and air forces surrounded the First Diversionary Attack Force and were closing in.

Given what Kurita knew, and his belief that his death and that of his men should not be meaningless, there should be absolutely no surprise that Kurita decided to head north and seek action with the supposed American carrier group there. Once he had made the decision, Kurita indicated after the war that his concerns shifted to the state of his fuel supply and the prospects of enemy air attacks in the Sibuyan Sea the following day. He never had a thought of turning back toward the gulf.[14]

Giving Kurita the benefit of the doubt in whether he carefully considered all options may be missing the bigger point. Was he up to the moment? His record throughout the war had been mixed and he had already made some tactical errors in the hours leading up to the final decision to halt the advance into the gulf. Among these errors was his decision to break off the pursuit of the carriers because the Americans had escaped, when in fact the American carriers were still in sight of his force. Breaking off the pursuit gave no guarantee that this would result in lessening the scale of air attacks; in fact, the opposite would probably be true. Kurita had reformed his force headed away from Leyte Gulf instead of toward it. This was a mistake if he really intended to press the attack into the gulf, but actually may have revealed his true intentions.

In the end, Kurita had no good choice. He could either follow orders and press into Leyte Gulf where he would have been in all likelihood annihilated for little or no gain, but in the process he would have fulfilled the intent of *Sho-1* and entered naval Valhalla. The other choice was to seek battle against another American force, knowing it was unlikely he could engage it, and avoid meaningless suicide. He declined a meaningless death. Only a Japanese admiral could be condemned for such an enlightened selection; had he been an American or British admiral, the choice would have not been remarkable in any way. In the 1950s, during an interview with Ito Masanori, a respected Japanese journalist on naval issues considered to be friendly with former Imperial Navy officers, Kurita changed his tune and stated that he had made a mistake by not attacking into the gulf. In 1978 Kurita told an old schoolmate that he ordered the retreat just because he did not think it was right to sacrifice his men.[15]

The real reason or reasons for Kurita's decision will almost certainly never be known. The author believes that Kurita made the correct decision and that there was no likelihood he could have acted any differently. Kurita never signed on to the suicide pact that was *Sho-1*. From the earliest point in the planning process he expressed his skepticism over it and his preference to seek a more meaningful death against the USN's main force. His reluctance to die without purpose came through on the afternoon of October 24 when he retreated in the face of unrelenting air attack in the Sibuyan Sea. When the air attacks stopped, he resumed his mission. Kurita expected to have to fight his way through the San Bernardino Strait, but, incredibly to him, this fight did not occur. When he encountered Taffy 3 off Samar, Kurita fought a half-hearted battle which he broke off prematurely. When given the chance to achieve a glorious sacrifice by attacking into Leyte Gulf, Kurita declined. Given that this gesture would have meant the annihilation of this force for only the possible opportunity to destroy empty transports, there was no question what he would do. The mystery message describing an American task force to his north, probably a fabrication, gave him an honorable alternative.

THE MYTHS SURROUNDING KURITA'S CHOICE

The controversy of Kurita's choice is driven by two key myths. The first is that Kurita had nothing in his way and once in the gulf he could have destroyed everything in sight. This is a constant theme ever since the dean of American World War II naval historians, Samuel Morison, declared there was nothing to prevent Kurita from charging into Leyte Gulf.[16] The corollary to this supposition is that once inside the gulf, Kurita could have proceeded to sink everything in sight, including all transports in the gulf.[17] The second myth, even more prevalent and pernicious than the first, is that the destruction of all the American shipping in the gulf would have constituted a major setback to future American advances. Thus by foregoing his attack into the gulf, Kurita threw away a chance for a decisive victory.

The first myth is the easiest to deal with. There was no guarantee Kurita could have fought his way into the gulf. In fact, it is unlikely that he would have succeeded in doing so. To block the entrance of a Japanese force into the gulf from the east, Kinkaid and Oldendorf had assembled a force much larger than what remained in Kurita's force. They decided that this force would wait for Kurita at the approaches to the gulf rather than charge east and meet Kurita's force in the open sea. Using a plan like that at Surigao Strait, the Seventh Fleet would ambush the Japanese on the way into the gulf. This force would have been supported by the remaining aircraft of the escort carriers and, later in the day, by the approximately 330 aircraft of TG 38.1. Given its performance against Taffy 3 just hours earlier, it is very difficult to construct a scenario in which Kurita's force would have been able to brush aside the Seventh Fleet and enter the gulf. Had any of the Japanese force been able to do so, finding the American shipping in the northern part of the gulf and then systematically destroying it, all the time under intense air and surface attack, would have been beyond imagination. The Battle off Samar provided empirical evidence of how Kurita and his force would have conducted a large-scale surface battle and the evidence shows that the Japanese would not have performed well. The odds against Kurita's 15 ships would have been great, since the Americans would have held a significant advantage in every category of combatants.

As detailed in more depth in the final chapter, the nature of a hypothetical battle inside the gulf is not hard to discern. Given the correlation of forces, it is unlikely the Japanese would have penetrated into the gulf. Assuming the possibility that some of Kurita's ships had made it into the gulf, it would have been extremely unlikely that the Japanese would have been able to methodically identify, engage, and destroy a significant number of the 28 Liberty ships and 23 LSTs present. It might have been possible the Japanese would have had fleeting opportunities to target a small number of transports, leading to the destruction of a handful. The elimination of a handful of Liberty ships or LSTs could have been shrugged off by the Americans. Even in the extremely unlikely event that divine assistance gave Kurita the opportunity to sink all the Liberty ships and LSTs present, and Kurita executed this opportunity flawlessly, their destruction, while not entirely unimportant in the short run, could also have been overcome and would have had little impact on future operations. To put these hypothetical losses into context, the United States bult 2,710 Liberty ships and 1,051 LSTs during the war. Had the Japanese reaped a rich harvest of shipping at Leyte Gulf, American shipyards would have made up the losses in short order. The myth that the Japanese could have successfully attacked into Leyte Gulf and that this attack had the probability to generate strategic effects is ridiculous on every level.

KURITA'S FLIGHT

Even after deciding to forego an attack into Leyte Gulf, the survival of the First Diversionary Attack Force was not assured. The first threat to Kurita's fleet was continued attacks from Taffy aircraft. At 1100 the commander of *Kitkun Bay*'s air group took off from *Manila Bay* in Taffy 2 and headed north to attack Kurita's retreating force. This attack consisted of 16 Avengers escorted by a similar number of Wildcats.

Another group of equal strength under the command of the *Kadashan Bay*'s air group commander also took part. After coming across the obviously doomed *Suzuya*, the Americans pressed on and spotted the Japanese fleet at 1220. The attack began at 1245. Minor damage was inflicted on *Nagato*. *Tone* was hit by a bomb at 1249 that temporarily disabled her steering and reduced speed to 15 knots.[18]

Taffy 2 launched its sixth and final strike of the day just after 1500 with 26 Avengers and 24 Wildcats. Only some of the Avengers carried torpedoes. By this point Kurita's force, with several ships trailing oil, was 135nm to the north. This attack wave was even less successful than the previous one; no hits were recorded against any Japanese ship.

Better results were expected from TG 38.1. This was the most powerful of Halsey's carrier task groups, with fleet carriers *Wasp*, *Hornet*, and *Hancock*, and light carriers *Cowpens* and *Monterey*. After breaking off from refueling, it was steaming west at high speed to get within range of Kurita's fleet. When its strike was launched at 1045, Kurita was some 335nm away, making this one of the longest carrier strikes of the war. The strike consisted of 48 Hellcats, 33 Helldivers, and 19 Avengers with bombs instead of torpedoes. Reaching its target at about 1315, the strike placed only a single hit on *Tone*, but the bomb failed to explode.

Hornet and *Hancock* launched another strike at 1255 comprised of 20 Hellcats, 20 Helldivers, and 13 Avengers. This attack had to cover 320nm to reach its target. Beginning at 1500, this failed to hit or damage a single Japanese ship. McCain's aviators had flown over 150 sorties with nothing to show for their efforts. Losses were high, with 14 aircraft being lost to combat or to operational causes. This dismal performance puts the results gained by the Taffy aviators earlier in the day in a much better light.

As the Japanese continued to dodge bombs and torpedoes, they were still looking for the American task force reported to be to their north. Six hours after turning north, Kurita had found nothing. The contact north of Suluan had turned out to be illusory. With no aircraft remaining to search, and no reliable communications with land-based air forces, Kurita realized there was no hope of finding the enemy.

Toyoda and his staff received Kurita's 1236 message that he was abandoning *Sho-1* at about 1600. Combined Fleet headquarters sent its reply at 1647.[19] When the response was received by Kurita and his staff at 1925, it confirmed that Toyoda agreed with their assessment that *Sho-1* was indeed dead. Unlike Toyoda's order the previous day that prodded Kurita to advance trusting in divine assistance, this order was resigned to the fact that *Sho-1* had failed. If Toyoda still believed in his plan, he could have given Kurita a direct order to change course and attack into the gulf. Even Toyoda knew such an order would have served no purpose. Some of his staff officers thought that Kurita should be ordered to head into the gulf, where some portion of the American fleet and many transports could surely be found. Toyoda decided against this because he had no way of understanding the situation Kurita was facing and did not want to restrict his freedom of action.[20] Instead he issued a vague order for Kurita to:

> If there is an opportunity to do so, the First Diversion Attack Force will contact and destroy what is left of the enemy tonight. The other forces will coordinate their action with the above. If there is no chance of engaging the enemy in a night engagement tonight, the Main Body of the Mobile Force and the First Diversion Attack Force will proceed to their refueling points as ordered by their respective commanders.[21]

At sundown, about 1830, Kurita turned to the west and headed for San Bernardino Strait.

Unless the Third Fleet could intervene, Kurita looked assured of escaping through the San Bernardino Strait. In a last effort to block the strait, Halsey detached the fastest ships from his battle line at 1622. Designated TG 34.5, and comprised of battleships *Iowa*, *New Jersey*, light cruisers *Biloxi*, *Vincennes*, and *Miami*, along with eight destroyers, this small but powerful force raced ahead to beat the Japanese to the strait. They arrived too late. At 2140 a night-capable aircraft from *Independence* spotted Kurita's force filing through San Bernardino Strait. The only ship not to make it was destroyer *Nowaki* loaded with survivors from *Chikuma*. Soon after arriving off the strait, the Americans detected the overloaded destroyer on radar at 0054 on October 26. Light cruisers *Biloxi*, *Miami*, and *Vincennes* opened fire at the surprised destroyer from 18,300 yards. After a four-minute barrage, the cruisers ceased fire to gauge its effectiveness. Seeing that the target was still moving, a second barrage began at 0101, joined by the 5-inch guns from two destroyers. This brought *Nowaki* to a stop. The two American destroyers closed in to finish her off. A massive explosion at 0132 marked the end of *Nowaki*, her crew of some 240, and all survivors from *Chikuma*.[22] This forgotten action accounted for over 1,000 Japanese sailors, an amount equal to the total number of American dead in the Battle off Samar. This was the final surface action of the Battle of Leyte Gulf and was the only time surface ships from Third Fleet encountered a unit from the First Diversionary Attack Force.

As Kurita's force transited to the west in the Sibuyan Sea on October 26, Halsey planned another major strike from TG 38.1 and TG 38.2. Both groups launched strikes at 0600, and McCain followed with two more. During October 26, TG 38.2 put up 83 aircraft and TG 38.1 another 174. This was a comparable effort to that on October 24 that resulted in *Musashi*'s destruction.

Despite the huge numbers of sorties, little additional damage was inflicted on Kurita's fleeing force. *Hancock*'s air group decided to attack *Kumano* which was proceeding alone after being torpedoed by *Johnston* the day before. The tough cruiser survived two attacks by TF 38 aircraft on October 25 and succeeded in getting through San Bernardino Strait before the arrival of Halsey's forces. Now, steaming south of Mindoro Island, she faced *Hancock*'s strike of 12 Hellcats, four Helldivers, and seven Avengers. In an attack from 0810 to 0850, the cruiser was hit by three bombs that knocked out seven of eight boilers and inflicted 40 dead or wounded. By 1000, she was able to restore speed to ten knots and was ordered to head to Manila. She arrived there on October 28.[23]

Most of TG 38.1's strike decided to go after Kurita's main force. The initial strike of some 80 aircraft from *Hornet*, *Wasp*, and *Cowpens* lasted from 0834 until just before 0900. *Yamato* came in for the most attention from the American aviators, and at 0845 she was hit by two bombs. Both bombs hit forward of Turret Number 1, where they penetrated the forecastle to explode on the upper deck below. No flooding resulted, and overall damage was light. *Nagato* was also subjected to attack, but four near misses from bombs caused no damage. *Haruna* was attacked by Avengers, but the battleship evaded all three torpedoes aimed at her. *Haruna* was not attacked by the first wave. A single bomber attacked *Haguro* at 0855 but achieved only a non-damaging near miss.[24]

Inexplicably, many American aircraft selected *Noshiro* for attack as the light cruiser steamed at the front of the Japanese formation. The first blow against the cruiser was delivered at 0846 in the form of a bomb that hit near one of the two forward 6.1-inch turrets. The explosion started a fire, but the ship's speed was unaffected. The nimble light cruiser proceeded to evade six torpedoes, but at 0852 a torpedo struck one of the port-side boiler rooms with devastating effect. Progressive flooding knocked out the propulsion system and within minutes *Noshiro* developed a 26-degree list to port, which was corrected to only eight degrees by counterflooding.

A second wave appeared over Kurita's force at 1031. Aircraft from *Hornet* decided to finish off the crippled *Noshiro*, which was dead in the water. A second torpedo hit the cruiser forward at 1039, and the ship began to settle by the bow. At 1113 *Noshiro* disappeared bow first. Two destroyers rescued 628 men, but 82 men were lost, including her captain.[25]

In addition to the heavy air attacks by carrier aircraft on October 26, the First Diversionary Attack Force was subjected to attack by US Army Air Force heavy bombers. The 307th Bomb Group dispatched 27 B-24 bombers that caught up with Kurita's force between Panay and Cuyo Islands. At about 1055 the group commander conducted the attack from 9,500 to 10,000 feet and selected *Yamato* and *Haruna* as the targets. Two squadrons were allocated to each target. Not surprisingly, the bombers failed to score a single hit, though near misses accounted for several personnel casualties on *Yamato* due to shrapnel. Among the wounded was Rear Admiral Koyanagi. *Haruna* suffered only minor splinter damage from the six bombs that exploded close on her port side.[26] The Japanese fought back fiercely, opening up with Type 3 antiaircraft shells from the battleship's main batteries at a range of almost eight miles. Against the constant altitude and speed of the B-24 formation, the barrage fire of the Japanese 5-inch guns proved very effective, with three bombers shot down and 14 damaged.[27] This was the last air attack on the First Diversionary Attack Force.

Kurita's straggling destroyers were the final ships of the First Diversionary Attack Force to come under air attack. By October 26 some of Kurita's destroyers were down to their last few tons of fuel, forcing them to reduce speed. Due to hull damage on October 25 from air attack, *Hayashimo* was down to only five tons of fuel by the morning of October 26. To make necessary hull repairs, the destroyer temporarily anchored off Semirara Island south of Mindoro. She was attacked by Avengers from 1045 to 1050 and had her bow blown off by a torpedo. *Okinami* came alongside to transfer fuel but was forced to depart when both ships came under air attack. The next day, October 27, *Fujinami* was ordered to complete the refueling and bring *Hayashimo* to Coron

Bay. The rescue effort was short lived; at about 0920 *Fujinami* was attacked by aircraft from *Franklin* and took a bomb amidships that resulted in the explosion of the torpedoes in the forward mount. The destroyer broke in two and sank. The entire crew was lost, as well as all survivors from *Chokai*.[28] Destroyer *Shiranui*, originally assigned to Shima's Second Diversionary Attack Force, was then given the task of rescuing *Hayashimo*. At 1330 carrier dive-bombers sank her trying to render assistance. Again, the ship's entire crew was lost. As the rescue attempts foundered, *Hayashimo* was subjected to additional attacks that rendered her steering gear inoperable and resulted in further flooding that forced her aground. Fires broke out which gutted her engine room. By October 28, with the ship firmly aground on a reef, it was obvious she could not be salvaged. Eventually, most of the crew was saved and the hulk not totally abandoned until December 3.[29]

Five other destroyers (*Hamanami*, *Kishinami*, *Akishimo*, *Shimakaze*, and *Urakaze*) reached Coron Bay and refueled. The last ships of Kurita's force, four battleships, three cruisers, and destroyers *Isokaze* and *Yukikaze* (both refueled by battleships) headed for Brunei Bay by way of the Dangerous Ground (instead of the Palawan Passage). Finally, on October 28, the sojourn of the First Diversionary Attack Force ended with the arrival of the last nine ships at Brunei Bay. Of the 32 ships assigned to Kurita's force at the start of the battle, only 22 were afloat by October 28. In addition to the ten ships sunk, three heavy cruisers were damaged so severely that they never made it home or never again saw active service.

In addition to the ships sunk between October 23 and 27, personnel casualties were very heavy. It is impossible to arrive at an exact count because of incomplete or conflicting records, but approximately 4,765 men were killed between October 23 and 27. It needs to be pointed out, though, that Kurita's decision to forego a suicidal attack into the gulf saved another 15,000 Japanese sailors, at least temporarily.

9

Halsey's Race to the North – Folly or Justified?

Of the two key decisions of the Battle of Leyte Gulf, those being Kurita's decision not to attack into the gulf and Halsey's decision to focus on Ozawa's carriers and leave San Bernardino Strait unguarded, Halsey's decision was clearly the most important. In the last chapter Kurita's decision was analyzed, and it was made clear that even if Kurita had proceeded into the gulf, the only thing that would have resulted was his own destruction. On the other hand, Halsey's decision had greater implications. By not guarding San Bernardino Strait, he created the conditions for the Battle off Samar to occur with the resulting heavy American casualties. Taking all of TF 38 north to fight Ozawa only to bring significant parts of it back south to support Taffy 3 meant that the full weight of the USN's most powerful force was never brought to bear against a single objective. Ozawa's force was heavily battered but not annihilated, and Kurita never faced the combined power of TF 38's air and surface forces. Halsey's decisions meant he threw away the potential for an epic victory in the largest naval battle in history.

Worst of all, the success of the diversionary aspect of *Sho-1* set up the mythology that the Japanese came close to victory. If only Kurita would have stuck to the plan! However clever the diversion of Halsey to the north was, it did not constitute victory nor did it lay the foundation for victory. Nothing could save *Sho-1* from itself. The lack of a decisive victory by Halsey's immensely powerful Third Fleet and the battering of Taffy 3 have been used by many to paint the battle as an American defeat, in spite of the shattering losses suffered by the Japanese.

THE OPERATIONS OF OZAWA'S
MOBILE FORCE, MAIN BODY

The operations of Ozawa's carrier force have been touched on only briefly. After inserting the Mobile Force, Main Body into *Sho-1* and giving it a diversionary responsibility, Ozawa and his staff assembled scratch air groups for his four carriers. The Main Body possessed very little striking power. The four carriers committed to the operation embarked only 116 aircraft, and most of these were flown by very poorly-trained aviators. Carrier Division 4, comprised of the hybrid battleship-carriers *Ise* and *Hyuga*, carried no aircraft. Ozawa planned to use whatever striking power he had to contribute to the air attacks planned against TF 38 on October 24. This was the key day for Ozawa. With the penetration of Leyte Gulf set for October 25, it was crucial that Ozawa's force be detected the day before so that TF 38 would focus on it and not Kurita's force. Ozawa was not very sanguine about his prospects of fulfilling his decoy mission:

> I had not much confidence in being a lure, but there was no other way than to try.
>
> I figured that you might concentrate and attack Kurita or you might concentrate the attack on my carriers, and let events take care of themselves; I just assumed it would be 50–50 chance. I knew that the decoy operation even using regular surface vessels is a very difficult operation, and also that using carriers for decoy operations would be more difficult than regular surface forces as a decoy.[1]

After a late start caused by having to load the aircraft by crane instead of flying them on the carriers, Ozawa's force departed the Inland Sea on October 20 at about noon. Passing through the Bungo Strait, the force made a diversion east along the coast until turning south at about midnight.[2] The American submarine wolfpack which had been positioned to monitor Japanese movements through the Bungo Strait had been pulled off station after October 18. Thus, Ozawa entered the open Pacific undetected.[3]

Things did not go according to plan for Ozawa on October 24. Land-based Japanese aircraft generated multiple contacts on TF 38, but Ozawa declined to launch his strike until he could confirm the enemy's location with one of his own search aircraft. The necessary conformation was received at 1115 with a report of an American carrier task group only 180nm to the southwest. Ozawa launched his strike and about half of the aircraft attacked TG 38.3. Before heading to Luzon, the strike reported seriously damaging two carriers (in fact, none were hit). Kurita reported that he had launched his strike to both Toyoda and Kurita. Neither ever received the message because of transmitter problems on *Zuikaku*.[4]

More important than the failure of Ozawa's only strike was that no American aircraft found the Mobile Force, Main Body until late afternoon on October 24. The Japanese had been making no attempt to maintain radio silence, sending messages from October 22, but the transmitter problems on flagship *Zuikaku* may have explained why none of these were intercepted and geolocated by the Americans. Ozawa's chief of staff thought it was very strange no American aircraft attacked on October 24, but assumed they were busy attacking Kurita's force.[5]

After the launch of his strike, Ozawa formed an Advance Guard and sent it south by 1500 hours. This force, under Rear Admiral Matsuda Chiaki (commander of Carrier Division 4), was comprised of *Ise* and *Hyuga*, escorted by the four large Akizuki-class destroyers. Ozawa informed Kurita of his operations, but again the message was never received. Matsuda's force had the nominal mission of mopping up the remnants of the carrier task force just attacked by Ozawa's strike, but it also increased the likelihood of being detected as it approached the known location of the American carrier force. According to Matsuda, his force continued south to attack the damaged American task force. With two carriers damaged, the task force was reduced to one carrier and two battleships. His two battleships and four large destroyers could defeat them in a night battle.[6]

HALSEY'S DECISION

All of TF 38, but especially TG 38.3, had a tumultuous day on October 24. Sherman's task force was the focus of Japanese air attacks during the morning and early afternoon, during which *Princeton* was crippled and later scuttled. TG 38.3 also managed to launch two strikes against Kurita's force. What it did not do was find Ozawa's carriers until late in the afternoon. Ozawa had done his best to allow the Americans to detect his force, including sending regular radio transmissions, launching morning searches, and then launching a full strike on October 24. Sherman believed the Japanese carriers were located to his north, so he asked Mitscher if he could conduct a search in that direction.[7] The aircraft took off at 1405 and soon thereafter spotted Matsuda's Advance Guard at 1540. An hour later, the search sighted Ozawa's carriers. The carrier force was identified as being comprised of four carriers, two light cruisers, and about five destroyers (a very close report; there were actually four carriers, three light cruisers, and four destroyers). The force was steaming west at 16 knots.[8] Ozawa was sure that he had been detected, since the uncoded transmission of the American contact report was intercepted. Ozawa sent a message at 1650 that he had been detected. This was a critical piece of information for the other Japanese commanders, but again the defective transmitter on *Zuikaku* prevented it from reaching Toyoda and Kurita.

Once it detected the Japanese carriers, it was too late in the day for TF 38 to launch an immediate strike. Halsey now had time to decide how to employ Third Fleet the following day. The destruction of Nishimura's force in Surigao Strait left only two remaining threats – Kurita's force in the Sibuyan Sea and the carrier force to Halsey's north. Halsey had three possible courses of action: he could take TF 38 north to deliver a crushing blow to the Japanese carriers while ignoring Kurita's force; he could keep TF 38 off San Bernardino Strait to defeat Kurita's force if it tried to transit the strait into the Philippine Sea en route to Leyte Gulf and ignore the newly-discovered carriers; he could divide his force in such a manner to deal with both Japanese forces at once. For the reasons discussed below, Halsey decided to order a full attack on Ozawa's force the next day. TG 38.2 and TG 38.4 were ordered north to join with TG 38.3 to attack the Japanese carriers during the morning of October 25. All of the battleships and escorts that would make up TF 34 stayed with the carriers. Before the battle was joined, TF 34 would be formed and deployed in advance of the carriers so it could complete the destruction of the Japanese force. This decision meant that San Bernardino Strait was not just undefended, but entirely unwatched.

Despite the obvious controversy of this decision, leading as it did to the costly Battle off Samar, the reasons, at least to Halsey, were not complex. In his message to Nimitz late on October 25, immediately after the battle and before he had a chance to "get his story straight" after making an apparent blunder, Halsey explained his action in the following manner:

> Searches by my carrier planes revealed the presence of the Northern carrier force [Ozawa's force] on the afternoon of October 24, which completed the picture of enemy naval forces. As it seemed childish to me to guard statically San Bernardino Strait, I concentrated TF 38 during the night and steamed north to attack the Northern Force at dawn. I believed that the Center Force [Kurita's force] had been so heavily damaged in the Sibuyan Sea that it could no longer be considered a serious menace to Seventh Fleet.

Halsey should be taken at his word. He had been ordered to attack the Japanese fleet if given the opportunity, and now he was selecting the main threat to TF 38 and preparing to crush it with overwhelming force. To Halsey, perhaps inclined to view complex matters without finesse, his choice was clear and decisive. This choice has been condemned, certainly after the fact, as disastrous.

As with any complex situation, there is important background to Halsey's decision. The outcome of the Battle of the Philippine Sea, fought just four months earlier, was important for two reasons. The battle resulted in a decisive defeat for the Combined Fleet. The Japanese carrier force, still seen as the most important element of the Combined Fleet, had been defeated. However, the full extent of that defeat was not knowable to the Americans, nor was the fact that the Battle off Formosa fought just days before the invasion of Leyte had further devastated Japanese prospects of rebuilding its carrier force. All that was knowable after Philippine Sea was that as many as three Japanese carriers had been sunk by air and submarine attack, but that most of the Japanese carriers had survived. These survivors were set to be reinforced by new construction ships. At least numerically, the Japanese carrier force still looked formidable. Of course the number of carriers possessed by the Japanese did not tell the whole story regarding the state of Japanese naval air power. As important as the number of flight decks was the state of training for the airmen flying off them. After facing extremely well trained Japanese air crew early in the war, the Americans witnessed the steady decline in the state of Japanese naval aircrew training. Philippine Sea seemed to represent the nadir of Japanese aircrew training. Nevertheless, it was not knowable to the Americans that the

Japanese had no prospects of retraining enough naval aviators before the American invasion of Leyte to fully equip their remaining carriers. In fact, the once powerful Japanese carrier force was an empty shell, but this was unknown to the Americans. Because the majority of the carriers themselves survived Philippine Sea, and the Americans knew other carriers were being added to the force, the Japanese carrier force was still considered a threat. In every other major battle of the war, the Japanese carrier fleet was the main threat. The Pacific War had become a carrier war, with carriers firmly supplanting battleships as a navy's primary striking force. The Americans had no way of knowing that by necessity the Japanese had turned this paradigm around in their planning for Leyte Gulf.

The second major implication from Philippine Sea was that the Pacific Fleet had only gained an incomplete victory. Nimitz wanted to complete the destruction of the Combined Fleet and thus gain increased operational freedom for future operations. He was disappointed that this did not occur at Philippine Sea and thus had inserted the instruction to Halsey that the destruction of the Japanese fleet would be his primary objective if the opportunity was presented. This part of Halsey's orders was totally unnecessary, as Halsey needed absolutely no prodding to aggressively seek out and destroy the Japanese fleet.

Halsey's desire to destroy the Combined Fleet was complicated by the geographic dispersion of the various elements of *Sho-1* and the sequence in which they were detected. Both Kurita's and Nishimura's forces had been detected early on October 24. After briefly attacking Nishimura's force, Halsey decided it could be handled by Kinkaid's Seventh Fleet. Kurita's force was clearly the bigger threat, so it was the focus of TF 38 attacks on October 24. Reports from the aviators indicated this force was heavily damaged, so much that it turned to the west at about 1400. Halsey and other members of his staff believed the aviators, leading to the assessment that Kurita's force no longer posed a threat. No surface force could withstand that kind of pounding and remain a threat. With the information available to him, Halsey had no way of knowing that his strikes had overconcentrated on *Musashi*, leaving most of Kurita's force battle ready. When Kurita turned back to the east after the air attacks were over and headed for San Bernardino Strait, his force was tracked by night-capable aircraft from *Independence*. Halsey received this information, but clung to his belief that this force had been so battered by air strikes that it did not pose a major threat to the Seventh

Fleet. By this point, the discovery of the Japanese carriers to the north had already captivated Halsey.

The decision-making process used by Halsey and his staff was part of the problem. Halsey had demonstrated throughout the war that he was an aggressive and at times bold commander who was familiar with taking risks. He was a man of immediate action. From his time as a carrier task force commander early in the war, he felt he had nothing to learn about the art of carrier warfare. Even as a fleet commander, he seemed most comfortable playing the part of task force commander, much to Mitscher's dismay. The staff he had built, and then brought with him when he took over Third Fleet, was unable to check Halsey's rash impulses. In the discussion of what to do in the aftermath of the discovery of Ozawa's carriers, Halsey focused on his fear of Japanese land-based air power. Coming from a man who had just led TF 38 in a two-month rampage in the face of Japanese land-based air power without damage, this was a curious fixation. To be fair, though, the loss of *Princeton* earlier in the day may have affected his calculations about the effectiveness of land-based Japanese aircraft. Nevertheless, this over-inflated fear of land-based Japanese aircraft led to the discarding of the idea of sending TF 34 and a single carrier task force to cover San Bernardino Strait. It was safer to adhere to the principle of concentration of force. If TF 38 remained concentrated, it had the power to utterly destroy the Japanese carrier force; in turn, this could affect the future course of the war. During this discussion of the best course of action, Halsey and his staff failed to consult principal subordinates, like Mitscher, and the staff did not come up with a viable alternative course of action to consider. When one staff officer failed to agree with the consensus to go after the Japanese carrier force with the entirety of TF 38, Halsey cut off debate.[9]

Given all these factors, it remains a foregone conclusion that at 1950 Halsey ordered his entire force north to crush what he assessed as the primary threat – Ozawa's carrier force. He decided to do so with the entirety of his resources – all three carrier task groups available to him and the battleships of TF 34. By so doing, he decided to ignore the threat posed by Kurita's force which was headed toward San Bernardino Strait. Even if Kurita's force did advance through the strait, Halsey and his staff assessed that it lacked the power to conduct anything more than hit and run attacks. The Seventh Fleet should be able to contend with this force and its reduced capabilities.[10]

He kept TF 38 together because that was how TF 38 fought and because, as he stated after the war, he did not want to divide his force in the face of the enemy. It kept the initiative in his hands and increased the possibility of surprise, Halsey assessed. A decisive victory was most likely if the carriers of TF 38 worked with the battleships of TF 34. This was USN doctrine and Halsey fully supported it. The final destruction of the Japanese carrier force would constitute a decisive victory. Not only would it eliminate the main threat to the invasion, but it would cripple the IJN's ability to interfere with future operations.

After making his decision, Halsey and his staff received word at 2006 that an *Independence* night aircraft had spotted the Japanese force in the Sibuyan Sea headed toward San Bernardino Strait at 12 knots. Halsey ordered that the contact report be sent to Kinkaid and then went to get his first sleep in two days.[11]

Some of Halsey's commanders did not agree with the 1950 order that sent TF 38 racing to the north to engage Ozawa. Rear Admiral Bogan, commanding TG 38.2 that included the light carrier *Independence* and its night-capable air group, was tracking the movement of Kurita's force toward San Bernardino Strait with *Independence's* commanding officer. Not only was Kurita tracking toward the strait, but the navigation lights in the strait were turned on. Bogan passed this information personally to Halsey's flagship, but was brushed off by a staff officer who indicated that the staff already had the information from *Independence's* aircraft. Bogan stated well after the war that he would have used TF 34 and TG 38.2 to guard the strait and sent the rest of TF 38 north to deal with Ozawa. He failed to pass that suggestion to Halsey.[12] Vice Admiral Lee had a similar experience, sending two messages to Halsey that he believed Ozawa was a decoy and that Kurita would attempt to come through the strait. He was also ignored.[13] Mitscher took a much more passive approach. After his staff received the 2305 report from one of *Independence's* aircraft confirming the continued movement of Kurita's force to the strait, they urged Mitscher to intervene with Halsey. After confirming whether Halsey was a recipient of the 2305 report, he told his staff, "If he wants my advice, he'll ask for it."[14]

Faced with two threats, Halsey should have divided his force to account for both. Certainly, TF 38 had the strength to do so. But he resisted this notion for several reasons. The first was his adherence to the military principle of concentration of force. To divide TF 38 meant it might be defeated in detail. This ruled out leaving TF 34 and TG 38.2 to cover San Bernardino Strait. Only if TF 38 remained concentrated could it deliver a decisive blow against the Japanese carrier force.

There were other reasons why Halsey declined to fight two different battles several hundred miles apart, one against Kurita's force and one against Ozawa's carriers. The simplest one is that there was no battle plan on how to do so. Existing doctrine focused on concentration of force at the decisive point, and there was no guidance on how to fight two major battles at once. Given Halsey's command style, it would have been difficult for Halsey and his staff to fight a distributed battle, since they were intent on performing as both fleet and task force commanders.

A final reason was that Halsey was working under conditions of extreme fatigue. Just as Kurita had not had any sleep for several days leading to his momentous October 25 decision, Halsey had not slept for nearly two days.[15] The fatigue enveloping Halsey and his staff reduced the chances that they would step beyond existing doctrine and procedures to devise an entirely new approach for an entirely new problem.[16] In the end, Halsey decided to take his entire force to go after Ozawa. Not a single ship was left to defend or even watch San Bernardino Strait.

Though some of Halsey's principal subordinates had serious issues at the time with Halsey's plan to take his entire force north, most criticism against Halsey has been made with the benefit of 20/20 hindsight. Knowing after the fact that Ozawa's force was toothless, that Kurita's force was still combat effective and was intent on transiting San Bernardino Strait, and that Japanese land-based air forces had expended most of their capabilities on October 24, makes it much easier to recommend a different course of action than the one Halsey selected. Given perfect intelligence of the above factors, it becomes obvious that Halsey should have divided his force to engage both Ozawa's and Kurita's forces simultaneously. To defend the strait, TF 34 should have been formed and been provided air cover by TG 38.2. As TG 38.1 reached the battle area later on October 25, it could have joined those forces off the strait. TF 34 had been allocated six fast battleships, two heavy cruisers, five light cruisers, and 18 destroyers, compared to Kurita's four battleships, six heavy cruisers, two light cruisers, and 11 destroyers. The Americans would have also had the benefit of air superiority, making it easy to find Kurita's force and to attack it incessantly during any surface engagement. TF 34, though it did not have any opportunities to work together and was rusty in the basic skills of surface warfare, was still superior in every measure of surface warfare compared to Kurita's force which just a few hours later performed with alarming mediocrity off Samar.

Meanwhile, TG 38.3 and TG 38.4 still brought about 450 aircraft to bear against Ozawa's force. This force could have mounted a similar level of sorties as TF 38 actually did on October 25 since TG 38.2 was the smallest of the three task groups. This would have been sufficient to cripple Kurita's four carriers, but probably insufficient to completely destroy Ozawa's force, just as happened historically. Ozawa did have two battleships against none in the two American task forces, but air superiority would have made it extremely unlikely that these would have been able to employ their 14-inch guns against an American ship (in fact, the historical result). The aggressive Ozawa would probably not have fled as soon as he came under attack, but upon hearing of Kurita's fight off San Bernardino Strait would have attempted to go to his aid. This would simply have prolonged the period his force would have been exposed to air attack and increased his losses, perhaps to levels above that which he suffered historically. In any event, TF 38 clearly had enough forces to deal both Kurita and Ozawa crippling defeats.

While it is interesting to explore this counterfactual and even more compelling to explore what TF 34's battleships would have done against *Yamato* and Kurita's other three battleships, there was never a chance that Halsey was ready to employ such a nuanced approach. It was simply against Halsey's character, against existing USN doctrine, and beyond Halsey's ability to command distributed forces. Once Halsey made up his mind that the Japanese carrier force was the primary threat, and that this was the golden opportunity the USN had waited the entire war for to crush it, his actions were virtually preordained.

THE BATTLE OFF CAPE ENGANO

The result of Halsey's decision was that the entirety of TF 38 headed north at 2022 hours. McCain's TG 38.1 was not included, since it was still steaming west from Ulithi, but the other three task groups still possessed an overwhelming advantage against Ozawa's force.

Forces Participating in the Battle off Cape Engano				
Ship Type	TG 38.2	TG 38.3	TG 38.4	Mobile Force, Main Body
Fleet carriers	1	2	2	1
Light carriers	2	1	2	3
Operational aircraft	145	220	240	29
Battleships	2	2	2	2
Heavy cruisers	0	0	2	0
Light cruisers	3	3	0	3
Destroyers	16	14	11	8

With Halsey's 65 ships bearing down on Ozawa's 17, supported by an overwhelming air power advantage, Ozawa was going to pay a high price for successfully drawing Halsey away from Leyte. Ozawa expected that his force would be completely annihilated; had Halsey been allowed to conduct the battle to its conclusion, Ozawa's force did face the real prospect of total annihilation. Finally, the Fast Carrier Task Force would get a chance to fight a set-piece battle according to doctrine. The battle would open with a series of air strikes from five fleet and five light carriers. Following these crippling blows, Task Force 34, with six battleships, two heavy cruisers, five light cruisers, and 18 destroyers, would finish off the cripples and chase down any survivors.

After the rendezvous of three of Halsey's four carrier task groups just before midnight on October 24, TF 38 headed north with every expectation of achieving a great victory. However, the Japanese had to be spotted first, and there had been no contact since the afternoon contact the day before. Just before 0100 on October 25, five radar-equipped aircraft departed from *Independence* to search out to a distance of 350nm. Contact was gained at 0205 on Matsuda's Advance Guard, with contact being gained on Ozawa's carriers at 0235. Because of a transmission error, the reported position of the Japanese forces was incorrect. The erroneous position plotted out some 120nm nearer to TF 38 than was actually the case; at this point TF 38 and Ozawa's carriers were actually about 210nm apart.

Just before midnight, Mitscher assumed tactical command of TF 38. At 0240 Mitscher ordered Lee to begin the process of forming TF 34. It was an intricate and time-consuming process to pull the six battleships, seven cruisers, and 18 destroyers that made up Lee's force from the three existing task groups to form TF 34 some ten miles north of Mitscher's flagship *Lexington*. To safely form TF 34 in the middle of the night, the entire force slowed down to 15 knots. Formation of TF 34 was an urgent matter, since if Ozawa's force had maintained its course, it could have potentially run into TF 38 as early as 0430 hours.

As this ballet was taking place, the *Independence* aircraft holding contact on Ozawa's force was forced to return because of engine problems. A relief aircraft was launched, but it developed problems with its radar. As a result, the location of the Japanese was unknown when Mitscher planned to launch his morning strike. Mitscher and his staff had a well-developed routine for conducting large-scale strikes. Fearful the Japanese might be trying to escape, Mitscher wanted to hit them as soon as possible. He ordered all carriers to have their first strike ready to launch at dawn. The strike would be launched concurrently with the morning search and then be vectored onto the target when the Japanese were located. Accordingly, at earliest dawn just before 0600, the ten flight decks in TF 38 became a beehive of activity. First the CAP was launched, then the search aircraft, and finally the first strike consisting of some 180 aircraft. TG 38.2's contribution was eight Hellcats, ten Helldivers, and eight Avengers.[17] The strike was ordered to head north 50–70nm and then orbit until the search aircraft reported contact.

Things became very tense when the search aircraft failed to find anything at the expected time and place. The planned search was looking too far to the west. Two members of Mitscher's staff thought that the Japanese were located to the east and were given permission to vector part of the CAP to look in that direction. Thankfully for the Americans, a Hellcat from *Essex* gained contact on Ozawa's now reunited force at 0710 and sent an accurate contact report. The Japanese were only 150nm away, headed to the northeast at 20 knots. Because of the proximity between Ozawa's force and TF 38, when the 0710 contact report was issued, the airborne strike was able to arrive over the target in an hour. At about 0830 the first of five strikes began. The overall strike coordinator of the initial blow was Commander McCampbell, air group commander of Air Group 15 from *Essex*.

By 0600, Matsuda's force had rejoined Ozawa's main force and by 0700 the Japanese had assumed a daytime antiaircraft formation. The Mobile Force, Main Body was divided up into two sections. The lead group consisted of *Zuikaku* (Ozawa's flagship), *Zuiho*, battleship-carrier *Ise*, light cruiser *Oyodo*, escorted by destroyers *Akizuki*, *Hatsuzuki*,

Wakatasuki, and *Kuwa*. The second group, under the tactical command of Matsuda, contained *Chitose* and *Chiyoda*, battleship-carrier *Hyuga* (Matsuda's flagship), light cruisers *Isuzu* and *Tama*, and destroyers *Shimotsuki* and *Maki*. The final two destroyers, *Kiri* and *Sagi*, had been detached on the evening of October 24 to rescue downed airmen. They never received the proper location of the rendezvous point between Ozawa's and Matsuda's sections and failed to rejoin the fleet.[18]

The Japanese were aware of the impending arrival of the initial strike, since lookouts on *Hyuga* had spotted American search aircraft at 0712 and radar aboard *Zuikaku* detected the American strike at 0804 about 110nm to the southwest. When the American aircraft were in sight, the entire fleet went to 24 knots. Four Zeros were assigned morning CAP; these were joined by the last nine fighters on *Zuikaku*. Thirteen Zeros were totally inadequate for an effective CAP. If Ozawa's ships were to survive, they would be totally dependent on the volume and accuracy of their antiaircraft fire, and perhaps more importantly, the ability of their skippers to conduct adroit evasion maneuvers in the face of dive-bombing and torpedo attack.

With excellent weather in the area, the Americans had no problems spotting the Japanese formation at 0810 some 25nm ahead. McCampbell assigned targets after he observed the Japanese were operating in two groups; the northern group was centered on *Zuikaku* and *Zuiho*, with a southern group built around *Chitose* and *Chiyoda*.

According to American pilots, Japanese antiaircraft fire was heavy and began with a display of multi-color explosions at 15nm out as *Ise* and *Hyuga* fired Type 3 *sanshiki-dan* incendiary shells from their 14-inch main battery. The small Japanese CAP raced toward the approaching American formation, but the escorting Hellcats prevented them from reaching the Helldivers or Avengers. *Essex* Hellcats claimed nine Zeros, but one Hellcat was shot down and its pilot left in the water to witness the unfolding attack; this unwilling spectator was rescued after the battle. For the next hour, Ozawa's ships came under unrelenting air attack, with the carriers serving as the main targets. The Helldivers went in first, followed by strafing Hellcats. Last to attack were the torpedo-laden Avengers. Once under attack, the Japanese ships began to maneuver individually.

Zuikaku, by far the largest of the four Japanese carriers, came under attack from dive-bombers from *Intrepid* and torpedo bombers from *Intrepid* and two light carriers. Within five minutes, *Zuikaku* was hit by three bombs amidships that created a fire on her lower and upper hangar decks. Only minutes later, a torpedo launched by an Avenger from either *Intrepid* or *San Jacinto* struck the big carrier on her port side. One of the engine rooms was flooded, and one of the shafts was damaged and had to be shut down. The ensuing flooding caused a severe list, but this was quickly corrected to a manageable six degrees. The veteran carrier's experienced and capable damage control team performed well. By 0850, the fires were extinguished, and 23 knots was restored using the starboard shafts. However, steering was uneven, and the ship's transmitters were out of commission.[19] Since she was no longer suitable as a flagship, plans were made to transfer Ozawa and his staff to cruiser *Oyodo*, which was well-fitted to act as a flagship having just been converted to serve as Toyoda's Combined Fleet flagship. It took much convincing to get Ozawa to agree to abandon his flagship. Before the transfer could happen, the second American strike showed up.

Enterprise's strike group targeted the veteran light carrier *Zuiho*, which was known to her crew as a lucky ship since she had survived three earlier carrier battles. Reports from *Enterprise* aircrew stated the carrier was left dead in the water and on fire. One *Enterprise* Avenger was heavily damaged by antiaircraft fire and had to be rolled over the side when it landed back onboard. Another *Enterprise* Hellcat was lost to Zero attack. *Intrepid* Helldivers also selected *Zuiho* for attack and claimed hits. According to Japanese records, *Zuiho* suffered three near misses followed by a direct bomb hit on the aft section of the flight deck at 0835. The explosion caused fires on the hangar deck, but these were out by 0855. A minor list and steering problems were soon corrected.[20] After the dive-bombers did their work, torpedo bombers from *Essex* and *Lexington* attacked *Zuiho*, but no hits were gained.

McCampbell assigned the *Essex* air group to attack *Chitose*. Beginning at 0835, Helldivers from *Essex* reported dropping 12 bombs and claimed eight hits, leaving the carrier burning and listing. In fact, *Chitose* suffered three near misses along her port side. This was sufficient to rupture the carrier's unarmored hull. The resulting flooding knocked out two boiler rooms and caused a severe 27-degree list. Damage control efforts reduced the list and kept the power on, but steering was only accomplished by using the engines. At 0915 progressive flooding forced the starboard engine room to be abandoned and speed fell below 14 knots. The crew was unable to stop the progressive flooding; ten minutes later, all power was lost and the list increased to a dangerous 30 degrees. *Hyuga* was ordered to tow the carrier, but her condition was beyond salvage. *Chitose* sank stern first at 0937, the first of Ozawa's carriers to go under.[21] *Isuzu* saved 35 officers and 445 men and *Shimotsuki* another 121 officers and men. The number of crewmen lost is unclear, but was probably 370.

Chitose's obviously dire condition prompted McCampbell to redirect the Avengers he had originally ordered to attack the carrier. Of the 16 Avengers reporting an attack on carriers or battleships during the first attack, ten claimed hits. This was another example of gross over-claiming, since the only successful torpedo attacks were the single hits on *Zuikaku* and *Tama*.

In addition to the attacks on three carriers, the first attack also struck some of the escorts. Light cruiser *Tama* was attacked by torpedo bombers from *Belleau Wood* and *San Jacinto*. One torpedo hit the ship in her boiler room. After emergency repairs, the cruiser was ordered to proceed independently to Okinawa at her best speed of 14 knots.[22] *Oyodo* was also subjected to attack and was lightly damaged. At 0848, she was struck by a bomb and two rockets and recorded near misses from bombs. The cruiser's speed was unimpaired.[23]

Large destroyer *Akizuki* was also attacked in the first strike. At 0842 the ship was struck amidships and set afire. *Akizuki* lost power and fell out of formation. Within minutes, a large explosion was observed amidships and at 0856 the ship broke in two and quickly sank. The cause remains unclear, but was probably due to a torpedo or bomb hit that detonated torpedoes in the amidships torpedo mount. The ship's commanding officer and 150 other officers and men were pulled out of the water before more air attacks forced destroyer *Maki* to abandon rescue operations. Four more men were later killed when *Maki* came under attack. *Akizuki's* final personnel casualties were 183 men, but one was later rescued by the Americans.[24]

TF 38's second strike took off around 0835 and arrived in the target area at about 0945. This was comprised of 36 aircraft (14 Hellcats, six Helldivers, and 16 Avengers) from *Lexington*, *Franklin*, *Langley*, *San Jacinto*, and *Belleau Wood* from TGs 38.3 and 38.4. McCampbell remained active as target coordinator.

When the small strike arrived in the target area, it found Ozawa's force already in disarray. McCampbell selected the undamaged carrier *Chiyoda* for attack. Dive-bombers from *Lexington* and *Franklin* attacked first and claimed four hits. For once, this was not too far from the actual results of the attack. At 1000 the carrier was hit by a bomb on the port quarter of her flight deck, while damaging near misses were recorded on the starboard side. The magazines were flooded as a precaution after fires broke out. Combined with the hull damage from the near misses, the carrier assumed a 13-degree starboard list. When the flooding reached the starboard engine room, *Chiyoda* came to a stop. *Hyuga* and destroyers *Shimotsuki* and *Maki* were ordered to assist. *Hyuga* was ordered to tow the 11,200-ton carrier, but the attempt was suspended when the third American strike was spotted. At 1414 *Isuzu* returned to start a tow but was hit by a bomb forward of the bridge. More air attacks and a lack of fuel forced *Isuzu* to give up, and steering problems made it impossible for the light cruiser to close and pick up *Chiyoda*'s crew. *Isuzu* was later ordered to try again to pick up the crew and sink the carrier with torpedoes. At 1548, as *Isuzu* approached *Chiyoda*'s position, the carrier was observed to be under attack from American warships. *Isuzu* reversed course to the north, leaving *Chiyoda* to her fate.[25]

Launched between 1145 and 1200, the third strike was the largest and most effective of the day. It was active over Ozawa's force from about 1310 to 1400 with some 200 aircraft, 75 percent of which had taken part in the initial strike in the morning. The strike coordinator was Commander Theodore Winters from *Lexington*. Winters observed that Ozawa's formation was in a shambles. Two carriers (*Zuikaku* and *Zuiho*) were located to the north with a battleship and what was reported as two cruisers. Another carrier (*Chiyoda*; *Chitose* had already sunk) was located some 20nm to the south, on fire and listing. A second battleship, a cruiser, and a destroyer were standing nearby the crippled carrier.

Winters ordered TG 38.3's 98 aircraft from *Essex*, *Lexington*, and *Langley* to go after the two operational carriers. Aircraft from *Lexington* focused on *Zuikaku*. By 1100 Ozawa and 11 members of his staff had departed *Zuikaku* and transferred to *Oyodo*. The nine surviving Zeros on CAP were forced to ditch around 1030, so for the rest of the day the Americans faced no air opposition. Upon spotting the third strike at 1308, *Zuikaku* worked up to 24 knots. Winters made *Zuikaku* the focus of the third wave. On this occasion, the attack by Helldivers and Avengers was well coordinated, with the Avengers coming in from both bows in an anvil attack at the same time as the Helldivers were conducting their attacks.

Twelve Helldivers from *Lexington* went in first, dropping 1,000-pound armor-piercing bombs and claiming several hits. On their heels were nine Helldivers from *Essex*, who also claimed success. The follow-up attack by Avengers inflicted mortal damage on the Pearl Harbor veteran. In less than ten minutes, *Zuikaku* was subjected to six torpedo hits – two on the starboard side and four on the port side. The first was a hit forward on the port side at 1315 that failed to detonate. Simultaneously, one hit the starboard side forward and did explode, flooding one of the boiler rooms. At about the same time, three bombs hit the flight deck aft. At 1321 three torpedoes hit in quick succession, all on the port side. Another bomb hit between the center and aft elevators. The ship assumed a 14-degree list and fires took hold on the hangar deck. A final torpedo struck the ship two minutes later on the port quarter. By 1325 the attack was over, but it was clear that the ship was doomed. The list increased to 20 degrees, all power was lost, and flooding and fires were unchecked. At 1327, with the list increasing to 21 degrees, the crew was ordered up to the flight deck. The captain gave a final address and then the ensign was lowered. Only after this touch of the dramatic was the crew ordered to abandon ship at 1358. The ship rolled over and sank by the stern at 1414, taking her captain, 48 other officers, and 794 enlisted men with her. Destroyers *Wakatsuki* and *Kuwa* fished 47 officers and 815 men out of the water.[26]

After surveying the damage to *Zuikaku*, Winters decided it was unnecessary for additional attacks to hit the obviously crippled carrier. Since nearby *Zuiho* looked to be steaming normally, he directed the strike groups from *Franklin*, *Enterprise*, and *San Jacinto* to attack her. When the aircraft from TG 38.4 arrived, including *Enterprise*'s second strike of six Hellcats, ten Helldivers, and five Avengers, they began their attack at 1310, followed by another wave at 1330. At 1317 one torpedo hit *Zuiho* on her starboard bow, followed by a bomb hit on the aft elevator. In the second wave, another torpedo hit on the starboard quarter at 1330, with a bomb hitting aft on the starboard side, joined by seven more near misses. The Japanese claimed that 60 more near misses followed, but this was impossible given the number of aircraft involved. In any event, the near misses inflicted great damage on the unarmored carrier that had been converted from a submarine tender. Bomb fragments cut steam pipes and caused flooding of the starboard engine room, while shrapnel on the ship's port side flooded a boiler room and caused slow flooding of the port engine room. This reduced propulsion to a single shaft, dropping the ship's speed to 12 knots. The flooding created a 13-degree list to starboard. By 1445 the port engine room had also completely flooded, and *Zuiho* came to a stop.[27]

A few aircraft, including some from *Franklin*, attacked the ships standing nearby the crippled *Chiyoda*. This attack prompted the remaining escorts to leave the stationary carrier at about 1410. No aircraft were reported lost in the third strike, but at least one *Essex* Helldiver returned so badly damaged it was dumped over the side.

Mitscher's fourth strike of the day was launched at about 1315 and reached the target area at about 1445. It was comprised of 40 aircraft from *Essex*, *Lexington*, and *Langley*. Twenty-seven aircraft went after *Zuiho* despite the fact she was dead in the water. Ten more near misses inflicted more hull damage, which increased the carrier's list to 23 degrees. This prompted her captain to order abandon ship at about 1510. At 1526, the carrier rolled over to starboard and disappeared. Casualties were fairly light given the pounding received, totaling seven officers and 208 men. *Ise* and destroyer *Kuwa* saved most of the crew – 58 officers and 701 men.[28] *Essex* dive-bombers attacked *Ise* and claimed eight hits, flying through what was described as a very heavy barrage of antiaircraft fire. The Japanese confirmed only four near misses.

The next effort consisted of a large strike launched at 1610 with aircraft from the five fleet carriers. The 85 aircraft in the fifth strike did their work between 1710 and 1740. Only three of the 13 Avengers in the strike carried torpedoes.[29] Because no further air opposition was expected, Mitscher ordered the 52 fighters in the strike to carry bombs or rockets. The strike coordinator was Commander Malcom Wordell from *Langley*, who was in control of the fourth and fifth strikes. Because of the lateness of the hour, the aircraft attacked as soon as they encountered a target, with little coordination between air groups.

Since they were the largest targets left, Wordell directed the last strike to hit the two hybrid battleship-carriers, which were in two different groups separated by 10nm. For most of the pilots, this was their third sortie of the day, and this was the second day in a row of flying multiple missions. The results indicate that pilot fatigue was at work. Located further to the north, *Ise* received the most attention. Japanese accounts state that she was attacked by the impossible total of 85 bombers and 11 torpedo bombers. All 11 of the supposed torpedoes were evaded, and only a single bomb hit outboard of the port catapult. The Japanese recorded 34 near misses, which caused the outer hull plates to rupture and resulted in minor flooding. Five crewmen were killed and 71 wounded.[30] American pilots reported that the Japanese ships put up a tremendous volume of antiaircraft fire. Adept maneuvering by *Ise*'s skipper, combined with pilot fatigue, prevented major damage. Sister ship *Hyuga* was also attacked. The Americans gained seven non-damaging near misses, but not a single bomb hit its target. The American aviators were sure they had seriously damaged both ships. After trying to eliminate duplicate claims against *Ise* and *Hyuga*, the official tabulation was 22 hits on one and 15 on the other, and these included ten torpedo hits.[31] In reality, both ships had suffered only minor damage and retained full combat effectiveness.

At the conclusion of the final strike, Ozawa's force was in a shambles. Three of the four Japanese carriers had sunk, and destroyer *Akizuki* had also been dispatched. *Ise*, *Oyodo*, and three destroyers were recovering *Zuikaku* and *Zuiho* survivors. Some 10nm south was another group consisting of *Hyuga*, light cruiser *Isuzu*, and a couple of destroyers. The wounded *Tama* was proceeding independently, trailing oil. To the south by another 60nm was *Chiyoda*, still dead in the water with her entire crew on board.

Ozawa's force had been subjected to a total of 527 sorties from TF 38. No other force in naval history had ever been subjected to such massive air attacks over such a compressed period. The level of effort against Ozawa's force on October 25 was twice that directed at Kurita's force the day before. As was the case against Kurita's force, the overall damage inflicted on Ozawa's force must be seen as disappointing. Once again, TF 38 strike aircraft faced virtually no air opposition and heavy, but generally ineffective, antiaircraft fire. The four carriers present were all sunk or crippled; in addition a destroyer was sunk, major damage was inflicted on a light cruiser, and several other ships suffered various degrees of light damage. Ozawa's chief of staff stated after the war, "I saw all this bombing and thought the American pilot is not so good."[32] Three reasons contributed to this relatively modest return on what was a massive effort: heavy antiaircraft fire, good ship handling, and fatigue on the part of TF 38 aircrew. American after-action reports confirmed that pilot fatigue was a major factor in operations. It must be kept in mind that many TF 38 pilots had flown five missions in two days against the heaviest antiaircraft barrages in naval history. Also noteworthy was the ineffectiveness of Japanese antiaircraft fire throughout the day. Despite the impressive barrage of fire put up by the Japanese, only ten American aircraft were lost to antiaircraft fire throughout the day. Japanese fighters also accounted for a handful of American aircraft.

HALSEY CHANGES HIS MIND

The start of the battle went extremely well for the Americans. Against a very weak Japanese CAP, the first waves of Mitscher's aviators methodically went about attacking the four Japanese carriers. With TF 34 already formed and ready to be unleashed, it seemed that Halsey would get his wish of fighting a battle of annihilation. This began to change at 0822 when Halsey received the first message from Kinkaid, sent without being encoded, that Taffy 3 was being attacked by Japanese battleships and cruisers. Kinkaid sent another message at 0725 that Taffy 3 came under attack by Japanese battleships and cruisers at 0700; an immediate air strike was requested and support from TF 38's heavy ships, since Kinkaid's six old battleships were low on main battery ammunition. This reached Halsey at 0922. This was followed at 0727 by an even more urgent request, also sent without being encoded: "Our CVEs being attacked by 4 BBs 8 cruisers plus others. Request Lee cover Leyte at top speed. Request fast carriers make immediate strike." Halsey got this message at 0900. Sprague sent a direct plea to Halsey at 0735. This was followed by two more urgent requests for Kinkaid at 0739 and 0829, the last of which read, "Situation critical, battleships and fast carriers strike wanted to prevent enemy penetrating Leyte Gulf." At 1000, Halsey received another plea from Kinkaid: "Where is Lee. Send Lee."

None of these fazed Halsey. He remained focused on his battle of annihilation. His only response, sent at 0927, was that he was engaged with the Japanese carrier force, but that he had ordered TG 38.1 to assist Kinkaid.

This all changed at 1000 when Halsey received a message from Nimitz, who had been following the action from his headquarters in Pearl Harbor and had become alarmed when he learned that San Bernardino Strait had been left unguarded. It was brief: "Where is repeat where is Task Force 34 RR The World Wonders." Nimitz meant it "as a reminder to Halsey."[33] Because of an error in handling the message, the last three words of padding were left in after the double consonant meant to mark the end of the message. When Halsey read what looked like a direct insult from Nimitz, he went into an emotional tirade. Throwing his cap to the deck, he yelled, "What right does Chester have to send me a God-damned message like that!" Halsey's chief of staff led him off the flag bridge to cool off.[34] This dramatic episode has been the focus of many accounts of the battle, but within minutes Halsey knew that the message had been mishandled and was not meant as an insult.[35] After his tantrum, Halsey got to business on formulating a new battle plan. While this was occurring, TF 38 continued north at 25 knots.

Nimitz's "reminder" had the desired effect, but it was not until 1055 that Halsey broke off his battle of annihilation. He ordered TG 38.2 (less eight destroyers and the four battleships originally in TG 38.3 and TG 38.4), to steam south.[36] According to Halsey's battle report, at this point TF 34 was only 42nm away from Ozawa's shattered force. At 1115 the battleships and Bogan's TG 38.2 executed the order to turn south.

By waiting until 1115 to turn his battleships around, Halsey made it unlikely that he would be able to intercept Kurita before he retreated through San Bernardino Strait. The only chance of catching the Japanese force before it escaped was that it would not move directly for the strait. But as we have already seen, Kurita did not linger and entered the strait at about 2140. Compounding the fact that the Americans got a late start, Vice Admiral Lee did not move with alacrity. The battleship force was limited to a top speed of 27 knots (the maximum speed of *Alabama*, *Massachusetts*, and *South Dakota*), but Lee set his speed at a somewhat leisurely 20 knots. From 1345 until 1622, this was reduced to 12 knots when the battleships slowed down to refuel destroyers in need of replenishment. Finally, when the refueling was complete, Lee formed a fast group of battleships *Iowa*, *New Jersey*, three light cruisers, and eight destroyers, designated TG 34.5 under the command of Rear Admiral Oscar Badger. Halsey did not give the order for TG 34.5 to take off for San Bernardino Strait at 28 knots until 1701.

Halsey's and Lee's lack of desire to bring Kurita to battle meant that Badger's force arrived off San Bernardino Strait at 0100 on October 26. Since Kurita had slipped through some three hours earlier, Badger followed his orders to sweep south along the coast of Samar. The only Japanese ship in the area was destroyer *Nowaki*, which had fallen behind Kurita's main body after rescuing the survivors of heavy cruiser *Chikuma*. *Nowaki* was sunk by gunfire, but this was the only time in the battle that Third Fleet surface ships encountered any part of Kurita's force.

It is curious why neither Halsey nor Lee moved with urgency to cut off Kurita's force before it escaped through the San Bernardino Strait. Had they done so, it is likely that elements of TF 34 would have arrived off the strait before Kurita. Of course, this would have taken a much different sequence of events. Halsey would have had to decide to break off TF 34 as soon as he received the first distress calls from Kinkaid, and then he and Lee would have had to push the battleships south at top speed, leaving the destroyers behind if need be. The prize was worth the effort — the first reports indicated that Sprague was being attacked by four battleships and numerous cruisers. Surely this was the bulk of the Imperial Navy's remaining strength and a much more appropriate target for Lee's battleships than the crippled escorts of Ozawa's force. If Halsey's decision to go north with the entirety of TF 38 was inevitable, as this author believes, and that this decision was an error as was demonstrated beyond a doubt when the first reports were received that Sprague's force was under attack, then Halsey's half-hearted and tardy efforts to address his mistake are even harder to defend than his original error. If TF 34 had arrived off San Bernardino Strait before Kurita, it had the capabilities to give Halsey the battle of annihilation he so desperately sought. As it was, the big guns of TF 34 remained silent during the largest naval battle of the war.

TF 38 SURFACE FORCES IN ACTION

The climax of Halsey's battle of annihilation against the Mobile Force, Main Body should have featured an engagement by TF 34 with six of the world's most powerful battleships. This dream came to a disappointing end at 1115 when the bulk of TF 34 turned around only two hours' steaming time from the Japanese to go to the assistance of the Seventh Fleet. Another indication of the stubbornness of Halsey to give up his dream of completing the destruction of Ozawa's force with surface units was that he kept elements allocated to TF 34 with the carriers as they continued the battle with Ozawa. This was a strong force consisting of heavy cruisers *New Orleans* and *Wichita*, light cruisers *Mobile* and *Santa Fe*, and nine destroyers.

Mitscher had to be careful how to use this force because of the presence of the two Japanese battleships. At 1330, when TF 38 was only 60nm from the nearest Japanese ships, he ordered that the carriers go no farther north. He discussed with Rear Admiral Laurance DuBose when to unleash his cruiser force, but DuBose was hesitant given the fact he would be outgunned by the two battleships. When Winters reported that the battleship standing by the southernmost cripples was headed north, Mitscher ordered DuBose to begin mopping up.[37] DuBose's force consisted of the four cruisers mentioned above and a total of 12 destroyers.

As the Americans streaked northward, they were vectored into their first victim by Winters, who was headed back to *Lexington*. He spotted the crippled *Chiyoda* dead in the water with light cruiser *Isuzu* nearby preparing to rescue survivors. Alerted to the presence of the Japanese, DuBose headed into action with his cruisers in a column led by *Santa Fe*. *Isuzu* quickly fled, leaving heavy cruiser *Wichita* to open fire with her 8-inch guns at 1625 from 19,000 yards.[38] *Chiyoda* responded weakly with a few salvos from her 5-inch dual-purpose guns, but against the stationary carrier American cruiser gunfire scored quickly and often. After a 15-minute barrage, the carrier was reduced to a mass of flames. *Chiyoda*'s final moments were marked by a towering column of black smoke. The carrier capsized at 1655. Many survivors were seen in the water, but the destroyers were denied permission to conduct any rescue operations and DuBose's formation continued north.[39] As a result, there were no survivors from her crew of about 970 men.[40]

After finishing off *Chiyoda*, DuBose reformed his column, launched two floatplanes for a night search, and continued north, with the destroyers arranged in four groups of three on each quarter. Strike coordinator Wordell, still airborne, reported two groups of Japanese ships ahead. DuBose chose to go after the group with three ships. The other contact was *Isuzu* operating by herself. At 1833 *Wichita* gained distant radar contacts at 35,200 yards. These contacts were large destroyers *Hatsuzuki* and *Wakatsuki* and the smaller *Kuwa* in the process of picking up survivors from *Zuikaku* and *Zuiho*. Once again radar proved an incalculable advantage – DuBose ordered his light cruisers to open fire on the surprised *Hatsuzuki* at 1852. The outgunned destroyer returned fire at 1905 with her 3.9-inch guns as she fled north. The heavy cruisers with their longer-ranged 8-inch guns opened up on *Wakatsuki* and *Kuwa* at a range of 28,200 yards, but at that range they failed to hit anything.[41]

Surprised by a superior force, the Japanese fled with the Americans in hot pursuit at 30 knots. The cruisers kept the Japanese under fire, and at 1911 scored a hit on *Hatsuzuki*. The destroyer turned broadside several times to feint launching torpedoes and laid smoke to slow down her pursuers. These maneuvers allowed *Isuzu*, *Wakatsuki*, and *Kuwa* to make their escapes, but DuBose's ships continued to gain on *Hatsuzuki*. Three of DuBose's destroyers took the lead to close the range for a torpedo attack. Launched just after 2000 from a range of 6,800 yards, all 15 torpedoes missed. Eventually, the unceasing barrage from the cruisers decided *Hatsuzuki's* fate. During this action alone, *Santa Fe* fired 954 6-inch rounds and *Mobile* another 779. The heavy cruisers were not as prolific with their 8-inch rounds, but *Wichita* fired 173 shells. As the cruisers closed the range eventually down to 6,000 yards, observers noted the destroyer was literally being torn apart by shells. *Hatsuzuki* fought back gamely and placed shells near two of the American cruisers without scoring a hit. After her desperate fight, the destroyer slipped under at 2059. From her crew of about 330, 25 men survived, reaching Formosa two weeks later in a small boat. Among the survivors were eight men from *Hatsuzuki* and 17 from *Zuikaku*.[42]

After the tough *Hatsuzuki* was finally dispatched, DuBose's search aircraft reported that the next group of Japanese ships was 46nm to the north. With his destroyers running low on fuel, and the nearest Japanese ships steaming north at 22 knots, DuBose decided to break off his pursuit at 2130. *Hatsuzuki* had issued a call for help at 1915 which prompted Ozawa to head south with *Ise*, *Hyuga*, *Oyodo*, and destroyer *Shimotsuki* at 2041. *Wakatsuki* joined the force at 2230 and reported that the Americans had attacked with a strength of two modern battleships, two cruisers, and a destroyer squadron.[43] In spite of this exaggeration, Ozawa continued south seeking battle. Finding nothing, he ordered a retreat at 2330. The fourth and final large engagement of the Battle of Leyte Gulf was over.

SUBMARINE ATTACKS ON OZAWA'S FORCE

Air attacks and DuBose's surface ships accounted for six of Ozawa's 17 ships. The final obstacle facing Ozawa before he could get his surviving ships back to Japan was a large force of Pacific Fleet submarines under Vice Admiral Charles Lockwood. To support the Leyte invasion, Lockwood deployed 22 submarines around the Philippines. Several of these were positioned in the chokepoint of the Luzon Strait, which was rich in Japanese merchant traffic. Their proximity to the area where the Battle off Cape Engano was fought placed them in a potential position to strike Ozawa's retreating force.

On the day of the action off Cape Engano, Mitscher informed Lockwood of the upcoming battle and provided a breakdown of the Japanese force. That morning, Lockwood had already ordered two wolf packs, each with three submarines, to establish scouting lines across Ozawa's predicted path of retreat. By 1830 on October 25 they were in position. *Pintado*, *Jallao*, and *Atule* were stationed along the eastern part of the line, with *Haddock*, *Tuna*, and *Halibut* manning the western part. The second group was so well positioned it was close enough to hear explosions and radio transmissions of pilots conducting the last strike of the day. Following the end of the air strikes, *Halibut* spotted *Ise* at 31,000 yards coming toward her at 1742. As the Japanese approached, *Halibut* went to periscope depth and also sighted *Oyodo* and a destroyer. A full salvo of six torpedoes was fired at the battleship-carrier at 1844. Despite the Americans hearing what they thought were five explosions, followed by the noises of a ship breaking up, *Ise* was undamaged after making a last-second zig. *Haddock* also chased *Ise* and *Hyuga* but could not get into firing positions. *Halibut* reported contact on a group of five ships at 2300 but also failed to get into firing position after a seven-hour chase.

After taking a torpedo in the first air attack, light cruiser *Tama* was proceeding independently to Okinawa at 14 knots. At 2004 the wounded cruiser was detected by radar on submarine *Jallao* from a range of 27,000 yards. *Jallao* was a brand-new boat on her first war patrol, but by 2301 her captain and crew set up for a submerged attack from 1,000 yards on the oblivious Japanese. The first three torpedoes from the bow tubes all missed, so the skipper brought the boat around and fired all four stern tubes from 800 yards. This time, three of the four hit, and two exploded. *Tama* broke in two and sank within minutes. There were no survivors from her crew of some 450 men.[44]

Ozawa predicted that his force would be annihilated in the course of its mission to draw the power of TF 38 on to itself. Of all the Japanese forces in *Sho-1*, Ozawa's was the only one to accomplish its mission. The cost of doing so was high, but it was not the annihilation that Ozawa feared. Of his 17 ships, seven were sunk, including all four aircraft carriers. Almost miraculously, given the weight of air attacks directed at them, both of Carrier Division 4's hybrid battleship-carriers survived. They played little part in the rest of the war, other than transporting a load of petroleum products and specialists from the Singapore area to Japan in February 1945. Ozawa's operations as part of *Sho-1* were the last time the Imperial Navy employed a carrier force during the war.

10

Final Actions

THE BIRTH OF THE KAMIKAZE

Aside from being the world's largest naval battle, the Battle of Leyte Gulf included the first formal Japanese endorsement of a radical new tactic. For the first time in the war, the Imperial Navy organized units with the express purpose of deliberately crashing bomb-laden aircraft onto the decks of American ships. Of course, this had happened many times earlier in the war, but these were acts of self-sacrifice by individual pilots and were not the result of an endorsed policy. For example, on October 13, a G4M Betty bomber crashed on carrier *Franklin* in the air-sea battle off Formosa. The pre-planned attacks were conducted by the Special Attack Corps and soon took the label of *kamikaze* or Divine Wind attacks.

The first formal suicide attacks were endorsed and created by the officers in command of the land-based air forces in the Philippines. Adoption of these tactics was the final recognition that the war had turned badly against Japan and that conventional tactics, flown by poorly trained aviators, had no chance of reversing the tide of war. The ensuing suicide attacks during the Battle of Leyte Gulf gained great initial success. Their use increased later in the Philippines campaign and became the centerpiece of Japanese strategy to defeat American naval operations for the remainder of the war.

The prime proponent of suicide tactics was Vice Admiral Onishi. He was among the Imperial Navy's most vocal air power zealots. At the start of the war he was the chief of staff for the 11th Air Fleet, the

Combined Fleet's principal land-based air formation. After serving in two shore billets, he was assigned command of the Fifth Base Air Force on October 2, but was not able to fly to Manila to assume his new command until October 17. What he found upon taking command gave him no confidence. Responsible for defending the Philippines, his formation was totally inadequate for the task.

In 1943, Onishi argued against adopting suicide tactics. After the debacle in the Philippine Sea, during which the futility of using conventional tactics against the USN was fully demonstrated, the increased calls for the necessity of suicide tactics convinced Onishi to support them. Using the veiled language of "special attacks," he sounded out chief of the Naval General Staff Admiral Oikawa Koshiro and Navy Minister Yonai Mitsumasa on his desire to shift tactics. Oikawa instructed that all pilots taking part in such attacks should be volunteers, but neither man objected.

Upon arriving in the Philippines, Onishi became more determined to implement the use of special attacks. The state of the Fifth Base Air Force left him no other choice. He was known as a man of action, and he believed that quick action was necessary before the situation for Japan got worse. Onishi believed that if he demonstrated how the actions and sacrifice of a small number of airmen could achieve disproportionate results against the superior might of the American Navy, then his ideas would catch fire. He intended to organize fighter units first, hoping that other land-based naval air units would follow. If the Imperial Navy embraced the notion of sacrificial attacks, the Imperial Army would follow.[1]

Onishi wasted no time taking his new concept to the fliers who would have to execute it. The unit Onishi selected to be the first to employ suicide attacks was the 201st Air Group based in Mabalacat. This was a fighter unit flying the once formidable, but now obsolescent, Zero. Onishi arrived at the unit on the evening of October 19, called the officers together, and issued the following statement:

> The situation is so grave that the fate of the empire depends on the outcome of the *Sho* Operation. Missions have been assigned. A naval force under Admiral Kurita is to penetrate Leyte Gulf and there annihilate enemy surface units. The First Air Fleet has been designated to support that mission by rendering enemy carriers ineffective for at least one week. In my opinion this can be accomplished only by

crash-diving on the carrier flight decks with Zero fighters carrying 250-kilogram bombs.[2]

With little debate, the officers of the 201st Air Group agreed to Onishi's proposal. Twenty-three pilots were assigned to the first suicide group, led by an experienced aviator, Lieutenant Seki Yukio. All were volunteers. The initial group was named *Shinbu* (after the divine wind that saved Japan from invasion from the Mongols in the 13th century) and was divided into four sections, each with a patriotic name: *Asahi*, *Shikishima*, *Yamato*, and *Yamazakura*. By October 20 they were organized and ready to conduct missions. On the evening of October 20, Onishi informed his superior, Vice Admiral Mikawa, of his plans and gained his approval.

The first suicide operations did not go smoothly. On October 21 the *Shikishima* section took off from Mabalacat to attack American carriers located north of Leyte, but failed to find a target. On the same day, the *Yamato* section deployed to Cebu with eight Zeros. They were under orders to organize another special attack unit at Cebu. After five aircraft were destroyed that afternoon by strafing Hellcats after being prepared for a mission, the other three aircraft were launched to attack a carrier group located in the approaches to Leyte Gulf. After finding nothing, the flight leader ordered the other two aircraft to return to base while he pressed on to find something to attack. He disappeared, and there is no record of an Allied ship being attacked at this time. The *Asahi* section was sent to Davao to organize a special attack unit there. This resulted in the creation of the *Kikusui* (Floating Chrysanthemum) section being established.

A similar pattern of frustration repeated itself over the next several days. Due to bad weather, American attacks on Mabalacat, Cebu, and Davao, and a lack of scouting aircraft, the special attack unit failed to find suitable targets. Not any target would do – suicide attacks were reserved for high-impact targets like carriers. Nevertheless, on October 24, two suicide attacks were made on shipping in Leyte Gulf. In the morning, a group of G4M bombers attacked ships in the anchorage. One bomber, already on fire and perhaps out of control, made a suicide dive on freighter *Augustus Thomas* with fleet tug *Sonoma* nearby. The bomber crashed between the two ships, but bomb explosions damaged both ships. The freighter was saved by beaching her, but *Sonoma* sank a few hours later. Also hit the same day was the small landing craft *LCI(L)*

1065. This attack was conducted by an Imperial Army Ki-21 bomber. Again, the bomber was ablaze before it hit the landing ship, but the impact took the ship down quickly, killing seven, wounding nine, with five more sailors missing. Neither of these attacks were conducted by the designated special attack unit, which flew only Zeros. In any event, the first American ship lost to a suicide attack in the largest naval battle of the war was a mere fleet tug.

Failure of conventional and suicide attacks against TF 38 before October 24 resulted in Halsey's aviators pounding Kurita's First Diversionary Attack Force. On the following day, Kurita ran into Taffy 3 and for over two hours subjected it to intense gunnery attacks. Taffy 1 and 2 were not involved in the surface battle, but all three Taffy task units were operating just east of Leyte and Samar and were easily detected by Japanese aircraft. By fate and not design, the first target of a pre-planned suicide attack was Taffy 1. The attackers from the *Asahi* and *Kikusui* sections came from Davao with six Zero fighters with bombs, with four Zeros without bombs acting as escorts.[3] Coming from Mindanao, the first group of carriers they spotted was Taffy 1, the southernmost group of escort carriers.

Taffy 1 consisted of three Sangamon-class escort carriers and one Casablanca-class escort carrier, plus escorts. The Sangamons were converted oilers with the capacity to take much greater damage than the escort carriers converted from smaller cargo ships or built on hulls to merchant standards. The Japanese spotted Taffy 1 at about 0730, just as Taffy 3 to the north was doing battle with Kurita. Radar aboard the ships of Taffy 1 had detected hostile aircraft, prompting the crews to go to General Quarters, but scattered clouds above the carriers prevented the Americans from spotting the incoming suicide aircraft. Using this cover well, the Zeros began their attacks. *Santee* was the first ship to be attacked. At 0740, a kamikaze commenced its dive out of a cloud above the carrier. Complete surprise was achieved, so no antiaircraft guns engaged the aircraft. The Zero hit the forward part of the ship and blew a large hole in the flight deck.[4] The bomb aboard the Zero penetrated to the hangar deck and exploded. Avengers were being armed for their next mission on the hangar deck, but in a stroke of very good luck for the crew of *Santee*, the explosion failed to start a fire. By 0751 the flight deck fire was out. The ship suffered relatively light damage, but the crash had killed 16 and wounded 27 crewmen.

Immediately on the heels of the first kamikaze, the second selected *Suwannee* for attack. The Zero came in from astern of the carrier and was engaged by antiaircraft fire. The damaged aircraft turned away from *Suwannee* and headed for *Sangamon*. Hit by additional antiaircraft fire, it crashed alongside the carrier's port bow and exploded. Damage was very minor and three men were wounded. Another was killed by strafing.[5] At the same time, a third Zero went after *Petrof Bay*. This aircraft was also hit by antiaircraft fire and crashed short of its target. The fourth Zero to attack began its dive at 0804 and also selected *Petrof Bay*. After this attacker was hit by antiaircraft fire and set ablaze, it switched targets to *Suwannee*. The Zero scored a direct hit on the starboard side of the flight deck just forward of the aft elevator. After leaving a 10-by-20-foot hole in the flight deck, the Zero's 551-pound bomb penetrated to the hangar deck and exploded. The explosion created damage to the hangar deck and the main deck below, but the ensuing fires were quickly extinguished. Personnel casualties were heavy, with 32 men killed immediately and another 39 dying of their wounds.[6] After temporary repairs to the flight deck, the carrier was able to resume flight operations just two hours later. Only four of the six suicide aircraft in this first attack have had the efforts recorded. The fates of the other two are unknown.

The first formal kamikaze attack had achieved limited results, but the second attack was more deadly. Nine Zeros from the *Shikishima* section took off from Mabalacat. Led by Seki, the section was comprised of five Zeros with bombs and four escorts.[7] Flying from the west, the first group of carriers they spotted was Taffy 3. By this time, the five remaining carriers of Taffy 3 were turning into the wind to recover aircraft. Seki led his group in at low altitude to avoid radar detection. Only when they increased altitude to about 5,000 feet to gain altitude for their attack dives were they detected on radar; by this point, a successful interception by the Wildcats on CAP was impossible.

Kalinin Bay was attacked by three Zeros. The first to dive on the carrier was Seki's aircraft. According to American observers, it was hit several times by antiaircraft fire but remained in control. The Zero hit the flight deck at a shallow angle and skidded off the flight deck without penetrating. Though the impact caused an intense fire, the aircraft's bomb did not explode. After the fire was put out, all that was left was a gouge in the flight deck. Two more kamikazes followed Seki down against *Kalinin Bay*. The second aircraft was engaged by antiaircraft fire, which appeared to spoil the pilot's aim. The Zero crashed on the catwalk on the carrier's port side. The third kamikaze missed the ship altogether despite not being engaged by antiaircraft fire. The two glancing blows to *Kalinin Bay* killed five and wounded 55.

Kitkun Bay was attacked at 1049. One Zero crossed ahead of the ship, climbed, and then headed directly toward the bridge. It missed the bridge only to hit the port catwalk before crashing into the sea just off the port bow. The bomb exploded upon impact, causing minor fires and damage.[8] One man was killed and 16 wounded.

The last two Zeros selected *White Plains* for attack. The first came in from astern. Though undamaged, it missed the ship and hit the water close aboard the port side. Only 11 crewmen were injured by the debris that rained down, but the bomb explosion caused considerable shock damage. The second Zero was deterred by *White Plains'* antiaircraft fire and headed toward *St Lo*.

This attack was the most skillful and the deadliest. At 1053 the Zero came in over the stern of *St Lo*, almost as if he was trying to land, according to an observer, and dropped its 551-pound bomb before performing a shallow dive into the flight deck amidships. Because of the shallow angle, the aircraft failed to penetrate the flight deck. The aircraft slid off the bow, leaving a trail of fire on the flight deck from its fuel tanks. The fire was dealt with quickly, but damage from the bomb was much more troublesome. It penetrated the flight deck and exploded in the hangar deck where six aircraft were being fueled and armed. As the fire mains serving the hangar were damaged by the explosion, the crew was unable to contend with a series of explosions from the aircraft on the hangar bay. One explosion was so powerful it blew a hole in the flight deck and threw the aft elevator hundreds of feet into the air. When the conflagration reached the magazines, more explosions ensued. Only 32 minutes after being struck, *St Lo* rolled over and sank; 114 crewmen did not survive.

The first day of kamikaze attacks had rendered promising results. One of the escort aircraft from Seki's group returned to Cebu and reported that he had witnessed one carrier and a light cruiser sunk and another carrier set ablaze.[9]

The next day, kamikazes returned to attack Taffy 1. This was mounted by the *Yamato* section from Cebu which was reinforced by three surviving escort Zeros from the *Shikishima* section's attack the previous day.[10] From these slender assets, the Japanese organized two attack groups. The first was comprised of two suicide aircraft and one escort fighter; the second was comprised of three kamikazes and two Zero escorts. The first group took off at 1015 and simply disappeared. No record of any attack on an Allied target was recorded. The second group took off after the first, headed east, and found Taffy 1.

Taffy 1 was down to three carriers – *Suwannee*, *Sangamon*, and *Petrof Bay*. Despite detecting the approaching Japanese aircraft on radar at 14nm and having CAP up, the suicide aircraft avoided interception and began their dives at 1237.[11] *Suwannee* was the first to be attacked and was caught in the middle of flight operations. Ten aircraft were on the forward part of the flight deck after landing, including an Avenger on the forward elevator. Ten more aircraft were sitting on the hangar deck ready to be brought up to the flight deck for launch. One Zero appeared above the carrier and commenced a dive from about 3,000 feet. It survived the ship's antiaircraft fire, hit the flight deck, and skidded into the elevator where the just-landed Avenger was sitting. A huge fireball resulted. Soon the flames engulfed the other nine aircraft located on the forward part of the flight deck. Even worse, the flames spread down the elevator to the hangar deck where the other fully-fueled aircraft were sitting. With the help of the hangar deck fire suppression system, and with the good luck of the ordnance aboard the Avengers not exploding, the hangar deck fire was contained and then extinguished. The flight deck fire took longer to bring under control. After the fires were finally put out over two hours later, the crew could count the toll for saving their ship. Another 17 men were killed instantly and another 22 died later from the wounds. In addition, 162 crewmen were wounded over the course of the two days.[12] This was the highest casualty list yet resulting from a kamikaze attack and was a portent of things to come.

The other kamikazes selected a different carrier to attack. *Sangamon* reported being near missed by a suicide attack. The after action report from *Petrof Bay* stated she was missed by a Zero 15 feet off her fantail and by another just 20 yards off her starboard bow.[13] Neither ship was damaged.

Following this initial burst of activity, suicide attacks slowed to an intermittent pace while the Japanese organized more special attack units.

When Fukudome's Sixth Base Air Force moved to the Philippines on October 22–23, the pool of potential suicide attackers grew. On October 26 the Fifth and Sixth Base Air Forces merged into the First

Combined Base Air Force. Fukudome assumed overall command and Onishi became his chief of staff.[14] Onishi immediately began efforts to convince Fukudome to endorse suicide attacks. To sustain his kamikaze campaign, Onishi needed additional aircraft and volunteers. Fukudome resisted the shift to suicide attacks, fearing it would destroy the morale of the aviators. After the obvious successes of the initial suicide attacks on October 25, Onishi pressed Fukudome for the third time to embrace the kamikaze spirit and allow his men to conduct suicide attacks. Early on October 26, Fukudome relented.[15] Additional special attack units were quickly set up from the large numbers of volunteers available. Kamikaze attacks became a staple for the remainder of the Philippines campaign and for the rest of the war.

Over the two days of suicide attacks, the success of this new tactic was undeniable. The debut of the kamikaze enjoyed a stunning initial success. Two groups of escort carriers were attacked over October 25–26. Of the nine carriers present, one was sunk and five were damaged to varying degrees. The table below provides an overview of the carnage.

Results of Suicide Attacks on American Escort Carriers, October 25–26		
Carrier	Fate	Casualties
Santee	Damaged; three months of repair	43
Kalinin Bay	Damaged; almost two months of repair	55
Kitkun Bay	Damaged; no repair required	17
White Plains	Damaged; almost two months of repairs	11
St Lo	Sunk	114
Suwannee	Damaged; two months of repair	289

This was just the opening phase of the kamikaze storm. Much worse was to come.

THE JAPANESE COUNTERLANDING OPERATION

The Combined Fleet's effort to land reinforcements on Leyte in response to the American invasion are usually lost in the shadow of the four major battles fought between and October 24 and 25, 1944. The actions of the small Japanese force assigned to make a counterlanding operation were relatively unimportant, but they did set a pattern for the next two months of Japanese reinforcement missions to reinforce their garrison on Leyte. These operations were very costly in terms of ships and men, but they were successful enough that the battle for Leyte was extended until late December.

Cruiser Division 16, comprised of heavy cruiser *Aoba*, light cruiser *Kinu*, and destroyer *Uranami* and under the command of Vice Admiral Sakonjo Naomasa, originally constituted the Fourth Section of the First Diversionary Attack Force. As plans began to firm up for the movement of Imperial Army forces to Leyte in response to the American landing there, on October 18 Sakonjo's force was removed from Kurita's command and placed under Shima's Second Diversionary Attack Force. The force arrived at Brunei at 1200 on October 20 and was instructed to remain at Brunei on alert. Orders came the next day for Cruiser Division 16 to lead the counterlanding operation. It departed Brunei at 1700 en route to Manila to rendezvous with five transport ships slated to carry the 41st Infantry Regiment from Cagayan, Mindanao to Ormoc on the western side of Leyte. At this point Sakonjo's force was designated as the Southwest Area Guard Force, and the transport mission was named No. 1 TA Transport Operation. Once in Manila, Cruiser Division 16 would escort three T.1-class fast transports (the Japanese version of destroyer transports) and two LSTs.

As Sakonjo's force was approaching Manila, it was detected on radar by submarine *Bream* in the approaches to Manila Bay. After tracking the Japanese force for over an hour, at 0424 the submarine fired a full salvo of six torpedoes at *Aoba*. One hit the cruiser in one of her engine rooms. This brought the cruiser to a stop and created a 13-degree list.[16] Light cruiser *Kinu* managed to tow her into Cavite Navy Yard for emergency repairs. In November *Aoba* departed Manila for Japan. She arrived at Kure on December 12, at which point her damage was deemed too extensive to repair. In April 1945, American carrier-based aircraft heavily damaged *Aoba*, which settled on the bottom of Kure harbor. In July, the hulk was destroyed by carrier and B-24 attack.

After losing his flagship, Sakonjo took *Kinu*, *Uranami*, and the five transports out of Cavite on October 24 bound for Cagayan. Beginning at 0700, and for the next three hours, the force was attacked by aircraft from *Lexington* and *Essex* of TG 38.3. No direct hits were suffered, but the ships were heavily strafed; 47 men were killed on *Kinu* and 25 on *Uranami*. The force arrived at Cagayan the same evening where *T 6*, *T 9*, and *T 10* embarked 350 men each and *T 101* and *T 102* 400 each. All the transports departed Cagayan on the morning of October 25. *Kinu* and *Uranami*, delayed by the necessity to repair damage to *Uranami*, departed at 1730 for Ormoc after the cruiser loaded 347 men and the destroyer 150. Since TF 38 and the aircraft from the escort carriers were occupied attacking higher priority targets on October 25, all the Japanese ships and their embarked troops arrived safely at Ormoc early on October 26.

After unloading their troops, *Kinu* and *Uranami* departed with three of the transports for Manila. Only two hours after leaving Ormoc, *Kinu* and *Uranami* were attacked by aircraft from Taffy 2. A total of 23 Avengers and 29 Wildcats from *Manila Bay* and *Natoma Bay* struck the Japanese, followed by a second wave from Taffy 1 with another 13 Avengers with torpedoes and 15 Wildcats. The American aircraft launched repeated attacks on Sakonjo's two ships, which were completely without air cover. *Uranami* was heavily strafed and hit by a bomb in a boiler room, reducing her speed. A second bomb hit at 1110 caused flooding severe enough that the captain ordered the ship to be abandoned. *Uranami* sank just after noon; 103 of her crew were killed, and only 94 were rescued.[17] *Kinu* took a direct bomb hit and three near misses near the aft engine room at 1130. The cruiser went dead in the water, took a minor list, and began to settle by the stern. The flooding could not be checked. By 1400 the stern was under water, and by 1700 the list reached a dangerous 26 degrees. The order to abandon ship was given at 1720. Ten minutes later, *Kinu* sank by the stern.[18] Most of the crew was saved by the three transports, but another 83 men were killed and 51 wounded. In exchange, the Americans lost only an Avenger and a Wildcat.[19]

This first Japanese transport mission to Leyte set the pattern for future Japanese reinforcement operations that extended into December. These missions were necessitated by the need to support the Imperial Army's efforts to fight the decisive ground campaign in the Philippines on Leyte instead of Luzon. The Japanese mounted another eight convoy operations to Leyte from Manila and other points in the Philippines to move four divisions to the island. Many of the surviving destroyers from the First Diversionary Attack Force were used in these missions. In spite of heavy losses in ships and men, the Japanese delivered an estimated 45,000 troops and 10,000 tons of supplies and equipment to Leyte. Though the Americans had won a decisive victory in the Battle of Leyte Gulf, they did not exploit the opportunity to gain control of the waters west of Leyte. This failure extended the ground campaign, just as MacArthur feared.

THE JAPANESE SUBMARINE OFFENSIVE

Another forgotten aspect of *Sho-1* is the operations of the Combined Fleet's submarine force. The Imperial Navy spent considerable resources to develop its submarine force before the war and gave it a prominent role in its planning against the USN. Because of a doctrine of focusing on heavily-defended USN main fleet units, faulty tactics, and an insufficient number of submarines, the Japanese submarine force had badly underperformed up until October 1944.

When the Americans landed on Leyte, the Japanese submarine force was at a low point. The dedicated submarine command, the Sixth Fleet, was caught on Saipan when the Americans invaded the Marianas. The commander and his staff were killed. Vice Admiral Miwa Shigeyoshi was given the task of rebuilding the fleet headquarters. He also faced the problem of insufficient submarines to meet all his mission requirements. On paper, the Sixth Fleet possessed the impressive total of 55 boats. However, of these 15 were training boats. The availability of the remaining boats was reduced by other factors; seven boats were working up after joining the fleet or following refits, four subs were being converted to carry *kaitens* (manned torpedoes), four were conducting operations against merchant shipping in the Indian Ocean, seven were operating as transports to isolated Japanese garrisons, and several were unaccounted for.[20] Miwa formed the First Submarine Group to support *Sho-Go*. This was comprised of 15 boats: 11 fleet type (called I boats) and four short-ranged coastal defense subs (RO boats).

Combined Fleet orders issued in August gave Miwa six pre-planned deployment zones and target priorities. Miwa convinced the Combined Fleet to authorize patrol areas instead of using picket lines, which had proved so disastrous for the Sixth Fleet in the defense of the Marianas. Attack priorities were aircraft carriers, battleships, and then troop convoys. Confusingly, this was not in accordance with *Sho-1*, which focused on attacking the invasion force. The Combined Fleet reserved the option to order the submarines to make a dash to the location of the American landing.[21]

When Halsey attacked Formosa, Miwa was ordered to deploy his submarines. The four units comprising the "A" Unit departed first; *I-26* and *I-45* sortied on October 12, followed by *I-54* and *I-56* on October 15. On October 21, after the activation of *Sho-1*, seven boats of the "B" Unit departed (*I-38, I-41, I-44, I-46, RO-41, RO-43,* and *RO-46*). The

"C" Unit (*RO-109* and *RO-112*) departed the Inland Sea on October 23. All boats were assigned patrol areas stretching along the coasts of Samar and Mindanao, and in the approaches to Leyte Gulf. By October 27, the patrol areas were modified so that all five RO boats were operating off southeastern Luzon and Samar, leaving all the fleet boats off the approaches to Leyte Gulf.[22]

The first group of boats had worked their way down to Leyte Gulf by the time the Americans landed on October 20. The Americans had tracked the movement of these boats through decrypted communications and direction-finding of their radio transmissions. On October 21, *I-26*, one of the most successful Japanese boats of the war having already sunk light cruiser *Juneau* and damaged carrier *Saratoga*, attacked Taffy 1 and fired torpedoes at *Petrof Bay*. The torpedoes missed, and a counterattack by one of the escorts probably accounted for *I-26*, since she was never heard from again. *I-54* had a similar fate. On October 28 the boat actually penetrated the formation of TG 38.4. However, two destroyers detected her before she could launch an attack, sinking her with depth charges. As far as Miwa knew, another boat had disappeared.

I-56 was the most active Japanese submarine during the battle. She reported making an attack on a convoy off Leyte Gulf on October 24 and the following day made an attack on *Santee* in Taffy 1. The attack occurred just 16 minutes after the ship was hit by a kamikaze. While the Americans were focused on the air threat, *I-56* approached undetected and fired a spread of torpedoes against the escort carrier. At 0756 one struck the carrier amidships on the starboard side. The blast created a large hole, flooded four compartments, and created a list.[23] Being a converted tanker with good compartmentation, *Santee* was not crippled by a single torpedo, and after emergency repairs was actually able to shrug off all her damage and resume flight operations. *I-56's* captain managed to survive the attacks of the escorts by going deep. The submarine returned to port, making her the only "A" Unit boat to survive. The final "A" Unit boat enjoyed some success, but it was after the period of the Battle of Leyte Gulf. During the early morning hours of October 29, *I-45* put two torpedoes into destroyer escort *Eversole* 60nm off Dinagat Island, which sank immediately. Within hours, destroyer escort *Whitehurst* detected and sank *I-45*.

The only other success gained by any of the boats that deployed before or during the battle was recorded by *I-41*. On November 3 the submarine hit light cruiser *Reno*, part of TG 38.3, while the task group was operating off Leyte. A single torpedo hit aft caused severe flooding. The ship was saved by good damage control and was towed to Ulithi by November 10. This was the first time in almost two years that a Japanese submarine had successfully attacked a ship operating with the fast carrier task force. *I-41* enjoyed her success only briefly, being sunk on November 18. Another "B" Unit boat, *I-38*, was sunk on November 12.

During the course of the Imperial Navy's last attempt to fight a decisive battle, its submarine force contributed almost nothing. It was able to record only a handful of attacks against the hundreds of Allied ships active in and off Leyte Gulf. Its only success was a single hit on an escort carrier which caused minimal damage. Compared with the operations and impact of American submarines during the battle, it was just another example of the Imperial Navy being unable to perform on a modern naval battlefield.

11

The Reckoning

In most battles, it is said that the side that makes the fewest mistakes wins. In the Battle of Leyte Gulf, both sides made many mistakes, but there was never any possibility that an American misstep was going to hand the battle to the Japanese. Leyte Gulf was the most decisive naval battle of the entire Pacific War. After October 1944, the Imperial Navy was finished as a force capable of large-scale operations. The USN gained control of the Pacific and prepared to launch the final offensives of the war against Japan without fear of a response from the IJN's surface fleet.

LEYTE GULF — THE COST TO THE IMPERIAL NAVY

Toyoda committed virtually every operational major combatant in the Combined Fleet to *Sho-1*. Even with this level of effort, the Japanese failed to achieve their objectives. They neither sank the American amphibious invasion fleet, stopped or slowed the invasion of Leyte, nor inflicted severe losses on the Pacific Fleet. From any perspective, *Sho-1* was an abject failure.

In the process, the Combined Fleet suffered extremely heavy losses. Over the span of five days (October 23–27), the Japanese lost more ships in combat than any other navy in modern naval history. Losses totaled just short of 310,000 tons, or about 45 percent of the total tonnage involved.[1] Losses during the five days of the battle constituted some 26 percent of total IJN losses suffered during the entire war.[2] Of the 69 ships involved, 28 were sunk and another four were so heavily damaged that they never saw action again. The table below details the carnage:

Combined Fleet Losses During *Sho-1*				
Force	Ships assigned on October 23	Sunk October 23–27	Heavily damaged	Ships operational October 28
First Diversionary Attack Force	32	10	3	19
First Diversionary Attack Force, Third Section	7	6	0	1
Second Diversionary Attack Force (including Destroyer Division 21)	10	3	0	7
Mobile Force, Main Body	17	7	0	10
Southwest Fleet Guard Force	3	2	1	0
Totals	69	28	4	37

The 28 ships lost included one fleet carrier, three light carriers, three battleships, six heavy and four light cruisers, and 11 destroyers. This represented the heaviest losses ever suffered by a navy in combat in such a brief period. In contrast, the Imperial Navy lost only 18 principal combatants over the entire period of the Guadalcanal campaign, which encompassed six months.

Of the 28 ships sunk, most (17) were sunk by American air power. Of these, all but one (light cruiser *Abukuma*) were sunk by carrier-based aircraft. Interestingly, of the 16 sunk by carrier aircraft, nine were sunk by Third Fleet and seven by the hard-fighting escort carriers.

Eight Japanese ships were sunk by American surface forces. Third Fleet surface forces accounted for only three; the remainder were sunk by the Seventh Fleet at Surigao Strait. The final three Japanese ships lost, all of which were cruisers, were sunk by submarines. Submarines also accounted for two of the four ships irreparably damaged, with the other two being split between surface and air attack (all of these were also cruisers).

Those ships that escaped destruction, primarily the six battleships, did not constitute a balanced force. Most of their supporting ships were destroyed, and the Combined Fleet's carrier force was definitely destroyed. In the words of Ozawa:

> After this battle the surface forces became strictly auxiliary, so that we relied on land forces, special attack, and air power. There was no further use assigned to surface vessels, with the exception of some special ships.[3]

Of the 69 ships committed to *Sho-1*, only 24 ever returned to Japan.

Personnel casualties were extremely high. On the 28 ships that were sunk, at least 12,943 men were killed. This was by far the highest number of sailors lost during a single battle of the war. An extraordinary fact was that the entire complement of six ships was lost. Another six ships lost all but a handful of their crews; only 20 men survived from the over 3,250 onboard *Fuso* and *Yamashiro*. Japanese sailors paid an appalling price for the vanity of their leaders.

Following its devastation at the Battle of Leyte Gulf, the Combined Fleet was only able to mount a handful of operations for the remainder of the war. One of these was the result of the Japanese decision to make Leyte the place of the decisive battle for control of the Philippines. To support their defense of Leyte, the Japanese ran a series of troop convoys to the island between October and December. With little air cover, these were very costly affairs. Seven of the destroyers that survived *Sho-1* were used to escort these high-priority convoys, and most were sunk. Two minor surface engagements were also fought inside Ormoc Bay between Japanese and American destroyers.

In late December, the Japanese caught the Americans by surprise by sending a surface task force of two cruisers and six destroyers from Cam Ranh Bay in Indochina to attack the beachhead at San Jose on Mindoro Island. Facing only PT boats and air attacks, the Japanese force conducted a brief and ineffective bombardment of the beachhead before fleeing, losing a destroyer in the process.

The only fleet operation conducted by the Combined Fleet for the remainder of the war was the most controversial. Following the American invasion of Okinawa on April 1, 1945, it was decided to use what remained of the Second Fleet to attack the invasion force. The operation had many similarities to *Sho-Go*. A massive air operation had been pre-planned to respond to an American invasion of Okinawa. It was named *Ten-Go* (Heaven Operation) and was scheduled for April 6.

Toyoda, still in command of the Combined Fleet, was convinced by April 4 that *Ten-Go* needed a surface component. By adding *Yamato* to the operation, the Imperial Navy could refute charges of cowardice from the Imperial Army, answer the emperor's query from March 29 as to why no surface ships were included in the operation, and avoid the embarrassment of having *Yamato* remain intact as the nation struggled for survival.

Although not formally considered a suicide mission, there was little likelihood that *Yamato* would survive a mission to Okinawa in the face of overwhelming American air power. *Ten-Go*, just like *Sho-Go* before it, was not a serious plan with any hope of making a real contribution to victory; instead, it was another ceremonial vehicle for the Imperial Navy to demonstrate its willingness to die fighting. In addition to *Yamato*, all that was available was light cruiser *Yahagi* and eight destroyers (six of which were *Sho-1* veterans). Predictably, the operation ended in utter disaster. Departing on the afternoon of April 6, *Yamato* was spotted by American submarines, and then aircraft, and brought under air attack in the early afternoon of April 7. After two hours, the attack was over. *Yamato*, *Yahagi*, and four destroyers were sunk. On *Yamato* alone, 3,055 men perished; another 1,187 died on the escort ships. This massive sacrifice was pointless. The sortie was not even coordinated with the planned air attacks. On April 7, only 54 kamikaze sorties were mounted, and only half of these found a target.

The Combined Fleet's carrier fleet was largely inactive after the Battle of Leyte Gulf. Never again did a Japanese carrier with an embarked air group leave the relative safety of home waters. Devoid of aircraft, Japanese carriers were used as transports, mostly for carrying troops and equipment to aid in the defense of the Philippines. On December 9, on her second mission with high-priority cargo to the southern area, *Junyo* was hit by two torpedoes. She was able to return to Japan but was never fully repaired. On December 19 in the East China Sea, the new fleet carrier *Unryu* was torpedoed. The carrier was en route to Manila with high-priority cargo, including suicide rocket bombs. The ship quickly sank after receiving a second torpedo. *Ryuho* made a delivery of 58 suicide rocket bombs to Formosa in January 1945, the last time a Japanese carrier ventured outside Japanese home waters.

Counting the number of Japanese ships that survived the Battle of Leyte misses the larger point. As Toyoda had foreseen, the remaining elements of the Imperial Navy were crippled by a lack of fuel. This was especially true with those ships sent back to Japan. In July 1945 Halsey made a point of destroying the last major Japanese ships idled in harbor. TF 38 air attacks destroyed many of the survivors of Leyte Gulf, among them battleships *Hyuga*, *Haruna*, and *Ise*; heavy cruisers *Tone* and *Aoba*; and light cruiser *Oyodo*. The new carrier *Amagi* was also sunk and *Katsuragi* damaged. Halsey had finally achieved his battle of annihilation.

LEYTE GULF – THE COST TO THE UNITED STATES NAVY

Five days of intense combat only cost the Americans six ships sunk. TF 38 lost light carrier *Princeton*. The other five ships were all from Taffy 3 – escort carriers *Gambier Bay* and *St. Lo*, destroyers *Hoel* and *Johnston*, and destroyer escort *Samuel B. Roberts*. The total tonnage of these ships was 36,600, or about 12 percent of the losses suffered by the Japanese. The tonnage lost represents about 3 percent of the overall tonnage of American ships involved in the battle.[4] Clearly, these losses were insignificant to a navy with the resources and ship-building capability of the USN in late 1944.

Personnel losses were another matter. Total American naval casualties were 473 killed, 1,110 missing, 1,220 wounded – a total of 2,803 men.[5] The vast majority of these casualties, 75 percent, were suffered by Taffy 3; 311 dead, 877 missing, and 914 wounded.[6] Had Taffy 3 not been exposed to surface attack, overall American personnel casualties would have been extremely light. To put these losses in perspective, they were only surpassed by those suffered during the Guadalcanal campaign, in which 4,770 sailors were killed or missing, and the fierce battle off Okinawa, in which 4,907 were killed and missing.

Given the scale of losses, the Battle of Leyte Gulf was a great American naval victory. If any naval battle in the Pacific War can be considered decisive, the closest would be Leyte Gulf. While a case can be made for calling Midway, Guadalcanal, and Philippine Sea decisive battles, they were not decisive in the sense that the Imperial Navy, even after having suffered defeats in those battles, was still a viable force and still exerted strategic influence on the course of the war. From this perspective, Leyte Gulf was the decisive naval battle of the Pacific War. It was conclusive in that after Leyte Gulf the Imperial Navy ceased to exist as a force capable of large-scale naval operations. Through a combination of heavy losses and the creation of a situation in which the Japanese were unable to replace their naval losses or even provide fuel for the remainder of the fleet, Leyte Gulf was the death knell of the Imperial Navy.

The small scale of American naval losses had no impact on future operations. With command of the seas established, the occupation of Leyte was concluded in December. The Philippines campaign came to a climax in January 1945 with the massive landing in Lingayen Gulf. In April 1945, even under a barrage of Japanese suicide attacks, the Americans advanced to the doorstep of Japan with a landing on Okinawa. The decisive battle of Leyte Gulf, designed by the Japanese to stop the onslaught of the American Navy, made no difference to the pace of the American advance during the last months of the war.

THE IMPERIAL NAVY AT LEYTE GULF – AN EVALUATION

Even given the fact that the Combined Fleet had no hope of victory, it is still worthwhile to examine the performance of the Japanese.

In the area of strategic and operational planning, the shortcomings of *Sho-Go* have already been detailed. On the strategic level it was a plan without a purpose. There was no hope of defeating the invasion before it occurred, and without this the entire operation lacked a strategic rationale.

Toyoda failed to synchronize his force employment at the strategic level. He decided (actually his chief of staff, but he was carrying out Toyoda's intent) to employ his air forces first during the air-naval battle off Formosa without the involvement of the Combined Fleet's surface forces. When he employed his surface forces a week later, it was with a weakened air arm. At this point, the employment of the surface fleet was too late to achieve the strategic objective.

On the operational level, *Sho-1* was a complex plan that required a high level of timing, reliable and timely communications, accurate intelligence, and excellent coordination to have even a chance of success. None of these were present, but Toyoda wished away all these potential issues. All of these problems were exacerbated by *Sho-1's* dramatic division of forces. During the battle, the Combined Fleet was divided into four main forces. None of these were in a position to provide mutual support to the other. The division of the two main forces, Kurita's and Ozawa's, was unavoidable due to fuel issues, but it does not change the fact that they ended up fighting different battles hundreds of miles apart. The Japanese realized this was a severe weakness and planned to reunite the fleet as soon as conditions allowed. Perhaps the battle should not have been fought at all until the fleet could fight as a single entity.

The decision by Kurita to divide his force, as "recommended" by Combined Fleet headquarters, was against the principles of war and only increased the likelihood that the First Diversionary Attack Force would be defeated piecemeal. However, in this case, the decision to split Nishimura off from the main force was correct, since it meant only a minor reduction in the offensive power of Kurita's fleet and provided a useful diversion that occupied the bulk of the Seventh Fleet. If this secondary attack through Surigao Strait was worthwhile, then it should have been allocated all available forces. The Second Diversionary Attack Force was in a position to easily provide support to Nishimura's force, but never did so. The refusal of Toyoda and his Combined Fleet staff to rectify the curious situation in which two forces operated in the same water space, almost at the same time, with the same objective, but with no attempt to coordinate their actions, adds another level to the inchoate planning surrounding the implementation of *Sho-1*.

The Japanese demonstrated almost no ability to coordinate operations during the battle. This was most apparent in the lack of coordination between air and naval attacks. At a superficial level, the Japanese should have had an advantage in this area, since they enjoyed a unified command structure during the battle. But this did them little good. Because of command ineptitude and poor communications, the Japanese exhibited a very limited ability to coordinate forces and benefit from mutual support.

Command and control in general was a glaring problem. From the faulty transmitter onboard *Zuikaku* to the general inability to share timely information among the principal commanders, communications proved to be an Achilles heel. The lack of information affected the way Japanese commanders conducted their operations, as evinced by Kurita's actions on October 24 and 25.

The linchpin of large-scale fleet operations is logistics. The Combined Fleet fought the battle on a logistical shoestring. Logistical issues affected the Japanese across the board. The nature of *Sho-1* itself was shaped by logistical constraints, as were tactical actions. The fuel status of their units was a constant worry for every Japanese commander. Not only were they constantly monitoring ships' fuel states, but they were concerned if the next planned fueling was even going to occur. In particular, this had an impact on the operations of Kurita's force.

It is worth underlining the extreme peril the Combined Fleet was in with regard to logistics. Logistics decided when, where, and how the Combined Fleet could fight. It is critical to keep in mind that even if the Japanese had scored a "decisive" victory during the battle, it would not have translated to sea control of the region. Lack of fuel and munitions meant that it would have been weeks or months before the Combined Fleet could have mounted another major operation in the Philippines area. By this point in the war, the Combined Fleet had been reduced to a raiding force, not a power projection force.

Intelligence was never a strength of the Imperial Fleet, and this was again the case at Leyte Gulf. This was a critical weakness, since the entire *Sho-1* plan was highly dependent on accurate intelligence. At the strategic level, the Japanese did a good job of discerning overall American intentions. At the operational level, they understood the basic American order of battle and how the Americans planned to fight. However, the critical date of when the Americans would land on Leyte was unknown, which impacted when *Sho-1* could be activated. At the tactical level, lack of reconnaissance gave the Japanese an abysmal level of situational awareness. This had a huge impact on operations, from Kurita's inability to determine which American naval force he was fighting on October 25, to Nishimura's rash charge up Surigao Strait against overwhelming odds, to Ozawa's failure to divert the Third Fleet earlier in the battle.

On the tactical level, the Combined Fleet was outclassed in every warfare area. The common theme throughout these areas was the lack of modern radar.

The lack of air capabilities by October 1944 was the central weakness of the Imperial Navy in general and of *Sho-1* in particular. The total weakness of the carrier fleet left the burden of air combat to Japanese land-based air forces. The weakness of the land-based air force was perhaps the key Japanese weakness in the entire battle, as both Kurita and Ozawa remarked after the war. The weakness was not just in attack, but also for reconnaissance. Tasked to neutralize the American carrier force, Japanese land-based air forces failed spectacularly. They did register an unusual success by sinking light carrier *Princeton*, but this fell far short of what was required to protect Kurita's force from attack. This weakness drove the Japanese to employ suicide tactics.

After a spectacular debut on October 25, the Japanese thought they had a game-changing tactic. Early results from October and November 1944 demonstrated that the kamikaze was seven to ten times more likely to cause damage compared to conventional attacks, but it was not the game changer the Japanese hoped. For the entire Philippines campaign, the Japanese expended between 500 and 600 suicide aircraft, causing some degree of damage to 140 ships and craft. Seventeen of these were sunk, with the largest being an escort carrier. These were significant losses, but were not on the level to generate an operational or strategic impact. Even so, it is interesting to ponder what the result would have been if the Japanese had been prepared to unleash massive suicide operations at the beginning of *Sho-1*.

Air defense was a critical weakness for the Japanese during the battle. Over the period of four days, American carrier aircraft pounded three of the four major Japanese forces, inflicting heavy losses. Air attack was the primary agent of destruction of Japanese ships during the battle. Japanese antiaircraft was voluminous but was generally inaccurate.

Since *Sho-1* focused on the striking power of Japanese surface forces, an examination of the Japanese performance in surface warfare is warranted. The focus of this examination is the Battle off Samar, where the Japanese have been criticized for not making short work of Taffy 3. For the most part, this criticism is unfair and fails to put this battle into proper context with other Pacific War surface battles fought during the day at long ranges.

For any navy, it is difficult to hit a target at long range with gunnery. The Battle off Samar was fought during the day, which was unusual during the Pacific War. However, there are a few comparable battles that we can use to place the Battle off Samar into proper context.

The Imperial Navy stressed long-range gunnery and trained hard to master this skill. It was Japanese doctrine to engage targets at long range; actions at extended range reduced the likelihood of an effective response by the enemy. Nevertheless, hitting a target at extended ranges is extremely difficult. Even the Japanese expected very low hit rates, in the area of 6 percent for heavy cruisers. Even this turned out to be exceedingly optimistic. Using this doctrine of long-range gunnery, a Japanese force led by heavy cruisers *Nachi* and *Haguro* engaged an Allied force of similar size in the Java Sea on February 27, 1942. During this multi-hour clash fought under the best possible conditions for long-range gunnery, only five of 1,619 8-inch shells from *Nachi* and

Haguro hit a target. A couple of days later, *Ashigara* and *Myoko* fired 1,171 rounds at a British heavy cruiser, of which two shells hit. On neither of these occasions were the Japanese ships under air attack.

Comparable results were recorded in the Battle of the Komandorski Islands fought on March 27, 1943. On this occasion, heavy cruisers *Maya* and *Nachi* opened fire at 20,000 yards on an American heavy cruiser. Over several hours, *Maya* fired 904 8-inch rounds and *Nachi* fired another 707 8-inch shells. Exactly two shells hit their target.

On October 25, 1944 in the Battle off Samar, the gunnery crews of the Japanese battleships and heavy cruisers faced the worst possible conditions. Their ships were under incessant air attack. Maneuvering to avoid air attack makes it much more difficult to generate a target solution. The Japanese were firing into smoke and bad weather without the benefit of radar. Given the innate difficulty of long-range gunnery and the severe conditions, the gunnery results should have been marginal at best. Nevertheless, the Japanese have been criticized for not sinking every ship in Taffy 3 within minutes. This was clearly impossible; in fact, Japanese gunnery performance was not as bad as has been portrayed. Though it is very difficult to get an accurate count of the number of hits scored by the Japanese, an accepted figure is 45 hits on the escort carriers. Most of these (26) were on *Gambier Bay* after she was damaged – it is much easier to hit a target dead in the water at reduced range. Hits on the American escorts are even more difficult to calculate. *Hoel* was sunk by at least 23 hits, and *Samuel B. Roberts* by six. *Johnston* was crippled by six shells fired from long range (20,000 yards) and then sunk by an indeterminate number of hits at shorter ranges. Destroyer escort *Dennis* was also hit three times. On the other hand, on many occasions American escorts came as close as 4,000 yards to heavy Japanese ships and were not hit by fire. Overall, Japanese gunnery was a mixed bag during the battle. It was not as atrocious as is often portrayed, but to claim it should have had much greater success is not based on an examination of prevailing conditions.

More telling than the performance of the Japanese gunnery crews at Samar was the lack of success by the torpedo crews. Torpedo combat was an essential component of Japanese surface combat doctrine. Of the 40 torpedoes fired during the battle, not a single one found a target.

Another Japanese weakness was in the area of antisubmarine warfare. Whenever they gained contact on a Japanese force, American submarines attacked with near impunity. The five cruisers sunk or severely damaged by American submarines during the battle accounted for more total tonnage than the Combined Fleet sank during the entire battle.

Japanese commanders performed with varying levels of effectiveness. All were forced to wield blunt instruments against an American Navy nearing the peak of its power. Based on whether or not their force achieved its mission, Ozawa must be judged as the most effective Japanese commander. He not only performed his decoy mission effectively but did so at a fairly low cost. However, his actions would have been more effective if his force had been discovered earlier. This was not really due to his shortcomings, but to lackadaisical TF 38 reconnaissance efforts.

Kurita is a hard figure to judge. On the one hand, he fought his way through the most unrelenting series of attacks ever faced by a naval commander. On the other hand, he did so while committing a series of errors. His inattentiveness to antisubmarine preparations on October 23 is hard to explain. As has already been explained, his tactics on October 25 off Samar were understandable given the fact he believed he was facing a carrier force capable of high speed. His pivotal decision not to go into the gulf and be destroyed for no reason was an act of conscience, not one of cowardice. However, the overall performance of the First Diversionary Attack Force was his responsibility, and it was mediocre at best. It displayed poor antisubmarine tactics, poor antiaircraft gunnery, atrocious ship recognition abilities, and only average gunnery skills. In the final analysis, Kurita was the victim of a bad plan and of the Combined Fleet's declining tactical skills.

Nishimura was a man focused on his mission, and he did everything he could to accomplish it. Of note, he was the only Japanese commander to press his attack to the point of destruction. In moving his force with haste, he allowed his force to be discovered early, which gave the Americans ample time to prepare an elaborate ambush. In the darkness of Surigao Strait, he failed to appreciate the nature of the threat he was facing, which meant his force was almost annihilated before the main phase of the battle had even begun.

Shima's performance was inexplicably bad. With his small force, he had no ability to strike a powerful blow by himself. Nevertheless, he refused to join up with Nishimura's larger force or even to coordinate his actions. Shima fought hard to get his force into the battle, but when he actually had the chance to engage the Americans, he squandered it. After firing a desultory torpedo barrage, he left the battle.

Onishi must also be given mention. Though talk of the need for adoption of suicide tactics had been floating around Japanese command circles for months, he had the determination to implement them. By doing so, he transformed the nature of the war in the Pacific just as the ships of the Imperial Navy were disappearing from the surface of the world's largest ocean. Kamikazes were a fearsome weapon, but one that caused widespread carnage without affecting the course of the war. Overlooking the fact that kamikazes only increased the human toll of the war without influencing its decision, Onishi can be faulted for not taking all steps necessary to introduce the new tactics in a more massive scale, instead of with just 24 initial pilots.

With there being so little chance that *Sho-1* would achieve a strategic result and so high a probability that the Combined Fleet would be sacrificed in the process, the Japanese should not have fought the battle at all. Combined Fleet headquarters was more concerned about the image of the Imperial Navy instead of what was best for the nation. With the loss of the Japanese fleet, Nimitz gained the strategic flexibility he sought. Planning for the invasion of Luzon, Okinawa, and for Japan itself went ahead without concern for a Japanese naval threat.

THE UNITED STATES NAVY AT LEYTE GULF – AN EVALUATION

The decision to invade Leyte directly and skip the Mindanao operation was bold. It undoubtedly sped up the pace of the war. Halsey must be given primary credit for this. It was bold because it was the first time MacArthur had conducted an operation beyond the range of land-based air cover. The size of the operation required that Nimitz provide significant reinforcements to MacArthur's Seventh Fleet and task the Third Fleet with providing overall cover to the invasion. This was the cause of the divided command structure that bedeviled the Americans during the battle.

The USN's principal weakness going into the battle was the divided command structure and the unresolved command relationships between supported and supporting commanders.[7] This laid the foundation for the troubles to come. The split command structure was the result of a compromise between the Army and the Navy in spring 1942. The fact that it was still in effect in October 1944 was the responsibility of the Joint Chiefs of Staff. The only possible solution to the convoluted command structure was if the Joint Chiefs of Staff had intervened to solve it. This would have required the appointment of an overall commander, who would have been either MacArthur or Nimitz. Given the intense service rivalries at play, even the Joint Chiefs might not have been able to arrive at a solution palatable to both services, making this an issue that only President Roosevelt could have addressed. Had there been a unified command structure, it is impossible to believe that San Bernardino Strait would have been left unwatched and undefended.

Nimitz also held part of the blame for the events of October 24–25. Instead of making clear to Halsey that support for the invasion was his top priority, he inserted an additional task in his orders that gave Halsey free range to channel his overriding desire to attack the Japanese fleet whenever the opportunity arose. By October 1944 Nimitz knew exactly who he was dealing with in Halsey, but he failed to take the necessary steps to channel his aggressiveness. Though it was not his style to meddle in the operations of his fleet commanders, Nimitz did intervene when he became concerned over Halsey's handling of the battle. He should have done so earlier.

A corollary to the divided command structure was the poor communications between the Third and Seventh Fleets. Because of the time delay getting information between fleets, neither Halsey nor Kinkaid fully understood what the other was doing. Since the two fleets were under different commanders, they could not communicate directly. Getting a message from one fleet to the other was an arduous and time consuming process. If Kinkaid wanted to communicate with Halsey, a message was drafted, then encoded, and then sent to the radio station at Manus in the Admiralty Islands. It was then transmitted on the "Fox" fleet broadcast, which was monitored by all units. Each ship or command would copy and decode only those messages addressed to it. In order to understand what Third Fleet was doing, Kinkaid's staff monitored and decoded all of Halsey's communications against orders. Adding to the problem was the time delay between transmission by the originator and its receipt. It is human nature to think that whatever you are doing is important, so many messages were incorrectly prioritized as "urgent." This meant that the truly urgent messages were mixed up with ones that really were not. At Manus, communications personnel handled urgent messages in the order they were received or made a rudimentary attempt to triage truly important messages. This led to messages being received out of order or taking hours to be received at all.[8] Most urgent messages were received within an acceptable 30 to 60 minutes, but even this lag was an issue in a crisis situation.[9] Another layer of difficulty was the imprecise wording of key messages. Writing clear messages was not a skill possessed in abundance by either of the staffs of Third or Seventh Fleet. All these factors led to American commanders making decisions on late or incorrect information.

The American advantage in intelligence has become one of the underlying assumptions of Pacific War battles. This was not the case at the Battle of Leyte Gulf. The Combined Fleet made its biggest effort of the war since Midway, and Allied intelligence completely failed to provide details of the Japanese operation. The fundamental error of Allied intelligence analysts was examining Japanese intentions rather than their capabilities. The Combined Fleet clearly had the capability to mount a major operation to contest the operation, as well as the intention to do so. The Allies failed to discern Japanese intentions while glossing over their capabilities.

This had real implications for the battle. Despite the fact that Ultra intercepts were generally not useful in tracing the movements of Japanese naval forces because they usually maintained radio silence at sea, Ultra was very useful in tracing the movements of land-based air units and logistics arrangements for naval forces. These indications were present in the days leading to the battle, but American naval intelligence analysts failed to "connect the dots." As a result, the massive Japanese reaction caught Halsey by surprise, as evinced by his sending two carrier task groups to Ulithi just days after the invasion. Obviously, the Japanese intent to use their carriers as a diversion and the extremely limited capabilities of those carriers was a major intelligence failure. There was evidence for this tactic as well, but it was also missed by intelligence analysts. As a result, American naval commanders had to respond to Japanese moves as they occurred without a high degree of insight into the overall Japanese plan.

On the operational level, American commanders can be faulted for poor battle management. Despite bringing the largest fleet yet assembled to the battle, they were unable to bring the full power of this superior force to bear. If anything, they adhered to existing doctrine and were guilty of overconcentration of force both at Surigao Strait and during Halsey's abortive attempt to annihilate Ozawa's force.

An overlooked area of excellence was the USN's proficiency in amphibious warfare. The initial assault force landed on Leyte, comprised of four divisions, was bigger than the initial American assault at Normandy with only three divisions. The invasion was conducted without major difficulties. Also overlooked was the speed of the assault. By the end of the first day, half of the invasion fleet had unloaded and departed, with most of the second half following the next day. This impressive performance undermined the very purpose of *Sho-1*.

Another area of excellence was the American submarine force. Not only did submarines sink or damage five Japanese cruisers during the battle, but they continued the ongoing massacre of Japanese merchant shipping. In October 1944, American submarines accounted for 314,906 tons of shipping (out of a total of 511,643 tons sunk that month), much of it in the Luzon Strait. This was a fraction of the 2,388,709 tons sunk by American submarines in 1944.[10] By the end of the year, the flow of raw materials to Japan had virtually stopped, just as Toyoda had feared. This was not due solely to the loss of the Philippines, as shipping losses to American submarines had already become prohibitive even before the Philippines were invaded. But the loss of the Philippines was the final nail in the coffin of Japanese dreams of keeping their SLOCS from Japan to the southern resource areas open.

However, the performance of American submarines during the battle could have been enhanced by better deployment. The problem was that the number of submarines devoted to direct support of the invasion was inadequate to cover all major chokepoints. The deployment of those submarines available was wanting. The wolf pack covering the major exit from the Inland Sea, the Bungo Strait, was removed before Ozawa's departure. Even more hard to explain was the fact that not a single submarine was assigned to watch Lingga Roads where the main Japanese fleet was based.

The USN reached high levels of proficiency in the fundamental warfare areas by October 1944. In the area of air defense, existing tactics and doctrine provided a high degree of protection from conventional Japanese air attacks. Only *Princeton* was hit by conventional attacks during a period of maximum effort from Japanese land-based air forces. The single hit was well placed, though, and led to the loss of the ship. Defense against kamikazes was much more problematic. The first use of these caught the Americans by surprise. Of all the various fleet elements, the escort carriers were the least capable in terms of defense and damage resistance, so initial damage from kamikaze attacks was significant.

The striking power of American carrier air groups was unsurpassed by this period of the war. A case can be made that the 1,043 offensive sorties by TF 38 on October 24–25 against Japanese surface forces without air cover should have inflicted greater damage, but during the period of the battle American carrier aircraft still sank 16 ships. The Third Fleet accounted for nine of these, including one of the world's biggest battleships, three carriers, one light cruiser, and four destroyers. On a level of effort basis, the aviators from the escort carriers were much more efficient. Though attacking Japanese warships was not their primary mission, they still sank four heavy cruisers (to be fair, one of these, *Mogami*, was already heavily damaged by surface action), one light cruiser, and two destroyers.

In the area of surface warfare, the Americans were also successful, sinking eight Japanese warships and losing four in return. All but one of the eight ships sunk were engaged at night. Five were sunk at Surigao Strait and the other three were dispatched by the Third Fleet on October 25–26. American naval gunnery was generally good because of modern fire control radar. Torpedo combat was even more deadly, since American destroyer tactics fully exploited the offensive potential of those ships.

EVALUATING THE PERFORMANCE OF AMERICAN NAVAL COMMANDERS

Any discussion of how American naval commanders performed at Leyte Gulf begins with Halsey. It seems most accounts of the battle make Halsey the scapegoat for a lost American victory or even an American defeat. Of course, Leyte Gulf was not an American naval defeat but a tremendous victory. Halsey's controversial decisions often overshadow that fact. In trying to assess Halsey's performance, two key decisions are held up for examination – his decision to go north after Ozawa late on October 24, and his decision to bring his battleships and a carrier task force back south late in the morning of October 25. These certainly were key decisions that shaped the entire battle, but focusing solely on them leaves out the bigger issue of Halsey's handling of TF 38 for the entire period of the battle. Even more damning than his shortcomings in the two decisions mentioned above is the fact that the full power of TF 38 was never brought to bear at any time in the battle. Before the full scope of the Japanese response to the invasion was known, Halsey decided to send two of his four carrier task forces to Ulithi for replenishment. One of these was so far along the way to Ulithi that even after being recalled it was unable to play any role in the operations of October 24 and no meaningful role in the next day's operations. Halsey's decision to fragment his force before it was clear that the Japanese had decided not to oppose the largest American amphibious operation of the war up to that point was based on poor intelligence, but remains beyond comprehension.

Halsey's decision to go after Ozawa and leave Kurita alone was the correct one, given what he believed at the time. The problem with this decision was that it was based on the assessment that Kurita's force had been severely damaged by TF 38's air strikes on October 24 and that it was no longer a threat, even if it came through San Bernardino Strait. This stemmed from the fact that Halsey and his staff chose to believe the reports from his aviators that they had delivered severe blows to Kurita's force. Attacking a surface force without air cover was bound to result in severe damage, but Halsey and his staff should have known from experience that basing decisions on unfiltered aviator damage assessments was not wise.

Even if Halsey was correct in his assessment that the Seventh Fleet could have dealt with Kurita's force, the only correct reason to pursue Ozawa's force was because it posed the greater threat to the invasion. In this assessment Halsey was entirely correct. Not only were there four carriers to his north, but also two battleships. The fact that the carriers were practically devoid of aircraft by the evening of October 24 was unknowable to him. Without knowing that the carriers carried no aircraft, they were a bigger threat than Kurita's force led by four battleships. In addition, the destruction of the carrier force promised the removal of the primary Japanese threat to future operations.

Another factor in Halsey ignoring the potential threat from Kurita was his desire to keep his force concentrated. This is a principle of war much valued by the USN, but concentration of force meant certain things to Halsey at certain times. He kept his force together to attack Ozawa's fleet with overwhelming power. But only 24 hours later the Third Fleet was splayed all over the Philippine Sea. Mitscher and two carrier task groups were about 250nm east of the northern tip of Luzon (Cape Engano, where the battle got its name from). North of Mitscher was a large surface force under DuBose. To the southwest of Mitscher was Halsey on *New Jersey*, leading TG 34.5 to cut off Kurita at San

Bernardino Strait. Behind TG 34.5 was TG 38.2 and the other four battleships of TF 34. Finally, far to the south, and only able to launch a very long-range strike against any target on October 25, was TG 38.1, the most powerful of any of Halsey's forces. This deployment provides powerful evidence that Halsey had lost control of the battle.

During the crucial period of October 24–25, only a fraction of Halsey's forces contacted the enemy. His largest carrier task force and all his battleships were not engaged on October 24. TG 38.1 was able to launch an ineffective strike late on October 25, but the battleships were never able to fire a single shot at a Japanese surface target. Halsey had mismanaged his forces to such a degree that he engaged two Japanese forces on consecutive days without bringing his full power against either one.

The "perfect" solution of dividing TF 38 into two sections to take on both Ozawa and Kurita concurrently can only be arrived at with hindsight. If Halsey had allocated two carrier task forces and two modern battleships to engage Ozawa's four carriers and two old battleships, and the other carrier task force with TF 34's other four modern battleships had been sent after Kurita's force, Halsey would have had a measure of superiority over both Japanese forces. Halsey wanted to achieve an overwhelming advantage leading to a decisive victory, not just a measure of superiority. Dividing his force was a risk, and it was not a risk Halsey was prepared to take. With what Halsey knew at the time, his decision to focus his efforts on Ozawa's carrier force was justified. Halsey believed this until he died.

On his second major decision, turning TF 34 south as it was on the brink of a great victory, Halsey made an error. The mass of TF 38 with TF 34 in the lead was on the verge of closing with Ozawa's force. It was only at this point that Halsey changed his mind and turned a big part of his combat power south to catch Kurita. If Halsey had made the right decision to concentrate his force and crush Ozawa, then he should not have broken up his force on the verge of achieving his objective. If he was going to change his mind, the time to do so was upon receipt of the first indication that Taffy 3 was under attack. Waiting until 1100 to detach TF 34 after receiving the prompt from Nimitz meant TF 34 would engage neither Japanese force. The last minute detachment of TG 34.5 was also a wrong decision. While the two battleships were the best in the world, had they arrived off San Bernardino in time to engage Kurita, they would have faced four Japanese battleships. Though the Americans had the speed to disengage if required without fear of pursuit, sending two battleships to fight four was more evidence that Halsey had a variable definition of concentration of force.

It is important to point out that Halsey was never called to account for his actions by his superiors. Nimitz never criticized Halsey for his performance. When Halsey met King for the first time after the battle in January 1945, King put him at ease with, "You've got a green light on everything you did."[11] On balance, though, Halsey's performance at Leyte was poor.

While Halsey receives the most criticism for his actions during the battle, Kinkaid's performance has been largely overlooked. As previously mentioned, he and his staff may have been expert in the conduct of amphibious operations, but they had no experience in large fleet operations. This showed during the battle. On the positive side, he oversaw the destruction of Nishimura's force in Surigao Strait. This was a function of Kinkaid's assumption that Halsey would cover San Bernardino Strait. Having made that assumption, he could allocate almost all of his combat power to Oldendorf to take on the Japanese threat from the south. The battle plan he provided Oldendorf was sound.

The fact that Kurita was able to transit San Bernardino Strait and surprise the escort carriers off Samar was as much Kinkaid's fault as it was Halsey's. Kinkaid had the forces and the responsibility to provide direct protection to the landing, and this meant keeping the strait under observation, or at least confirming that Halsey was going to perform that key function. Kinkaid did neither. He simply assumed the strait was being defended when in fact it was not. His assumption was based on the skimpiest of facts. Halsey issued battle plans at 1512 on October 24 to his principal commanders. Included in the order was a list of ships that would form TF 34. This was meant as a battle plan, not the actual order to form TF 34. Kinkaid, who was not an addressee on the battle plan message but had intercepted it, interpreted the order very differently. Not only did he assess that TF 34 had actually been formed, but that it was assigned responsibility for guarding San Bernardino Strait. Halsey clarified when TF 34 would be formed later in a message sent by voice radio: "If the enemy sorties TF 34 will be formed when directed by me."[12] Because this message was sent by line-of-sight voice radio, it was not picked up by Kinkaid. When Halsey sent his order to Third Fleet at 2022 on October 24 detailing plans for the attack against Ozawa's force, there was no mention of TF 34. The reason was because it had not been formed and all the ships allocated to form it were still in their respective task groups. This should have made clear that TF 34 did not exist and that Third Fleet had made no plans to guard the strait.

By Kinkaid's latter admission, sometime between 0300 and 0330 a discussion with his staff raised the critical point that they had based their planning on the presumption that TF 34 was in place off San Bernardino Strait, but that they had never confirmed this. Only at 0412 on October 25 did Kinkaid send a direct question to Halsey regarding the status of TF 34. Halsey got his message at 0648; within minutes he and his staff sent a response at 0705 – TF 34 was with the carriers headed north. For the first time Kinkaid understood the strait was unguarded; of course, Kurita had already taken advantage of the situation by using it to enter the Philippine Sea some six hours earlier.

Kinkaid's placement of Taffy 3 was an error. Any Japanese force coming through San Bernardino Strait on its way to Leyte Gulf was bound to encounter it. In the event of surprise, as happened on October 25, there was no opportunity to move Taffy 3 out of danger.

Having placed Taffy 3 in potential danger, Kinkaid's response to the worst case of Taffy 3 being caught by surprise was poor. When Kurita fell upon Taffy 3, Kinkaid sent a series of panicky messages, some in the clear, to Halsey. There was no possible way Halsey could provide immediate aid to Taffy 3, as Kinkaid knew. This put Halsey in a tough position. He was eventually forced to turn away from the destruction of Ozawa's force to come to the aid of Kinkaid, even though there was little chance he would get there in time. In the final analysis, Kinkaid's Seventh Fleet had the resources to protect the beachhead from Japanese forces approaching from both the south and north. He failed to deploy his forces to do both. By not covering or monitoring San Bernardino Strait, which he clearly had the resources to do, he sacrificed the chance to move the escort carrier groups out of the way of Kurita's heavy ships. Failure to do so led to the majority of American losses (in both ships and personnel) during the battle.

Another blemish on Kinkaid's performance during the battle was the botched effort to save survivors from Taffy 3. Immediately after the battle, Sprague informed Seventh Fleet headquarters that he had lost four ships and requested the commencement of rescue operations.

Because of an incorrect initial report of the survivors' position and a lack of coordination between searching aircraft and surface ships, the first contact with *Gambier Bay* survivors was not made until midnight on October 26 – 39 hours after the men went into the water. Men from the three sunken escorts were subsequently discovered, but it was not until 1000 on October 27 that all survivors were picked up. The delay resulted in the death of at least 116 men from *Johnston, Hoel*, and *Samuel B. Roberts*, who had been seen in the water alive but did not survive until rescue.[13]

The ambush set up by Oldendorf in Surigao Strait was nearly perfect, as were the attacks executed by the forces under his command. What was not perfect was his uninspired pursuit that allowed Shima's force to escape. In retrospect, however, it was beneficial that Oldendorf did not order a full pursuit, as this would have taken his forces farther away from the gulf as the threat from Kurita was looming.

Clifton Sprague gave by far the best performance of any American commander. He kept his calm and used every advantage he had to defeat a more powerful enemy. Using smoke, rain, interior position, air and surface attack, he and his valiant sailors and airmen turned a survival situation into victory. Every decision he made was right, and all were made under intense pressure. The other two escort carrier commanders, Stump and Thomas Sprague, provided prompt and able assistance to Taffy 3.

A CRITICAL REVIEW OF THE BATTLE
OF THE SIBUYAN SEA

All accounts of this battle focus on the death of superbattleship *Musashi*. It was a remarkable feat for carrier aircraft to destroy such a well-protected ship. But the simple fact is that TF 38 failed to accomplish its mission in this encounter. Though an American strike coordinator was present during the attacks on Kurita's force, this failed to avoid the overconcentration on *Musashi*. The battle resulted in what was the best possible outcome for Kurita. A maximum effort by TF 38 resulted in only two ships from his force being sunk or damaged enough that they were forced to turn back (combat actions before the Battle off Samar also forced Kurita to detach four destroyers to escort crippled ships or conduct rescue operations). The fact that Kurita's force remained combat effective made this battle a tactical defeat for the Americans.

A CRITICAL REVIEW OF THE BATTLE
OF SURIGAO STRAIT

Though not fully apparent to Kinkaid and Oldendorf at the time, they possessed an overwhelming numerical and firepower advantage over Nishimura's and Shima's combined force. Added to this was favorable geography that restricted Japanese maneuver room and forced them to run the gauntlet of Oldendorf's set piece battle plan. Also not apparent to the Americans was the fact that the two Japanese forces were operating independently and therefore were ripe for destruction in detail. Finally, the degree to which Japanese night-fighting skills had atrophied and the resulting gap between the Americans and Japanese navies in night combat was not fully appreciated.

Given all these factors, a decisive Japanese defeat was the most probable outcome. In the last major night surface battle of the war, the Japanese fought very poorly. Despite having radar on all their ships, the Japanese were caught by surprise at every turn by American ships with much better radar. The usual Japanese prowess with night optics was also not in evidence. The result was a series of shattering blows by American destroyer-launched torpedoes. Compared to the daring attacks launched by American PT boat and destroyer commanders, both Nishimura's and Shima's forces fought with little aggression. The only survivor from Nishimura's force, destroyer *Shigure*, left the battle without firing a single torpedo. Shima's four destroyers exhibited the same timidity. Japanese gunnery was lackluster, with only *Yamashiro*'s secondary battery being able to hit a target.

Kinkaid and Oldendorf devised a simple plan to maximize their firepower and geographic advantages. Radar gave the Americans a decisive edge by providing a degree of situational awareness never possessed by the Japanese and critical targeting data for torpedoes and guns. The most effective American weapons at Surigao Strait were destroyer-launched torpedoes. Destroyers and torpedo combat were highlighted in Oldendorf's plan, and the result was that Nishimura's force was shattered before it came into contact with Oldendorf's main force.

A CRITICAL REVIEW OF THE BATTLE OFF SAMAR

Almost 80 years after the fact, the Battle off Samar has not emerged from the shroud of mythology surrounding it. In this engagement, the cream of the Combined Fleet's surface force battled with an American force never intended to fight a surface engagement. According to all observers, including the American participants at the time, the result should have been the immediate destruction of Taffy 3. But the battle did not turn out as predicted. The American force took a beating, but inflicted more losses (at least in tonnage) than it incurred. How could such a result be possible?

The outcome should have surprised nobody. Since the first day of the Pacific War, aircraft had established mastery over surface ships. Why should it be any different at the Battle off Samar just because the aircraft were flying off slow and unprotected escort carriers? The situation that both sides found themselves in off Samar on the morning of October 25 was unlike any other in naval history. A force of surface ships engaged a carrier force while under air attack.[14] Two primary reasons were responsible for the Japanese defeat.

Long-range gunnery against surface targets is difficult. As outlined above, the Japanese demonstrated this difficulty earlier in the war, when long-range cruiser fire scored microscopic hit rates in day actions. And this was under ideal conditions. On October 25, conditions were far from ideal. Without the benefit of radar good enough to direct gunnery, for much of the action the Japanese were forced to shoot through squalls and smoke without having direct visual contact on their targets. Accordingly, hit rates were low. When the Japanese worked their way around to the east and south of Taffy 3, thus gaining a better view, hit rates went up. Another factor affecting Japanese gunnery was the fact that their heavy ships were being subjected to constant, though not continual, attack by aircraft and surface ships. Gunnery control is always difficult, and the degree of difficulty increases if the ship is constantly maneuvering to avoid air attack. Given all these issues, the Japanese should be given credit for what they did manage to hit, not what they failed to hit. They managed to sink four ships by gunfire and damage another three. Under the circumstances, this was a creditable achievement. Expecting more would be unrealistic.

Japanese torpedoes should have added to the damage done by gunfire. But in the largest surface action of the Pacific War, the Japanese failed to score a single torpedo hit. Only 40 torpedoes were fired, and all missed. Even a single hit on an escort carrier or a destroyer could have been fatal. The lack of aggression on the part of the two destroyer squadrons at the battle was noteworthy and defies explanation. Kurita decided to hold back his destroyers from the action. This was either driven by fuel concerns or a desire to hold them in reserve. However, if this was the decisive battle against a portion of the Third Fleet as Kurita believed, the aggressive employment of the destroyer squadrons was essential for victory.

The Battle off Samar was not just a surface battle. It was an air-sea battle. The primary American weapon was not the brave and much-heralded attacks by the escorting destroyers, but the aircraft aboard the escort carriers. The almost 500 aircraft aboard all three Taffy task units was a real threat to surface ships, and as outlined above Taffy aviators were more efficient ship-killers than their Third Fleet brethren. All three Japanese ships sunk during the battle were claimed by Taffy airmen. It should be no surprise that aircraft carriers defeated surface ships, even if the carriers concerned were slow and poorly-armed.

A CRITICAL REVIEW OF THE BATTLE OFF CAPE ENGANO

Halsey's strikes against Ozawa's carrier force resulted in an undisputed American victory, but it was clearly an incomplete one. Just as Nishimura's force was almost annihilated in the face of a much more powerful opponent, Ozawa's force faced the same prospect. Given the disparity of forces, and Halsey's intent to fight a battle of annihilation, it is not hard to envision a scenario in which most, if not all, of Ozawa's 17 ships would be destroyed. In fact, only seven were sunk, so the battle must be viewed as only a tactical American victory. With over 500 sorties thrown at the Japanese by TF 38, the haul was not commensurate with the effort – three carriers sunk, one carrier damaged, one light cruiser damaged, and one destroyer sunk. The reason the aviators did not account for more destruction was simple – exhaustion. TF 38 had been in constant action since October 6. Just over the period of October 24 and 25, most of the aviators had flown four, and sometimes five missions, all in the face of indescribably heavy antiaircraft fire. The escape of *Ise* and *Hyuga* can only be chalked up to utter exhaustion on the part of TF 38 aircrew, since neither ship was fast or nimble. The general ineffectiveness of Japanese antiaircraft fire was evinced again. Throughout the day, the Japanese only managed to shoot down ten American aircraft with antiaircraft fire. The surface action between DuBose's cruisers and destroyers provides additional evidence that superior radar made the Americans deadly in a night engagement.

THE UNFOUGHT BATTLE OF LEYTE GULF

The Battle of Leyte Gulf featured four major engagements. However, there was another battle that was never fought and is never even considered as possible in accounts of the battle. This was the unfought Battle of Leyte Gulf – an attempt by Kurita to enter the gulf on the afternoon of October 25. Since most accounts of the battle condemn Kurita for not doing this, it is necessary to examine what would have happened if he actually had.

Most accounts of the battle, and even participants in it, simply assume that Kurita was in a position to waltz into the gulf and deal a serious blow to the Americans. MacArthur's view is typical. He refrained from giving advice to his naval commanders during the battle, but after the war he framed the situation on October 25 as such:

> Should the naval covering forces allow either of the powerful advancing thrusts to penetrate Leyte Gulf, the whole Philippines invasion would be placed in the gravest jeopardy… It was a dramatic situation fraught with disaster… Should the enemy gain entrance to Leyte Gulf, his powerful guns could pulverize any of the eggshell transports present in the area and destroy vitally needed supplies on the beachhead. The thousands of US troops ashore would be isolated and pinned down helplessly between enemy fire from ground and sea. Then, too, the schedule for supply reinforcement would not only be completely upset, but the success of the invasion itself would be placed in jeopardy…[15]

The Sixth Army's Operations Report, inserted into the US Army's official history of the Leyte campaign, takes an even more dramatic tone:

> Had the [Japanese] plan succeeded, the effect on the Allied troop[s] on Leyte in all likelihood would have been calamitous, for these troops would have been isolated and their situation would have been precarious indeed. If it had been victorious in the naval battle, the Japanese fleet could have leisurely and effectively carried out the destruction of shipping, aircraft, and supplies that were so vital to Allied operations on Leyte. An enemy naval victory would have had an adverse effect of incalculable proportions not only upon the

Leyte Operation, but upon the overall plan for the liberation of the Philippines as well.[16]

In 1995, the Royal Navy's history of the Pacific War stated the following:

The damage his [Kurita's] battleships could have done to the invasion shipping and on shore was enormous. Kinkaid, with his ships low on ammunition, could have put up little resistance; whilst the 150,000 men in the beachhead and command posts ashore were all within range from the sea.[17]

The British were not alone in this assessment. As late as 2020, a respected naval historian wrote:

Kurita had held a smashing victory in his grasp, and let it slip through his fingers. That was an egregious command failure, never convincingly justified by the array of rationales offered later.[18]

Prevailing mythology is that with nothing in his way, Kurita would have destroyed all shipping in the gulf. Of all the myths surrounding the battle, the origin of this one is hardest to understand, but it is also the easiest to refute. Kurita's force did not have unblocked access into the gulf. In fact, had it attempted to move in that direction, it faced a force larger than itself. The Seventh Fleet was waiting for Kurita in the approaches to the gulf and possessed a multitude of advantages.

Seventh Fleet vs First Diversionary Attack Force, 1200, October 25[19]		
Ship Type	Seventh Fleet	First Diversionary Attack Force
Battleships	6	4
Heavy Cruisers	4	2
Light Cruisers	5	2
Destroyers	39	8
PT Boats	Approx. 30	0

The ammunition situation for Kinkaid's ships is often cited as a reason they stood no chance against the Japanese. This has been overblown. The American battleships certainly had enough ammunition for an ambush as Kurita tried to push his way into Leyte Gulf, but not enough for a prolonged running gunfight. *Maryland, Tennessee*, and *Pennsylvania* had 24, 27, and 30 rounds of armor-piercing rounds remaining for each of their guns respectively. *West Virginia* had almost 14 rounds per gun, *California* almost 15, and *Mississippi* almost 16. The count for high-explosive rounds was higher: *West Virginia* 31.5, *Maryland* over 55, *Tennessee* almost 22, *California* 6.5, *Mississippi* over 45, and *Pennsylvania* just over 1.[20]

Seventh Fleet was in position to contest a potential Kurita attack into the gulf. At 0850 Oldendorf received orders from Kinkaid to take his entire force to a position north of Hibuson Island (located near the southern approaches to Leyte Gulf) and await further orders. At this point he received an important reinforcement in the form of five destroyers from Destroyer Squadron 21 and four from Destroyer Squadron 49. At 1015, the other five destroyers from Destroyer Squadron 49 were ordered to proceed back to the gulf. These were important additions, since all of these ships carried full torpedo tubes. At 0953 Oldendorf was ordered to take half his force north to assist the escort carriers, but this was canceled when it appeared Kurita was breaking off his advance. The order was reissued at 1127 when Kurita made his abortive move toward the gulf. At about 1300, the order was canceled for good.[21]

In positioning his forces, Oldendorf would have enjoyed favorable geography, just as he had at Surigao Strait. A glance at a chart of the eastern approaches to Leyte Gulf reveals the problem that Kurita would have faced. There are two ways into the gulf from the east, either north or south of Homohon Island that sits astride the eastern entrance. The northern passage between Homohan and Samar was less than 10nm wide. The main entrance south of Homohan was less than 20nm across to Dinagat Island. In a day engagement in which every American ship was equipped with radar, there was no possibility that Kurita could have slipped undetected into the gulf. Oldendorf would have used this geographic advantage to set up another ambush.

In addition to superior numbers and a superior position, the Americans would have enjoyed a huge advantage in gunnery conferred by their superior fire control. Their biggest edge was plentiful air support. Though Taffy 3 had lost two carriers sunk and two damaged, and Taffy 1 had two carriers damaged and forced to leave for repairs, this still left Taffy 2 with all six of its carriers and the remaining air power of the two battered Taffies. In total, this represented ten escort carriers and some 300 aircraft.

This is how Halsey saw a hypothetical clash inside the gulf playing out:

> That Kurita's force could have leisurely and effectively carried out the destruction of shipping, aircraft, and supplies in Leyte Gulf was not in the realm of possibilities... Kurita would have been limited to a hit-and-run attack in the restricted waters of Leyte Gulf. He would further have been subjected to the attack of the cruisers present in Leyte Gulf. He would have been limited to minor damage... The statement that an enemy naval victory would have an effect of incalculable proportions... can only be premised on the thought that our naval forces would be almost totally destroyed. The prognostication of such a condition could be reasoned on none of the facts existing during this three days' engagement.[22]

Kurita's force was not a juggernaut at this point. His men must have been exhausted after two straight days of action. His fuel supplies were low, at least for the destroyers. What would have probably ensued if Kurita had pressed into the gulf was an even larger version of the Battle off Samar, with the Japanese facing battleships instead of destroyers. Oldendorf had fought a tightly controlled battle defending Surigao Strait. He would have tried to replicate this in the eastern approaches to Leyte Gulf, perhaps even gaining the tactical advantage of capping Kurita's "T" as he entered the gulf. In any event, he almost certainly would have been successful in denying Kurita's entrance.

Possible insight into how a Japanese attack against the Leyte beachhead would have developed is provided by a real-world example later in the Philippines campaign. Following the landing at San Jose on Mindoro Island on December 15, the Japanese decided to attack the beachhead. Rear Admiral Kimura Masanori, formerly one of Kurita's destroyer squadron commanders, was given command of the operation and ordered to sink Allied shipping off the beachhead and to shell the installations ashore. Collecting heavy cruiser *Ashigara*, light cruiser *Oyodo*, and six destroyers, Kimura departed Cam Ranh Bay in Indochina and headed across the South China Sea. The so-called San Jose Intrusion Force gained almost complete surprise. It was not spotted until 1600 on December 26, when it was only 180nm from its objective.

There were no American naval forces able to intervene, so defense of the beachhead rested with Army Air Force aircraft flying from the airfield at Mindoro and 20 PT boats. The approaching Japanese were first detected on radar by the PT boats at 2048. Kimura's force was harassed by the Mindoro-based Army aircraft, eight Navy flying boats, and the PT boats. Under continual air attack, Kimura braved the PT boats and headed toward the beachhead. According to Army accounts, at 2130 the Japanese began a brief bombardment (20–40 minutes) of the airfield, the beach, and the town of San Jose. The bombardment was inaccurate, inflicting only superficial damage on the airfield. It was impossible to conduct an accurate bombardment while under air attack and surface harassment. To add further insult, the PT boats managed to torpedo and sink destroyer *Kiyoshimo* in the early morning hours of December 27. Every other ship was damaged to some degree by air attack.[23]

Though obviously on a much smaller scale than a hypothetical Kurita attack against the American beachheads on Leyte, this incident replicated what Kurita would have had to deal with. He would have faced continual air attacks, combined with attacks from surface ships that were much more deadly than PT boats. In these conditions, any sustained and accurate bombardment of the beachhead would have been impossible. Locating and destroying shipping in the gulf, probably hidden behind smoke screens, would have been a difficult task, as Kurita had already experienced in the Battle off Samar.

At the point Kurita planned to storm into the gulf, there was considerable shipping remaining inside. This included 23 LSTs, 28 Liberty ships, two medium landing ships, one attack cargo ship, and three amphibious command ships. Assuming some portion of Kurita's force had managed to get into the gulf, it might have sunk a handful of the shipping present and shelled targets ashore, inflicting minor damage on the supplies ashore and killing personnel. It would not have changed the fact that the invasion force was fully established ashore with enough supply for a full month of operations. The delay caused by such an attack could probably have been measured in hours or perhaps days, but would have had no significant impact on the Leyte invasion or future invasions.

THE FINAL RECKONING

The Japanese fought a hopeless battle at Leyte Gulf. There was never a prospect of a Japanese victory in any real sense. Toyoda knew this, as did Kurita, and every other Japanese naval officer in a position to understand Japan's position in October 1944. *Sho-1* was an exercise in total stupidity. Even Japanese naval officers had a limit on following idiotic and hopeless orders, as Kurita and Shima demonstrated.

As a military operation, *Sho-1* was a complete failure. For the Americans, the loss of six ships and 2,803 casualties was painful, but by no means significant. It in no way changed the correlation of naval forces in the Pacific. If the point of the operation was to employ the Combined Fleet to get better peace terms, this was also a failure, since American losses were so low.

Of all the "decisive" battles in the Pacific War, only the Battle of Leyte Gulf lives up to its name. After the battle, one navy was destroyed, and one gained virtually unfettered operational flexibility for the remainder of the war. This is the definition of decisive. Within a little over five months, the Americans were landing on Okinawa, the last Japanese bastion before Japan itself. In the final analysis, the Battle of Leyte Gulf was the last gasp of a dying navy and an empire unable to defend itself. Under no circumstances was there a chance for any meaningful Japanese victory. Leyte Gulf was a battle fought by a navy too proud to admit defeat and too irresponsible to decline a hopeless last battle. However, it will always remain a testament of the willingness of brave men to fight for a cause, whatever the cost.

Appendix 1

Third Fleet (Admiral William F. Halsey aboard New Jersey)
Task Force 38 (Vice Admiral Marc A. Mitscher aboard *Lexington*)
The precise composition of the various task groups kept changing as ships, particularly destroyers, often changed subordination. Also, several ships had been detached after the Air Battle off Formosa to escort the torpedoed cruisers *Canberra* and *Houston* and were just returning to their original task groups. This is the best assessment of TF 38's composition on October 23.

Task Group 38.1 (Vice Admiral John S. McCain aboard *Wasp*)		
Carriers		
Hancock	Air Group 7	
	VB-7 (Bombing Squadron)	42 SB2C-3/3E
	VF-7 (Fighter Squadron)	37 F6F-5, 4 F6F-5N
	VT-7 (Torpedo Squadron)	18 TBM-1C
Hornet	Air Group 11	
	VB-11	25 SB2C-3
	VF-11	40 F6F-3/3N/3P/5/5N/5P
	VT-11	18 TBM/TBF-1C
Wasp	Air Group 14	1 F6F-3
	VB-14	10 F6F-3/5, 25 SB2C-3
	VF-14	42 F6F-3/3N/3P/5/5N
	VT-14	18 TBM/TBF-1C/1D

Light carriers		
Monterey	Air Group 28	
	VF-28	23 F6F-5/5P
	VT-28	9 TBM-1C
Cowpens	Air Group 22	
	VF-22	26 F6F-5/5P
	VT-22	9 TBM-1C

Screen:

Heavy cruisers *Chester, Pensacola, Salt Lake City*

Destroyers *Bell, Boyd, Brown, Burns, Caperton, Case, Cassin, Charrette, Cogswell, Conner, Cowell, Cummings, Downes, Dunlap, Fanning, Grayson, Ingersoll, Izard, Knapp, McCalla, Woodworth*

Task Group 38.2 (Rear Admiral Gerald R. Bogan aboard *Intrepid*)		
Carrier		
Intrepid	Air Group 18	1 F6F-5
	VB-18	28 SB2C-3
	VF-18	43 F6F-3N/5/5P
	VT-18	18 TBM-1C
Light carriers		
Cabot	Air Group 29	
	VF-29	21 F6F-3/5
	VT-29	9 TBF/TBM-1C
Independence	Night Air Group 41	
	VFN-41	19 F6F-3/5/5N
	VTN-41	8 TBM-1D

Screen:

Battleships *Iowa, New Jersey*

Light cruisers *Biloxi, Miami, Vincennes*

Destroyers *Benham, Colahan, Cushing, Halsey Powell, Hickox, Hunt, Lewis Hancock, Marshall, Miller, Owen, Stephen Potter, Stockham, The Sullivans, Tingey, Twining, Uhlmann, Wedderburn, Yarnell*

Task Group 38.3 (Rear Admiral Frederick C. Sherman aboard *Essex*)		
Carriers		
Essex	Air Group 15	1 F6F-3
	VB-15	25 SB2C-3
	VF-15	50 F6F-3/3N/3P/5/5N
	VT-15	20 TBF/TBM-1C
Lexington	Air Group 19	1 F6F-3
	VB-19	30 SB2C-3
	VF-19	41 F6F-3/3N/3P/5/5N/5P
	VT-19	18 TBM-1C
Light carriers		
Langley	Air Group 44	
	VF-44	25 F6F-3/5
	VT-44	9 TBM-1C
Princeton	Air Group 27	
	VF-27	25 F6F-3/5
	VT-27	9 TBM-1C

Screen:
Battleships *Massachusetts*, *South Dakota*
Light cruisers *Birmingham*, *Mobile*, *Reno*, *Santa Fe*
Destroyers *Callaghan*, *Cassin Young*, *Clarence K. Bronson*, *Cotton*, *Dortch*, *Gatling*, *Healy*, *Porterfield*, *Preston*

Task Group 38.4 (Rear Admiral Ralph E. Davison aboard *Franklin*)		
Carriers		
Enterprise	Air Group 20	1 F6F-5
	VB-20	34 SB2C-3
	VF-20	39 F6F-3N/5
	VT-20	19 TBM-1C
Franklin	Air Group 13	1 F6F-5
	VB-13	31 SB2C-3

	VF-13	38 F6F-3/3N/5/5N/5P
	VT-13	18 TBM/TBF-1C
Light carriers		
Belleau Wood	Air Group 21	
	VF-21	25 F6F-3/5
	VT-21	7 TBM-1C
San Jacinto	Air Group 51	
	VF-51	25 F6F-5/5P
	VT-51	9 TBM-1C

Screen:

Battleships *Alabama, Washington*

Heavy cruisers *New Orleans, Wichita*

Destroyers *Bagley, Gridley, Helm, Irwin, Laws, Longshaw, Maury, McCall, Morrison, Mugford, Nicholson, Patterson, Prichett, Ralph Talbot, Swanson, Wilkes*

TF 34 (formed October 25)

Battleships *Alabama, Iowa, Massachusetts, New Jersey, South Dakota, Washington*

Heavy cruisers *New Orleans, Wichita*

Light cruisers *Biloxi, Miami, Mobile, Santa Fe, Vincennes*

Destroyers *Bagley, Cogswell, Caperton, Clarence E. Bronson, Cotton, Dortch, Healy, Hickox, Hunt, Ingersoll, Knapp, Lewis Hancock, Marshall, Miller, Owen, Patterson, The Sullivans, Tingey*

TG 34.5 (formed October 25)

Battleships *Iowa, New Jersey*

Light cruisers *Biloxi, Miami, Vincennes*

Destroyers *Hickox, Hunt, Lewis Hancock, Marshall, Miller, Owen, The Sullivans, Tingey*

Cruiser-destroyer Group formed on October 25 under Rear Admiral DuBose to pursue remnants of Mobile Force, Main Body

Heavy cruisers *New Orleans, Wichita*

Light Cruisers *Mobile, Santa Fe*

Destroyers *Bagley, Cogswell, Caperton, Callaghan, Cotton, Clarence K. Bronson, Dortch, Healy, Ingersoll, Knapp, Patterson, Porterfield*

Pacific Fleet Supporting Submarines

Task Force 17 (Vice Admiral Charles A. Lockwood)

Atule, Barbel, Besugo, Blackfish, Drum, Gabilan, Haddock, Halibut, Icefish, Jallao, Pintado, Ronquil, Salmon, Sawfish, Seadragon, Shark, Silversides, Snook, Sterlet, Tang, Trigger, Tuna

Seventh Fleet
Task Group 77.2 (Rear Admiral Oldendorf aboard *Louisville*)
Battle Line (Rear Admiral Weyler aboard *Mississippi*)
> Battleship Division 2
>> Battleships *California, Pennsylvania, Tennessee*
> Battleship Division 3
>> Battleship *Mississippi*
> Battleship Division 4
>> Battleships *Maryland, West Virginia*
> Destroyer Division X-ray (Commander Hubbard)
>> Destroyers *Aulick, Claxton, Cony, Sigourney, Thorn, Welles*
Left Flank Force (Oldendorf)
> Cruiser Division 4 (Oldendorf)
>> Heavy cruisers *Louisville, Minneapolis, Portland*
> Cruiser Division 12 (Rear Admiral Hayler)
>> Light cruisers *Columbia, Denver*
> Destroyer Squadron 56 (Captain Smoot)
>> Destroyer Division 111 (Smoot)
>>> Destroyers *Bennion, Heywood L. Edwards, Leutze, Newcomb, Richard P. Leary*
>> Destroyer Division 112 (Captain Conley)
>>> Destroyers *Albert W. Grant, Bryant, Halford, Robinson*
Right Flank Force (Rear Admiral Berkey aboard *Phoenix*)
> Cruiser Division 15 (Berkey)
>> Heavy cruiser HMAS *Shropshire*
>> Light cruisers *Phoenix, Boise*
> Destroyer Squadron 24 (Captain McManes)
>> Destroyers HMAS *Arunta, Beale, Bache, Daly, Hutchins, Killen*
Special Attack Force (Captain Coward aboard *Remey*)
> Destroyer Squadron 54 (Coward)
>> Destroyer Division 107 (Coward)
>>> Destroyers *Remey, Monssen*
>> Destroyer Division 108 (Commander Phillips)
>>> Destroyers *McDermut, McGowan, Melvin*

Task Group 70.1 Motor Torpedo Boat Squadrons (Commander Bowling)
> Surigao Strait Patrols (Lt. Commander Leeson)
>> Section 1: *PT-130, PT-131, PT-152*
>> Section 2: *PT-127, PT-128, PT-129*
>> Section 3: *PT-146, PT-151, PT-190*
>> Section 4: *PT-191, PT-192, PT-195*
>> Section 5: *PT-150, PT-194, PT-196*
>> Section 6: *PT-132, PT-134, PT-137*

Section 7: *PT-324, PT-494, PT-497*
Section 8: *PT-523, PT-524, PT-526*
Section 9: *PT-490, PT-491, PT-493*
Section 10: *PT-489, PT-492, PT-495*
Section 11: *PT-321, PT-326, PT-327*
Section 12: *PT-320, PT-330, PT-331*
Section 13: *PT-323, PT-328, PT-329*

Task Group 77.4 Escort Carrier Group (Rear Admiral Thomas L. Sprague)

Task Unit 77.4.1 "Taffy 1" (Rear Admiral Thomas L. Sprague)		
Escort carriers		
Sangamon	Air Group 37	17 F6F-3/5, 9 TBM-1C
Suwannee	Air Group 60	22 F6F-3, 9 TBM-1C
Chenango	Air Group 35	22 F6F-3, 9 TBM-1C
Santee	Air Group 26	24 FM-2, 9 TBF/TBM-1C
Saginaw Bay	Composite Squadron 78	15 FM-2, 12 TBM-1C
Petrof Bay	Composite Squadron 76	16 FM-2, 10 TBM-1C

Screen:

Destroyers *Hazelwood, McCord, Trathen*

Destroyer escorts *Coolbaugh, Edmonds, Eversole, Richard M. Rowell, Richard S. Bull*

Escort carriers *Chenango* and *Saginaw Bay* and destroyer escorts *Edmonds* and *Oberrender* (from Taffy 2) detached at 1645 hours October 24.

Task Unit 77.4.2 "Taffy 2" (Rear Admiral Felix B. Stump)		
Escort carriers		
Natoma Bay	Composite Squadron 81	16 FM-2, 12 TBM-1C
Manila Bay	Composite Squadron 80	16 FM-2, 12 TBM-1C
Marcus Island	Composite Squadron 21	12 FM-2, 11 TBM-1C
Kadashan Bay	Composite Squadron 20	15 FM-2, 11 TBM-1C
Savo Island	Composite Squadron 27	16 FM-2, 12 TBM-1C
Ommaney Bay	Composite Squadron 75	16 FM-2, 11 TBM-1C

Screen:

Destroyers *Franks, Haggard, Hailey*

Destroyer escorts *Abercrombie, Leray Wilson, Oberrender, Richard W. Suesens, Walter C. Wann*

Task Unit 77.4.3 "Taffy 3" (Rear Admiral Clifton A. Sprague)		
Escort carriers		
Fanshaw Bay	Composite Squadron 68	16 FM-2, 12 TBM-1C
St Lo	Composite Squadron 65	17 FM-2, 12 TBM-1C
White Plains	Composite Squadron 4	16 FM-2, 12 TBM-1C
Kalinin Bay	Composite Squadron 3	16 FM-2, 12 TBF/TBM-1C
Kitkun Bay	Composite Squadron 5	14 FM-2, 12 TBM-1C
Gambier Bay	Composite Squadron 10	18 FM-2, 12 TBM-1C

Screen:

Destroyers *Hoel, Heermann, Johnston*

Destroyer escorts *Dennis, John C. Butler, Raymond, Samuel B. Roberts*

Supporting Submarines
Seventh Fleet – Task Group 71.1 (Rear Admiral Ralph W. Christie)
Darter, Dace, Angler, Bluegill, Bream, Raton, Guitarr

Appendix 2

Combined Fleet (Admiral Toyoda Soemu in Tokyo)
(Divisions were called *sentai* by the Japanese without reference to type, but are rendered in the US Navy style for convenience)

Mobile Force, Main Body (Vice Admiral Ozawa aboard *Zuikaku*)
Carrier Division 3 (Ozawa)
>   Fleet carrier *Zuikaku*
>   Light carriers *Zuiho, Chitose, Chiyoda*
>   Air Groups 653 and 601 with a total strength of 80 A6M5 "Zero" fighters and fighter bombers, 25 B6N2 "Jill" torpedo bombers, 4 B5N2 "Kate," 7 D4Y "Judy" dive-bombers

Carrier Division 4 (Rear Admiral Matsuda)
>   Battleship-carriers *Ise, Hyuga* (neither ship embarked any aircraft)

Light cruisers *Oyodo, Tama*

Destroyer Division 61
>   Destroyers *Akizuki, Hatsuzuki, Wakatsuki*, plus *Shimotsuki* from Destroyer Squadron 41

Escort Squadron 31
>   Light cruiser *Isuzu*
>   Destroyer Division 43
>>   Destroyers *Kiri, Kuwa, Maki, Sugi*

Supply Unit
>   Destroyer *Akikaze*
>   Escort ships *CD-22, CD-29, CD-33, CD-43, CD-132*
>   Oilers *Jinei Maru, Takane Maru*

First Diversionary Attack Force (Vice Admiral Kurita aboard *Atago*)

First Section (Kurita)
Battle Division 1
   Battleships *Musashi, Nagato, Yamato*
Cruiser Division 4
   Heavy cruisers *Atago, Chokai, Maya, Takao*
Cruiser Division 5
   Heavy cruisers *Haguro, Myoko*
Destroyer Squadron 2
   Light cruiser *Noshiro*
   Destroyer *Shimakaze*
   Destroyer Division 2
      Destroyers *Akishimo, Hayashimo*
   Destroyer Division 31
      Destroyers *Asashimo, Kishinami, Naganami, Okinami*
   Destroyer Division 32
      Destroyers *Fujinami, Hamanami*

Second Section (Vice Admiral Suzuki Yoshio aboard *Kongo*)
Battleship Division 3
   Battleships *Haruna, Kongo*
Cruiser Division 7
   Heavy cruisers *Chikuma, Kumano, Suzuya, Tone*
Destroyer Squadron 10
   Light cruiser *Yahagi*
   Destroyers *Kiyoshimo, Nowaki*
   Destroyer Division 17
      Destroyers *Hamakaze, Isokaze, Urakaze, Yukikaze*

Third Section (Vice Admiral Nishimura aboard *Yamashiro*)
Battleship Division 2
   Battleships *Yamashiro, Fuso*
Heavy cruiser *Mogami*
Destroyer Division 4
   Destroyers *Asagumo, Michishio, Yamagumo, Shigure*

Second Diversionary Attack Force (Vice Admiral Shima aboard *Nachi*)
Cruiser Division 16
   Heavy cruisers *Nachi, Ashigara*
Destroyer Squadron 1
   Light cruiser *Abukuma*
   Destroyer Division 7
      Destroyers *Akebono, Ushio*

Destroyer Division 18
    Destroyers *Kasumi, Shiranui*
Destroyer Division 21
    Destroyers *Wakaba, Hatsushimo, Hatsuharu*

Southwest Area Fleet Guard Force (Vice Admiral Sakonju aboard *Aoba*)
Cruiser Division 16
    Heavy cruiser *Aoba*
    Light cruiser *Kinu*
    Destroyer *Uranami*

Sixth Fleet (Vice Admiral Miwa Shigeyoshi)
First Submarine Group
"A" Unit *I-26, I-45, I-54, I-56*
"B" Unit *I-38, I-41, I-44, I-46, RO-41, RO-43, RO-46*
"C" Unit *RO-109, RO-112*

Land-based Air Forces
Fifth Base Air Force (formerly First Air Fleet) (Vice Admiral Onishi Takijiro)
Number of operational aircraft fluctuated; on October 24 about 60 aircraft were operational

Sixth Base Air Force (formerly Second Air Fleet) (Vice Admiral Fukudome Shigeru)
    202 Air Group (fighters)
    341 Air Group (fighters)
    763 Air Group (medium bombers)
    141 Air Group (dive-bombers, reconnaissance aircraft, night fighters)

Approximately 350 aircraft moved from Formosa to the Philippines by October 23; approximately 200 were operational on October 23

On October 25 the Fifth and Sixth Base Air Forces were unified under the First Combined Base Air Force.

Appendix 3

CHARACTERISTICS OF PRINCIPAL
SEVENTH FLEET WARSHIPS

Ships Present at the Battle of Surigao Strait				
Ship	*Tonnage (full load)*	*Principal Weapons*	*Main Armor*	*Top Speed*
Battleships				
Maryland, West Virginia	33,590	8 16-inch guns, 16 5-inch/38 dual-purpose (DP) guns (*Maryland* 6 5-inch/25 DP, 10 5-inch/51)	Main belt 16 inches, horizontal 7.9–9.1 inches	21 knots
California, Tennessee	40,345	12 14-inch/50, 16 5-inch/38 DP	Main belt 13.5 inches, horizontal 7–8 inches	20.5 knots
Mississippi	33,000	12 14-inch/50, 8 5-inch/25 DP, 6 5-inch/51	Main belt 13.5 inches, horizontal 6.75 inches	21 knots
Pennsylvania	32,567	12 14-inch/45, 16 5-inch/38 DP	Main belt 13.5 inches, horizontal 6.25 inches	21 knots
Heavy Cruisers				
Louisville, Portland, Minneapolis	11,420–12,493	9 8-inch/55, 8 5-inch/25 DP	Main belt between 3 and 5.75 inches; horizontal between 1 and 2.5 inches	32.5 knots

Shropshire (Royal Australian Navy (RAN))	13,315	8 8-inch, 8 4-inch	Main belt 4.5 inches, horizontal 1.375 inches	32 knots
Light Cruisers				
Boise, Phoenix	12,207	15 6-inch/47, 8 5-inch/25 DP	Main belt 5.37 inches, horizontal 2 inches	32.5 knots
Columbia, Denver	14,131	12 6-inch/47, 12 5-inch/38 DP	Main belt 5 inches, horizontal 2 inches	32.5 knots
Destroyers				
Fletcher class	2,500	5 5-inch/38, 10 21-inch torpedo tubes	None	36.5 knots
Tribal class (RAN)	2,122	6 4.7-inch, 4 21-inch torpedo tubes	None	36.5 knots

Ships of the Escort Carrier Group				
Ship	*Tonnage (full load)*	*Weapons*	*Armor*	*Top Speed*
Sangamon-class escort carriers	23,875	2 5-inch/38, 18 40mm, 19 20mm	None	18 knots
Casablanca-class escort carriers	10,900	1 5-inch/38, 16 40mm, 20 20mm	None	19 knots
Fletcher-class destroyers	2,500	5 5-inch/38, 10 40mm, 7 20mm, 10 21-inch torpedo tubes	None	36.5 knots
Butler-class destroyer escorts	1,773	2 5-inch/38, 4 40mm, 10 20mm, three 21-inch torpedo tubes	None	24 knots

Appendix 4

Ships Assigned to the First Diversionary Attack Force				
Ship	*Tonnage (full load)*	*Weapons*	*Armor*	*Top Speed*
Battleships				
Yamato, Musashi	73,000	9 18.1-inch guns, 6 6.1-inch guns, 24 5-inch guns (*Musashi* 12), 152 25mm (*Musashi* 130)	Main belt 16 inches, horizontal 7.9–9.1 inches	27.5 knots
Nagato	46,356	8 16-inch/45, 18 5.5-inch/50, 8 5-inch/40, 96 25mm	Main belt 12 inches, horizontal 8.1 inches	25 knots
Kongo, Haruna	36,601	8 14-inch/45, 12 6-inch/50, 8 5-inch/40, 122 25mm	Main belt 8 inches, horizontal 4.75 inches	30.5 knots
Heavy Cruisers				
Haguro, Myoko	15,933	10 8-inch/50, 8 5-inch/40, 52 25mm, 16 24-inch torpedo tubes	Main belt 4 inches, horizontal 3 inches	33 knots
Atago, Chokai, Maya, Takao	15,641	10 8-inch/50 (*Maya* eight), 8 5-inch/40 (*Maya* 12), 38-66 25mm, 16 24-inch torpedo tubes	Main belt 4 inches, horizontal 3 inches	35.5 knots

Kumano, Suzuya	15,057	10 8-inch/50, 8 5-inch/40, 50-56 25mm, 12 24-inch torpedo tubes	Main belt 3.9 inches, horizontal 2.95 inches	35 knots
Chikuma, Tone	15,239	8 8-inch/50, 8 5-inch/40, 45-57 25mm, 12 24-inch torpedo tubes	Main belt 5.7 inches, horizontal 4.76 inches	35 knots
Light Cruisers				
Noshiro, Yahagi	8,534	6 6-inch/50, 4 3.15-inch, 32 25mm, 8 24-inch torpedo tubes	Main belt 2.36 inches, horizontal .78 inches	35 knots
Destroyers				
Kagero class	2,540	4 5-inch/50, 21-28 25mm, 8 24-inch torpedo tubes	None	35 knots
Yugumo class	2,520	6 5-inch/50, 26 25mm, 8 24-inch torpedo tubes	None	35 knots
Shimakaze	3,300	6 5-inch/50, 21 25mm, 15 24-inch torpedo tubes	None	39 knots

Ships Assigned to the First Diversionary Attack Force, Third Section and Second Diversionary Attack Force

Ship	Tonnage (full load)	Principal Weapons	Armor	Top Speed
Battleships				
Fuso, Yamashiro	39,154	12 14-inch/45, 14 6-inch/50, 8 5-inch/40 DP	Main belt 12 inches, horizontal 5.1 inches	24.75 knots
Heavy Cruisers				
Nachi, Ashigara	15,933	10 8-inch/50, 8 5-inch/40 DP, 16 24-inch torpedo tubes	Main belt 4 inches, horizontal 3 inches	33 knots
Mogami	15,057	6 8-inch/50, 8 5-inch/40 DP, 12 24-inch torpedo tubes	Main belt 3.9 inches, horizontal 2.95 inches	35 knots

Light Cruisers				
Abukuma	7,094	5 5.5-inch, 2 5-inch/40 DP, 8 24-inch torpedo tubes	Main belt 2.36 inches, horizontal .78 inches	35 knots
Destroyers				
Fubuki class	2,050	4 5-inch/50, 9 24-inch torpedo tubes	None	38 knots
Shiratsuyu class	1,802	4 5-inch/50, 8 24-inch torpedo tubes	None	34 knots
Asashio class	2,370	4 5-inch/50, 8 24-inch torpedo tubes	None	35 knots
Kagero class	2,490	4 5-inch/50, 8 24-inch torpedo tubes	None	35 knots

Appendix 5

Fates of First Diversionary Attack Force Ships	
Unit	*Fate*
Battleships	
Yamato	Survived Leyte Gulf; sunk April 7, 1945 by air attack off Okinawa
Musashi	Sunk by air attack October 24
Nagato	Survived Leyte Gulf; surrendered September 1945
Haruna	Survived Leyte Gulf; sunk June 1945 in Inland Sea
Kongo	Survived Leyte Gulf; sunk November 21 by submarine *Sealion* attempting to return to Japan
Heavy Cruisers	
Haguro	Survived Leyte Gulf; sunk by British forces on May 16, 1945
Myoko	Damaged by air attack October 24; surrendered September 1945
Atago	Sunk by submarine attack October 23
Chokai	Sunk by air attack October 25
Maya	Sunk by submarine attack October 23
Takao	Heavily damaged by submarine attack October 23; surrendered September 1945
Kumano	Survived Leyte Gulf in a heavily damaged condition; sunk by air attack November 25
Suzuya	Sunk by air attack October 25
Chikuma	Sunk by air attack October 25
Tone	Survived Leyte Gulf; sunk by air attack in Inland Sea July 1945
Light Cruisers	
Noshiro	Sunk by air attack October 26
Yahagi	Survived Leyte Gulf; sunk April 7, 1945 by air attack off Okinawa escorting *Yamato*

Destroyers	
Shimakaze	Survived Leyte Gulf; sunk by TF 38 aircraft on November 11 escorting convoy to Leyte
Akishimo	Survived Leyte Gulf; sunk by TF 38 aircraft on November 14 following damage received while escorting convoy to Leyte
Hayashimo	Hit by torpedo on October 26 and beached; later abandoned
Asashimo	Survived Leyte Gulf; sunk April 7, 1945 by air attack off Okinawa escorting *Yamato*
Kishinami	Survived Leyte Gulf; sunk December 4 by submarine *Flasher*
Naganami	Survived Leyte Gulf; sunk by TF 38 aircraft on November 11 while escorting convoy to Leyte
Okinami	Survived Leyte Gulf; sunk by TF 38 aircraft on November 13 in Manila harbor
Fujinami	Sunk October 27 by air attack with all hands
Hamanami	Survived Leyte Gulf; sunk by TF 38 aircraft on November 11 while escorting convoy to Leyte
Kiyoshimo	Survived Leyte Gulf; sunk December 26 by aircraft and PT boats while attacking American beachhead on Mindoro
Nowaki	Sunk by surface attack October 26 with all hands
Hamakaze	Survived Leyte Gulf; sunk April 7, 1945 by air attack off Okinawa escorting *Yamato*
Isokaze	Survived Leyte Gulf; sunk April 7, 1945 by air attack off Okinawa escorting *Yamato*
Urakaze	Survived Leyte Gulf; sunk November 21 by submarine *Sealion* off Formosa attempting to return to Japan
Yukikaze	Survived Leyte Gulf and the war, the only ship from the First Diversionary Attack Force to do so

Bibliography

ARCHIVAL DOCUMENTS

Commander Destroyer Squadron Twenty-Four – Action Report October 24–25 1944

Commander Destroyer Squadron Fifty-Six War Diary

Commander Task Group Thirty-Eight Point Two Action Report October 6 Through November 3, 1944

COMTASKFOR 38 – Summary of Task Force 38 Ops 8/28/44–10/30/44

Commander Third Fleet Operational Summaries of Carrier Strikes October 24–26

History of the USS *Kalinin Bay* CVE 68

History of the USS *Kitkun Bay* CVE 71

History of the USS *Santee*

History of the USS *White Plains*

Report of Action of USS *Gambier Bay* (CVE-73), culminating in its loss October 25, 1944

United States Navy, Pacific Fleet, *Admiral Nimitz Command Summary, Running Estimate and Summary, 1941–1945*

USS *Birmingham* (CL-62) Action Report October 3–4, 1944

USS *Fanshaw Bay* War Diary for October 1944

USS *Intrepid* War Diary for October 1944

USS *Petrof Bay* War Diary for October 1944

USS *Princeton* Action Report October 24, 1944

USS *Sangamon* War Diary for October 1944

USS *Suwannee* War Diary for October 1944

OFFICIAL HISTORIES

Bates, Richard, et al., *The Battle for Leyte Gulf, October 1944: Strategical and Tactical Analysis*, vols I–III and V, US Naval War College, Newport, 1953–58

Buchanan, A.R., ed., *The Navy's Air War*, Harper & Brothers Publishers, New York, undated

Canon, M. Hamlin, *United States Army in World War II: The War in the Pacific, Leyte: The Return to the Philippines*, Office of the Chief of Military History, Department of the Army, Washington, DC, 1954

Craven, Wesley, F. and James L. Cate, eds, *The Army Air Forces in World War II. Vol. 5: The Pacific: Matterhorn to Nagasaki, June 1944 to August 1944*, Office of the Air Force History, Washington, DC, 1983

General Headquarters, Southwest Pacific Area, *General Douglas MacArthur's Historical Report on Allied Operations in the Southwest Pacific Area, Vols I–II*, Government Printing Office, Washington, DC, 1966

Ministry of Defence (NAVY), *War with Japan: Vol VI; Advance to Japan*, Her Majesty's Printing Office, London, 1995

Morison, Samuel Eliot, *Leyte: June 1944–January 1945* (Volume XII of *The History of United States Naval Operations in World War II*), Little, Brown and Company, Boston, 1975

Morison, Samuel Eliot, *The Liberation of the Philippines, Luzon, Mindanao, the Visayas 1944–1945* (Volume XIII of *The History of United States Naval Operations in World War II*), Little, Brown and Company, Boston, 1975

US Department of the Army Far East Command, General Headquarters Supreme Commander for the Allied Powers, *Japanese Monograph No. 5, Submarine Operations in the Philippines Area (September 1944–March 1945)*, Tokyo, 1947

US Department of the Army Far East Command, General Headquarters Supreme Commander for the Allied Powers, *Japanese Monograph No. 82, Philippines Area Naval Operations, Part I January–September 1944*, Tokyo, 1947

US Department of the Army Far East Command, General Headquarters Supreme Commander for the Allied Powers, *Japanese Monograph No. 84, Philippines Area Naval Operations, Part II October–December 1944*, Tokyo, 1947

United States Strategic Bombing Survey (Pacific), *The Campaigns of the Pacific War*, United States Government Printing Office, Washington, DC, 1946

MEMOIRS AND ACCOUNTS BY PARTICIPANTS

Barbey, Daniel E., *MacArthur's Amphibious Navy. Seventh Amphibious Force Operations 1943–45*, Naval Institute Press, Annapolis, 1969

Evans, David C., ed., *The Japanese Navy in World War II: In the Words of Former Japanese Naval Officers*, 2nd edn, Naval Institute Press, Annapolis, 1986

Halsey, William F. and Bryan, J., *Admiral Halsey's Story*, Zenger Publishing Co., Washington, DC, 1947

Inoguchi, Rikihei and Nakajima, Tadashi, with Pineau, Roger, *The Divine Wind: Japan's Kamikaze Force in World War II*, Naval Institute Press, Annapolis, 1994

MacArthur, Douglas, *Reminiscences*, McGraw-Hill, New York, 1964

Sherman, Frederick C., *Combat Command*, Bantam Books, Toronto, 1982

Solberg, Carl, *Decision and Dissent*, Naval Institute Press, Annapolis, 1995

Ugaki, Matome, *Fading Victory*, University of Pittsburgh Press, Pittsburgh, 1991

United States Strategic Bombing Survey (Pacific), *Interrogations of Japanese Officials* (Volumes 1 and 2), United States Government Printing Office, Washington, DC, undated

Willoughby, Charles A. and Chamberlain, John, *MacArthur 1941–1951*, McGraw-Hill, New York, 1954

BIOGRAPHIES

Borneman, Walter R., *MacArthur at War*, Little, Brown and Company, New York, 2016
Borneman, Walter R., *The Admirals: Nimitz, Halsey, Leahy and King – The Five-Star Admirals Who Won the War at Sea*, Little, Brown and Company, New York, 2012
Buell, Thomas B., *Master of Sea Power: A Biography of Fleet Admiral Ernest J. King*, Little, Brown and Company, Boston, 1980
Hoyt, Edwin P., *How They Won the War in the Pacific: Nimitz and His Admirals*, Weybright and Talley, New York, 1970
Hughes, Thomas Alexander, *Admiral Bill Halsey*, Harvard University Press, Cambridge, 2016
Potter, Elmer B., *Bull Halsey*, Naval Institute Press, Annapolis, 1985
Potter, Elmer B., *Nimitz*, Naval Institute Press, Annapolis, 1976
Sweetman, Jack, ed., *The Great Admirals: Command at Sea, 1587–1945*, Naval Institute Press, Annapolis, 1997
Symonds, Craig L., *Nimitz at War*, Naval Institute Press, Annapolis, 2022
Taylor, Theodore, *The Magnificent Mitscher*, Norton, New York, 1954
Wheeler, Gerald R., *Kinkaid of the Seventh Fleet*, Naval Institute Press, Annapolis, 1996

REFERENCE WORKS

Campbell, John, *Naval Weapons of World War Two*, Naval Institute Press, Annapolis, 2002
Evans, David C. and Peattie, Mark R., *Kaigun: Strategy, Tactics and Technology in the Imperial Japanese Navy 1887–1941*, Naval Institute Press, Annapolis, 1997
Friedman, Norman, *Naval Anti-Aircraft Guns & Gunnery*, Naval Institute Press, Annapolis, 2013
Friedman, Norman, *Naval Firepower*, Naval Institute Press, Annapolis, 2008
Lacroix, Eric and Wells, Linton, *Japanese Cruisers of the Pacific War*, Naval Institute Press, Annapolis, 1997
Lengerer, Hans and Ahlberg, Lars, *The Yamato Class and Subsequent Planning*, Nimble Books, Ann Arbor, 2014
Stille, Mark E., *The United States Navy in World War II*, Osprey Publishing, Oxford, 2021
Stille, Mark E., *The Imperial Japanese Navy*, Osprey Publishing, Oxford, 2014

SECONDARY SOURCES

Blair Jr, Clay, *Silent Victory: The US Submarine War Against Japan*, J. B. Lippincott, New York, 1975

Boyd, Carl and Yoshida, Akihiko, *The Japanese Submarine Force and World War II*, Naval Institute Press, Annapolis, 1995

Carpenter, Dorr, and Polmar, Norman, *Submarines of the Imperial Japanese Navy*, Naval Institute Press, Annapolis, 1986

Carter, Worall Reed, *Beans, Bullets, and Black Oil: The Story of Fleet Logistics Afloat in the Pacific During World War II*, Government Printing Office, Washington, DC, 1953

Chambers, Mark, with Holmes, Tony, *Nakajima B5N 'Kate' and B6N 'Jill' Units*, Osprey Publishing, Oxford, 2017

Como, Byron G., *The Defenders of Taffy 3*, 2018

Como, Byron G., *The Raiders of Taffy 3*, 2017

Cox, Robert J., *The Battle off Samar*, 5th edn, Agogeebic Press, Wakefield, 2010

Cutler, Thomas J., ed., *The Battle of Leyte Gulf at 75: A Retrospective*, Naval Institute Press, Annapolis, 2019

Cutler, Thomas J., *The Battle of Leyte Gulf*, HarperCollins, New York, 1994

Dull, Paul S., *A Battle History of the Imperial Japanese Navy (1941–1945)*, Naval Institute Press, Annapolis, 1978

Falk, Stanley L., *Decision at Leyte*, W. W. Norton, New York, 1966

Field, James A., *The Japanese at Leyte Gulf*, Princeton University Press, London, 1947

Fletcher, Gregory G., *Intrepid Aviators*, NAL Caliber, New York, 2012

Friedman, Kenneth I., *Afternoon of the Rising Sun*, Presidio Press, Navato, 2001

Holmes, W.J., *Undersea Victory: The Influence of Submarine Operations on the War in the Pacific during World War II*, Naval Institute Press, Annapolis, 1979

Hornfischer, James D., *The Last Stand of the Tin Can Sailors*, Bantam Books, New York, 2004

Hoyt, Edwin P., *The Men of the* Gambier Bay, Lyons Press, Guilford, 2002

Hoyt, Edwin P., *The Kamikazes*, Arbor Press, New York, 1983

Hoyt, Edwin P., *The Battle of Leyte Gulf: The Death Knell of the Japanese Fleet*, Weybright and Talley, New York, 1972

Ito, Masanori, *The End of the Imperial Japanese Navy*, W. W. Norton, New York, 1962

Lundgren, Robert, *The World Wonder'd: What Really Happened off Samar*, Nimble Books, Ann Arbor, 2014

Lundstrom, John B., *The First Team and the Guadalcanal Campaign*, Naval Institute Press, Annapolis, 2005

MacDonald, Rod, *Task Force 58*, Naval Institute Press, Annapolis, 2021

Mansfield, John G., *Cruisers for Breakfast*, Media Center Publishing, Tacoma, 1997

Mawdsley, Evan, *The War for the Seas*, Yale University Press, New Haven, 2019

Miller, John G., *The Battle to Save the* Houston *October 1944 to March 1945*, Naval Institute Press, Annapolis, 1985

Millot, Bernard, *Divine Thunder: The Life and Death of the Kamikazes*, McCall Publishing, New York, 1971

O'Hara, Vincent P., *The US Navy Against the Axis*, Naval Institute Press, Annapolis, 2007

Parillo, Mark P., *The Japanese Merchant Marine in World War II*, Naval Institute Press, Annapolis, 1993

Potter, E.B. and Nimitz, Chester W., eds, *The Great Sea War*, Bramhall House, New York, 1960

Prados, John, *Storm over Leyte*, NAL Caliber, New York, 2016

Prados, John, *Combined Fleet Decoded: The Secret History of American Intelligence and the Japanese Navy in World War II*, Random House, New York, 1995

Reynolds, Clark, *The Fast Carriers*, Naval Institute Press, Annapolis, 1992

Rielly, Robin L., *Kamikaze Attacks of World War II*, McFarland, Jefferson, 2010

Sears, David, *The Last Epic Naval Battle*, Praeger, Westport, 2005

Smith, Peter C., *Kamikaze*, Pen & Sword, Barnsley, 2014

Stafford, Edward P., *The Big E*, Naval Institute Press, Annapolis, 1988

Stern, Robert C., *Fire from the Sky*, Naval Institute Press, Annapolis, 2010

Stewart, Adrian, *The Battle of Leyte Gulf*, Scribner, New York, 1980

Symonds, Craig L., *World War II at Sea: A Global History*, Oxford University Press, New York, 2018

Thomas, Evan, *Sea of Thunder*, Simon & Schuster, New York, 2006

Thornton, Tim, *Air Power: The Sinking of IJN Battleship* Musashi, *Warship XII*, Naval Institute Press, Annapolis, 1991

Toll, Ian W., *Twilight of the Gods: War in the Western Pacific, 1944–1945*, W.W. Norton, New York, 2020

Tully, Anthony P., *Battle of Surigao Strait*, Indiana University Press, Bloomington, 2009

Vego, Milan, *The Battle for Leyte, 1944*, Naval Institute Press, Annapolis, 2006

Warner, Dennis, Warner, Peggy, with Seno, Sadao, *The Sacred Warriors: Japan's Suicide Legions*, Van Nostrand Reinhold, New York, 1982

Willmott, H.P., *The Battle of Leyte Gulf*, Indiana University Press, Bloomington, 2005

Woodward, C. Vann, *The Battle for Leyte Gulf*, W. W. Norton, New York, 1947

Y'Blood, William I., *The Little Giants: US Escort Carriers against Japan*, Naval Institute Press, Annapolis, 1989

Yoshimura, Akira, *Build the* Musashi, Kodansha International, Tokyo, 1991

ARTICLES

Thomas, Evan, "Understanding Kurita's 'Mysterious Retreat,'" *Naval History*, October 2004: 22–26

Thorne, Phil, "Battle of the Sibuyan Sea," *Warship International*, volume 59, issue 1, March 2022: 34–65

Tully, Anthony P., "Solving Some Mysteries of Leyte Gulf: Fate of *Chikuma* and *Chokai*," *Warship International*, 3, 2000: 248–58

WEBSITES

www.combinedfleet.com (accessed between February and June 2022)

Notes

INTRODUCTION

1 Daniel E. Barbey, *MacArthur's Amphibious Navy. Seventh Amphibious Force Operations 1943–45*, Naval Institute Press, Annapolis, 1969, p. 237.
2 In comparison, the Battle of Jutland fought in 1916 between the Royal Navy and the High Seas Fleet included 154 ships of all types and only a handful of aircraft. The tonnage of these ships was approximately 1.6 million tons, as opposed to the over 2.0 million tons of warships that fought at Leyte Gulf.

CHAPTER 1

1 Paul S. Dull, *A Battle History of the Imperial Japanese Navy (1941–1945)*, Naval Institute Press, Annapolis, 1978, pp. 26–34. Japanese naval operations related to their seizure of the Philippines have been largely ignored, but Dull provides a good summary.
2 Richard Bates et al., *The Battle for Leyte Gulf, October 1944: Strategical and Tactical Analysis*, vol. II, US Naval War College, Newport, 1955, p. 9.
3 Milan Vego, *The Battle for Leyte, 1944*, Naval Institute Press, Annapolis, 2006, p. 3
4 Vego, *Battle for Leyte*, p. 6.
5 M. Hamlin Canon, *United States Army in World War II: The War in the Pacific, Leyte: The Return to the Philippines*, Office of the Chief of Military History, Department of the Army, Washington, DC, 1954, p. 2.
6 Vego, *Battle for Leyte*, p. 11.
7 Canon, *Return to the Philippines*, p. 8.
8 Samuel Eliot Morison, *Leyte: June 1944–January 1945* (Volume XII of *The History of United States Naval Operations in World War II*), Little, Brown and Company, Boston, 1975, p. 13.
9 Morison, *Leyte*, pp. 12–15; Vego, *Battle for Leyte*, pp. 12–13.
10 Morison, *Leyte*, p. 14; Vego, *Battle for Leyte*, p. 14.
11 Douglas MacArthur, *Reminiscences*, McGraw-Hill, New York, 1964, p. 212.
12 Morison, *Leyte*, pp. 56–57.

13 Bates, *Battle for Leyte Gulf*, Vol. I, pp. 15–16.

14 Morison, *Leyte*, p. 58.

15 Bates, *Battle for Leyte Gulf*, Vol. I, p. 17; Elmer B. Potter, *Nimitz*, Naval Institute Press, Annapolis, 1976, pp. 325–26.

16 Vego, *Battle for Leyte*, pp. 101–02.

17 Ibid., pp. 103–05.

18 John Prados, *Storm over Leyte*, NAL Caliber, New York, 2016, pp. 112–13.

19 Bates, *Battle for Leyte Gulf*, Vol. I, p. 447.

20 John B. Lundstrom, *The First Team and the Guadalcanal Campaign*, Naval Institute Press, Annapolis, 2005, pp. 484–88.

21 Potter, *Nimitz*, p. 221.

22 Elmer B. Potter, *Bull Halsey*, Naval Institute Press, Annapolis, 1985, p. xii; Clark Reynolds, *The Fast Carriers*, Naval Institute Press, Annapolis, 1992, pp. 256–57.

CHAPTER 2

1   Stanley L. Falk, *Decision at Leyte*, W. W. Norton, New York, 1966, pp. 49–50.

2   C. Vann Woodward, *The Battle for Leyte Gulf*, W. W. Norton, New York, 1947, p. 22.

3   Evan Thomas, *Sea of Thunder*, Simon & Schuster, New York, 2006, pp. 74–79, 176–78.

4   Anthony P. Tully, *Battle of Surigao Strait*, Indiana University Press, Bloomington, 2009, pp. 30–33.

5   Tully, *Surigao Strait*, p. 22.

6   General Headquarters, Southwest Pacific Area, *General Douglas MacArthur's Historical Report on Allied Operations in the Southwest Pacific Area, Vol II, Part I*, Government Printing Office, Washington, DC, 1966, pp. 304–07.

7   *MacArthur's Report, Vol II, Part I*, p. 309.

8   Vego, *Battle for Leyte*, pp. 59–60.

9   Falk, *Decision at Leyte*, pp. 45–46.

10 *MacArthur's Report, Vol II, Part I*, pp. 329–30.

11 Vego, *Battle for Leyte*, pp. 55–56.

12 David C. Evans, ed., *The Japanese Navy in World War II: In the Words of Former Japanese Naval Officers*, 2nd edn, Naval Institute Press, Annapolis, 1986, pp. 358–61.

13 Woodward, *Battle for Leyte Gulf*, p. 23.

14 Vego, *Battle for Leyte*, pp. 56–58.

15 Ibid., p. 58.

16 Evans, *Japanese Navy in World War II*, p. 359.

17 Vego, *Battle for Leyte*, p. 67.

18 Ibid., p. 67.

19 Bates, *Battle for Leyte Gulf*, Vol. II, p. 108.

20 Vego, *Battle for Leyte*, pp. 211–12.

21 *MacArthur's Report, Vol II, Part II*, pp. 381–82.

22 Vego, *Battle for Leyte*, p. 215.

23 Ibid., p. 220.

24 James A. Field, *The Japanese at Leyte Gulf*, Princeton University Press, London, 1947, p. 35.

25 Vego, *Battle for Leyte*, pp. 228–29.

26 Field, *Japanese at Leyte Gulf*, p. 39; Vego, *Battle for Leyte*, p. 231.

27 Rikihei, Inoguchi, and Tadashi, Nakajima with Pineau, Roger, *The Divine Wind: Japan's Kamikaze Force in World War II*, Naval Institute Press, Annapolis, 1994, pp. 51–52.

28 Tully, *Surigao Strait*, pp. 20–21.

29 Ibid., p. 21

30 Ibid., p. 25.

31 Ibid., p. 54.

32 Ibid., p. 44.

33 Ibid., p. 47.

34 Woodward, *Battle for Leyte Gulf*, p. 21.

35 Thomas J. Cutler, *The Battle of Leyte Gulf*, HarperCollins, New York, 1994, p. 66.

36 Ibid., p. 67.

37 H.P. Willmott, *The Battle of Leyte Gulf*, Indiana University Press, Bloomington, 2005, p. 50.

38 Vego, *Battle for Leyte*, pp. 72–74.

39 United States Strategic Bombing Survey (Pacific), *Interrogations of Japanese Officials (Vol. 2)*, United States Government Printing Office, Washington, undated, p. 317.

CHAPTER 3

1   Two escort carriers departed the battle areas at 1645 hours on October 24.

2   No land-based American tactical aircraft were within range of the battle area. The Army Air Force heavy bombers and USN long-range patrol aircraft that were are not included in this total.

3   This total includes all destroyers allocated to Third and Seventh Fleet task forces, and Seventh Fleet destroyers assigned to convoy escort duty during the first week of the invasion.

4   Only includes destroyer escorts assigned to the Escort Carrier Group and thus directly involved in the battle.

5   Rod MacDonald, *Task Force 58*, Naval Institute Press, Annapolis, 2021, p. 228.

6   Theodore Taylor, *The Magnificent Mitscher*, W.W. Norton, New York, 1954, p. 316.

7   Willmott, *Battle of Leyte Gulf*, pp. 318–20. See Appendix 1 for a more detailed composition of each task group.

8   Ibid., p. 319.

9   Reynolds, *Fast Carriers*, p. 223.

10 See Appendix 3 for key characteristics of Seventh Fleet surface combatants.

11 Vego, *Battle for Leyte*, pp. 119 and 134.

12 Morison, *Leyte*, p. 420.

13 See Appendix 4 for details on these ships.

14 Bates, *Battle for Leyte Gulf*, Vol. I, pp. 195–96.

15 Edwin P. Hoyt, *How They Won the War in the Pacific: Nimitz and His Admirals*, Weybright and Talley, New York, 1970, p. 424.

16 Morison, *Leyte*, pp. 75–76.

17 Morison, *Leyte*, pp. 428–29.

18 Morison, *Leyte*, pp. 80–83.

19 Field, *Japanese at Leyte Gulf*, p. 12.

20 Vego, *Battle for Leyte*, p. 54.

21 Field, *Japanese at Leyte Gulf*, p. 35.

22 Willmott, *Battle of Leyte Gulf*, p. 73.

23 Morison, *Leyte*, p. 319, Field, *Japanese at Leyte Gulf*, p. 36, and *Zuikaku* Tabular Record of Movement (TROM) found at www.combinedfleet.com and accessed March 19, 2022.

24 See Appendix 4 for the principal characteristics of the First Diversionary Attack Force's ships.

25 Masanori Ito, *The End of the Imperial Japanese Navy*, W. W. Norton, New York, 1962, p. 115.

26 Norman Friedman, *Naval Firepower*, Naval Institute Press, Annapolis, 2008, p. 241.

27 For the principal characteristics of these ships, see Appendix 4.

28 For the principal characteristics of these ships, see Appendix 4.

29 Norman Friedman, *Naval Anti-Aircraft Guns & Gunnery*, Naval Institute Press, Annapolis, 2013, p. 145.

30 Friedman, *AA Guns*, p. 291.

31 Field, *Japanese at Leyte Gulf*, p. 5.

32 Willmott, *Battle of Leyte Gulf*, p. 55.

33 Field, *Japanese at Leyte Gulf*, p. 19.

34 Vego, *Battle for Leyte*, p. 68.

35 Morison, *Leyte*, p. 165.

36 Bates, *Battle for Leyte Gulf*, Vol. 1, p. 22; Vego, *Battle for Leyte*, p. 165.

37 Fukudome's operations officer stated after the war that of the Fifth Base Air Force's 100 and the Sixth Base Air Force's 300 aircraft, two-thirds were operational (*Interrogations of Japanese Officials, Vol. 1*, p. 178); Bates believed that Fukudome had 178 operational aircraft (Bates, *Battle for Leyte Gulf*, Vol. III, p. 677); *MacArthur's Report* states the Japanese had 246 operational aircraft on October 23 (*MacArthur's Report, Vol. II*, pp. 336 and 359).

CHAPTER 4

1 Canon, *Return to the Philippines*, pp. 42–43.

2 Ibid., p. 43.

3 Vego, *Battle for Leyte*, p. 156.

4 Morison, *Leyte*, p. 91.

5 Vego, *Battle for Leyte*, p. 162.

6 Ibid., p. 163.

7 Bates, *Battle for Leyte Gulf*, Vol. I, p. 222. Actual Japanese air strengths are difficult to determine, but Bates gives a detailed table.

8 Evans, *Japanese Navy in World War II*, pp. 342–44.

9 Morison, *Leyte*, p. 92.

10 Evans, *Japanese Navy in World War II*, p. 346.

11 Ibid., p. 350.

12 Bates, *Battle for Leyte Gulf*, Vol. I, p. 101.

13 Ibid., pp. 104–06.

14 Ibid., p. 108.

15 Ibid., pp. 110–11; Mark Chambers with Tony Holmes, *Nakajima B5N 'Kate' and B6N 'Jill' Units*, Osprey Publishing, Oxford, 2017, pp. 84–85.

16 Bates, *Battle for Leyte Gulf*, Vol. I, p. 113.

17 Ibid., p. 116.

18 Ibid., p. 125.

19 Ibid., pp. 135, 138.

20 Ibid., p. 132.

21 Ibid., p. 143.

22 Ibid., p. 123.

23 Evans, *Japanese Navy in World War II*, p. 353.

24 Morison, *Leyte*, pp. 60–61.

25 Ibid., pp. 139–40.

26 Ibid., p. 155.

CHAPTER 5

1 Willmott, *Battle of Leyte Gulf*, p. 84.

2 Ito, *End of the Imperial Japanese Navy*, p. 120.

3 John G. Mansfield, *Cruisers for Breakfast*, Media Center Publishing, Tacoma, 1997, pp. 150–61.

4 Field, *Japanese at Leyte Gulf*, pp. 51–52.

5 *Takao* TROM, accessed April 7, 2022.

6 Mansfield, *Cruisers for Breakfast*, pp. 163–67.

7 Reynolds, *Fast Carriers*, p. 264; Willmott, *Battle of Leyte Gulf*, p. 105.

8 Willmott, *Battle of Leyte Gulf*, p. 92.

9 Prados, *Storm over Leyte*, p. 196.

10 Morison, *Leyte*, p. 177.

11 Edwin P. Hoyt, *The Battle of Leyte Gulf: The Death Knell of the Japanese Fleet*, Weybright and Talley, New York, 1972, p. 104.

12 Frederick C. Sherman, *Combat Command*, Bantam Books, Toronto, 1982, pp. 249–50.

13 USS *Princeton* Action Report October 24 1944, pp. 3–11.

14 Ibid., pp. 14–17.

15 USS *Birmingham* (CL-62) Action Report October 3–4 1944, p. 15.

16 Field, *Japanese at Leyte Gulf*, p. 62.

17 *Zuikaku* TROM, accessed April 10, 2022.

18 Willmott, *Battle of Leyte Gulf*, p. 111.

19 Field, *Japanese at Leyte Gulf*, p. 63.

20 Willmott, *Battle of Leyte Gulf*, p. 112.

21 Cutler, *Battle of Leyte Gulf*, pp. 156–57.

22 Evan Mawdsley, *The War for the Seas*, Yale University Press, New Haven, 2019, p. 455.

23 Thomas J. Cutler, ed., *The Battle of Leyte Gulf at 75: A Retrospective*, Naval Institute Press, Annapolis, 2019, p. 118.

24 Bates, *Battle for Leyte Gulf*, Vol. V, pp. 164–65; Cutler, *Battle of Leyte Gulf at 75: A Retrospective*, p. 118.

25 Commander Task Group Thirty-Eight Point Two Action Report October 6 Through November 3 1944, p. 13; Phil Thorne, "Battle of the Sibuyan Sea." *Warship International*, volume 59, issue 1, March 2022, p. 39. There is some conflict between the TG 38.2 Action Report and the after-action reports of the ships concerned; these numbers reflect the reports from *Cabot* and *Intrepid*.

26 Gregory G. Fletcher, *Intrepid Aviators*, NAL Caliber, New York, 2012, pp. 40–51.

27 Field, *Japanese at Leyte Gulf*, p. 66.

28 Hans Lengerer and Lars Ahlberg, *The Yamato Class and Subsequent Planning*, Nimble Books, Ann Arbor, 2014, p. 447. The information from this source comes from the semi-official Japanese history of the Pacific War (*Senshi Sosho*).

29 Lengerer, *Yamato Class*, p. 430.

30 Fletcher, *Intrepid Aviators*, pp. 240–50.

31 Eric Lacroix and Linton Wells, *Japanese Cruisers of the Pacific War*, Naval Institute Press, Annapolis, 1997, p. 347.

32 Cutler, *Battle of Leyte Gulf at 75: A Retrospective*, p. 120.

33 Commander Task Group Thirty-Eight Point Two Action Report, p. 14.

34 Lengerer, *Yamato Class*, p. 431.

35 Fletcher, *Intrepid Aviators*, p. 260.

36 Lengerer, *Yamato Class*, p. 431.

37 Tim Thornton, *Air Power: The Sinking of IJN Battleship* Musashi, Warship XII, Naval Institute Press, Annapolis, 1991, p. 30.

38 Lengerer, *Yamato Class*, p. 431.

39 Cutler, *Battle of Leyte Gulf at 75: A Retrospective*, p. 121.

40 Lengerer, *Yamato Class*, p. 447.

41 Field, *Japanese at Leyte Gulf*, p. 67.

42 Cutler, *Battle of Leyte Gulf at 75: A Retrospective*, p. 121.

43 Ibid., p. 122.

44 Lengerer, *Yamato Class*, p. 432.

45 Ibid.

46 *Yamato* TROM, accessed April 11, 2022.

47 *Yahagi* TROM, accessed April 11, 2022.

48 Lengerer, *Yamato Class*, pp. 432–33.

49 Thornton, *Air Power*, p. 31.

50 Lengerer, *Yamato Class*, p. 432.

51 Cutler, *Battle of Leyte Gulf at 75: A Retrospective*, p. 123.

52 Lengerer, *Yamato Class*, p. 433.

53 Thornton, *Air Power*, p. 31.

54 *Tone* TROM, accessed April 13, 2022.

55 Thorne, "Battle of the Sibuyan Sea," p. 49.

56 *Yamato* TROM, accessed April 13, 2022.

57 Thorne, "Battle of the Sibuyan Sea," p. 49.

58 Cutler, *Battle of Leyte Gulf at 75: A Retrospective*, p. 123.

59 Ibid., p. 124.

60 Ibid.

61 *Nagato* TROM, accessed April 14, 2022.

62 *Tone* TROM, accessed April 14, 2022.

63 Cutler, *Battle of Leyte Gulf at 75: A Retrospective*, p. 125.

64 Commander Task Group Thirty-Eight Point Two Action Report, p. 14.

65 Cutler, *Battle of Leyte Gulf at 75: A Retrospective*, p. 126.

66 Lengerer, *Yamato Class*, pp. 434–35.

67 Ibid., pp. 435–36.

68 Thornton, *Air Power*, p. 33.

69 Akira Yoshimura, *Build the Musashi*, Kodansha International, Tokyo, 1991, p. 140.

70 Field, *Japanese at Leyte Gulf*, pp. 70–71.

71 USS *Intrepid* War Diary for October 1944, pp. 36–37.

72 COMTASKFOR 38 – Summary of Task Force 38 Ops 8/28/44–10/30/44, pp. 250–51.

73 Willmott, *Battle of Leyte Gulf*, p. 133.

CHAPTER 6

1 Field, *Japanese at Leyte Gulf*, p. 82.

2 *Yamashiro* TROM, accessed April 24, 2022.

3 *Fuso* TROM, accessed April 24, 2022.

4 *Mogami* TROM, accessed April 26, 2022.

5 Tully, *Surigao Strait*, pp. 70–71.

6 Ibid., p. 24.

7 Ibid., p. 64.

8 Bates, *Battle for Leyte Gulf*, Vol. 5, p. 154.

9 Tully, *Surigao Strait*, pp. 82–83.

10 Morison, *Leyte*, pp. 201–02.

11 Ibid., pp. 203–06.

12 Ibid., *Leyte*, p. 198.

13 Ibid., p. 202.

14 Ibid., p. 207.

15 Willmott, *Battle of Leyte Gulf*, p. 141.

16 Bates, *Battle for Leyte Gulf*, Vol. 5, p. 276.

17 Tully, *Surigao Strait*, p. 120.

18 Morison, *Leyte*, pp. 210–11.

19 *Yamagumo* TROM, accessed April 23, 2022.

20 *Michishio* TROM, accessed April 23, 2022.

21 *Yamashiro* TROM, accessed April 24, 2022.

22 *Fuso* TROM, accessed April 24, 2022.

23 Ibid.

24 Tully, *Surigao Strait*, p. 214.

25 Vincent P. O'Hara, *The US Navy Against the Axis*, Naval Institute Press, Annapolis, 2007, p. 254.

26 Morison, *Leyte*, pp. 224–26.

27 Ibid., p. 227.

28 Ibid.

29 *Yamashiro* TROM, accessed April 24, 2022.

30 O'Hara, *US Navy Against the Axis*, p. 255.

31 *Yamashiro* TROM, accessed April 24, 2022.

32 *Mogami* TROM, accessed April 26, 2022.

33 Tully, *Surigao Strait*, p. 124.

34 *Abukuma* TROM, accessed April 26, 2022.

35 Tully, *Surigao Strait*, p. 238.

36 O'Hara, *US Navy Against the Axis*, p. 258.

37 Bates, *Battle for Leyte Gulf*, Vol. 5, p. 630.

38 *Asagumo* TROM, accessed April 27, 2022.

39 Tully, *Surigao Strait*, p. 252.

40 Morison, *Leyte*, p. 420.

41 William I. Y'Blood, *The Little Giants: US Escort Carriers against Japan*, Naval Institute Press, Annapolis, 1989, p. 152.

42 *Mogami* TROM, accessed April 26, 2022.

43 O'Hara, *US Navy Against the Axis*, p. 255.

44 Wesley F. Craven and James L. Cate, eds, *The Army Air Forces in World War II. Vol. 5: The Pacific: Matterhorn to Nagasaki, June 1944 to August 1944*, Office of the Air Force History, Washington, DC, 1983, pp. 366–67; Tully, *Surigao Strait*, pp. 264–65.

CHAPTER 7

1 Morison, *Leyte*, p. 245.

2 Ibid., p. 246.

3 *Interrogations of Japanese Officials (Vol. 1)*, p. 173.

4 Matome Ugaki, *Fading Victory*, University of Pittsburgh Press, Pittsburgh, 1991, pp. 492–93.

5 *Interrogations of Japanese Officials (Vol. 1)*, p. 173.

6 Prados, *Storm over Leyte*, p. 295.

7 USS *Fanshaw Bay* War Diary for October 1944, p. 12.

8 Report of Action of USS *Gambier Bay* (CVE-73), culminating in its loss October 25, 1944, p. 2 to Enclosure A.

9 History of the USS *Kitkun Bay* CVE 71, p. 29.

10 Y'Blood, *Little Giants*, p. 163.

11 Ibid., p. 195.

12 Ibid., p. 200.

13 Ibid., p. 199.

14 *Interrogations of Japanese Officials (Vol. 1)*, p. 173.

15 Lacroix and Wells, *Japanese Cruisers*, p. 499.

16 Ibid., p. 599.

17 History of the USS *White Plains*, p. 31.

18 Robert Lundgren, *The World Wonder'd: What Really Happened off Samar*, Nimble Books, Ann Arbor, 2014, pp. 32–35.

19 Prados, *Storm over Leyte*, p. 319.

20 Byron G. Como,, *The Raiders of Taffy 3*, 2017, pp. 67–78.

21 Prados, *Storm over Leyte*, p. 319.

22 Ibid.

23 Ibid.

24 Como, *Raiders of Taffy 3*, pp. 190–92.

25 Ibid., p. 173.

26 History of the USS *Kalinin Bay* CVE 68, p. 23.

27 Y'Blood, *Little Giants*, p. 184.

28 USS *Fanshaw Bay* War Diary, pp. 14–17.

29 History of the USS *White Plains*, p. 32.

30 Report of Action of USS *Gambier Bay*, p. 4 to Enclosure A; Part IV, p. 2.

31 *Interrogations of Japanese Officials (Vol. 1)*, p. 174.

32 Morison, *Leyte*, pp. 286–87.

33 *Suzuya* TROM, accessed May 9, 2022; Lacroix and Wells, p. 499.

34 Morison, *Leyte*, p. 285.

35 Lacroix and Wells, *Japanese Cruisers*, p. 349.

36 Anthony P. Tully, "Solving Some Mysteries of Leyte Gulf: Fate of *Chikuma* and *Chokai*," *Warship International*, 3, 2000: 248–51.

37 Lacroix and Wells, *Japanese Cruisers*, p. 533.

38 *Haguro* TROM, accessed May 9, 2022.

39 Lacroix and Wells, *Japanese Cruisers*, p. 599.

40 Morison, *Leyte*, p. 288.

41 Field, *Japanese at Leyte Gulf*, p. 100.

42 Ibid.

43 *Interrogations of Japanese Officials (Vol. 1)*, p. 174.

44 Field, *Japanese at Leyte Gulf*, p. 109.

45 *MacArthur's Report*, Vol. II, part II, p. 397.

CHAPTER 8

1 Field, *Japanese at Leyte Gulf*, p. 122.
2 Prados, *Storm over Leyte*, p. 307.
3 Field, *Japanese at Leyte Gulf*, p. 125.
4 Morison, *Leyte*, p. 300.
5 Lundgren, *The World Wonder'd*, p. 210.
6 Ibid., p. 12.
7 Thomas, *Sea of Thunder*, p. 309.
8 Ibid., p. 310.
9 Evan Thomas, "Understanding Kurita's 'Mysterious Retreat,'" *Naval History*, October 2004: 22–26, p. 26.
10 Ito, *End of the Imperial Japanese Navy*, p. 156.
11 *Interrogations of Japanese Officials (Vol. 1)*, p. 152.
12 Evans, *Japanese Navy in World War II*, pp. 355–84.
13 Field, *Japanese at Leyte Gulf*, p. 125; *Interrogations of Japanese Officials (Vol. 1)*, p. 45.
14 Ito, *End of the Imperial Japanese Navy*, p. 167.
15 Thomas, "Understanding Kurita's 'Mysterious Retreat,'" p. 26.
16 Morison, *Leyte*, p. 297.
17 An example of this line of reasoning can be found in Craig L. Symonds, *Nimitz at War*, Naval Institute Press, Annapolis, 2022, p. 334.
18 *Tone* TROM, accessed May 15, 2022.
19 Ito, *End of the Imperial Japanese Navy*, p. 168.
20 Vego, *Battle for Leyte*, p. 275.
21 Lundgren, *The World Wonder'd*, p. 237.
22 O'Hara, *US Navy Against the Axis*, p. 278.
23 Lacroix and Wells, *Japanese Cruisers*, p. 498.
24 Lundgren, *The World Wonder'd*, pp. 244–46.
25 Lacroix and Wells, *Japanese Cruisers*, pp. 599–600; *Noshiro* TROM, accessed May 14, 2022.
26 *Haruna* TROM, accessed May 15, 2022.
27 Craven, *Army Air Forces in World War II. Vol. 5: The Pacific*, p. 367.
28 *Fujinami* TROM, accessed May 16, 2022.
29 *Hayashimo* TROM, accessed May 15, 2022.

CHAPTER 9

1 *Interrogations of Japanese Officials (Vol. 1)*, p. 221.
2 Ibid., p. 156.
3 Bates, *Battle for Leyte Gulf*, Vol. III, pp. 203–04.
4 Field, *Japanese at Leyte Gulf*, p. 63.
5 *Interrogations of Japanese Officials (Vol. 1)*, p. 157.
6 Ibid., p. 279.
7 Reynolds, *Fast Carriers*, p. 266.
8 Morison, *Leyte*, p. 192.

9   Jack Sweetman, ed., *The Great Admirals: Command at Sea, 1587–1945*, Annapolis, 1997, p. 496.
10 Reynolds, *Fast Carriers*, pp. 267–68.
11 Ibid., p. 268.
12 Morison, *Leyte*, p. 195.
13 Ibid.
14 Ibid.
15 Reynolds, *Fast Carriers*, p. 268.
16 Cutler, *The Battle of Leyte Gulf at 75: A Retrospective*, p. 92.
17 Commander Task Group Thirty-Eight Point Two Action Report, p. 16.
18 Field, *Japanese at Leyte Gulf*, p. 73.
19 *Zuikaku* TROM, accessed May 22, 2022.
20 *Zuiho* TROM, accessed May 22, 2022.
21 *Chitose* TROM, accessed May 20, 2022.
22 *Tama* TROM, accessed May 20, 2022.
23 *Oyodo* TROM, accessed May 20, 2022.
24 *Akizuki* TROM, accessed May 20, 2022.
25 *Chiyoda* TROM, accessed May 20, 2022.
26 *Zuikaku* TROM, accessed May 20, 2022.
27 *Zuiho* TROM, accessed May 20, 2022.
28 Ibid.
29 Willmott, *Battle of Leyte Gulf*, p. 200.
30 *Ise* TROM, accessed May 21, 2022.
31 Woodward, *Battle for Leyte Gulf*, p. 155.
32 *Interrogations of Japanese Officials (Vol. 1)*, p. 158.
33 Symonds, *Nimitz at War*, p. 332.
34 Carl Solberg, *Decision and Dissent*, Naval Institute Press, Annapolis, 1995, p. 154.
35 Potter, *Bull Halsey*, p. 335.
36 Commander Task Group Thirty-Eight Point Two Action Report p. 17; Morison, *Leyte*, p. 329.
37 Woodward, *Battle for Leyte Gulf*, p. 153.
38 O'Hara, *US Navy Against the Axis*, p. 275.
39 Woodward, *Battle for Leyte Gulf*, p. 154.
40 *Chiyoda* TROM, accessed May 19, 2022.
41 O'Hara, *US Navy Against the Axis*, p. 275, *Chiyoda* TROM, accessed May 19, 2022.
42 O'Hara, *US Navy Against the Axis*, p. 276.
43 Field, *Japanese at Leyte Gulf*, p. 121.
44 Lacroix and Wells, *Japanese Cruisers*, p. 383.

CHAPTER 10

1   Vego, *Battle for Leyte*, p. 232.
2   Evans, *Japanese Navy in World War II*, p. 421.

3 Dennis Warner and Peggy Warner with Sadao Seno, *The Sacred Warriors: Japan's Suicide Legions*, Van Nostrand Reinhold, New York, 1982, p. 103.
4 History of the USS *Santee*, pp. 22–23.
5 USS *Sangamon* War Diary for October 1944, p. 5.
6 USS *Suwanee* War Diary for October 1944, p. 9.
7 Inoguchi and Nakajima with Pineau, *The Divine Wind*, p. 59. Six Zeros carried out attack dives, so maybe one of the escort fighters decided to conduct an attack.
8 History of the USS *Kitkun Bay* CVE 71, p. 34.
9 Inoguchi and Nakajima with Pineau, *The Divine Wind*, p. 59.
10 Ibid., pp. 60–61.
11 USS *Sangamon* War Diary, p. 6.
12 USS *Suwanee* War Diary, pp. 9–17.
13 USS *Petrof Bay* War Diary for October 1944, p. 7.
14 Vego, *Battle for Leyte*, p. 233.
15 Inoguchi and Nakajima with Pineau, *The Divine Wind*, pp. 67–68.
16 *Aoba* TROM, accessed May 23, 2022.
17 *Uranami* TROM, accessed May 23, 2022.
18 Lacroix and Wells, *Japanese Cruisers*, p. 416.
19 *Kinu* TROM, accessed May 23, 2022.
20 Prados, *Storm over Leyte*, pp. 281–82.
21 Carl Boyd and Akihiko Yoshida, *The Japanese Submarine Force and World War II*, Naval Institute Press, Annapolis, 1995, p. 153.
22 Boyd, *Japanese Submarine Force*, pp. 153–56.
23 History of the USS *Santee*, p. 23.

CHAPTER 11

1 Woodward, *Battle for Leyte Gulf*, p. 229.
2 *MacArthur's Report*, Vol. II, part II, p. 40.
3 *Interrogations of Japanese Officials (Vol. 1)*, p. 225.
4 Woodward, *Battle for Leyte Gulf*, p. 230.
5 Willmott, *Battle of Leyte Gulf*, p. 250.
6 Ibid., p. 372.
7 Vego, *Battle for Leyte*, p. 293.
8 Potter, *Bull Halsey*, p. 290.
9 Vego, *Battle for Leyte*, p. 337.
10 Mark P. Parillo, *The Japanese Merchant Marine in World War II*, Naval Institute Press, Annapolis, 1993, p. 243.
11 Willmott, *Battle of Leyte Gulf*, p. 247.
12 Vego, *Battle for Leyte*, p. 260.
13 Morison, *Leyte*, pp. 313–16. Morison attempts to absolve Kinkaid of blame in this matter, but the period required to effect the rescue speaks for itself.
14 The only other instance during the war in which a carrier was engaged by surface ships was in June 1940, when German battleships *Scharnhorst* and

Gneisenau surprised the British carrier *Glorious* off the coast of Norway. The comparison with the Battle off Samar is not apt, however, since *Glorious* was never able to launch aircraft.

15   MacArthur, *Reminiscences*, pp. 227–28.

16   Canon, *Return to the Philippines*, p. 92.

17   Ministry of Defence (NAVY), *War with Japan: Vol VI; Advance to Japan*, Her Majesty's Printing Office, London, 1995, p. 92.

18   Ian W. Toll, *Twilight of the Gods: War in the Western Pacific, 1944–1945*, W.W. Norton, New York, 2020, p. 298.

19   For the Americans, this assumes all forces present at the Battle of Surigao Strait plus the following: light cruiser *Nashville*, and the 14 destroyers of Destroyer Squadrons 21 and 49. The one destroyer damaged at Surigao Strait has been deleted from the total. The total of PT boats is somewhat speculative, but of the 39 present at Surigao Strait, one was sunk and nine were damaged to varying degrees. The Japanese totals reflect Kurita's actual force at the time.

20   Morison, *Leyte*, p. 295.

21   Ibid., pp. 295–96.

22   Canon, *Return to the Philippines*, p. 92.

23   Samuel Eliot Morison, *The Liberation of the Philippines, Luzon, Mindanao, the Visayas 1944–1945* (Volume XIII of *The History of United States Naval Operations in World War II*), Little, Brown and Company, Boston, 1975, pp. 37–42.

Index

Note: Page numbers in **bold** refer to maps and those in *italic* refer to tables.